MYTHOGRAPHY

The Study of Myths and Rituals

MYTHO

WILLIAM G. DOTY

GRAPHY

The Study of
Myths and Rituals

THE UNIVERSITY OF ALABAMA PRESS

Library of Congress Cataloging in Publication Data

Doty, William G., 1939–
  Mythography: the study of myths and rituals.

  Bibliography: p.
  Includes index.
  1. Myth. 2. Ritual. I. Title.
BL304.D58 1986   291.1'3   85-991
ISBN 0-8173-0269-7

for Joan T. Mallonee

Contents

Acknowledgments

Permission to quote is gratefully acknowledged as follows:

Material from *The Snow Poems*, A. R. Ammons, copyright © 1977 by W. W. Norton & Company, Inc. Used by permission of the publisher, W. W. Norton & Company, Inc.

Material from William G. Doty, "Mythophiles' Dyscrasia: A Complex Definition of Myth," *Journal of the American Academy of Religion* 48/4(1981)531–62. Used by permission of Robert P. Scharlemann, editor.

Material from *Purity and Danger: An Analysis of Pollution and Taboo*, by Mary Douglas, copyright © 1966 by Mary Douglas. Used by permission of Routledge & Kegan Paul, PLC, London.

Material from Morris Freilich, "Myth, Method, and Madness," *Current Anthropology* 16/2(1975)207–226. Used by permission of The University of Chicago Press.

Excerpts from *Fables of Identity* by Northrop Frye, copyright © 1963 by Harcourt Brace Jovanovich, Inc. Reprinted by permission of the publisher.

Eric Gould, *Mythical Intentions in Modern Literature*. Copyright © 1981 by Princeton University Press. Scattered quotes reprinted with permission of Princeton University Press.

Material from *Beginnings in Ritual Studies*, by Ronald Grimes, copyright © 1982 by University Press of America. Used by permission.

Material from *The Drums of Affliction: A Study of Religious Processes Among the Ndembu of Zambia*, by Victor Turner, copyright © 1968 by Oxford University Press. Used by permission.

Material from Victor W. Turner, *The Ritual Process: Structure and Anti-Structure*. New York: Aldine Publishing Company. Copyright © 1969 by Victor W. Turner. Used by permission.

Preface

There is a kind of intellectual frontier within which he must be who will sympathize
with myth, while he must be without it who will investigate it, and it is our fortune
that we live near this frontierline and can go in and out.

Edward B. Tylor, *Primitive Culture*

The traditional term for the compilation of mythological accounts is
mytholography; the term *mythography* means the application of critical
perspectives to mythological materials, and I will expand that here to
include rituals as well.[1] I will be focusing not on materials from antiquity but on modern approaches to myths and rituals, on the major
schools of interpretation that still have some viability in various contexts
of critical study.

To a large extent the study of the history and applicability of mythographies is a study in the history of ideas; thus attention is focused
primarily upon understanding why we approach myths and rituals the
way we do at the present time—whence writers may be coming, in
terms of both worldview and hermeneutics. My focus will be largely
methodological, to be sure, but methodologies involve worldviews, and
worldviews both create hermeneutical (interpretive) systems and are
created by them.

Too much of the history of mythography has been marked by the
assumption that a single approach must be chosen: myths are considered to have only one function, to be of only one type. Mythology is
considered to be only the preliminary stage that leads to scientific thinking, for example, or rituals represent reality as enacted, myths only
ideally; myths are only psychological, or they are only a way of passing
on yesterday's values. My own preference is for a multilayered, multi-
functional working procedure, and I will indicate some of its contours as
the survey and the arguments are developed in this book.

Although it has been heeded by mythographers only rarely, the sentiment of Percy S. Cohen's statement may stand as a sort of motto:

> There are many theories of myth, but they are not necessarily rival theories: the reason for this is that different theories often explain different statements about myth. Particular theories may, of course, explain several statements about myth and they may therefore compete, partly or wholly, with other theories. (338)

Cohen's point is that theorists should make clear which aspects of myth their own theory is designed to clarify. But because most theorists aim at myth in general, or ritual in general, one purpose of historical surveys such as those Cohen and others undertake—and those I engage in the substance of this book—is to perform a sort of archaeology of mythography. What is being sought is not so much the "bricks"—the mythological microunits (*mythemes*) or ritual symbols and ritemes, or mythic themes (*mythologems*)—as the various ways these have been charted, organized, and considered integral to coherent systems of belief, to symbologies and ritual praxis.

The presentation here will be primarily chronological, but I am not suggesting that the most recent approaches (structuralism, say, or semiotics) are any more competent or inclusive than any other, any more than particular stages in the development of a mythic or ritual performance pattern may be said to be "better" than any other. The success and strength of a multidisciplinary, synoptic approach depends upon recognizing the sources of its components as well as its inherent problems. Psychoanalytical theories, for example, often stress the individual and de-emphasize the societal context; and structuralist analysis may be halted prematurely at the level of the para-algebraic coding. The proof of the pudding is always in the usefulness of the method or theory within a complex and multilevel approach and in the ways the mythic or ritual pattern satisfied its original adherents.

It often will be necessary to characterize schools of interpretation, or the approach of an individual mythographer, in a less subtle way than representatives of a particular methodology might use in describing their own approaches. But for the purposes of our broad survey, it seemed most helpful to portray the specific and distinct features of each approach rather than to emphasize points held in common.

In the period when I was finishing this book I began to be aware that contemporary critical theory is something of a "field-encompassing field," that in Jonathan Culler's formulation works alluded to in recent discussions as "theory" "are those that have had the power to make strange the familiar and to make readers conceive of their own thinking, behavior, and institutions in new ways" (1982). And as I began to try to parcel out distinctions between post-Saussurean methodologies, especially in Chapters 6 and 7, I found it difficult to avoid discussing specific issues before the general discussions. I hope I have been successful in keeping things straight in this regard, but the reader should know that often theories introduced in one chapter are discussed more fully later.

If this were a more thetic or "constructive" (or perhaps in more contemporary frames, a more "deconstructive") work, perspectives with which I now operate (stemming from Jacques Derrida, Michel Foucault, John J. White, and others) would demand a very different order of presentation. But what I have done is to remain with a more or less chronological, sequential presentation (technically, a synchronic assessment of diachronic developments). Except in the last chapter, the emphasis is upon the origination and development of various approaches to myths and rituals, rather than upon arguing that particular historical developments must now be foregrounded. In fact my working use of a multidisciplinary mythography is already in tune with much of contemporary critical theory, without, however, utilizing so many of the technical terms (absence, desire, *différance,* and others like them) that now permeate many areas of academic writing.

The production of texts spans a particular biographical period, and the period here, in my biography, spans roughly 1971–83, a period in which I developed a comprehensive survey of the various mythographic approaches of the modern period and began to work with it in classes and in other writings. Were I to start from the end point of this time span, it is likely that my mode of expression, as well as my interests, would be quite different, but I continue to think that résumés of research procedures and interests remain crucial to the historian and myth analyst.

I know of no single volume that provides a comprehensive overview of the approaches to the study of myths and rituals current today. The available historical surveys mostly focus upon scholarship of the late nineteenth and early twentieth centuries, or else they argue the case for a particular approach represented by a writer or editor.

This book is intended to serve as an English-language bibliographic resource, not only through the references but also by means of the notes and the bibliographic recommendations at the end of the book. References within the text are cited according to the "social science format": name of the author, if it has not been cited in the text; year of publication, if the author has more than one publication listed in the References

Cited; and page number(s). Other parentheses function in customary ways but especially here to avoid footnotes as much as possible. When manageable, references to illustrative rituals or myths have been provided; to include illustrative applications of each method, as was desired by several readers, would have led to a volume at least twice as long as this one dares to be. Joseph Campbell's Masks of God series is readily available in paperback and at least partly serves that lack, although primarily from psychological and literary perspectives.

With respect to the actual study and interpretation of myths and rituals, the following list of questions will give some indication of what I think the attentive reader ought to be able to garner from this mythography for practical study of myths and rituals. To apply the list of questions to any particular myth or ritual account would require another book at least this size!

Social contexts: How does the material function within the society where it is indigenous? What are its macro- and microcontexts (its widest functioning context within the society's language-world, its immediate applicability)? To what extent does it justify social roles, organize hierarchies of social interaction, convey moral values, express familial or other relational interaction models? How "realistic" is the material? Does it model social experience or idealize it or criticize it?

Psychological aspects: To what aspects of the psyche/personality/self does the myth or ritual speak? Does it speak primarily to individual issues or to the corporate "self"-understanding? How is it related to issues of gender behaviors, to images of maturity, to career modeling? Does it express experiential truths that have their apparent basis in the biogenetic structures of the human race? How does the material function as a means of emotional expression? How does it relate to cultural patterns of expressing and controlling anxiety, anger, joy, creativity?

Literary/textual/performative aspects: What are the literary characteristics of the materials (the dramatic aspects of rituals)? How is the myth or ritual related to other similar materials in the culture (is it a typical genre, or an antigenre, or unique)? What materials may have influenced its formation and development? To what subsequent rites or myths or other forms may it have given rise, or has it exerted influences upon others? How were the materials transmitted, performed, diffused, codified? Are there for this material particular dramatistic or literary markers that are not found elsewhere in other rituals or literary genres? Are there indications within the material about the correct context for performance (during certain seasons, during particular ritual contexts, and so forth)?

Structural aspects: What are the innate dynamics of the myth or ritual, and do they correspond to those found in the wider context of the host culture? To what extent does the example represent a class of similarly structured materials, and to what extent is it unique? How does the material fit within the society's conceptual, aesthetic, and semiotic (signifying) systems? Does it refer to other privileged codes, or does it function as a "master code" that rules other materials?

Other interpretive matters: What are the symbolic and iconographic traces left by this material? (And correspondingly, what must we know about the imagery and iconographic conventions of the society to be able to understand the signifying systems of this particular ritual or myth?) Where is the ritual or myth now situated within the society? For which persons is it a primary experience as opposed to an antique or outmoded relic? How self-evident is its meaning to the hearer-participant? Does it require extensive secondary interpretation?

I was impressed when I first encountered Elizabeth Sewell, through her remarkable critical writings on the history of ideas and literature (such as her 1960 work), then by her poetry, and then in person. A statement from the 1960 work has guided me in the several revisions of this book:

> An author can do three things with myth. He can study its nature and its origins, in its traditional form; interpret myths according to his own theories; or mythologize himself, either by thinking himself into existing myths and using them as instruments for his own thought, or by inventing new myths and using them in the same way. The first activity may be poetical, although it need not be. The third must be poetical. The second is wholly nonpoetic, indeed antipoetical. (82)

Or one may recall Martin Heidegger's marvelous "Poetically, man dwells on the earth," which I would transform to "Mythically and ritually, humans live. . . ." At any rate, mythopoesis ultimately constitutes the matrixing mode and activity for any and all our endeavors. I will be pleased if books such as this one can provide some of the poetic and mythic yeast to ferment something newly creative through the heavy dough of our present style of life.

I hope that few readers will agree with Robert Graves when he states that "Mythology is the study of whatever religious or heroic legends are so foreign to a student's experience that he cannot believe them to be true" (introduction to Guirand:v). There is a disjointedness with the everyday, a strange-making quality about mythic figures that gives us distance upon them, and this is an important distance, necessary so that the figures/incidents can remain "out there" as models, as possible developments for what we know "in here."

I don't find myths particularly "foreign," in Graves's term, but rather the opposite: they often reveal to me parts of myself or my society that I might otherwise ignore. Myths and rituals have a way of disclosing us to ourselves, either as we are or as we might be—and as we might be in either a negative *or* a positive light. Hence I refer to myths as "projective psyche models," understanding that "psyche" in a fully social sense as in a fully historical sense: the traces of the process by which the psyche/soul is determined to be real or unreal, major or minor in the scheme of things, will be the traces of the cultural sophistication of that culture.

Perhaps even more as a teacher in the humanities than as a specialist in religious studies, I am dedicated to the explication of the ways the psyche grows and develops and values; to hear in Ravel's *La Valse* the clashing discords of the early twentieth century's chaos of values may be more important (to me) than detailed documentation of European economic trends from 1900 to 1930—or more significantly, ought to be included *along with* such documentation. Even within the disciplines of the social sciences and the humanities the sorts of abrupt disclaimer of any knowledge of fields other than the specialist's own have left us living like so many transients in a vast academic Holiday Inn: this book seeks to show that some of that isolation and fragmentation can be overcome. But steps toward reintegration of our knowledges remain only very preliminary; we are a long way from realizing how absurd it is for our academic specialists to continue to hone their tools in rigid isolation from one another, or to expect students to forget in an anthropology class what they have just heard about in classics or English.

For the student whose work in mythography begins with this book, I hope I have shown that that work cannot be developed within any one traditional academic speciality; for the specialist in any one of the five or six fields I touch upon here, I will be satisfied if she or he finds that a dialogue with at least one other specialty simply must be begun.

We need only suffer through a compilation such as Susan Griffin's painful *Woman and Nature* (1978) to gain some sense of the ways one of the mythic orientations of our own culture operates: frequently we have used masculine forms for generic humankind, and we have objectified and abstracted Nature herself. In my own writings, such as in this book, I make a conscious effort to avoid the implicit male-dominance diction, but many of the authors quoted do not.

Several sections of this book were strengthened by the critiques of members of a National Endowment for the Humanities seminar at Harvard University during the summer of 1984. It was in the Lamont Library at Harvard that I came across the extensive annotated bibliography by Ron Smith, *Mythologies of the World: A Guide to Sources* (1981), which can be recommended as a means of gaining access to mythological materials themselves, augmenting considerably the second section of the Selected Introductory Bibliography at the end of this book (note that Smith uses the term "mythography" to refer to myth collections, pp. 3, 15, whereas I use it to refer to studies of myth and ritual).

I would like to thank the several colleagues who have taught alongside me, read parts of the manuscript, or tried to push me in the direction of mythopoetic creation. I am also grateful to the Office of the Dean of the College of Arts and Sciences, The University of Alabama, for a typing grant and for word-processor equipment and supplies. Marsha Baines and Anna Yee were wonderful in helping with the manuscript preparation, and Margaret Vines often helped me balance administrative, teaching, and writing functions.

Having accepted her husband's obsession with writing across a span of twenty years and some eight previous books, Joan T. Mallonee receives the last word of thanks in this Preface—but then she often deserves, and gets, the last word!

MYTHOGRAPHY

The Study of Myths and Rituals

The Many Dimensions of
Myths and Rituals

1

Myth study at present has not so much the purity and
integrity of an homogeneous regional cooking as it has
the syncretistic flavor of international *cuisine*: a dash of
Cassirer, a dollop of Freud, a gram of Frazer, a minim of
Graves, a pinch of Harrison, a smidgeon of Jung, a taste
of Thompson, all intriguing flavors in themselves,
excellently cooked, but, still and all, not really a style.
                    Herbert Weisinger, *The Agony and the Triumph*

THE FIRST TASK IS TO GAIN AN OVERVIEW OF THE many ways myths and rituals can be studied: this chapter treats definitions and notes problems that arise. Following the tracking of some beginnings is a study of subsequent historical meanings of "myth." Next is a proposal of a comprehensive definition, the development of which will constitute the bulk of the chapter.

Myth the Mother

The sort of glaze that comes over our eyes when someone chants "In the beginning . . ." is phased only slightly by recent scholarly translations of the initial verse of that late-biblical source responsible for what now begins the Tanak/Old Testament. Genesis 1:1 is translated more adequately with a processive verbal form: "When the gods began creating . . . ," or in the striking rendering by Doria and Lenowitz, "At the first of the gods' godmaking skies and earth, the earth was all mixed up—darkness on top of deepness; so the gods' spirit swooped down on the waters" (37). That glaze on our eyes surely is related to the veneration our culture ascribes to anything that goes "way back"—especially to anything that goes way back to "the beginnings."

Those familiar with the many studies of the contemporary mythographer Mircea Eliade will recognize the theme; it is the theme, often repeated by Eliade, of the importance of the *cosmogonic myth,* the account of first-beginnings that remains a potential source throughout the life of a culture, a powerful source that, in the many examples Eliade cites, can be renewed and made present repeatedly in retellings of the cosmogonic myth and in rites (see extracts in Beane and Doty). While I do not consider the cosmogonic myth to have the absolute priority of place Eliade would assign it and its kin, there is no doubt that Western civilization since the days of the Greeks—who used to compile lists of the "first-finders" of all sorts of cultural practices or objects—has been devoted to the psychic reality of Beginnings rather than of Now as "the place to start." Even our narrative tales are structured not from a present instant backward but by "Once upon a time there was . . ."; and the habit reaches even into academe: woe betide the graduate student whose dissertation does not begin with a review of previous research (a pattern established by the German *Forschungsbericht*).

Following this tradition, the mythography begins here literally at the beginning—or at least at the beginning of words. It begins with the *mother,* whose Proto-Indo-European root appears to be *ma-, identified by the *American Heritage Dictionary* as "An imitative root derived from the child's cry for the breast (a linguistic universal found in many of the world's languages . . .)"; and it begins with the similar root of the word *myth,* the P-I-E root of which is **mu-.* The Greek stem is apparently the noun *my,* pronounced "muh" or "moo," and referring to a mu-ttering sound made with the lips. So from the similar *ma-* and *mu-,* or as I would arbitrarily connect them, "mother-myth," we have the noun *mythos* in Greek, as the term for what was made as a sound with the mouth, that is, for "word" (cf. the French cognate *mot*); *mythos* came to designate a particular organization of words in story form.

In Homer and the early Greek poets *mythos* signified the ways words are treated on the surface level of the text, that is, the ornamental or fictional use, or the beauty of arrangement of the words in a literary work. Plato considered myth to be an art of language alongside of and included within poetry, and he cited mythic stories at the same time he suggested that the creativity of the poet-artist ought to be overseen closely by the state. Plato moved to the mythic or legendary mode, or at least to extended metaphors, precisely at those points where his "rational" discourse needed to be amplified emotionally or aesthetically, at those points where the logical mode exhausted the subject rather than elucidated it (see especially Friedländer: chap. 9; Detienne 1981: chaps. 4 and 5). In his *Poetics,* Plato's pupil Aristotle used *mythos* more restrictively to refer to what we now call plot or fabula, indicating that the organization of words and actions of a drama into a sequence of narrative components was the most important dramatic element.

In addition *mythos,* "word" or "story," could be combined with a second Greek noun for "word," namely *logos* (related to the verb *legein,* "to speak"). The result: *mythologia* (mythology), which might mean most literally "words concerning words." However apart from its place in *mythologia, logos* gained the sense of referring to those words making up doctrine or theory, as opposed to *mythos* for those words having an ornamental or fictional, narrative function. The outcome of this development was that the mythological came to be contrasted with logic (the *logos*-ical) and later with "history" in the sense of an overview or chronicle of events (*epos* or *historia,* not necessarily chronologically distant from the present).

Mythology as the imaginative rather than the historical: that is something of the end product of this course of linguistic development, and it influenced the Latin adaptations of these terms. *Mythos* came into Latin as *fabula,* which is the basis of both "fable" and "fabulous" (and as indicated above, it is used as a synonym for plot also). Now the emphasis is purely upon the poetic, inventive aspects of mythological creations. And it is precisely this fictional aspect that has colored the majority of approaches to mythology, especially when knowledge in the sciences (science is from *scire,* P-I-E **skei-,* to know by separating things; cf. scission, from the same root) is conceived of as being based in the concretely experienced, the empirical, the study of that which can be measured and quantified. In these cases the realm of science is considered to be the opposite of the mythological (or the religious, or the metaphysical) as the realm of fiction, fantasy, imagination. (This sort of technical usage of myth as the nonscientific may be what brought the term myth into modern usage—as late as 1830 in English, 1815 in German, 1818 in French; on the role of the concept in French intellectual history, see Detienne 1981.)

One of the underlying intentions of this book is to question this distinction, to raise up some qualifications to this separation between science and mythology as both terms usually are conceived. I will suggest that our myths are fictional, to be sure, but that fictional need not mean unreal and certainly not unempirical; myths are "mysterious" (another side-formation from the hypothetical Proto-Indo-European stem, **mu-*), but they are not incomprehensible.

But that is to anticipate somewhat; the main point I want to convey here is that the heavy burden of our cultural background lies upon the weighting of mythology with the sense "unreal, fictional." We will see that it is precisely this rationalizing approach to myths that has dominated the study of mythology through the years. Later phases of a myth's situation within a culture are marked by increasing rationalization, and most of the theories of myth and ritual we shall be discussing also derive ultimately from the tendency to rationalize, to substitute abstract social or philosophical-scientific meanings for the graphic imagery of narrative myths and performed rituals.

Sophisticated rationalizing or ridiculing of myths is by no means a purely modern phenomenon. It began in late Hellenic allegorization of Homeric mythology (Thales, ca. 624–547) and reached a peak with Euhemeros of Messene (330–260). In his novelistic travel book entitled *Sacred Scripture (Hiera anagraphē),* Euhemeros claimed to have seen, supposedly on an island in the Indian Sea, an ancient temple of Zeus in which a golden column displayed magnificent deeds of Ouranos, Kronos, and Zeus, who were portrayed as mortal and fairly ordinary human heroes rather than as gods. By Euhemeros's time these three figures were regarded as powerful deities, so he concluded that the gods of popular worship originally had been mere human kings and conquerors to whom humankind expressed appreciation by offering them the worship due to gods. When the human status was later forgotten, they were regarded as having been deities from the beginning.

Euhemeros's rationalistic anthropology was not paid much heed by his Greek contemporaries—after all, Greek religion included no rigidly exclusive distinctions between gods and human heroes. But it was revitalized and developed by Roman writers, and subsequently it became an important apologetic tool in the hands of early Christian writers, who used euhemeristic analysis to demonstrate the secondary nature of the Greek pantheon and to contrast Greek deities with Jesus Christ, who was regarded as a nonlegendary, nonmythological figure of history.[1]

As a technical term, euhemerism now refers to attempts to trace the human precursors of mythical deities, or specific practices behind mythical situations, an analysis that has found many favorable echoes in classical anthropology. An example of a modified euhemerism is found in the early work of F. Max Müller (1823–1900), who understood myths as representing false etiologies (explanations of origins), especially as people sentimentalized and personalized natural forces. So the sun's progress, made analogous to the human life cycle, was personalized as the course of a sun deity across the sky.

In each case mythologies were thought by Müller to have been inventions intended to explain underlying causes for natural phenomena. Müller also proposed, with respect to the evolution of language, that the original mythological terms first had been understood metaphorically but eventually were understood to be referring to real persons or deities. So Kephalos ("head" of light) and Prokis ("fading dew," bride of Kephalos) were personalized and worked into a mythological story about a mortal youth and his bride. Hence Müller saw mythology as a problem: humankind ought to be able, by means of philology (tracing the derivations of the terms), to push through such confusion to a clearheaded thinking that could overcome this mythological "disease of language."

Not only Müller, but Sir James Frazer (whose work will be discussed in Chapter 6) and many other nineteenth-century scholars, saw myth almost exclusively as a problem for modern rationality. Many of the attempts at "explaining" myth that we will survey (sociofunctionalism in Chapter 2, the ritual-dominant school in Chapter 3, psychological approaches in Chapter 5) are rooted in "euhemeristic" substitutions of one thing for another: for a mythic story about the family of the gods we may substitute historical reflections of the founding political dynasties; for a mythic account of primeval earth-shaping we may substitute modern geological eras; and so forth.

On the whole our mythographic sciences have sought to replace the mythic imagery with abstractions, particularly with recent philosophical or psychological categories, and much of the analysis in this book will be devoted to demonstrating how such approaches developed as well as to what they may continue to contribute to a complex mythography that is not just based upon euhemeristic principles, substituting one set of abstract categories for another set of mythic images or ritual actions.

Positive and Negative Uses of "Myth"

Before we begin the survey of mythographies, we need to touch down briefly into our own social setting, where to say "myth" or "ritual" is to say so many different things to so many different people that we almost founder in the "things" at the start. The terms myth and ritual are used with a multitude of different meanings in the many disciplines where they are studied, even when scholars attempt to avoid the casualness of everyday speech. We can list some of the fields of inquiry where the terms are central:

- in the study of religions, especially the study of primitive religions or non-Western religions, where there is often a tendency to refer to "their" *myth* but "our" *theology* or beliefs
- in analyzing "mythic elements" or "legendary plots" in the study of poetry, drama, and fiction
- in the anthropological and ethnological analysis of cultures other than one's own—where there is an unfortunate history of referring to the premodern as "the mythic period"
- in political science, where one may find treatments of the "myth" of democracy or of socialism
- in sociology, both with respect to belief systems and their creation and with respect to ritualized forms of behavior—which are also of interest in clinical psychology

And the list could be extended much further.

In most of these instances myth and ritual are positively approached: they are seen as really existing, as important social entities that express and mold cultures. Myth is understood as referring to the basic religious or philosophical beliefs of a culture, expressed through ritual behavior or through the graphic or literary arts.

But alongside such generally positive uses are the negative tones that frequently surface when someone wants to denigrate an issue or an opponent. When we read, for instance, about "the myth of the upper class," or "the myth of youth," or "the myth of psychology," we often are to understand myth as having a negative, pejorative connotation. Indeed the phrase, "But it's only a myth!" may be used to justify personal actions that go against societal norms.

Such a negative use of the term myth is hardly a modern invention, inasmuch as ancient Greek rationalists also considered themselves to be "above" such crude concepts as "myths." But I think there is a definite echo of modernity in the vehemence with which the negative sense is used today: especially when myth refers to the nonscientific, science being understood as the rational, the empirically provable. Myth tends to be lumped together with religion or philosophy or the arts as a superfluous facet of culture that may be considered enjoyable but not particularly functional. In this sense myth suffers from the same ambiguity that prevails with respect to the arts or aesthetics in general: today an "interior decorator" may be called in to supply the finishing flourishes to a new office building, but the architectural engineer or the building contractor is thought of as the more important worker, and customers are seldom aware of the symbolic significance of the type or shape of the building.

And finally there is the negative sense of myth by which one refers to a negative stereotype. I have found that I must stress this point, ever since students in one of my "Myth and Ritual" classes proposed making a film on the mythic patterns of male-female relationships at the two colleges of the university where I was teaching (the colleges were at that time exclusively male or female in student population). The film's "book," which I had asked to see before the actual filming took place, centered around male and female stereotypes of the behaviors of the other sex: long lines of wolf-fanged men charging a women's dormitory, prissy coeds afraid of drinking a single beer, and the like. Myth had been understood by my students as referring to a joking caricature of the other sex. To be sure, there were deep mythic patterns involved, and I encouraged the students to seek out the underlying sociomythic models leading to their proposed scenario. But essentially the original focus had been upon dating and interactional habits in a very immediate and limited fashion, not upon underlying societal models and tensions.[2] Myth had been understood as deceit, as a falsifying construct, an understanding mirrored in many dictionaries where myth is first described as "primarily fictitious."

At one level I agree with that definition: I see myths as a particular kind of fiction, and I see myths and other literary fictions as having an important function in our society—that of modeling possible personal roles and concepts of the self. But "fictional" today usually means "unreal," and it carries a negative connotation (being opposed to "reality"), with a further connotation of "something unnecessary." It is this negative connotation that we often confront in book titles when an author wishes to expose what he or she thinks is actually happening, as opposed to what is superficially apparent. Any number of political exposés, for instance, are entitled "The Myth of ———."

Such a negative connotation, however, is only a much reduced secondary development. My understanding is that myth includes primary, foundational materials. It provides information about the structure of the society or its customs in a narrative form; it is experienced at some point in its development as both true and crucial to those who believe in it (see Geertz 1973:129); and the events of the narrative are most often supposed to take place in a foundational period (the primal times, the times of beginnings and creations; the times when new patterns are established and old ones reformulated—times that need not be chronologically distant but usually are).

Mythic themes may be present in a less than foundational way, just as many other thematic materials may guide composition, but mythic narratives themselves are ultimately "special." They are not little but big stories, touching not just the everyday but sacred or specially marked topics that concern much more than the immediate situation. And myths generally concern themes that humans face over and over again, rather than problems that are relevant only to one person or one group or at one particular period of life. We have many myths about sexuality as a basic human perplexity, for example, but few about masturbation or "how far to go" on a first date.

I find it helpful to distinguish between myth in the sense of narrative, that is, a mythic story or thematic pattern, and "mythicity." The latter term refers to a generalized orientation to the cosmos based upon a myth or series of myths (the concept of mythicity is developed by Gould). For myth as narrative, or for mythicity, the question is where a myth actually is situated within the dynamics of a culture. We must attempt to recognize whether a myth we are studying is so vital or "alive" that it shapes and "in-forms" the culture directly and immediately, or if it has become secondary or tertiary, so that only its themes and characters still appear, no longer represented within the intensely vibrating matrix of the original power-packed story but functioning merely as thematic materials added to or utilized within a later work.

A number of the issues noted in the last three paragraphs will resurface in the rest of this chapter; others (such as "where" myth "is" in a society—its level of mythic vitality) will resurface in Chapter 2. In turning now to matters of defining myth, we continue some aspects of that social game we all have learned to play along with "In the beginning. . . ." I mean, of course, the classical gambit of defining what it is that one intends to discuss or analyze. In "The Range of Definitions," which follows immediately, I begin to draw the net tight by noting just how vast is the number of ways "myth" is used in our culture; then in "A Comprehensive Working Definition" I develop a complex definition of a mythological corpus and the ways mythologies exercise their powers. I develop the complex definition at this point rather than waiting until the end of the book because I do not think a reader ought to have to keep guessing at the author's position; but it puts me at something of a disadvantage, inasmuch as the definition itself was attained only after several years of working with the various mythographic approaches and after utilizing what seem to me to be their lasting values: to some extent, then, the reader gets here the end results before the presentation of the data.

The Range of Definitions

Casually collecting definitions as I studied the literature on myths and rituals, I now have a list of more than fifty individual definitions, chosen on the basis of eliminating duplications. Fifty! And I emphasize the "casual collection," for I have made no sustained effort with index cards or computer-searches. I have organized these definitions into ten categories and have grouped the fifty definitions within them. I assign students the project of coming up with their own definitions, rather than providing the professor's favorite; the whole assignment aims at evoking a sense of the multiplicity of what may be encompassed by the terms myth and ritual, as well as a sense of the importance of the historical context of the persons writing the definitions. (It will be helpful if you turn from this page to jot down your own definitions of myth and ritual before you read further; you will see the results of my taking that assignment to heart in the next subsection.)

Abstracting from the categories I use, here are some of the components that appear in the definitions:

- myth as aesthetic device, narrative, literary form
- subject matter having to do with the gods, the "other" world
- explaining origins (etiology)
- as mistaken or primitive science
- myth as the words to rituals, or myth dependent upon ritual, which it explicates
- making universals concrete or intelligible
- explicating beliefs, collective experiences, or values
- "spiritual" or "psychic" expression

The wide range of definitional sets is striking, given the amount of energy spent over the years in classifying and defining both myths and rituals.

A number of inclusive definitions are included in the materials I prepare for classes; we will meet some of them, and some of the fifty definitions just abstracted, throughout the rest of this book. Henry A. Murray's essay, "The Possible Nature of a 'Mythology' to Come" (1968b), is strongly recommended as a thorough and provocative work that can lead to reflection on the necessary inclusiveness of whatever definition one uses. Murray refers approvingly to a definition by Mark Schorer:

> Myths are the instruments by which we continually struggle to make our experience intelligible to ourselves. A myth is a large, controlling image that gives philosophical meaning to the facts of ordinary life; that is, which has organizing value for experience. A mythology is a more or less articulated body of such images, a pantheon. . . . Myth is fundamental, the dramatic representation of our deepest instinctual life, of a primary awareness of man in the universe, capable of many configurations, upon which all particular opinions and attitudes depend. (Murray 1968a: 355–56)

The strength of Murray's discussion lies in his attempt to spread his definitional net as widely as possible. Instead of reducing components in myths to essential common denominators, Murray expands his definition into a multileveled exposition. He includes formal, referential, functional, conditional, and causal modes of definition, and the result is a rich study of mythological definitions that opens to a rewarding precision in facing issues such as the "part-myth" or "covert myths" in literary fictions and works of art.[3] (Such issues will be confronted repeatedly, especially in Chapter 6, where the problem of precision in mythological literary criticism is noted.)

A Comprehensive Working Definition

Rather than simple and easily memorized statements that suggest that myth does this . . . or that, a definition is provided here that includes many more factors than normally are included in traditional definitions. It should provide a step toward an inclusive matrix for understanding many types of myths, myths that function differently within different social settings yet share a sufficient number of common features among those of the definition to be recognizable as "myth."[4] Such a definitional matrix ought to be helpful to focus myth analysis; my aim is to provide a previsualization and a conceptualization of how many myths are constituted and how they function (more on function in the next chapter) in order to foster a type of myth appreciation that recognizes mythic multidimensionality in both origination and application. Obviously a more complex, even algebraic, taxonomy could be developed, so that particular myths could be indexed by numerical values, but that is not my concern here.

"Language is haunted by myth," suggests Albert Cook, "and the act of defining myth is an act of something like exorcism" (10). So I will begin my exorcism by first stating the complex definition, delineating its components sequentially, and then discussing the components in greater or lesser detail in the subsections of the rest of this chapter.

A mythological corpus consists of (1) a usually complex network of myths that are (2) culturally important (3) imaginal (4) stories, conveying by means of (5) metaphoric and symbolic diction, (6) graphic imagery, and (7) emotional conviction and participation, (8) the primal, foundational accounts (9) of aspects of the real, experienced world and (10) humankind's roles and relative statuses within it.

Mythologies may (11) convey the political and moral values of a culture and (12) provide systems of interpreting (13) individual experience within a universal perspective, which may include (14) the intervention of suprahuman entities as well as (15) aspects of the natural and cultural orders. Myths may be enacted or reflected in (16) rituals, ceremonies, and dramas, and (17) they may provide materials for secondary elaboration, the constituent mythemes having become merely images or reference points for a subsequent story, such as a folktale, historical legend, novella, or prophecy.

Network of Myths

Items within a mythological network are interrelated. As when we trace the relationships of disparate branches of a large tree, we often can discover within a corpus relationships between mythemes and myths that have no apparent kinship at first glance; the same thing might occur when we are pursuing random cross-sectional sampling. The more one studies individual myths constituting a corpus, the more one becomes aware of common elements and internal connections between them. Obviously there is a problem for the analyst, in this context, when only fragmentary selections are extant, but the more familiarity the analyst has with mythemic units in a corpus, the more it is possible to make accurate guesses about gaps.

Within a network, various myths may actualize parts of the underlying cultural worldview. Seldom does a single myth actualize the entire worldview, because that seems to require a collection of many interlocked stories, a canon rather than one sample. In the processes of transmission, constant change and adaptation to new or changed contexts seem to be normal. A particular myth may undergo addition and expansion, deletion or substitution, of mythemic units. Transformations and variations may occur within a network, or between two or more territorially adjacent networks, or—at the most abstract conceptual level—across the astonishingly diverse range presented by the totality of human mythologies.

The quest for the earliest or purest version is often fruitless; it may be possible to posit a hypothetical primal version (an *Urtext*) by inference from transformations and variations sighted in cross-cultural myth analysis, but it is important first to study a particular network as one analyzes the variations of musical themes within a complex composition. The leitmotiv may be recognizable only after hearing all the variations—and then it may sound rather thin, played alone and without harmony or contrasts; similarly there are limits to the usefulness of analytical units being abstracted from mythological performance contexts.

What seems like the simplest, "purest" version may not be temporally early but the product of a late and sophisticated reworking; traditional materials are not always expanded but may be telescoped in the process of transmission if they have become familiar to everyone or if a reviser (such as Homer or one of the evangelists) imposes a single unified perspective upon a mass of originally diverse traditions.

While for purposes of historical or other analysis extrinsic to a myth it may be productive to track the meanings of versions within particular sociographic or temporal situations—as, for instance, the meaning of Oidipous for Freud—it is also important at some stage of the analysis to focus upon the myth *and all its transformations* simultaneously if we are to appreciate the full psychodynamic range of its powers and to comprehend the unique significance of any one version.

Myths within a network may belong to different classes, depending upon whether the mythographer classifies according to content, type of action, sphere of reference of images, or some other feature. Myths may fit several classifications simultaneously: belonging, for instance, to *collective, natural,* and *etiological* classes, depending upon the functions of the myth in the society or upon the external (etic) distinctions made by the analyst.[5] And myths within a network may have a plurality of functions and usages within a culture or cross-culturally, as we will see in the next chapter.

Many of the monomythic definitions of the past that emphasized just one primary aspect of the nature or function of myth—that myths provide social cohesion, for example, or that they antedate scientific and philosophical reflection—have seriously hampered our view of the poly-functionality of myths, even within one culture. Definitions operating with only one key function often are falsified so easily as to be useless to a subsequent generation.[6] The problem for definitions such as that used here is to provide for a wide range of constituent features and social function while recognizing that any particular feature or function may be actualized more or less completely in one or another context.

Culturally Important

The term "culturally important" is intended to differentiate myths from private fictions and to suggest that they are stories that uniquely represent particular societies. If ritual, in Victor Turner's phrase, is "quintessential custom," then myth is quintessential story, not just something extra.

We may describe many myths as being socializations of private dreams or visionary stories, recognizing that in many societies the inspiration of the individual dreamer or prophet is tested in the public arena for its corporate significance before its wider acceptance. Living myths are marked by social consensus as to their importance and often their implications. Hence we may speak of self-acknowledgment by the society that a myth is culturally important, which is one way of indicating that the myth is considered to provide a normative perspective on the whole framework of reality.

Culturally important myths, "big" stories as opposed to purely personal themes, reappear repeatedly within various frameworks of the society's oral and written literature and are represented thematically in rituals and iconography. Some materials may be considered highly significant yet reappear only upon specially marked occasions; in this case they often gain significance precisely by the infrequency of their use. Audience expectations set up by a regular pattern of myth use may be shattered disturbingly or intensified emotionally if use ceases or is transferred to another social sphere. Conscious manipulation of expectations is therefore possible, as when a scene of a primeval waterfall is used to merchandise cigarettes.

Many societies frame the recitation of certain important myth types by temporal sanctions: for example, myths about snakes may not be told during summer among the American Hopi, at the time when snakes are active above ground, for the Hopi believe that snakes may take offense and become dangerous to humans at that time if they overhear their stories being recited incorrectly. Other sanctions may indicate the cultural importance of certain myths: as late as 1760, Uriel Freudenberg was condemned by the local Swiss authorities to be burned alive because he published his opinion that the legend of Wilhelm Tell originated in Denmark rather then Switzerland!

Economic considerations may be involved: myths may be regarded as a personal or tribal possession, to be shared only for a price or as a gift, and considered a form of real property (see L. Allen:23; Rappaport's 1968 study of the relations between religious and economic-ecological systems has been widely discussed; see also 1979; and see Vecsey and Venables; Lincoln 1981b; Hultkrantz 1966 and 1974). The "inner meanings" of myths, ceremonies, or impersonators of deities most often are revealed only to initiates who have demonstrated their willingness to guard the cultural "properties" of the society from debasement by nonserious or nonindigenous onlookers.

It is sometimes possible to spot junctures where contemporary persons and events are considered so important that they are mythicized, as North Americans witnessed in the demiapotheosis of John F. Kennedy and after the first emplacement of astronauts on the moon's surface. Work of a critic upon one's own traditions may be required to see just "where" cultural materials are being interpreted mythically; it is not easy to operate both within and without the mythic perspective, to have additional and alternative visions of what a culture says about itself. This work is the analytic work of a critic—but also the creative work of a poet, whose double vision exposes, repositions the languages through which a culture speaks its meanings.

Imaginal

Images are the means by which social meanings are invented (Latin: *in* + *venire,* "come upon"), constructed, and conveyed. We may speak of imaginal "fictions," understanding fiction not as a pejorative term for the unreal but with reference to its roots in the Latin participle *fictus,* from *fingo,* hence "something made, constructed." Imaginal expressions and stories are the embodiments in which interpretations are applied schematically to experienced reality; meanings are "invented" and "fictionalized" onto the world.

In this sense the "fictional" range of a culture includes sacred myth and philosophical reflection as well as fable or anecdote, poem, or novel. Hence myths share a large imaginal spectrum, and it is the "culturally important" criterion in the definition used here that distinguishes their communal and lasting significance from the more idiosyncratic imaginings of the individual entertainer or artist. However, artistic images, like the dreams and visions mentioned above, may become images accepted into shared usage also; indeed it is frequently the artist—whose images may conflict at first with traditionally accepted interpretations—who provides the images and languages necessary to shape or to change cultural viewpoints.

To persons in a society where myths are very much alive and strongly determinative of everyday actions, myths are never devices of conscious deceit but are considered to be true experientially, whether or not they are recognized as projections of the subjective psyche as well as participants in the liminal or ludic dimension of human expression. Myths provide opportunities "to perform the world," that is, to engage in sacred play by reciting them or by ritually enacting them (which activities may be bracketed by specific markers of the play arena, such as those of initiation rituals). The participant "plays" at such expressions, inducing the metaphoric or "as if" dimension to state "fictionally" what otherwise will not be exposed directly or sufficiently.

In myth we are close to the inventive primacy of the imaginal, close to the poetic seizure of truth, which as Martin Heidegger emphasizes is an *alētheia* (the Greek term for truth that means literally an uncovering, a disclosure) of what makes itself present to us as significant. "In such cases," Kathleen Raine suggests, "myth is the truth of the fact, not fact the truth of the myth" (quoted by Duncan:5).

Hence mythological language is important as a way of viewing how people understand the discovery of meaning to have taken place or to take place. Recently I have analyzed almost four hundred epithets of Hermes, following the belief that analysis of mythic names and descriptions provides a mythographic approach that begins with original materials rather than from later taxonomic categories (Doty 1980a). Images-become-names are considered daily enablements of deific power, accessible or avoidable, but close to one's life as the abstractions of our mythological handbooks never can be.

Stories

The literary critic William Righter observes that "what the myth does is to present a concrete possibility. To our openness in the face of ultimate questions to which we have no answers and for which explanations are simply not explanatory the myth poses another question: 'It's like this, isn't it?' And what follows is a story" (94)—"a story," and not philosophical reflection, historical chronicle, legal dictate, demographic statistics, and the like. Although any of these may be reflected in mythological narratives, the primary shaping of the materials is in narrative. A story is told, whether or not the outward shape of the story is prose or poetry, formalized dialogue, or other conventionalized format peculiar to a national literature.

Narrative provides a mode of ordering significant events, that is, a plot (Greek *mythos,* Latin *fabula*) of experienced or ideal existence. Myths are the narrative fictions whose plots read first at the level of their own stories and then as projections of imminent transcendent meanings. Such plots mirror human potentialities, experiences with natural and cultural phenomena, and recognition of regular interactions between them. Myths thus provide possible materializations for otherwise inchoate or unrecognized instantiations, names for the possible. Yellowman, a Navajo storyteller, in reponse to the question as to why the trickster Coyote incorporates so many conflicting values and dualities, replied: "If he did not do all those things, then those things would not be possible in the world" (Toelken 1969:220).

Ordering within mythological stories is disciplined by narrative grammars, that is, by the constraints upon arrangement and manipulation of the traditional mythological formulas, sequences, mythemes, and the like, derived from tradition and from the internal (emic) sense of what is "appropriate" mythic subject matter (more on this in Chapter 6).

Narrative point of view is also important: perhaps we may speak of a mythological point of view as that feature in which the uniqueness of culturally important narratives is situated. Myths do not concern trivialities or mere idiosyncrasies but issues of substance for the whole society. They are not told primarily for comic effect (although there may be comedy or entertaining embellishments in any particular performance) but because telling them is regarded as symbolic participation in their own and the culture's own inner significance. The Taos elder who spoke with Carl Jung was convinced that his story had significance not only for his own people but for all humankind: "After all [he said] we are a people who live on the roof of the world; we are the sons of Father Sun, and with our religion we daily help our father to go across the sky. We do not do this for ourselves, but for the whole world. If we were to cease practicing our religion, in ten years the sun would no longer rise. Then it would be night forever" (Jaffé:252; a similar statement from the Delaware is in Tooker:123–24).

That sense of the importance of one's story doubtlessly is related to the sense of important "history" conveyed in myths. I do not refer to history-as-chronicle but to meaningful history, the historic rather than the historical. Myths convey what a culture has chosen as its most important symbolic interpretations, its quintessential codings of what "means" the most to humankind out of the myriad of possibilities. To tell a story is to pass along wisdom of the past: "story" derives from P-I-E *weid-, through Greek *histor,* "wise person," hence a story is something wise from the past, an idea that can serve as a guide or as part of a worldview (cf. the cognates from *weid-*: guide/wise, etc./guise/*eidos*/wit/view, etc./idea/Veda—"knowledge" or "I have seen").

We are becoming so accustomed to instant history (books about major happenings published within days of the events, the immediacy of television "specials" whose commentators go out of their way to inform us that "history is being made") that a longer-range view of the past is threatened. But in antiquity Cicero grasped the importance of the historical story in constituting the ways we humans develop to maturity: "Not to tell what happened before you were born is to be forever a child. For what is the span of a man unless it is tied to that of his ancestors by the memory of earlier events?" (*The Orator*:120). A contemporary poet from Acoma pueblo in New Mexico speaks to the formative power of such stories even today: "Your children will not survive unless you tell something about them—how they were born, how they came to this certain place, how they continued" (S. Ortiz:15).

Cicero in antiquity and Ortiz today remind us of the role of mythic stories in providing the frameworks for human consciousness, the necessary linkages between the generations, even the sequences and measurements of the human life span: in some societies the storyteller has to be called in to tell the story of each stage of the development of a child, as when the child first takes the mother's nipple, first eats solid food, and so forth (see Beane and Doty: §§ 19, 21–22, 50–52). Each of us develops a personal set of mythostories, a means of relating our own existence to the larger cultural and universal meanings that have been treasured in the past.

The framing stories are told most often at our most impressionable age, that of childhood; but there are also framing stories that determine what the researcher will analyze, and those that justify economic or racial stratification. Indeed the scientist who comes up with a new framing story—think of the careers of Galileo, Newton, Einstein, or Freud—will have a great deal of trouble getting her or his work accepted when it is not congruent with the ruling stories of the day (see Kuhn; Polanyi:chap. 6; L. Hudson).

Most of us have a considerable resistance to accepting such ruling stories as constructs or fictions. We suppose our own culture no longer needs to analyze the framing metaphors, because we now (it is assumed) deal directly and scientifically with raw nature, facts, data—forgetting that these very terms are already second-order abstractions. Thinking ourselves rational and above all objective, we would have trouble with a saying from Isleta pueblo that states "Say the words of a prayer [myth, story], even a child or a foreigner, and the gods will understand" (cited by A. Ortiz 1972:204). The type of speaking ("Say the words . . .") is considered to be of an entirely different type than that used in scientific discourse, and we think we have outgrown the *do ut des* pattern that suggests that the deities must respond when the human performs a religious act. But often the metaphors of scientific discourse are treated as if they had just as much magical power, as can be noted when we listen to scientists from two or more different disciplines trying to agree on a common set of terms in which to frame a proposal for joint discussion. And naming the disease has as much power in the modern hospital as it does for the shamanic healer.

Some of the resistance to the traditional mythic stories is that they *are* traditional, that they are not the modern products of the research laboratory or the abstracting journals. Both the development of the physical sciences and the recent importance of existentialist philosophy have contributed to a certain resentment of ritual and myth in the modern world, a resentment against the repetitious, against that which is stated in informal and traditional rather than scientific or existential terms (of course the scientific or existentialist terms may become just as formulaic, but my contrast here is between the historical-traditional and the contemporary). We have become so dominated by the omnipresent Now! of the merchandisers and by the scientific "latest and best" that our attention is riveted so securely upon a narrow ribbon of time—the present—that we cannot hope to fulfill all of humankind's needs for continuity and meaning.

One of the main problems of our culture, therefore—one of the sources of what sociologists call anomie, rootlessness, the sense of having lost all foundations—is precisely our lack of attention to the "big" mythic stories or at least our unwillingness to live with the big stories considered as effective framing realities. The glib emphasis upon Now! is a shoddy substitute for consciousness of an eternal recurrence, an awareness of the human continuities that span peoples and periods of human civilization.

I do not want to be understood as calling for a new primitivism. I do not advocate a sort of head-in-the-sand retreat from contemporary life. Rather I want to point to the importance of reflecting on the traditional myths and rituals and to the dangers of ignoring the big stories. I want to point to the dangers of letting the dangerous and false mythical stories, such as the Nazi myth, racist myths, and the like, obtain dominance in our social order and in our personal lives because we have not given proper and sustained attention to the foundational mythic stories that have set us into motion and sustained us for generations.

Our contemporary appropriation of "old stories" may be an enterprise quite different from that of our ancestors: many of the ancient Greek/Roman/Jewish/Christian mythic accounts simply function no longer for us the way they once did. Mythography, critically pursued, may function as a curettage device, scalpeling away debris (from our present perspective) that should have been removed long ago. But it also may provide us with some of the tools for making moral choices among the vast range of myths that are available to us; it should provide us with a heightened dedication to forge the best possible personal and cultural mythostories, the stories that can serve as symbolic constructions of reality leading to individual freedom and social growth rather than a retreat into an automatically repeated and uncritical view of historical events that now may need to be drastically reshaped. Among the mythic/historic stories that we may have to revise are those of the literalistic interpretations of the Genesis creation stories (which have no relevance for dating a sequential series of geological periods but are concerned to make moral points about human behavior), the economic myths of free-market capitalism, or the Western understanding that humans are to conquer and rule over nature.

Myths also open toward the future, and perhaps there are, as many science-fiction advocates would argue, mythic dimensions to such speculative fictions. Gaston Bachelard suggests that "A myth . . . is a life line, a form of the future rather than a fossilized fable" (preface to Diel:xi).

Metaphoric and Symbolic Diction

Including as it does poetic, emotive, and attitude-conveying diction, mythic language is not just an arena for human rationality; it also engages sensual experience as a medium for the incarnation of mind. Metaphors and symbols touch upon, but do not exhaust, the sensual.

Gesturing toward rather than explicating, they picture out of the everyday at its very boundaries—calling forth images and experiences of the world beyond what is present, traditional, or corporate, to seed new appropriations of meaning and allow them to become embodied and spoken realities. W. B. Yeats spoke to the open-ended qualities:

> It is the charm of mythic narrative that it cannot tell one thing without telling a hundred others. The symbols are an endlessly inter-marrying family. They give life to what, stated in general terms, appears only a cold truism, by hinting how the apparent simplicity of the statement is due to an artificial isolation of a fragment, which, in its natural place, is connected with all the infinity of truths by living fibres. (Comments on Blake, quoted by Block:15; see Waardenburg)

And Richard Slotkin refers to the way a mythological corpus can dramatize "the world vision and historical sense of a people or culture, reducing centuries of experience into a constellation of compelling metaphors" (Slotkin:6–7, cited by Jewett and Lawrence 1977a:43).

As units of information that are not bound by the immediate contours of what presently is being experienced, mythical metaphors, symbols, and allegories provide concrete conveyances for (abstract) thought. Alive in a world of metaphoric and symbolic meanings, they allow experimentation and play with images, ideas, and concepts that otherwise would remain too incorporeal to be engaged. Rituals, likewise, provide physical and bodily means of acting out ideas dramatically: "ritual and myth provide the contexts which allow symbols to function" (Myerhoff 1974:240); "Ritual is the other half of the mythic statement: when myths speak only of the absolute reality, rituals ground it in the relative" (Sproul:26).

Mythemic units may be combined, correlated, clustered, condensed, and so on, and mythographic analysis often will have to concentrate upon the interconnections among them in order to bring into view the whole network. Nonmythological materials such as law codes may clarify a mythological image, and the reverse is certainly true. Justifications of the divine right of monarchs, or the concept of "the just war," for example, were not derived from rational arguments about administrative efficiency.

In supplying the root metaphors, the ruling images, of a society, mythological language provides a coding mechanism by means of which the apparent randomness of the cosmos is stabilized. Myths structure the overarching conceptualities of a society: prototypical mythical accounts may recall the first namings of the features of the landscape or of cultural activities; children are taught mythological stories as a means (albeit often only tacitly recognized) of socializing them into a worldview and an ethnic pattern of ethical behavior (Mannheim is still valuable on the development of ideologies from myths). Among the Lege (a Bantu people of East Zaire), initiates learn literally thousands of traditional proverbs; these are taught one by one, but the adult initiate comes to view the entire experienced universe through the lens of these parables: they have the function of naming and coding the universe in a way that gives it daily and immediate meaning (the example is from Zuesse 1979:6–8). Somehow we seem to be able to see this sort of coding operation much more easily when we look at another society, but it operates in any society; our very language is permeated with proverbial and mythological features by which we interpret reality (on one such coding, the future orientation in North America, see Dundes 1969).

Originally metaphors and symbols convey new, world-creative perceptions that resound with many different voices and meanings. We speak poetically or metaphorically when "hard language" or "stenodiction" (Philip Wheelwright's term for monovocal stabilized dictionary language) does not allow us the necessary linguistic flexibility to state what is just coming into view. However, by repeated usage, metaphors and symbols become locked into single-meaning codes, where each term "stands for" only one meaning. Then, instead of opening up multiplex insights, they close down alternative viewings and demand social conformity of usage.

Frequently myth tends to become so thoroughly internalized and intrasubjective that its inventiveness no longer is recognized but it is considered as "the way things are literally." Then mythical concepts are considered not as expressing tensile relations between concept and reality, not as metaphoric approximations to complex mysteries, but as literally functioning systems. (Contrast Western concepts of human dominance over the earth with Eastern and Amerindigen emphasis upon the continuity of the human and the earthly, upon flowing with nature rather than dominating it.)

One purpose of the study of mythological fictions and imagination may be to recover some of the original multiple and polyvocal dynamics of the metaphoric inventions, in order subsequently to speak anew in a repristinized mythopoesis that may be truly recreative. F. Dümmler suggests that "the preoccupation with mythology has something intoxicating about it, and the [person] who does research in myth must always become to a certain degree a poet of theogonies" (in a review quoted without publishing information by Robert B. Palmer, introducing his translation of Otto 1965:xx). The myth analyst as theogonist—

quite a striking suggestion!—or as locator and identifier of the goddesses and gods whose reality is still to be experienced!

At least we may speak of the mythographer's role as being that of an imaginal educator, who discloses or uncovers the metaphoric powers of mythological expression. Whether or not she or he also becomes "to a certain degree a poet" depends upon the individual and upon the receptivity of the mythographer's society to one's findings, which in turn reflects the society's openness toward its continuum of imaginative acts at a particular time. It may be the critic or historian, no less than the acknowledged "poet," who aids the recovery of the past tradition as lively-for-the-present; but the psychologically true may have to be defended or delimited from the stenodiction of particular academic or scientific hegemonies.

Graphic Imagery

When there is a widespread interest in mythology, as made evident by current book sales, university course electives, and successful programs and seminars on mythology, it is instructive to ask just why it is present—especially at this twentieth-century apex of scientific progress and social engineering. Why is it that mythological figures are so compelling today?

A personalistic answer would be that the goddesses and gods themselves are stirring us up, deliberately causing a discordant noise, in order once again to be experienced, redefined, and heard. Another explanation would focus upon the progressive tendencies toward abstraction and depersonalization in our increasingly fact-impacted society.

⌊Myths play out expression not abstractly but, as we have seen, in stories and images; because mythical language operates as an aesthetic device (and in other ways as well, of course), it expresses meanings through concrete and graphic imagic diction. I suspect that mythological figures speaking through myths will be listened to most receptively when the abstract has become problematic, when the abstract seems so removed from experience that people become painfully aware of a mind-body bifurcation that seems to exclude meaningful embodiment and incorporation of thought. (I am struck by how many contemporary speculative fiction stories culminate in disclosures that "perfect beings" live a completely disembodied existence.)

And if my hunch is correct, we may correlate the widespread contemporary fascination with "body movement"—yoga, tantrism, meditation, psychosynthesis, and the like—with a search for more satisfactory integration of flesh and spirit. The programs just mentioned emphasize this integration, and each reflects a frequent feature of mythological symbolism, namely the graphic use of the human body as a master symbol for spirituality. We can refer to traditional figures of speech such as the Christian church as the Body of Christ, or to the Jewish kabbalistic tradition, in which the arrangements of the elements of the Sephirothic diagram may be interpreted as a multidimensional interfacing of the worlds of reality and the component members of the human body.

The body serves as a rich source of mythological symbolism throughout the world; some even have argued that its white, red, and dark components contribute the essential color triad in myth and ritual (Douglas, 1966, 1970; Zahan; V. Turner 1965). And the extended body, society, also contributes graphic expression to mythic imagery; we need only refer to the biocosmological geography represented by images of the Earth Mother, or by the life-giving fluids of the various Rivers of Life. Myths highlight the experienced polarities of human physical and social existence, such as light versus dark, female versus male, living versus dead, and order versus disorder; and they graphically reflect awareness of the stages of human development and change (both physical and social) from infancy to old age.

While we seem to be awaiting yet the full developments of Claude Lévi-Strauss's "science of the concrete," attention to the actual types of graphic imagery employed in myths—for instance, conquests of gravity, winged flight, metamorphoses, and the like—may reveal conceptual patterns otherwise easily overlooked. It will be interesting, given developments in computer coding, to see if particular types of graphic imagery appear regularly in myths across many cultures.[7]

Introducing a collection of writings by Gaston Bachelard she translated, Colette Gaudin proposes that "material elements reflect our souls; more than forms, they fix the unconscious, they provide us with a sort of direct reading of our destiny" (preface to Bachelard 1971a:xv). If this proposal is so, and Bachelard's works provide a rich resource to demonstrate that it is, we should be able to move myth analysis closer to iconographic studies in order to obtain a more inclusive analytic perspective.[8]

Emotional Conviction and Participation

One of the first benefits of myths, suggests the fourth-century Saloustios, is that they stir up our intellects by causing us to ask questions about what they recount (Nock:par. iii). Mythic *narratives* are a form of *knowing* (note the Indo-European cognates from the stem **gno-*: know/cunning/ken/cognition/narrative/gnosis). The knowing is not just that of the rational, ideational aspects of human consciousness but that of the sensual-aesthetic, moral, and emotional as well. In fact, Murray Stein can speak correctly of a certain "elusiveness to the intellect" (32) as characteristic of myth; he refers, I suppose, to the coherence of feeling-tone that can draw us into the web of the mythic story, that quality of "deeper psychological reflection than would otherwise be likely" in, say, the daily newspaper. Similarly Toelken and Scott can refer to mythic tales as providing "a way of projecting and experiencing our anxieties" (97; Polanyi and Prosch, in chaps. 8 and 9, address the issue of the immediate appeal of lively myths).

Myths both convince the believer of their relevance and lead her or him to participate in them, when they are seen as part of oneself, when one recognizes how the personal mythostory is fused with the cultural or archetypal—or perhaps more acutely, when one discovers the presence of mythemes within one's own story or within the lives of those around us. "We are what we myth," and we are always in the process of becoming another realization of our potential selfhoods, another enactment of the deities within. Or as Herbert Mason would have it, "Instead of leading us on a journey to self, as some believe, [myth] leads us on a journey out of self. We leave the isolation of our perspective and enter the larger, if ultimately limited, universe in which others see what is true to them" (16).

We are convinced by the mythic story and recognize our participation within it when we feel its claim to unite rather than to separate aspects of our existence, when it both explains and honors the inexplicable, accepting rather than denying that what cannot be examined and demonstrated mathematically may have a very powerful reality indeed. Doria and Lenowitz speak to this totalizing aspect of myth:

> Myth has this value: it unites rather than separates or divides; it provides ways other than the purely sequential to grapple with undifferentiated experience; it preserves instead of eliminating unfathomed reaches and the discoverable/decipherable spaces that make up at least in part the totalities of our existence (i.e., there are mysteries after all; it is not "all there"). (xix)

An imaginally illiterate culture will have trouble with emotionally powerful images, demanding that common signs replace large, mysterious images and symbols. It will veer away from totalizing as from the nonrational, seeking to code the spiritually intense in sociological or statistical patterns, causing the soul's appearance to appear aberrant, the intensity of the mythic story a gaucherie. It will demand that the rite be totally rational, losing sight of the inexplicable ways mythic influences decide the sounds, colors, and emblems, even the shaping of the sacred and secular environments and the character of the priesthood. It will never understand Friedrich von Schlegel's romantic definition, which more than any other "explains" the emotional powers at work: "The myth is a hieroglyphic expression of environing nature under the transfiguration of imagination and love" (cited by Bogan:12).

The Primal, Foundational Accounts

Myths are perceived as essential accounts, the primary stories of a culture, the stories that shape and expose its most important framing images and self-conceptions, its "roots." So a Mexican Huichol begins a myth about the origins of the food plant maize (corn) this way: "This is the story of our roots. It is a story of the maize that we adore, that which we hold sacred, because it is our nourishment, it is our life. That is why we must know it well" (Myerhoff 1974:210).

Rather than chronological or logical primacy of place, such roots are what matter to a culture; and myths and rituals promise continuity with what is radically essential to "our life," to humanness as it is defined in the culture. So the Zuni creator god Kisklo ("tireless hearer"), who brought the myths of the Zuni people, is addressed by the chief of the Council of the Gods: "As a woman with children is loved for keeping unbroken the line of her kin, so you, tireless hearer, will be cherished by us and worshipped by men for keeping unbroken the Stories of Creation and all that we tell of past days and future" (cited by Tyler:63).

Zuni and other stories of creation define what "human" shall mean, and such stories often delineate the orders of relationships between "our people," "them," and "the gods." One who does not define oneself in terms of the culture's primary myths—that is, someone who belongs to another mythic mind-set, another nationality—may be considered barely human, as many field ethnologists have discovered. Clifford Geertz and his wife, arriving in Bali in 1958, discovered that: "We were intruders, professional ones, and the villagers dealt with us . . . as though we were not there. For them . . . we were nonpersons, specters, invisible" (Geertz 1973:412).[9]

Myths are resolutely chauvinistic in such matters: whatever cannot be related to origins in the primal accounts will have to be justified by often elaborate secondary interpretation. This phenomenon may be sighted quite readily in attempts to base modern social legislation upon what is said to be implicit in the national constitution; cognitive dissonance arises whenever the contemporary social setting differs so radically from that presupposed in the foundational document that sufficient reinterpretation seems impossible.

Many myths serve to justify contemporary practices, statuses, relationships, ritual performances, technologies, and the like, and/or to provide their etiological explanations. It is not only in medicine that etiology functions as a technological tool for manipulating the object—we referred earlier to the organization of the *Forschungsbericht* prefacing a scholarly thesis, and Freudian psychoanalysts argue that solutions to latter-day personality disorders lie in counteracting their etiological traumata at earlier stages of personality development.

An important religious function of mythic expression is that it reaffirms that the primal stories are the most perfect and the most potent, that salvation is attained by reconnecting with the spiritual energies that first were given expression in the myths in primal times. Rituals may seek to engage directly and to reactivate this potency, to make it available to the participants often as a form of healing either a personal maladjustment or a societal tension. Hence initial episodes of such rituals often include marking off a mythical geography that recapitulates that of "the primordial former condition . . . construed as the beginning" (Myerhoff 1974:252) as a first step toward identifying the spatial locus of health or salvation. The most modern religious ritual will include a ceremonial "processional" that introduces the boundaries of the sanctified space and identifies the statuses of the primary ritualists.

Mythic accounts, especially those that relate beginnings, embody ideas of wholeness, of order replacing chaos. Hence they may be emphasized strongly during periods when fragmentation or attenuation threaten social structures. A period of cultural *breakup* may produce a conservative reaction, leading to an almost magical reaffirmation of the normative *breakthrough* of order into chaos in the primeval era.[10] Those who question the sacral validity of the mythic origins at such a time may find themselves classified as traitors to the tribal or national cause.

The Real, Experienced World

The participant in the mythical cosmos ingredient to the network of myths does not perceive the represented events, persons, times, and so on, as primarily unreal or imaginary but sees them as reflections of what actually transpires on some level. In general mythical personages are believed really to have existed, or really to exist, at particular times in the mythic chronology. But such perception has reference to "mythic chronology," and that sort of time is "time experienced as bearing meaning." It is not the same as the sort of historicality to which we so often refer, that is, something that has merely happened. The German language distinguishes meaningful history, *Geschichte,* from history as chronicle, *Historie,* a distinction similar to my earlier distinction between the historic (German: *geschichtliche*) and the historical (German: *historische*). W. F. Otto observes that the myths around Dionysos, for instance, may not reflect actual historical events, yet "they contain much more that is real than if they were repeating that which had once occurred. They are not witnesses of that which once was but of that which will always be, as Sallustius says when he is speaking of the myths of Attis: 'This never happened but it always is' " (Otto 1965:75, quoting Saloustios, *Peri theōn* 4.9).

To the extent that myths are regarded as expressing lasting nodal points of human significance, they present unquestionable truths, which are considered unfalsifiable so long as sympathetic retelling or ritual reinforcement continues to evoke emotional participation. It is when someone from another framework calls into question the reality of the mythic framework that we begin to feel its nature as something human-made, imposed upon the world; hence Herbert Mason's comment that

> we might perceive myth to be, not a mere untruth, but a story rooted in a place where one has been in the past and that one has to reach urgently in the present and that someone at a crucial point on the way says does not exist. It is a story, like most, of facts familiar to oneself but to which, until something happens to make returning to them impossible in the familiar way, one gives almost no thought. (15)

As part of the real, experienced world, myths may establish a temporal network, an interior chronological continuum between contemporary and primal times, relating individuals and societies temporally, and providing relative rankings of "our time" to "as in days of yore" (cf. the remarkably persistent use of the Christian designations B.C. and A.D.). The extent to which chronological conceptions are mythically maintained even today may be seen in cases where for a long time scientists—such as archaeologists and cultural anthropologists—have ignored findings that would demand revisions of their operational time schemes. The Olduvai Gorge excavations by Louis and Mary Leakey, for example, were studiously ignored for some time.

As deposits of experience or as indicators of types of constant relations, myths pass along traditional adaptational patterns and thus serve survival functions; for those for whom the myths have become inert, however, conscious modeling of the self according to mythic prototypes may be rejected, while subterranean traces in consciousness live on. We see such traces in languages, which may harbor mythological associations long after the underlying myth is forgotten (and so tropical storms even today are given personal names), or in the unconscious psyche (although today few Western persons would posit a historical reality with respect to "Adam and Eve," doubtless the first image that occurs when these names are mentioned would be of a specific man and woman).

Structuralist analysis has taught us that the relationship of the mythic events to the real, experienced world may be dialectical in nature, expressing limit situations and possibilities that the society considers should be excluded from normal behavior; or it may reflect possibilities that the society has not yet actually experienced. In either case, the benchmark is the socially constructed and reinforced real, and myths establish systems of differences between components of existence, sometimes mediating between them and other times increasing the contrasts ("What have Athens and Jerusalem to do with each other?").

Humankind's Roles and Relative Statuses

As we have seen, myths model possible behavioral roles, thereby expressing the range of possibilities conceived as "human" within a particular society. Mythic figures provide projective mythic identities, even for highly sophisticated contemporaries, the figures functioning sequentially as objectively other psyche models, providing opportunities to play seriously at the various selves we may desire to explore or to become.

Myths may establish pecking orders, genealogical relationships, and the relative importance of various social groups within a society. Hence they may provide both pragmatic and psychological orientation toward the immediate social cosmos. Changes in social status may be reflected in and guided by myths and rituals, especially insofar as these both mirror roles and provide ceremonies that facilitate transitions within a society: hero myths, initiation, marriage, and so on. (In addition myths and rituals may inculcate social standards that are given public acquiescence, while the participant follows private models and goals: the modern practice of politics often seems based on such procedure!)

The role of heroines and heroes is especially marked: they seem to represent the extremes of human behavior on behalf of the collective, even though often imaged in terms of the lone individual's struggle to determine a proper course of behavior that initially seems antisocial. The heroine or hero—or perhaps every initiate—goes beyond the expected social norms in order to return to confirm the norms or to reshape them. The history of the ways the heroic is defined will be as well the history of the definition of selfhood: active or passive, conquering or receptive, critical toward or accepting of traditional models, and so on. The dominant myths of an era reflect its views of psychosocial maturity or health.

Various subgroups may support differing mythic models, leading to the presence of more than one norm for human fulfillment (making money, ruling a kingdom, attaining enlightenment). Tribal or familial myths may provide incentive to understand oneself as having a special status within a larger social whole (a leader, a servant, a prophet). In this way they may provide a justification for understanding one's group as "God's people" in a period of suppression by others. So the Okanagon (a Salish tribe) claim that the first Indians were made "from balls of red earth or mud, and this is why we are reddish-colored. . . . As red earth is more nearly related to gold and copper than other kinds of earth, therefore the Indians are nearer to gold, *and finer than other races*" (first published in 1917 after contacts with European-Americans; in Sproul:243, my emphasis).

Convey Political and Moral Values

Anthropology subsequent to Bronislaw Malinowski's emphasis upon myths as "charters" for social orders (discussed in Chapter 2) favors the position that political and moral values are conveyed by mirroring of the actual order as well as by idealistic paradigms: myths and rituals both reflect and project valuational frameworks; they provide scenarios for action as well as reflecting or distorting mirrors.

Values conveyed by myths within a network may be of different types: they may relate ideals for human interaction, responses toward non- or suprahuman realities, and so on. Myths are normative in supporting particular types of behavior and association and rejecting other *exempla*; they are educative and heuristic in highlighting adaptive and adjustive patterns. They provide social cohesion by creating a shared symbolic articulation of social patterns and relations, by leading to a releasing of tensions (as in rituals between age groups), and by blocking nonapproved explorations of relationship or behavior or inquiry (functioning today as scientific paradigms or models). While myths may well be cohesive within a monofocal society (Émile Durkheim's "social cement"), they may be divisive within a polyfocal society such as our own: myths such as those underlying anti-Semitism may perpetuate hatred among subgroups.

The tendency to justify values by referring them to a prototypical time of origins may reflect the desire to make social ideals and sanctions absolute by grounding them in a primordial scene that is not open to questioning the way immediate pragmatic decision making must be ("thou shalt not kill," but "anyone who wears the red shirt is fair game"). A period of severely heightened social change may herald a vast amount of confusion for religious and mythological concepts correlated with social institutions (cf. Geertz 1973:chap. 6, and Vogt); one party may urge maintenance of ancient standards while another urges accommodation to more recent pragmatisms.

Myths (and rituals) may emphasize values and conditions that are just the opposite of what is found in contemporary experience; for example, myths stressing coordination and peace may be prominent during a period of anarchy or warfare. "The Lady doth protest too much, methinks" applies, of course; or, to use a psychoanalytical term, we might speak of mythic compensation or of the attempt to recondition the present through magical repetition of what was understood to be effective primally. Hence the mythographer should proceed very cautiously in drawing conclusions about social situations from the mythology emphasized at any given period. The emphases of myths in repeated use may reflect idealizations rather than actualities.

Systems of Interpretation

Culture itself may be called a hermeneutical system of interpretation, a semiotics, or a language event. As a person is what she or he speaks, a culture is the mythic stories it tells; predilection for certain types of stories reflects the modes by which a society can best explain itself—the ways, in Talcott Parsons's phrase, it glosses perception. A survey of our own society's fiction can disclose important indications of the ways we gloss perception, the ways we more or less unconsciously accept certain parameters of what a fiction writer or novelist may or may not portray. Literary histories can track the first instances of the use of a particular narrative voice or style, for instance, or the growing acceptance of the way explicit sexual activities are portrayed. And within the fictions most recently considered "acceptable" in contemporary literature, de-emphasis upon sequential narrative plots, rejection of chronological or temporal conventions, and the shattering of the model of the omniscient narrator may reveal as much about our own social incoherence as volumes of sociological data.[11]

To the extent that myths provide essential frameworks for the language of a society, they provide systems or patterns for signifying meanings, especially meanings of the past (I referred to this provision of frameworks as "coding" earlier). These frameworks provide markers that establish the emotive and effective values of symbols and scriptures within the society; they enable value distinctions to be made among the elements of the world at hand; they intensify certain features, synthesize others, and establish relative rankings among the key and secondary symbols.

The relative validity of a particular mythemic system will determine the influence it exercises among other systems, varying from very significant to purely subordinate. Reform movements frequently seek to revivify the terms and concepts of an earlier stage of the mythological semantics and hence to reinstate an earlier system of interpretation. Revivalist "Back to the Bible" movements within Christianity provide one example.

The symbols may provide means of depotentiating forces that are experienced naively as being threatening (death, sexuality, weather phenomena). By the overlayering of symbolic interpretations, such dangers are reduced by being connected to experiences already recognized as safe. Ritual exorcists or shamans may encourage a patient to experience fully "the other world" into which the specialist takes her or him. Upon return to everyday reality the person will be able to operate more effectively, because she or he now recognizes the actual contours of that world's powers as interpreted by the society and no longer is controlled by fearful personal projections. By its behaviors—which may include disapproval or laughter—the ritual audience reinforces the societal understandings concerning how the two worlds are to be related.

Individual Experience within Universal Perspective

Myths delineate the *macrocosmic* dimensions of the perceived social and natural worlds in symbolic terms that enable individuals to situate themselves *microcosmically* within them. Because ritual facilitates the actual interfacing of the cultural macrocosm with the individual microcosm, we may say that it in turn performs a *mesocosmic* function (the term is from Zuesse 1975:522).

Myths highlight distinctions between "my people" (the immediate group: kin, socioeconomic, or geographical neighbors) and "them" (those medially removed: persons from another territory, enemies). Hence myths establish the personal boundaries of interpreted existence and guide one's adjustment to normative attitudes, statuses, and roles within it. In this manner myths and rituals may be anxiety reducing when they mesh the individual with the social order or provide associative identification within the immediate group. Even the "self-made person" has a family, and familial genealogy will be emphasized when the social role of the individual is unclear.

Situations of great social change often trail confusions in the patterns of individual-to-group identifications featured in the primary myths. In such periods it becomes more and more difficult to internalize the ways individuals recapitulate the development of the microcosm, as stressed in initiations, which may include a symbolic regression to chaos before a sequence of developmental stages leading to full adulthood (or full personhood: the uninitiated may not be considered fully human). Then the question of "role models" becomes acute, as seen most clearly in modern societies in the confusion around the nature of "identity," a theme that appears in many contemporary novels as well as "self-help" books.

Myths provide us with projective psyche models, perhaps not as immediately and insistently as do our parents and peers, but with models nonetheless—models of roles, of aspirations toward becoming something other than what we are, of ways of imaging new possibilities as to who we are. They function particularly—or at least they have so functioned—to give us role models of masculine and feminine behavior (as for instance the myth of Eros and Psyche). They educate us in ways of acting out maleness and femaleness, in interrelating the two, in reflecting on the best traits of each sex, and even in ways of reconceiving the social manifestations of masculinity and femininity within particular historical periods.

The danger is that mythological models are apt to become stereotypical models, merely enforcing patterns of behavior that are no longer adequate to our own social realities. A skeptical tension between the model and the reality is always necessary and must be cultivated carefully. (I am reminded of the formation of a group of one hundred Wonder Women at the annual convention of the National Organization of Women in Atlantic City in September 1974: the NOW organizers clearly understood the need to work against the Super*man* stereotype of our immediate heritage.)

Myths provide a sense of the person's roles in the universe, a centering upon ourselves as located within a cosmic as well as a local context. "Who am I?" evokes mythic answers: compare the Genesis creation myth with its positive evaluation of the role of human beings—or now negatively regarded, its picture of human beings so elevated above nature that we have felt free to manipulate and in the process destroy it. Such questioning and comparison might lead us to ask where the new ecological creation myths may be located, or to ask what happens to such a dichotomy between nature and culture when experiments seem to indicate that plants have nervous systems and feelings (Tompkins and Bird).

And myths elucidate our dreams and fantasies; they tie our imaginings into universal sharings, ancient postures of acting out that may be forgotten or replaced but reenter when least noticed: think of the recent fascination with magic and the occult. Part of what it means to study myths and rituals of other peoples, other times and places, is that one recovers parts of personal identity: the personal microcosm recreated from the impersonal macrocosm. "Who am I?" becomes "Who have humans like me been?" and "What are the possible ranges of human becoming?"

In these ways we can speak of personal guidance as a function of myths and rituals—not so much directly, answering to the moral decision, "How must I behave?" but informing that decision, educating the imaginative function that must assemble the possibilities for acting. With respect to the study of myths and rituals, the role of "universals" and cross-cultural comparisons is not so much to establish the exact meaning of a particular version as to open up the range of human possibilities in which such expressions otherwise occur—for we all too readily become trapped within the range of our own experience. Universals and cross-cultural comparisons also enable us to see whether or not any particular version of a myth or ritual is congruent with the norm in a particular culture, or whether it reverses it or otherwise adapts it to a specific context (see K. Kroeber 1981:88).

Intervention of Suprahuman Entities

Myths so frequently feature the intervention of deities or forces from "another world" discontinuous with this one that many definitions have taken the element "stories of the gods" to be necessarily ingredient to "myth" as such. However, the beings or forces are not always personal and are more accurately designated as being suprahuman. By using the term suprahuman I would emphasize that myths typify qualities associated with highly marked experiences that indicate something transcending (but not negating) ordinary personhood and yet stopping short of the *totaliter aliter* (absolute Otherness) of deity in Western theology.[12]

The suprahuman entities may be nonpersonal attitudes, as in myths where qualities of social behavior (eros, desire, vanity) are embodied in personal roles. Or the transcendent aspect may arise from summarizing and carrying in personal form the clearest expressions of corporate significance, be they the most noble or the most base (I think of the Greek personalization of Aretē, the hypostases of Gnosis, or the terrifying Balinese witch, Rangda). At the most abstract level, we might speak of archetypes represented in action, or embodied, as ultimate symbols of interior life and human interaction.

Here to a marked degree the myth analyst confronts differences in perspective between the analyst's and the society's interpretation. Those within a mythical worldview may regard as personal interventions of suprahuman powers what the external analyst regards as a mechanism illustrating a psychological displacement of affect. Respect for the society's own perspectives is crucial, and every effort must be made to listen in on the ways a mytheme is experienced at firsthand; contemporary myth gathering includes indications of tone of voice in which the materials are chanted or spoken, sound effects used, performance markers, and audience reactions.

The account of the disclosure of a numen or other power or deity ought not be disrespected or treated condescendingly, no matter how the analyst wishes to code it for her or his own metastructural purposes. Its appearance will be marked by a sense of "otherness" within the context where it has found a religious response. The observer may collate such phenomena into a wider context of the phenomenology and history of religion, but first every effort must be made to project oneself imaginatively into the primary context where the mythic forces are directly and affectively experienced. Creative mythopoesis may include a poesis of ethnomethodologies![13]

Sympathetically, therefore, the analyst asks such questions as: What is it that is revealing itself through this myth? What comes to expression here that has not been expressed—or which has been expressed—elsewhere under different forms? What mode of being discloses itself in such phenomena? How does such-and-such an element contribute to a total organization of societal meaning? Does the myth provide expression to meanings that cannot be expressed adequately through other forms of diction such as philosophical or theological reflection? And what would be relinquished if this particular item were deleted or altered?[14]

Aspects of the Natural and Cultural Orders

The nature of mythology is such that myths are originally statements in nonreligious language, that is, the mythological "bricks" are figured from daily life, not just from specially elevated religious subject matter or diction, however much they may become so marked in the course of transmission and development.

Natural imagery such as references to the seasons or metaphors of growth may be emphasized, but they hardly exhaust the vocabulary of myth, as we have learned from the misdirections of nineteenth-century mythography. Myths frequently reinforce a tribe's learned ecological adaptations to its natural contexts as well as its orderings of social behaviors within the tribe. Many mythic stories provide effective means of interrelating the natural/objective, the psychic/psychological, and the cultural/learned aspects of experience. So a person growing up within a mythically alive society learns a mythical gazetteer that may provide a great source of emotional connection with places never actually seen. Alfonso Ortiz recalls sharing a journey with a companion to an area in Colorado well described by Tewa mythology. His friend wept with joy as he recognized features of a place he had never actually visited before: "He had heretofore never journeyed here, but now it was as if he had come home. . . . He had never been here, but then he had never really left" (1973:90).

Our own alienation from our bodies, and from satisfying corporate ritual, may indicate that much is to be learned from other (earlier, more "primitive") societies in which the individual has been more consistently related to the universal, the ectypal to the archetypal, and the natural to the cultural orders. However, we must find some manner of operating without the traditional supports so important in those societies, if we no longer suppose that the deities reveal the inner rules of "nature," and emphasize instead the logos supremacy of human culture—although the well-known relativity of human standards across time and cultures makes even that questionable.

Rituals, Ceremonials, and Dramas

We no longer need to argue against the notion that myths *need be* enacted (a common methodological residue derived from the ritual-dominant school, to be discussed in Chapter 3), yet common sense also requires us to recognize the possible, or even probable, relation between the story and its enactment, between *mythos* and *cultus*. Often we may speak of mutual influence and reinforcement; but in many cases, especially from antiquity, we now have either the myth or the ritual but not both.

Ritual often implies a license to enact, within a specific spatiotemporal frame, the contents of a myth. Even when a record of the ritual performance is not available, elements of a myth may be clarified by reference to what is known about ritual usage in other contexts. (I will discuss ritual studies much more extensively in Chapter 3.)

Formalized as the texts of underlying or accompanying rituals, myths are loaded with expectations (such as those I have charted here); hence their canonical status may elevate them or otherwise separate them from other "texts" of the community. Many different societies differentiate culturally important myths from other materials such as tales and legends; and the specialist in reciting or enacting the myths may be specially venerated or surrounded by taboos.

Later retellings or descriptions— "desituations" from a performance context (the term is from Abrahams; also see Schechner)—affect subsequent receptions of the myth, not only for someone who may read a transcript of a public myth recitation that one has heard personally, but unavoidably for most of us, who must perforce only guess at the auditory, somatic, and kinetic clues accompanying the telling of mythical stories, as in, for example, archaic societies.

"Dramas" is included in our definition in light of Victor Turner's helpful use of the dramatistic analogy to clarify the dynamics of ritual behaviors, as well as to suggest that many myths have developed through a phase in which dramatic shaping was crucial—evident in Greece and other cultures—an argument especially associated with Theodor H. Gaster's work, *Thespis* (1961).

"Ceremonies" is included because even in a nonreligious or nonmythological setting mythical elements may form part of the vocabulary: compare the ritualistic invocation and benediction at university graduation services or political banquets (recent studies on nonreligious rituals: Moore and Myerhoff, with bibliog.; Lincoln 1977:157–60; and Grimes 1982b).

Secondary Elaborations

Various degrees of appropriations of myths within a network may be demonstrated, ranging from the most vital appropriation, where the myth is accorded cognitive status directly and immediately, to a relatively inert stage where it has become an empty image or an artificial frame of reference. It is extremely important, therefore, to recognize the relative level of functional vitality of a particular myth at a particular time; I will develop this analysis in Chapter 2. At one moment the same mythological material may be "heard" quite differently even by coequal members of the same society. Any number of instances could be cited of a graphic artist's figuring of a mythological scene with images that have been modified or rejected by contemporaneous literary artists: I think especially of Greek pottery illustrations but also of the development of paintings of the Nativity of the Christ.

Furthermore, it is important to recognize that a culture that does not appear to be concerned explicitly with mythology in terms of referring to mythological terminology formally, frequently, and emotionally (Kerényi 1962 cites the later Romans) may be embodying it, acting it out directly and constantly in social role differentiations, and hence taking it very seriously indeed.

We hardly can be ignorant today, for instance, of biblical influences upon the ways we have elevated masculinity while denigrating femininity. And Pearce's important study demonstrates how deep-mythic models influenced white European contacts with the Native Americans: the settlers simply could not "see" the natives as settled, peaceable *farmers,* even in the cases where they were, because of their own cultural models of "savages" as rapacious *hunters.* Similar stereotyping has contributed to the image many Western persons project toward the Native North American yet today—as a befeathered, seminaked warrior, riding bareback after the buffalo; yet the model, the Plains hunter, existed for barely a century of Native American history and was atypical of most Amerindigen societies (Niethammer:xvi).

In referring to secondary elaborations, I have in mind the stage of mythic vitality where the believed myths are the least believed, when the mythemes have become something more akin to arbitrary stereotypes and stenodiction than to language considered powerful enough to make the supranormal present and effective. In this case a recreative mythopoesis may be the only means of reobtaining access to the originative metaphoric dynamics.

The relationship between a lively access to myth and the believing social framework is expressed, in its contemporary problematic aspects, by the literary critics Wellek and Warren: "To speak of the need for myth, in this case of the imaginative writer, is a sign of his felt need for communion with his society, for a recognized status as artist functioning within society" (192). Literary myth criticism seems to have had its heyday, but we have only begun to appreciate the range of possibilities by which mythemes are elaborated secondarily in fictional and poetic works of our own recent literary history.

And we need to apply some of what we learn about mythic systems to the so-called high religions, to modern societies, and to intellectual activities in the sciences and the humanities. Clearly, mythical attitudes exist that touch how one lives one's life, quite apart from explicit affirmation of specific myth systems. I have focused here less on such ideological attitudes than upon myth proper, but the attitudinal question is also extremely important (see Smart:83).[15]

My own experience provides an illustration of the "use" of the study of myths and rituals in what I will call "comparative thematic elucidation." A few years ago I had a very detailed dream in which I wandered into a series of underground rooms decorated in Oriental motifs, coming eventually to a modern sound stage where a group of Japanese teenagers were playing Western rock music. After noting the rightness of the union of East and West in this scene, I ascended a staircase into the innermost chamber and was stunned by the beauty of some round stone sculptures set on pedestals in a reflecting pool. At the same instant I realized, first, that the stones were the most perfect items in the entire series of underground rooms, second, that these were my own creations and, third, that I had not yet created them.

There were many other details, but these are enough for our purposes here. In trying to come to grips with that dream (which struck me with great emotional affect), I reread Joseph Campbell's *Hero with a Thousand Faces* (1968b) and found that my dream had been imaged or experienced for centuries. It followed closely the pattern of the career of the typical mythical hero, the pattern called by Campbell the heroic monomyth, a pattern consisting of separation from the world, penetration to a source of power, and a life-enhancing return. I also found some important material in Herbert Fingarette's *The Self in Transformation* (1963) on the relationship between reality and fantasy, and that in turn led to materials in the Upanishads concerning dreams as an intermediate state between this world and "the other" world.

The dream and subsequent study of it gave me an existentially important lesson in what I am calling thematic elucidation, and although I did not obtain a new self-definition of myself as a mighty culture hero, I did find the exploration of great personal value. Later research on the hero motif for class lectures led to study of the literary hero archetype and the modern anti-hero, to study of the schizophrenic experience (with its motifs of separation-penetration-return), and to work on kingship patterns in the Ancient Near East. No one who is familiar with the Jungian analytical method of amplification will be surprised by my experience, but it was new to me at the time. Several years later I found that a similar method when studying the figure of Hermes led me to non-Greek parallels in South America, China, and elsewhere that greatly added to my appreciation of representations of Hermes: I literally saw things in the Greek materials I had not seen before the comparative study.

Comparative thematic elucidation is simply my term for a type of freely associative study that consists of tracking motifs and pattern similarities in mythology and folklore, no matter where they originally occur. Similar studies have led me and my students into analysis of shamanism and, with that phenomenon, the role of religious leaders in preliterary societies, the roots of drama and popular entertainment in shamanism, and study of healing-curing specialists, including the "poor, deaf, blind, and dumb boy," Tommy, in The Who's rock opera with that title.

Studying dreams in relationships to cultural myths (the frequently represented position is that myths are cultural dreams), we have learned about cultures supposedly more primitive than our own that practice dream analysis as a regular family activity (see Stewart); we have studied contemporary laboratory research on dreams, Gaston Bachelard's philosophical meditations on the role of reverie, Freud on dreams as repressed sexual problems, and Jung on dreams as anticipations of future vocations.

The subjects for this type of elucidation are almost infinite: I and my students have worked with the trickster image, emergence and creation narratives, witchcraft, magic, medieval Jewish mysticism, fairy tales . . . and many other subjects. Cross-cultural comparative research clearly differs from typical academic studies in anthropology and sociology, and it may be important to urge a renewal of such an approach that so contradicts the compartmentalizations and specializations of scholarship today.

Cross-cultural comparative analyses, as well as discussions of universals or archetypes, can be misleading if they are considered as providing genetic explanations. But when they are used to establish a projective matrix of possible realizations of a particular theme, they may be of great value in appreciating just what is unique to a particular realization (text, theme, motif, or performance). Comparative analysis seems extremely important in the fields of intellectual history, where it is one of the tools for establishing critical standards. The days of uncritical collation of many different accounts—such as marked Frazer's *The Golden Bough,* or William Graham Sumner's *Folkways*—are clearly in the past; no one today would accept as authoritative comparisons that ignore the original cultural contexts. But I suspect that we soon may see comparative thematic studies become popular once again, compiled now on the basis of paradigmatic linguistic structuralist criteria.

In concluding this definitional attempt, we may need to be reminded that we ought not to expect across-the-board consistency of understanding or application. Philip Slater writes that "a myth is a little like a political platform: there is something in it for everyone; and for that reason one should not expect psychological consistency for a myth any more than one would expect value consistency from a political platform" (1968:196).

I find the first part of Slater's comment most agreeable to the complex definition I have presented here. Only a polyphasic definition that makes use of the many strands of myth interpretation developed in modern research will enable us to catch sight of the many facets of myth and ritual situated within many contexts of individual and social life. And only an orientation that recognizes that myths do not speak consistently in only one voice within a society—whether because of the different levels of their vitality or because of the differing trainings and capacities of their interpreters—will enable us to approach this very complex topic adequately.

A hypothetically all-inclusive definition would need to treat other aspects as well; but we must bear in mind Jane Ellen Harrison's caution that "a definition however illuminating always desiccates the object" (1957b:487). If we have been able here to avoid desiccating myth but rather have pointed provisionally to its immense richness and utility, the movement toward adequate mythic understandings will have been satisfactorily begun. It remains to return to the various ways myths and rituals may be approached, and to the myths and rituals themselves; for as David Maclagan suggests in the commercial language of our own day: "Myth, like poetry, pays compound interest on each re-reading" (12).

The Functional Contexts
and Truths of
Myths and Rituals

Myths in general have the attributes of objective truth
largely because, perhaps, they are stories having a weight
of common consent. This does not mean that storytellers
cannot make their own additions to a particular myth;
but it does mean that the additions they make have to
obtain popular consent if they are to remain parts of the
myth. Myths are stories stamped large with social
approval.

Kenelm Burridge, Mambu

ONE OF THE UNDERLYING ASSUMPTIONS OF THE preceding chapter, an assumption that surfaced at several points somewhat tentatively, was the assumption that while we are forced to speak abstractly about "myth and ritual" when we want to gather global impressions, every single instance of the occurrence of either myths or rituals ought to be regarded as an occurrence shaped as much by the specific social contours in which the myths or rituals were localized as by the broader, more abstract terms of the definitions I discussed.

In this chapter I focus more specifically upon the tools for studying the actual social contexts in which myths and rituals appear, by means of a résumé of the work of the sociofunctional approach to myths and rituals and by means of a survey of what myths and rituals "do" within and for societies. I will be returning repeatedly to the question of the functioning contexts of myths and rituals and will have a look at the ways individual meanings of myths and rituals vary from individual to individual, and from subgroup to subgroup.

All that study is necessary before I discuss the often-perplexing question of the "truth" of mythical materials; I will suggest that there are truths and there are truths . . . , that myths may represent hypothetical truths which rituals manage to make more livable . . . , that rituals, in other words, may perform a function of mediating between the absolute values of myths and the relative values of the societies in which the rituals operate.

Sociofunctionalism: Myth as "Cement" and as "Charter"

Most modern myth analysis stands directly in the euhemeristic tradition discussed in Chapter 1. Almost all modern and contemporary study of myths and rituals from earlier periods, or from cultures other than one's own, has presupposed that myths and rituals of less modern folk must be reinterpreted, that they somehow must be redone in order to show what they are "really" about. The usual assumption is that the voice of the folk itself is not to be trusted. Even self-conscious and self-critical views from within particular societies will, according to this view, be tainted by overarching values and belief structures in such ways that the indigenous viewpoints can be safely disregarded in favor of the outside analyst's codings of the materials: "Aha! The fact that this mask is painted blue must mean that the social stratification no longer is tenable, and the resistance against it has been transformed into supposedly 'sacred' color systems. We'll have to substitute a sociopolitical framework here to see what is really being said."

The sociofunctional (or structural-functional) approach is studied here as the first of the modern methods of study of myths and rituals, as the first of the many attempts to reinterpret them into the analysts' own categories.[1] The reinterpretation in this case was primarily that myths and rituals should be treated not as excesses or errors of language referring to natural phenomena (a position typical of eighteenth-century and earlier studies) but as statements and activities that reflected or fulfilled social needs, needs that were seldom clearly so named but that nonetheless were the "real" reasons those less-modern folks told such incredible stories and performed such bizarre ritual activities.

We will see that there are major limitations to this view and that not all sociofunctionalists are content with such a bold statement of the issues. But by and large the classical statement of this position found in Clyde Kluckhohn's formulation would satisfy most sociofunctionalists: "Both myth and ritual satisfy the needs of a society and the relative place of one or the other will depend upon the particular needs (conscious and unconscious) of the individuals in a particular society at a particular time" (1942:47).

A clear exposition of a society in which such a situation clearly did prevail is provided for Roman society by Michael Grant (1971:chap. 7).[2] "The aim of the Roman myths," writes Grant, "was to justify the traditional Roman social institutions." Grant also documents the "use" of myths by Roman rulers; Quintus Mucius Scaevola, for instance, stated that "it is expedient that populations should be deceived in the matter of religion" (228, 226). Roman history frequently was rewritten in the interests of particular families or rulers, and religious materials were concerned with justifying rituals, which formed such a dominant feature of Roman public life. Myths—taken here in the broadest sense as the primary religious and political stories—clearly served the Romans as a justifying "charter" for their society, to use the functionalist term Malinowski made famous.

The French sociologist Émile Durkheim (1858–1917) often is considered the founder of the sociofunctional approach, although it is primarily Bronislaw Malinowski (1884–1942) whose name is linked explicitly with its beginnings. The equation, *Society = God*, while it never appears in this form in Durkheim's writings, is a helpful way of conceptualizing his thesis that social values are the highest and most important human constructs and that religious terms such as "god" are ciphers used to express these values. In this way religion is the means of supporting cultural and social values by grounding them in a transcendent realm, by projecting them outside the culture so that they become models for the society, forming a cohesive "social cement" that holds the society together. Myth and ritual are seen as the graphic media that enforce the community's values and make them visible to all its members.

The functionalist view has to be seen in its own historical context, namely as a reaction to the late-nineteenth-century view that myth and ritual were primarily entertainments, stories and activities intended for enjoyment and recreation—especially by the less-well-educated masses. (Goode:31 differentiates this view of functionalism from Malinowski's, using different criteria than I have.) Against such a view, Malinowski, in his very influential essay, "Myth in Primitive Psychology," considered myth to be "not an aimless out-pouring of vain imaginings, but a hard-working, extremely important cultural force" (97). And in pointing to the close connection between the stories of the myths, the deeds of the ritual, and the social organization of a culture, Malinowski presented the formulation that his followers often quote: "Myth, as it exists in a savage community, that is, in its living primitive form, is not merely a story told, but a reality lived" (100).

Even more so than Durkheim, Malinowski understood myth to be a direct statement of social realities, not as "symbolic" statement (he used the word symbol negatively) but as the establishment of the social order:

> Myth fulfills in primitive culture an indispensable function: it expresses, enhances, and codifies belief; it safeguards and enforces morality; it vouches for the efficiency of ritual and contains practical rules for the guidance of man. Myth is thus a vital ingredient of human civilization; it is not an idle tale, but a hard-worked active force; it is not an intellectual explanation or an artistic imagery, but a pragmatic charter of primitive faith and moral wisdom. (202; cf. 144; on "charter" and the "home" of a myth in a culture, see Peacock)

Since Malinowski's time, we operate with a broader perspective: essentially we may differentiate between models *of* society, setting out in a Durkheimian sense a particular mirror image of the culture, and models *for* society, as when the model makes visible the ideal standards to which a society aspires. Perhaps the best statement of this distinction—and of the necessary interpenetration of the two types of models—is in an important essay, "Religion as a Cultural System," by Clifford Geertz:

> The acceptance of authority that underlies the religious perspective that the ritual embodies . . . flows from the enactment of the ritual itself. By inducing a set of modes and motivations—an ethos—and defining an

image of cosmic order—a world-view—by means of a single set of symbols, the performance makes the model *for* and model *of* aspects of religious belief mere transpositions of one another. (1973:118; see also chap. 6, which portrays some of the problems with "static" types of functionalism)

It can be seen in this quotation that Malinowski's "pragmatic charter" has been modified considerably. Myths provide "charters" insofar as they justify and exemplify the social order, but there is always an interpenetration of the proscriptive and the prescriptive, the basis and the goal, and Malinowski's "charter" seems to emphasize only the basis.

The sociofunctionalists established clearly the interrelations between the social order and the myths and rituals that sustain it. Their great contribution to the study of myths was to establish this connection against the view that myths were purely something entertaining or merely mistaken perceptions of the environment that could be superseded by science. And in the hands of such practitioners of the method as William J. Goode, the approach could be expanded to include more than the merely sociological correlation between myths and social forms. Goode established four important points (222–23):

1. Religion must be seen as a form of social acting out, not merely as a set of philosophical reflections about another world. It is something in which people believe, to be sure, but this belief is acted out in social contexts.
2. Goode recognized the danger of stressing social integration as the primary function of myth and ritual at the expense of ignoring the internal meanings experienced by the participants in the society. "Emotion is intrinsic to religion," and participants in a culture accept and internalize the myths in many ways other than the purely intellectual.
3. Something more than sheer efficiency is involved when a people live out a myth-and-ritual complex: religion cannot be explained on the basis of hedonism, of acceptance of only those myths and rituals that are enjoyable entertainments or obviously beneficial to the societal well-being.
4. And, anticipating Geertz somewhat, Goode also recognized that religious myths are both models of and models for social cohesion: "Religion *expresses* the unity of society, but it also helps to *create* that unity."

A sociopsychological anthropologist, Anthony F. C. Wallace, expands the sociofunctional view by showing that it looks primarily at the various consequences of the performance (or nonperformance) of rituals in a given cultural setting, and by showing that such analysis must be balanced by attention to biological and psychological consequences (1966a:168). Taking hunting rituals as illustrations, Wallace shows *biological* needs being met when ritual is instrumental in fulfilling needs for continued food supply (hunting rituals that are part of food gathering). *Psychological* effects are demonstrated in the ways myths and rituals provide emotional satisfaction or establish among members of the society an emotional balance that contributes to overall operational effectiveness (killing an animal, for instance, as a displacement for killing a threatening father or other clan members). And *sociological* values can be seen in the way myths and rituals contribute to effective organization of the work group (hunting rituals that assure that every hunter in the group will approach the game in the same manner).

One of the most balanced statements of the functionalist viewpoint is found in an article by Kluckhohn, "Myths and Rituals: A General Theory" (1942). Basically Kluckhohn's argument turns on three interrelated theses:

1. Myths and rituals are "cultural forms defining individual behaviors which are adaptive or adjustive responses."
2. Mythology represents "a cultural storehouse of adjustive responses for individuals."
3. And myths provide "cultural solutions to problems which all human beings face" (Kluckhohn 1942:64–66; this essay has been reprinted frequently, with omissions).

Given these theses, myths and rituals can be studied in terms of their functional ability to provide social solidarity, to transmit cultural values, to provide stability in a threatening world, to reduce anxiety, to show relationships between cultural values and particular objects, to explicate origins, and so forth.

Kluckhohn's essay had a positive reception because it expanded the sociofunctional approach by including psychological and other aspects. In this sense it met the criticisms that early functionalists were too sociological in orientation and that they ignored the role of the individual in society (see Davis; the argument that functionalism is not a method and does not satisfactorily explain the role of religion in a society is developed by Penner). Both Clifford Geertz and I. C. Jarvie criticize functionalist studies for their inability to take into account social change. By favoring well-integrated societies, functionalists ignored the problematic tensions in societies where the mythic and symbolic structures were out of phase with the societal structures. And by ignoring these tensions, the method tended to represent myth and ritual in an overly conservative manner. Jarvie shows that the cargo cults of southeast oceanic societies are a result of external influences and that functionalist approaches are entirely inadequate to explicate situations where social changes are caused by outside factors. Christopher Crocker also notes that sociofunctionalists are apt to fail to recognize customs that are carried onward faithfully even after their social utility has been lost (78).

Studies by those who followed the primary period of sociofunctionalist study tended to be focused more precisely upon specific societies in specific historical frameworks, passing over the earlier questions of the roles of myth and ritual in culture as a whole. These later studies also tended to use perspectives derived from other disciplines and methodologies (our scope prohibits discussion of the work of A. R. Radcliffe-Brown, Fred Eggan, E. E. Evans-Pritchard, and others in the British tradition, or of the highly sophisticated tracing of the interrelations of social custom and religious praxis now appearing in the French journal *Annales*—see Forster and Ranum for representative essays).

An article by Alan Dundes, "Earth-Diver: Creation of the Mythopoeic Male" (1962a), for example, develops a psychological-functionalist view of the earth-diver creation motif (a bird or other animal dives to the bottom of the sea, returning with bits of mud that expand to form the earth). In developing his argument, Dundes shows the limitations of the strict sociofunctionalist method: it excludes the question of the origins and early history of mythic materials that predate the actual example being studied; it excludes features that have been introduced from a second culture group; and it deals insufficiently with the fact that many myths are found throughout the world in similar form but having different social functions. Dundes therefore moved toward cross-cultural and psychological interpretations.[3] Our own survey will move in that direction in Chapter 5, after we look at the approaches privileging ritual over myth (Chapter 3) and then those emphasizing the biogenetic nature of myth and ritual (Chapter 4).

How Myths Serve Society

There are lasting values to the sociofunctionalist approach that ought not be overlooked, even if the method itself is now considered dated. W. Richard Comstock's discussion of the social function of religion strikes me as exceptionally well balanced in that he shows the ways myth-and-ritual complexes accomplish socially integrative functions, overcoming threats toward disintegration of the social order, and strengthening social bonds through communal rites, rituals, and myth tellings. Comstock highlights six aspects of myths and rituals that are disclosed through modern sociofunctionalist analysis, and I will use five of his categories to summarize functionalism's lasting values (quotations are from Comstock:38–40).

1. Myth and ritual complexes provide "assistance in the *symbolic articulation* of the social patterns and relationships themselves." Here we have in view parallels between mythic personages and their performance roles in the sacred organization of deities as acted out in social dramas. What has come down to us as the divine right of kings is, for instance, clearly derived on a this-worldly level from a model considered to originate in an other-worldly hierarchy. (This feature of the this-worldly mirroring the other-worldly is especially prominent in Ancient Near Eastern mythologies.)

2. The myth-and-ritual complex serves *to validate the society:* by relating human social needs to divine or mythic prototypes, the organization of human society obtains consensus and justification. Perhaps it is not too farfetched to use as an illustration here the American presidents' patterns of public church attendance or even the much-reported prayer breakfasts. Mythically charged symbols articulate models for and of the society and may serve both to evoke and to enforce social conformity.[4]

3. The *performatory* function: by their performances, involving community members, rituals may bring about social integration, making members known to one another, establishing social roles, and publicizing the benefits of living together harmoniously. Often rituals can be seen, therefore, as a symbolic acting out of the community itself. Or, as Comstock puts it, "The family that prays together stays together because in doing their religious thing together they are together." Rituals acted out by or witnessed by the members of the community, myths told or read or explained to the community—these help create the community to which they refer.

4. What Comstock calls the *heuristic* function, that is, the educative function, is especially important. Myths and rituals focus energy upon adaptive responses, upon ways of utilizing social and individual energies that have proved their efficacy over time. Comstock gives the example of the hunter who recalls the story that animal speech is heard only when there is total silence: that person will be the hunter most likely to stalk game quietly and hence most likely to be successful. As cultural storehouses of useful information, myths and rituals are not merely entertaining but provide a reservoir or en-

cyclopedia of useful information. When the information no longer appears to be useful, reinterpretation is necessary or foreign materials are incorporated.

5. Another social function of myths and rituals is *solving personal and social dilemmas.* As Kluckhohn would put it, myths and rituals "reduce anxiety." They can provide a means of reducing interactional tensions by providing a forum for the acting out of familial and societal conflicts within a socially safe and socially approved manner. Such conflicts are regularized and given a context and social and behavioral controls. We may think here of the ritualized combat between elders and youths during initiation rites or, in terms of one common American interaction, of the traditional baseball games between varsity and alumni or between students and faculty members at school picnics and reunions.

I think it may be a bit difficult for the person educated in contemporary secondary schools and colleges to appreciate the impact of the development of the disciplines of sociology and anthropology, and subsequently of sociofunctionalism, at the beginning of this century. Most of us today are so accustomed to the apparent importance of sociological analysis that much of the sociofunctionalist approach seems almost self-evident. But in its historical context the movement provided an important corrective to the views that myths were only literary entertainments or only the preoccupation of the priestly classes.

The lasting influence of the sociofunctionalist approach ensures that we will not ignore the important social contexts of myths and rituals, their cohesive function in providing the social cement that binds societies together. Myths and rituals have importance in large measure because they represent corporate significances, meanings that transcend individual needs, desires, and values. They provide a mechanism for enabling holistic interaction between individuals who otherwise might remain independent and disengaged. Hence myths and rituals *mean* culture, *mean* social structure and interaction, and a sociofunctionalist view remains crucial to appreciate the ways they bring about and sustain the social worlds of their performers.

Levels of Operational Vitality

What the sociofunctionalist view has not always taken into account—what few analyses of the effective uses of traditional materials have taken into account—is the manner in which there may be great variation within a society in the ways traditional materials are applied or ignored. Think of the range within our own society with respect to the television series "Star Trek": there will be those (the Trekkies) for whom the actors are little less than gods, others for whom the series is primarily important as an indication of certain values of the youth culture, and others (such as myself) who have never seen an episode of the series and know only derivatively about its reportedly fantastic adventures.

We may distinguish three phases in the relative vitality of a myth, moving from the original, most powerful and dynamic context to the most rationalized form.[5] The first may be called the phase of *Primary Myth*. In it the myth addresses itself directly to the need of the culture to have answers concerning the significant questions and problems of human existance. We do not find developed mythic narratives in this phase, simply because this is the period of initial formulation when the rough edges and inconsistencies are not yet smoothed over. But we have a sense of the operational status of the Primary Myth stage when we think of it as the period when a new cultural model and a new mode of self-understanding begin to be assimilated. This is the period of compelling commitment, the time when the appeal of the myth is precisely its newly discerned ability to explain how the world got the way it is and how the parts of the experienced universe fit together. Think of someone undergoing conversion to a new religious or political theory at the point where the person has just begun to think it explains most of human history, and that will illustrate what I mean by Primary Myth. The convert *believes* the myth but has not yet explored all its ramifications or brought it into harmony with other myths.

The second phase is that of *Implicit Myth*. The central mythical story becomes widespread and accepted; internal contradictions are hammered out, and the mythic story begins to be accepted as part of the way things really are. Now the myth tends to drive out previous understandings and, as it becomes more and more widely shared, to support an orthodoxy antagonistic to other competing worldviews. It may assimilate some of these competitors by modifying them to fit within its own contours. At this stage of the development, the myth is so much a part of the culture that its terms seem to be the only "natural" way of conceiving the world (Richard Moore calls this the "subliminal" phase).

Finally a third phase is apparent when the myth no longer seems to have such compelling wholeness, when new competing myths massively threaten the views of reality presented by the myth in its primary and secondary stages. This is the phase of *Rationalized Myth,* because the concern at this point is to preserve the originating myth by rationalizing it, by utilizing interpretations that show that the original terms of the myth can be rewritten in such ways that they no longer conflict with more recent knowledge and understanding.

Richard Moore notes: "When members of a society begin to say, 'What the myth really means is . . . ,' they are fairly launched on the third or rationalized stage" (37).[6] It is at this stage that persons may follow unique private interpretations of a foundational myth even though giving lip service to the society's "official" interpretations. Within the West today, for example, there are many degrees of belief in the Jewish and Christian scriptures, and many interpretations of the United States Constitution, that would have astonished the original authors of these works.

The model of phases or levels I have proposed is introduced in order to stress that a myth means different things in terms of its actual use during particular phases of personal and societal development. "Development," however, may be somewhat misleading: I do not propose that the three phases of mythic development are necessarily progressive stages in the history of every myth (sometimes they may overlap considerably) or that the three phases coincide with the advance of societies from a primitive to a more sophisticated level. Indeed the model has the advantage of being applicable to any given period in a society's history, as seen if it is applied to any particular period in the history of Christianity or of Marxism.

There is always a dynamic relationship between myth and ritual and the social contexts in which they appear, and we seldom find an entire myth or a complete ritual pattern remaining unchanged over long stretches of time. Variations and new combinations of parts continually occur, and the total patternings must be perceived as dynamically interacting rather than as normalized once and for all. So Claude Lévi-Strauss remarks:

> a mythic system can only be grasped in *a process of becoming;* not as something inert and stable but in a process of *perpetual transformation.* This would mean that there are always several kinds of myths simultaneously present in the system, some of them primary (in respect of the moment at which the observation is made) and some of them derivative. And while some kinds are present in their entirety at certain points, elsewhere they can be detected only in fragmentary form. Where evolution has gone furthest, the elements set free by the decomposition of the old myths have already been incorporated into new combinations. (1973:354, my emphasis)[7]

At any particular moment, therefore, some mythic elements are very lively indeed, while others have become part of "the dead hand of the past."

Functional Contexts of Myths and Rituals

Just where within a particular society "some mythic elements are very lively indeed" is very much a matter of the varying contexts in which myths and rituals may function. An example of different functions may as well be our Star Trek example again: the adolescent (or grandparent, for that matter!) for whom the television series represented a means of voicing a radically new vision of the world could be expected to devote a larger portion of his or her waking hours to Star Trekking activities than would someone for whom the series was something seen as a silly and "unreal" waste of time.

But let us assume for now that we are talking about materials that truly matter, that have mattered in centering and guiding a society. An example would be the multiple accounts of emergence, or origin, or creation that appear in many cultures simultaneously: three or more appear at about the same period in Egypt, and within a few centuries others were widespread in ancient Israel and ancient Greece. It would be a fascinating cross-cultural study to correlate the types of origin myths with the types of political systems being developed in these so-cieties and to observe how the mythic stories served to recapitulate, or to reinforce, social stratification. (In Egypt, for instance, the various cre-ation myths were associated with the three main centers of priestly power, each competing for dominance, each seeking to be the headquar-ters of the "only" creation story.)

I am referring in these instances to ways myths and rituals function from the perspective of their function *within* working mythological sys-tems. And I think some of the most useful insights about the several functions such systems demonstrate have come from Joseph Campbell, who has distinguished four types of functions, the Mystical-Meta-physical, the Cosmological, the Sociological, and the Psychological (in several of his works: 1964:518–23; 1970a; 1972:214–25; the quota-tions in the following discussion are from these sources, except where noted).

The first function is the Mystical or Metaphysical, which deals with "the reconciliation of consciousness with the preconditions of its own existence," with "redeeming human consciousness from its sense of guilt in life." According to this first function the purpose of the great myths is "to waken and maintain in the individual a sense of awe and gratitude in relation to the mystery dimension of the universe" or to elicit and support "a sense of awe before the mystery of being."

This first function may be illustrated by introducing the myths of emergence/origins/creation that form one of the most important mythemic systems in the West.[8] Most of the great creation stories emphasize that creation was not accidental, that the world, even the universe, did not come into existence by chance coincidence; even contemporary indeterminancy theories would argue that the levels of probability are themselves matters of some design and rationality.

But mysterious—yes! That Something IS strikes most humans as both mysterious and awe inspiring; it also establishes, in the most primordial of stories (logically), the essential tension between Being and Not Being, a primordial duality that has structured Western thought throughout its known history. The metaphysical function of origin myths, then, is clear: they map the miracle of purposed coming-into-being and the threat of ceasing-to-be; they suggest that being alive is a matter of gift, perhaps even of intention and design. And the impressive Near Eastern creation stories go further to indicate that the primordial period is also the model for the end times. It is very striking in Israelite materials, for example, that the future, eschatological periods are figured with images drawn from the supposed primordial bliss in the "garden" or "paradise"—the same word lying behind the Garden of Eden stories—that the First People enjoyed.

The second function, the Cosmological, has to do with "formulating and rendering an image of the universe, a cosmological image in keeping with the science of the time"; it reinforces the mysterious aspects of the universe as revealed in the first function of myth: The "image of the universe . . . will support and be supported by this sense of awe before the mystery of a presence and the presence of a mystery." The cosmological conceptions must, however, also satisfy the logics and sciences of the day, and Campbell has brought devastating criticisms to bear upon contemporary forms of the world's great religions for failing to relate modern scientific worldviews to the metaphysics of traditional religion:

> If, in a period like our own, of the greatest religious fervor and quest, you would wonder why the churches are losing their congregations, one large part of the answer surely is right here. They are inviting their flocks to enter and to find peace in a browsing-ground that never was, never will be, and in any case is surely not that of any corner of the world today. Such a mythological offering is a sure pill for at least a mild schizophrenia. (1972:215)

Campbell's bitter critique of contemporary religions is based largely upon his understanding that Judaism and Christianity have indulged too long in what I sometimes refer to as "biblical antiques"—a persistent refusal to revise sacred belief systems in order to accommodate them to the wider world of the sciences. Certainly the cosmology assumed by medieval religionists to be the only possible true cosmology because it was discussed in the Bible has dominated a great deal of Western thinking and even scientific language. Those who have held tenaciously to the Genesis stories, for instance, have not even been interested in understanding the rich store of Babylonian, Assyrian, Phoenician, and other mythology from which the Israelite materials clearly were derived. In this case Campbell's "sense of awe before the mystery" has been more functionally effective than his requirement of accommodation to the logics and sciences of the day. Other contemporary persons seem to feel rather more comfortable holding the latest in scientific theory along with traditional religious positions with respect to cosmology; presumably they are able to expand their "awe" to encompass the developments of scientific hypotheses as well as an ancient cosmological system. (As an example of those who find a rapprochement possible, I will cite only Schilling's *The New Consciousness in Science and Religion* [1973], where the "and" expresses a possible continuum that Campbell apparently finds impossible. Ten Raa demonstrates with a Tanzanian example that the levels can coexist quite well.)

The Sociological is Campbell's third function, and it has to do with supporting "the current social order," integrating "the individual organically with his group." Hence myths can be said "to validate, support, and imprint the norms of a given, specific moral order," to authorize "its moral code as a construct beyond criticism or human emendation." It is this function of myths that goes hand in hand with dogmatic religious interests, and it is this function that the French sociological school around Émile Durkheim considered myth's primary role in human society.

Here my illustration of origin myths is particularly instructive: it is often possible to deduce all the various social strata into which a society is divided from the society's dominant emergence/origins/creation myth. Along the way of telling the primordial stories, we hear again and again of the (seemingly casual, even accidental) establishment of this or that sacred place, this or that hierarchical position, this or that dominance of gender or family or nation. Covenants are concluded between a deity and a particular clan, or a particular family is identified as the most qualified to lead, or the relation between humans and environing nature is specified (see who names whom in Genesis!).

Finally, the fourth function of myth according to Campbell is the Psychological, having to do with "shaping individuals to the aims and ideals of their various social groups" and guiding the individual "stage by stage, in health, strength, and harmony of spirit, through the whole foreseeable course of a useful life." In this manner myths relate the inner, personal, private human being to the outer, impersonal, public roles that are offered in a particular culture. Campbell is fond of stressing the tension between the local and particular, and the global and universal (Campbell: throughout, most recently 1975:11); and it is particularly the psychological function of myths that concerns the interrelation of these tensions within the individual psyche.

The person who has learned by means of an origin myth that there are various social roles available within the articulated social cosmos, various possible ways for him or her to fulfill a proper position within the social hierarchies or to find ways of operating meaningfully as a contributing member of his or her society—this person will have gained from the mythic stories, reinforced by ritual dramatizations, a very clear sense of what that society defines as psychological health. The person who is healthy is the person who "fits in," as we are fond of saying, and we can look either at traditional legendary stories or at modern mass-media plots to substantiate the pressure toward conformity that such a position implies. (Into such a position steps the heroine or hero, who seems initially to be "heroic" by challenging the conformisms that everyone else finds satisfactory; but I would argue that the historical heroes/heroines, after their initial challenge to the status quo, or even after altering the status quo somewhat, become in turn its defenders and resist further change.)

Joseph Campbell's own emphasis has been upon the fourth, the Psychological, function of myths, as is best seen in his *The Mythic Image* (1975), where the fourth and crucial chapter ("Transformations of the Inner Light") suggests that the psychological ramifications of Kundalini yoga represent a "master key to the inward dimension of *all* symbolic forms" (278).

As I suggested in a review essay on this book (1976), I am not as inclined as Campbell to search for *the* image or for one ultimate mythic answer. Rather I am impressed with the polyfunctionality of myths, and I am certain that both myths and rituals may "mean" different things at different developmental levels within a society, at different points within personal chronology, and within the meaning systems of two or more persons within the same culture.[9]

Obviously myths and rituals do have useful, even crucial functions within the societies that tell and perform them: but it is misleading to suggest that all myths and all rituals always represent the same functions. And it seems important to locate a particular myth or ritual within a culture as it is being told or performed, perhaps on the sort of three-part continuum I outlined above. One might then demonstrate, for instance, how it is that variant stories appear at different stages of cultural development and at different locations within the range of cultural enterprises such as religion, science, philosophy, and psychology.

We will be best served if we attempt to catch the dynamism of myths and rituals functioning throughout the strata and the history of cultures, regarding their polyfunctionality as an essential part of their very nature, and reaching toward overarching, archetypal, or other patterns only when we have accounted for the manifold ways in which these patterns precipitate out in particular social manifestations. The "pattern"—the "forms"—change and manifest differently even within a single social group; hence Richard Chase can state that: "The emotional necessity of myth is constant; the forms of myth are not" (113; cf. Larsen:18–22, 88; Kirk 1974).

Polyfunctional and Polysemantic Meanings

It may well be our own rationalistic perspective that has led us to assume that myths and rituals perform one or another function, and that alone. "An examination of myth as it still lives and functions among a modern primitive people is likely to show a surprising lack of homogeneity" (Chase:112): but perhaps it is "surprising" only from our own perspectives. In spite of my discomfort with Chase's references to "primitives" and "savages," what he has to say in continuing that statement is quite relevant:

> The same myth takes on the differing forms given it by different raconteurs; when a single myth appears among different peoples or endures over a period of time among one people, it will assume a variety of forms and nuances according to a variety of aesthetic climates—and this despite the savage's rather compulsive fear of or lack of interest in change. (113)

A lack of interest in change, perhaps: yet few mythic or ritualistic elements remain unchanged for very long, and the ways one believes in a myth element or a ritual moment may vary considerably during one's lifetime. Even the ways mythic materials are recounted may vary according to what the raconteur surmises about the particular interests of the listeners or according to the particular raconteur's skills, politics, and abilities.[10]

And rituals may vary in formality, as in the degree to which performers perceive themselves enacting ritual roles; there are "high" and "low" ranges to ritual behavior (Douglas 1966, 1970) and markers that say it is all right to wear casual clothing to one midweek evening ritual while formal clothing is required for the first-of-the-week midmorning ceremonial—even though both occasions may feature the same mythic or religious stories.

Mythographic studies seek, ideally, to recognize the situation of the mythic or ritualistic materials within the complex range of societal activities; an analogy might be drawn to emphasis upon the role of the hearer or reader in literary criticism (see J. White 1980:74, discussing the work of Stanley Fish).

Certain native distinctions are important not only as a means of understanding the societies from which the materials derive but for understanding whether a particular mythic or ritual element derives from the "great" or "little" traditional network of the society. These distinctions, developed by Robert Redfield, are summarized by Myerhoff (1978:256): the Great Traditions refer "to the abstract, eternal verities of a culture, are usually controlled by literati from a distance, interpreted and enforced by official institutions." The Little Tradition, on the other hand, represents "a local, folk expression of a group's beliefs; unsystematized, not elaborately idealized, it is an oral tradition practiced constantly and often unconsciously by ordinary people without external enforcement or interference" and may also be termed "domestic religion" or "folk culture ethnicity." (Charles Leslie's anthology includes studies of both types of tradition.)

Little Tradition symbols often pertain to the family, the home, the immediate community; those of the Great Traditions pertain to large, formal rituals and to scriptures and their study. It is more often than not the Great Traditions that are explicitly and formally recognized and studied, whereas the Little Traditions may not even seem to be recognized and reflected upon, yet they undergird at a familial and emotional level many of the actual day-to-day decisions made and actions taken.[11]

Obviously many Americans hold beliefs and values that belong more to the sphere of American civil-secular religion than to the rarified theology of Christian and Jewish theorists: few of us today pay any attention to the ways essentially secular values are interlaced with religious sentiments—or we would protest strongly at the display of the national flag within a religious sanctuary, or at the offering of a solemn prayer at the religious ceremonial meeting nearest to national elections.

But is our situation so different from that of ancient Egypt, where, as I noted earlier, various creation theories were held simultaneously and competitively? Or Rome, where several versions of the founding legends coexisted simultaneously (see Donlan)? Or Greece, where no fewer than three different versions of the ancient "golden age" coexisted (Kirk 1974:134; Guthrie:chap. 4)? Or the Algonkian Montagnais culture, where persons seem to have believed that after dying souls travel both to a distant place *on this planet* and to the Milky Way *in the sky* (Hultkrantz 1981:195)? It is all too easy for us to assimilate "variants" to a hypothetical master version, a lowest common mythic denominator: but we should remain fully aware that the "variants" were sometimes as politically charged, as economically consequential, as modern options such as capitalism and socialism.

Ronald Grimes, in his book *Symbol and Conquest* (1976), has shown a very wide range of meanings assigned to one contemporary festival, the Fiesta de Santa Fé in New Mexico: the actors in the annual pageant are chosen, from year to year, on the basis of attempts to placate competing ethnic and political groups. But multiple meanings may simply pile up on top of one another; Michael Dames (83) suggests that the ancient Silbury complex in Britain incorporated simultaneously some twelve symbolic representations:

1. The pregnant seated goddess.
2. The goddess half-buried in the ground.
3. The eye goddess, supreme intelligence.
4. The White Mountain in the primordial water.
5. The cosmic egg.
6. Sickly grain and root crops.
7. The royal throne.
8. The sacred stag.
9. Umbilical snakes.
10. Mother and child.
11. Woman with phallus—the androgynous being.
12. The spinning and weaving goddess.

Each of these symbols is known from elsewhere in the International Neolithic, and each has a great importance—but at the Silbury mound, Dames suggests, they appear to be fused into one massive symbolic complex that would indicate that no single meaning ought to be sought for this prehistoric construction. Or perhaps it suggests confirmation of Myerhoff's point that ideology is never completely systematized by a social group (1978:183), a point immediately illustrated when one is visiting another country and tries to elicit from casual contacts just why a particular observance is being held this time around in a manner vastly different from what the learned guidebooks had led one to expect.

Even Dames's listing of the complex interweaving of symbols at Silbury pales before the multiplicity of interpretations of the fundamental

Zuni emergence myth in the American Southwest. Dennis Tedlock notes no fewer than fourteen priesthood interpretations, plus thirteen medicine-society interpretations, plus the great range of interpretations given to the mythic cycle by each family that passes along the myth within the home (1981:47; 1980:131). Likewise Snyder (66) gives examples of a myth type varying in its interpretation (but not in its basic plot) across the face of North America.

Complexities such as I have sketched here, added to the range of possible interpretations by outside analysts, led Waardenburg to suggest some seven kinds of meanings a given myth might be understood as carrying (61–62). Adapting his list rather freely and selectively, the following may be suggested:

1. Original meanings of the myth or ritual in its earliest contexts, with all the symbolic overtones that may be determined by cosmological, sociological, psychological, or other levels. This focus may be narrowed to specific meanings as stated by the society in which the myth is at home.
2. Subsequent meanings of the myth or ritual in later contexts. Here we are often at the mercy of the tradition that has transmitted the myth, for later situations may highlight mythemes and rituals that were of lesser or greater importance at an earlier level of social development (whether "higher" or "lower").
3. Specific ways in which the myth or ritual has a role in providing explicit terms or frameworks for giving meaning to other aspects of the society: "political ramification" covers a good bit of what I have in mind here. An example can be found in the ways the Egyptians used the same word for the "appearance" (*khay*) of the primal light and for the way the pharaoh stood before his court; and Egyptian moral teachings about Maat (justice) related it to both contemporary politics and the characteristics of the first world order that appeared when chaos was overcome. Or we might mention David's clever ploy of moving Israelite headquarters to the insignificant Jerusalem and tying that move to a particular interpretation of the Holy City as divinely established, an earthly correlate to the Eden of the Genesis myths, which were being restructured at the same period.
4. Particular meanings that formal analysis of myths, or rituals, may provide. Here reference is to literary and phenomenological analysis, and with that the question of meanings found in many cultures, but also to the questions about possible implications formal analysis may have for such transcendent matters as "the way humans think," the way they structure existence.
5. Self-referencing importances: ways the myth or ritual has functioned

in order to secure its own significance. The ritual of crowning the king or queen of England would have little significance, for example, if it were held at midnight at a location disclosed only to a few intimate family members.

Some of these meanings will be explored in the rest of this book. The list given here is sufficient to illustrate Olson's comment that the very usage of the term "myth" has been substantially modified since the romantic definitions and especially since the theological confrontation over "demythologization" in the mid-1950s: "the meaning of the word 'myth' has moved in its semantic possibilities from univocity to equivocity and even to plurivocity" (3). Of necessity we will have to continue to speak of "myth" as if it were something particular and univocal; but I suspect that few future studies will be able to avoid the growing consensus that "myth" is a make-do term that implies singularity and univocity of meaning, whereas the reality continues to amaze us with its plurivocity and multiplicity. Even a single recital of a myth or performance of a ritual is already one form of criticism and interpretation, and the work of the myth-and-ritual analyst is but another layer, a layer that is determined by our own functional or generic expectations (Toelken and Scott [73] found that few Navajo interpret as etiological what our history of scholarship would lead us to expect as being such) as well as by our inability to appreciate the mysteries around which the myths or rituals have centered as they have come into being.

But perhaps myths and rituals themselves tolerate more coexistence of opposing valuations than our Western rationality finds comfortable.[12] And that in turn leads us to the awkward issue, long-discussed in anthropology, philosophy, and religious studies, of the relative "truth" of mythic materials—an issue that has tended since Lucien Lévy-Bruhl (see J. Z. Smith 1972) to be focused upon the supposed differences between "primitives" (or premoderns, or savages, or preliterates, or what have you: none of the terms quite work) and those of us who enjoy the benefits (as well as the detriments) of the modern sciences.

Myths, Science, and Truth(s)

The fundamental danger to a balanced interpretive perspective is that we tend to assume that *we* are above the primitive need for myth, that science does away with the necessity for mythic expression or belief, and that, being aware of the phases of mythic vitality, we will operate only at the most sophisticated level. However, I suspect that modern science is just as properly mythical in the sense used here as was medieval Catholicism. Modern science as a worldview rests upon a foundational (post-Cartesian) mythic story of reality, although this story is precisely one that *claims* to be anything but mythical. We are so impressed with our scientific advances that we soon label "primitive" or "unsophisticated" any viewpoints that call the underlying mythic frames into question.

Approaches that have treated myths as representing primitive as opposed to sophisticated levels of cultural advancement have been popular ever since the great mythographer James Frazer spoke of myths as a primitive science based on ignorance and misapprehension. A contemporary anthropologist, David Bidney, is typical of others in suggesting that myth "must be taken seriously precisely in order that it may be gradually superseded in the interests of the advancement of truth and the growth of human intelligence." "Myth originates," Bidney states further, "wherever thought and imagination are employed uncritically or deliberately used to promote social delusion" (1958:22; cf. the later elaboration, 1967:chap. 10; a strong statement against such reductionism is LeGuin 1976).

Bidney's perspective could not be further from my own; myths may function in quite critical ways to advance knowledge, and science itself has been used to promote social delusion. What seems to lurk behind such negative evaluations of myth as Bidney's is the assumption that there is, somewhere, a body of abstract truths or facts waiting to be discovered.[13] So long as we proceed from the model of facts out there, and the observer over here (the infamous Cartesian subject:object dichotomy), we are not going to gain any sort of sympathy for the myth-maker or myth believer, because the structure of the argument is set in just such a way as to deny any validity to the observer's entering emotionally into the relationship and thereby bridging the dichotomy.

But scientific observation and experimentation, and mythopoetic creation and belief, are approached most fruitfully as different planes of thought, not as a wrong and a right plane of thought. And myth at the Primary Myth stage is not an attempt at the sort of scientific description found in the laboratory of the physical sciences but is an attempt to express the quality and range of human existence, its emotional, aesthetic, and moral aspects. Myth is not unsophisticated science but sophisticated poetic enunciation of meaning and significance. W. Richard Comstock appropriately notes that "Myth, properly understood, is not an early attempt to do what modern science can now do better, any more than a poem is an early attempt to express what a geometrical theorem and proof can state more clearly and convincingly" (33). Mythological statements do convey a certain kind of knowledge but not so much the knowledge of the scientific laboratory as the knowledge of communal, even racial, experience that has proved itself useful and healthy. Myths convey the sorts of psychological and adaptational learning that enable us to live harmoniously within natural and cultural frameworks, that enable us to express and to be enriched by meanings and significances, by the realms of morally pregnant realities.

Facts may well be represented in myths, but it is often important to recognize that natural and cultural data may be represented dialectically or paradoxically as often as, or more often than, they are represented with pragmatic exactness.[14] Inasmuch as myths model possibilities—both positive and negative—we should not expect them to function along the lines of the evening news report. Myths function in quite different fashion, as Jean Houston argues, emphasizing the "myths of evocation and potentiation, myths of new ways of being" that seem to her to be emerging in our own time: "The myth is something that never was but is always happening—the coded DNA of the human psyche calling us to refresh the dream that has been pushed so far away. . . . The myth is always the stimulus, the alarm clock, the lure of becoming. It quickens the heart to its potential and prepares the ground for society's transformation" (6–7).

Somehow our love of absolute contrasts and oppositions—I think of us as an age of *either/or,* seldom of a *both/and*—has misled us into dichotomizing myth and science (or religion and science, or poetry and science) in our own societies as well as when analyzing those of the past. But what if they are to be regarded not as contrastive but as supplementary? Can we not speak of a mythic orientation as one of several complex human orientations?—and not necessarily an inferior orientation! Here I join Stephen Larsen (and earlier Paul Radin) in emphasizing that mythmaking is not a primitive stage of thinking that must be left behind when science develops. It is rather a facility, an "alternative mode of consciousness" (in Larsen's words) whose function is crucial for us no less than for persons living at an earlier stage of technological development. Larsen writes: "The faculty in [humankind], then, which is susceptible to and also generates myths is more than merely an archaic stage of cognitive development or a primitive curiosity about how things work; it is rather an alternative mode of consciousness, with an a-priori, instinctive impulse toward this different, sacred mode of comprehension" (28).

Myth considered as an "alternative mode of consciousness": this could lead toward an empathetic viewing of premodern cultures that fully recognizes their lasting contributions to ways of dwelling in the universe we still inhabit. It could lead to a questioning of the appropriateness of our excessively rational approach to the world—if by rational we mean the rejection of all that cannot be quantified and scientifically analyzed. It might help us appreciate Jamake Highwater's observation that "Science, and the philosophy based upon it, is one of the numerous ways by which we ritualize our experience. That ritual is undergoing constant alteration" (36).

We are now at the point in our own cultural history where we have begun to question whether modern scientific and technological advances truly have increased the *meanings* of our lives. We begin to ask about the human and poetic qualities of existence that seem increasingly suppressed by the usual scientific techniques. For all their impressive contributions, modern sociology and psychology, for example, have led more than one student to the recognition that there is more to human culture and the human psyche than statistics and quantifiable data. And even our much touted rationality has definite limitations. As one observer comments: " 'Rational thinking' lacks important ingredients that are necessary for the psychic balance and the stability of the individual" (Gallus:553; see also Larsen; Argüelles).

"Rational thinking" may be one extremely important phase of modern consciousness, but the failure of traditional culture and religions to wither away before it might suggest that it is not *all* that human consciousness needs to survive. In its own terms, however, rational thinking (cf. Freud's "our god Logos") is totalizing; it claims to explain all, to predict all, to be able to regulate all. But that sounds in turn like another religiosity; as Frank Kermode notes, "Myths of total explanation are religious; comment upon them is theology" (211). And that would indicate what other observers have noted (Sexson:36, 42; Jewett and Lawrence 1977a: notes to pp. 2 and 7), namely that the recurrent modern emphasis upon mythlessness is itself a myth!

Those who followed the biblical theologian Rudolf Bultmann in the sweeping post-1950s Protestant (and later Catholic) movement known as Entmythologizierung ("demythologizing"; see Bultmann 1953, and the initial debate in Bartsch) were perhaps buying in too soon to the understanding of the scientific worldview, the historical perception of the West as the epitome of mythless humanity. Already in the 1950s, Amos N. Wilder and others saw that Bultmann's program made most sense as a *deliteralizing* project, not as a project to strip away primitive Christian myths. Subsequently there have been many theological progressions toward recognizing the legitimacy of the religious imagination (see Hart; Barbour) as well as a revitalized appreciation of the roles of mythological thought in the development of the literature of ancient Israel and Christianity—not only in the Psalms and creation stories, where we have little trouble recognizing mythic materials, but also in the Prophets.[15]

Some theologians have seen that mythological language has an important place in religious expression and should not be treated in a uniformly negative manner (see Richardson; Dudley). The great philosophical theologian Paul Tillich presented a strikingly positive evaluation of myth and mythology in his article for the important German theological encyclopedia, *Die Religion in Geschichte und Gegenwart* (Religion: Historical and Contemporary). Tillich joins Mircea Eliade in speaking of the reality of myth: myth expresses what is absolutely real for people, the experiencing of the cosmos that seems to lend meaning to all its parts and that becomes the model for what humans do in all generations. Myth is understood by Tillich to represent "a symbol, built up from elements of reality, for the Absolute, the being beyond beings, which is the object of the religious act" (344).

Eliade especially emphasizes the role of myths as they set exemplary models for societies, and hence he emphasizes their contributions to later self-understanding. Humans understand themselves, in mythological terms, as having been constituted by events that happened in the primal times; and by recollecting the myths and reenacting them in rituals, one becomes contemporary with the powerful time of the beginnings once again (see Beane and Doty:chap. 1, for a selection of Eliade's statements of these themes).

Whether one reenters the powerful time of origins for the purposes of healing (that is, the patient is taken back into the time when life was perfect, identified with the perfect creations there, and hence reconstituted) or for purposes of controlling natural or human-made objects (that is, by knowing the origins of a tool, one gains knowledge of its use), there is a more-or-less technological view of myth and ritual implied here (see Eliade 1971; Beane and Doty:24). This is technology in a rather rarified sense, of course, but it is an important sense.

Perhaps my point is made more clearly by a quotation from Eliade: "knowing the origin of an object, an animal, a plant, and so on is equivalent to acquiring a magical power over them by which they can be controlled, multiplied, or reproduced at will" (Beane and Doty:5). We no longer refer very often to magical power, but I suggest that we are just as influenced by the concept that knowing the origin of the thing is power ("Where did you get it?"). How many history books and government reports, for example, begin with "The Origins of the XYZ Problem"? Or think of the vast technology of the medical research laboratory, harnessed to answer questions about the origins of a disease. Or think of the psychoanalyst searching in the personal past for the origins of a neurosis, or of the cultural anthropologist looking for the origins of a particular social pattern.

I suspect our immediate tendency is to accept the applicability of such a technology only for "primitive societies": *they* learn the secrets of the origins of things, whereas *we* know through science and technology. But surely the point to be made is that our "knowing" is mythological to a very similar degree. I am attracted by Marshall McLuhan's suggestion that a culture's language is its macromyth; our knowing is formed and shaped by what we look for, by the categories in which we think we apprehend the real or the nonreal. So in contemporary culture, indebted as it is to the printed word and the illustrated book, one conceives of the real as that which can be seen and observed, whereas in a more oral culture the real is more likely to be conceived of in terms of harmonies, that which is "heard."[16]

These are just a few indications that a more positive approach to myth may be incorporated into theological, religious, and even scientific reflection. I cannot here map an extensive program for incorporation of a more positive approach, but in treating the development of primitive Christianity, for example, what is needed is an approach to the early Christian theologies (within and outside the New Testament) that treats them as mythological constructs (cf. Doty 1980b; Henry).

There has to be some means of reconciling the negative approach represented by Bultmann and others—where mythology is merely the awkward expression in a particular age of the timeless truths that have to be stated in ever new ways—with the more positive relationship between theology and mythology advocated by those who see, in cross-cultural perspectives, the structural significance of mythological themes throughout human culture. Clearly one of the appeals of the work of Carl Jung has been his careful elaboration of the mythological and archetypal aspects of both communal religions and individual dreams. Not many people are satisfied with Jung's proposals or with those of subsequent Jungians. But Jung was a sophisticated researcher and thinker whose works may well provide the basis for a more creative future synthesis of approaches to the sociology and psychology of myth and religion, and I will review his contributions to mythography within his own historical context in Chapter 5.

The Smart and the Proper

A final consideration of the ways myths and rituals function within societies has to do with the ways they serve as adjustive devices, bridging the absolutes of a society with the pragmatisms of everyday life. Both Jonathan Z. Smith and Morris Freilich have discussed this function of myths and rituals. Smith (1980) differentiates between the unreal or ideal and the actual or situational, Freilich between the smart norm and the proper norm.

Smith's concern was with the apparent discrepancies between hunting rituals and the actual practices of those who hunted. The hunt of the bear has been documented and described in classic ethnological accounts from several cultural areas: a special language is invoked, a language that avoids all mention of hunting; the bear is represented as presenting itself as a gift to the hunter, who is the guest of the bear and the forest; many sanctions surround the actual killing of the animal—it may be killed only while running toward the hunter, it may not be killed while sleeping in its den, and so forth; and the reintegration of the hunters back into the home camp is elaborate, involving the hunters' women performing elaborate ceremonies but not partaking of the meat.

Smith asks some blunt questions about the practicality of such ritualizing of an actual hunt: are we to believe that any experienced hunter would expect game to remain stock-still while being addressed by the hunter in elaborate dithyrambs, ceremonial speeches, or even love songs? Or that—as stated in the rituals—the prey would be abandoned if it were imperfect in some physiological detail? Or that none but the hunters actually would share the meat?

From details of actual bear hunts, Smith responds that the practical, in-the-field behaviors of the hunters demonstrate very few, if any, of the ritual proscriptions. "There appears to be a gap," Smith suggests (123), "between their ideological statements of how they *ought* to hunt and their actual behavior while hunting." He then suggests that rituals may represent an ideal reality, a model of how reality might be or ought to be; in fact Smith suggests that one of the crucial functions of ritual is to highlight the incongruities between the actual and the ideal. The ritual therefore serves as a "focusing lens" that acknowledges the experienced threat the universe seems to offer even when human endeavors have been focused intensely upon doing "the proper." The ritual bear hunt, rather than reflecting the actual practices of actual bear hunts, represents a perfect hunt, with all possible threats and variables controlled (127); therefore it represents a "gnostic" occasion to reflect on what happened, an occasion to consider the strengths and weaknesses of the actual hunt vis-à-vis an ideal model.

Morris Freilich's point of departure is explicitly the gap between the mythically stated and the actual, as he develops a strategy for myth analysis based upon an observation by Claude Lévi-Strauss that behind the obvious sense of a mythic story there is nonsense, namely coded messages that are inconsistent with the messages of the myth itself (see also Bär, who develops a view of myths as "privileged false stories" based upon a neo-Freudian view of the irony of repression). What is being coded is the distinction that our abstract analytical tradition usually discusses as "nature versus culture." Freilich suggests working with a different contrast, that between "smart" and "proper" norms. Proper norms are those coming from a cultural, historical tradition; they are those that are presented to us frequently in "you should" sorts of statements, and they provide few answers other than "you should" to "why should I do xxx?" Smart norms, on the other hand, are direct reflections of "natural" pragmatic behaviors that have proven effective; and if proper norms (culture) are directly reflective of history and order, smart norms are spatially oriented—and can be proved or rejected quickly on empirical grounds.

If we learn smart norms to survive physically, Freilich suggests, we learn proper norms to survive psychically. Myth is mediative for both Lévi-Strauss and Freilich; for the latter, it is the agency within a society that functions as a switching point between the smart and the proper: "Myths must regularly and effectively transform the smart (that which seems to be effective, efficient and spatially useful) into the proper (that which becomes convention, a rule followed for its own sake)" (1975:209). Hence (selected from Freilich's strategy of myth analysis, 210, where they are Freilich's points 3, 4, 7, and 14):

- Myths attempt to resolve the fundamental human dilemma: to be smart and stay (physically) alive or to be proper and stay sane.
- Myths attempt to resolve contradictions, among them contradictory smart norms and contradictory proper norms. Myths attempt to explain paradoxes, including why properness sometimes leads to tragedy and why smartness sometimes leads to losses.
- Myths resolve dilemmas, contradictions, paradoxes, and puzzles by identifying mediators.
- The key subsystems that together constitute a myth are (a) content—"history," a story that amuses; (b) structure—technology, paired opposites that carry messages; and (c) hidden messages—instructions as to what is proper and what is smart.

Freilich applies his analytical nonsense-in-myth strategy to the Garden of Eden stories in Genesis 1–3, producing some startling, but I think quite valid, insights: "The Fall of man is completely alien to the spirit and content of the Old Testament, which is concerned with evolutionary progress, and the generally accepted belief that Eden is paradise finds no support in the text . . . Paradise is a state to which the human form slowly evolves, not a situation from which man is cast" (212). On the basic Eden story Freilich remarks:

> These bits of non-sense information provide a puzzling picture (i.e., within Hebraic culture and theology) of a tempting God, who lies; of a talking snake who must work hard to get a woman to act contrary to orders, while the "superior" male grabs the fruit almost without a second thought. Then, almost in a childish tantrum, God threatens Adam and his descendants with the terrible consequences for disobeying orders. Suddenly God becomes apologetic and presents Adam and Eve with clothes, clothes they really do not need. Finally, Adam and Eve are thrown out of Eden to keep them away from a tree whose fruits have not previously been forbidden. (214; Freilich 1977 repeats much of the 1975 essay, in a briefer and clearer presentation)

What Freilich finds that the basic story up to introduction of Adam has to convey concerns the nature of the Israelite deity, who is disclosed to be "a system concerned with order, immortal, moral, and creative" (1975:216; there partly in italics). Adam, as the mediator between the deity and the natural world, is by contrast an evolving system, and we learn that "Since he is made in the image of God and since he is a mediator, the link between the creator and his creations is *loneliness* and *growth*" (216).

And finally Freilich's analysis of the nonsense of Genesis 1–3 leads him to a restatement of some of its basic tenets in his own "non-sense" (for as he notes, "Every myth analyst is also a myth maker" [217]):

2. Loneliness lies behind creativity.
3. Creativity begins with Chaos.
4. Creativity finds its peak in relationship.
5. A perfect place can never be paradise for a creative system.
8. Morality is born in decision making, in challenge instead of security.
11. Everything evolves: [the deity,] man, morality, relationship, etc.

The analysis has led Freilich to modify Lévi-Strauss's emphasis upon mediation: "Myth's central purpose, I believe, is to provide certainty: to explain how things begin, how they end; to resolve paradoxes, dilemmas, and contradictions of all kinds" (Freilich 1975:224).

Freilich's notion of nonsense-in-myth may be qualified somewhat by asking about the *contexts* in which the nonsense is apparent: for myths may convey perspectives that seem nonsensical from one perspective yet entirely coherent and congruent with social rules from another. One of the great values of Lévi-Strauss's four-volume Introduction to a Science of Mythology (1969, 1973, 1978b, 1981) has been his emphasis upon the various mythic levels that can be separated by analysis. Lévi-Strauss calls these levels codes, aspects, frameworks, schemata, or orders of mythic presentation, and they are variously distinguished as the geographical, the acoustic, the astronomical, the culinary or alimentary, the techno-economic, the sociological, the cosmological, and the sociopolitical levels. The bulk of Lévi-Strauss's modestly named "Introduction" consists of the patient tracking of these various levels across some 1,600 myths and variations from North and South America.

When we are foiled in satisfactorily analyzing a myth with respect to its sociological message, we may well find that it conveys rather more of an astronomical message; or we may find (as Lévi-Strauss often does find) that apparently astronomical information in myths bears culinary, and hence sociological, significances. What is called for in mythical *analysis,* then, is mythical *analyses*: "It transpires, then, that if we wish to analyze two different levels of the myth we must also apply two different levels of analysis. In a single analysis the different projections clash with each other and even seem to present inversions" (ten Raa:340).

Eric ten Raa demonstrates this procedure with respect to a cluster of creation myths from the Tanzanian Sandawe people; he is able to demonstrate that for this cluster of myths both a cosmological and a sociological level are involved but that the "binary vision" of the Sandawe enables him or her to look at both levels simultaneously; "the eternal values of the cosmological level" are combined with the ideals of contemporary Sandawe social surroundings (343). Crucial to ten Raa's analysis, and a step forward in myth analysis, is his discussion of *projection,* the mechanism by which societies interrelate the various levels on which they code and interpret their myths: 'A projection is something which operates between two planes in such a manner that it creates on one of them an image that is derived from the other" (334).

In ten Raa's method, we must separate the myth as message from the technical expedience of telling it—what usually is referred to as its narrative expression. Projections represent relationships between the various levels, between the pure myth-as-story and the level of information it conveys; projections carry over from one framework or level to another rather the way expert allegory may tell one story while conveying another. What may appear to be mythical inversion, when two levels are analyzed from the basic perspective of only one level of analysis, appears instead to be differences in the apperception of the projected material from one level as it appears within the armature of another level. Hence (in ten Raa's analysis) apparently cosmological materials indeed may code sociological standards (exogamy and endogamy, who may marry whom); and we are able to separate secondary or tertiary materials from the "real" messages intended by the myth itself.

While I feel that ten Raa's analytical discussion is quite successful, and that his distinctions are very helpful, I am not always convinced that in every case myths must be treated in terms of the pragmatisms of our own mythic framework, within the pragmatisms that require a mythic account to have a socially useful "message." Or at least I am hesitant to accept the "usefulness" criterion as the ultimate criterion: surely many mythic stories are created and continued because of their nonutilitarian value. If we are to relate, in some way or another, the mythopoetic activities of societies where myths are very much alive to the work of our own poets, writers, and artists (and indeed it is for this purpose that most "creative" writers of our own day have turned to study of myth and ritual), I suspect we shall have to develop more profound ways of speaking of "the entertainment value" of myths and rituals. We are, in short, confronted once again by the "superplus" of meaning in myths and rituals, with the dilemma aesthetics must always engage, namely how we are to explain the continued appeal and impact of mythopoetic materials that do *not,* to all appearances, have apparently significant social values, cosmological values, and so forth.

Both Freilich and ten Raa point to the necessity of differentiating different levels of mythical expression; they both note myth's propensities to develop "tension-reducing techniques for self-deception" (Freilich 1975:210); and they both note ways various categories may modulate within analytical perspectives: from the spatial to the temporal (Freilich), from the historical to the mythic, or from the cosmological to the sociological (ten Raa). Neither of them has yet enabled us to spring the restraints of our own scientific/economic-determinist orientation toward making myths and rituals "do something" in terms of social expediency. But this focus upon social expediency, and the underlying assumption that mythic and ritual materials must "do something," are themselves results of our own modern mythological perspective, a perspective that determines how we value certain "givens" (data) and not others, a perspective that ultimately commercializes and weakens the living frameworks of both myths and rituals.

If we have no answers about the apparent nonexpediency of myths and rituals, nothing but gestures that suggest that we tell myths and perform ritual acts because they are nonproductively beneficial or satisfying to us, at least we have been placed once more before the question about why such answers should continue to fail us at this point in a highly complex and technical society. We also are sent back to the question as to what sorts of mythic frameworks are evolving and being reflected in our scientific methodologies. That question is one of the implicit questions behind this book: we have chosen to approach the issue by means of survey of methodological approaches that have been or currently are viable in one or another circle, rather than arguing from a particular philosophical or theoretical base. The questions about the natures of myths and rituals remain, it would seem, matters of hermeneutical orientation; or we might say that all hermeneutics reflect a mythical perspective, as they reflect the categories of "unreal:real" or "important:insignificant" according to which we pay our professors of technology or of literature differently, according to which we print photographs of the high school graduate and (usually) *his* family while (usually) *he* signs on for an athletic scholarship, while relegating the winner of a graduate fellowship in the humanities to the Social Life page of the weekly newspaper.

Ritual: The Symbolic Intercom

3

Looked at from the symbolic "inside out" (rather than the functionalist "outside in"), ritual can be seen as a symbolic intercom between the level of cultural thought and complex cultural meanings, on the one hand, and that of social action and immediate event, on the other.

Nancy D. Munn, "Symbolism in a Ritual Context"

UP TO THIS POINT, MYTH AND RITUAL HAVE BEEN
presented as a more or less undifferentiated whole; I focus here and in
Chapter 4 more directly upon ritual, especially inasmuch as the so-called
myth-and-ritual school that developed alongside sociofunctionalism
stressed ritual almost to the exclusion of myth. This analytical method
treated ritual as the primary phenomenon, while myth was considered
to be almost totally dependent upon and secondary to ritual. And having discovered that ritual origins could be discovered behind many of
the classical texts of antiquity, the myth-and-ritual scholars became pre-
occupied with finding tiny ritual fragments everywhere.

The Ritual-Dominant (Myth-and-Ritual) School

The method, therefore, most accurately is identified as the ritual-
dominant school, for the phrase "myth and ritual" has lost its historical
identification with a particular school of interpretation and has become
a catch phrase for the complex interrelation of myths and rituals in both
simple and complex societies.

The clearest statement of the ritual-dominant position is found in a
famous distinction by Jane Ellen Harrison: "[myth] is the spoken correlative of the acted rite, the thing done; it is *to legomenon* [that which is
spoken] as contrasted with or rather as related to, *to dromenon* [that
which is performed; cf. our drama]" (1957b:378).[1]

Harrison's distinctions between that which is spoken, the myth, and
that which is acted out, the ritual, were very influential, and they are
echoed several times in the materials cited in this chapter. She and
others brought a helpful corrective to the earlier view that myth was
primarily or exclusively a verbal or literary phenomenon. The ritual-
dominant school, however, stressed ritual almost exclusively, or at least
demanded that both elements, myths and rituals, be seen as necessarily
and always interdependent.

A statement of this perspective by Edmund R. Leach (who is not
himself a typical representative of the school) sums up this interdependence: "Myth, in my terminology, is the counterpart of ritual; myth
implies ritual, ritual implies myth, they are one and the same. . . . Myth
regarded as a statement in words 'says' the same thing as ritual regarded
as a statement in action" (1954:13–14, cited by Kirk 1970:23).

Contemporary analysts would want to hedge at the point of noting
that *in some societies* the relation between myth and ritual may be so
stated; but in others a more ambiguous relationship holds—hence the
importance noted in Chapters 1 and 2 of identifying the relative

viability of a myth or ritual in the developmental stage of the society being studied. Often we can study both the myths and the rituals, but for the study of many societies—especially ancient ones—we have to make do with one or the other, and today there are fewer attempts to extrapolate the component that happens to be lacking.

The ritual-dominant school derived its emphasis on ritual mostly from W. Robertson Smith (1846–1894) and James Frazer (1854–1941), both of whom were apt to discover rites lurking in the tiniest shadows of legends and myths and both of whom were influenced by the French sociologists whose studies centered around the work of Émile Durkheim (1858–1917). The main activity of the ritual-dominant school occurred at the first of this century, when its approach became well established in two areas: first in biblical and Ancient Near Eastern studies, especially those of writers associated with S. H. Hooke (1874–1968), and in Theodor H. Gaster's American works; here it was a means of making some of the ancient Hebrew materials more "acceptable" to modern interests.[2] (One lasting impact of this approach is in most modern treatments of the Hebrew Psalms, many of which can be shown to have had explicit ties to rituals, such as the enthronement of the king, cultic services of the royal court, public and private lamentation and accusation, and other acts of public ceremony.) Second, the school was influential in classics, where the Cambridge School included F. M. Cornford (who was strongly influenced by Durkheim), A. B. Cook, Jane Ellen Harrison, and Gilbert Murray.

Harrison's *Themis* (1957b, with added chapters by Murray and Cornford) and her *Prolegomena to the Study of Greek Religion* (1957a) are thick, richly detailed compendia of ritual-dominant interpretations of Greek ritual reflected in Greek mythology. The books remain substantial resources so long as the reader remains aware of the author's bias toward explaining almost all mythic themes as having been shaped directly by the rites that preceded them. So the mythological race of the Titans is considered a mythological by-formation from the roles of primordial leaders in initiation rites, and even the Olympian Games are considered to be derived from the (hypothetically) pervasive New Year's festivities. In one of the added chapters to *Themis*, Murray suggests bluntly that "Tragedy is in origin a Ritual Dance . . . representing the Aition, or supposed Historical Cause, of some current ritual practice" (J. E. Harrison 1957a:17, 216, 341).

In spite of the genuine contribution of the Cambridge School in classical studies—the school's influence led to a healthy insistence that classical materials were only fully understood when their historical and social contexts were fully recognized—it was the absolute character of the supposed derivation of materials from specific ritual contexts that was most suspect. Already Lord Raglan provided something of a modification of the ritual-leads-to-myth position, suggesting that myths that have no apparent connection with a ritual "were once associated with rites," that is, not necessarily derived from them, "and that the rites ceased to be performed but the myths survived in the form of stories" (1958:129).

Other anthropologists have attempted to relate myth to ritual in terms of functional equivalencies. So A. R. Radcliffe-Brown stresses the intensely practical expression of sentiments necessary to the continued existence of a society: "I have tried to show that the function of the myths and legends of the Andamanese is exactly parallel to that of the ritual and ceremonial" (1968:71). In such a statement we begin to see a mitigation of the absolute position of the ritual-dominant principles, and in a statement by Clyde Kluckhohn we see the broadening of focus in which analysts began to explore the parallel functioning of myths and rituals:

> Ritual is an obsessive repetitive activity—often a symbolic dramatization of the fundamental "needs" of the society, whether "economic," "biological," "social," or "sexual." Mythology is the rationalization of these same needs, whether they are all expressed in overt ceremonials or not. (1942:78; a classic statement of this position by Sigmund Freud is Freud 1959)

In spite of this emphasis upon the parallel aspects of myths and rituals, however, it was Kluckhohn who stated reservations about the ritual-dominant thesis as an answer to all myth-and-ritual patterns:

> At all events, the factual record is perfectly straight-forward in one respect: neither myth nor ritual can be postulated as "primary." . . . In sum, the facts do not permit any universal generalizations as to ritual being the "cause" of myth or vice versa. Their relationship is rather that of intricate mutual interdependence, differently structured in different cultures and probably at different times in the same culture. (1942:55–56)

Such reservations are especially important in light of one aspect of the ritual-dominant school's work, namely the recurrent emphasis upon a prototypical New Year's festival as the source of Ancient Near Eastern and Greek mythologies.

The most extreme statement of the supposed ritual pattern underlying the early religions of Egypt, Babylonia, and Canaan has been made by S. H. Hooke in his introduction to *The Labyrinth* (1935), the second volume of essays clearly derived from the ritual-dominant orientation in Ancient Near Eastern studies:

> [The religions he has just listed] were all essentially ritual religions aiming at securing the well-being of the community by the due performance of ritual actions. Each of these religions had certain rituals of central importance, and in each the central figure was the king, in whose person the fortune of the state was, so to speak, incarnate. In each religion these rituals presented the same broad general pattern.
>
> This pattern consisted of a dramatic ritual representing the death and resurrection of the king, who was also the god, performed by priests and members of the royal family. It comprised a sacred combat, in which was enacted the victory of the god over his enemies, a triumphal procession in which the neighboring gods took part, an enthronement, a ceremony by which the destinies of the state for the coming year were determined, and a sacred marriage.
>
> Together with the ritual and as an essential part of it there was always found, in some form or other, the recitation of the story whose outlines were enacted in the ritual. This was the myth, and its repetition had equal potency with the performance of the ritual. In the beginning the thing said and the thing done were inseparably united, although in the course of time they were divorced and gave rise to widely differing literary, artistic and religious forms. (1935:iv–vi; see also 1933, 1958)

Joseph Fontenrose brings to bear a devastating critique of this position, noting that while the New Year's festival most likely included creation myths, for instance, that is not the same thing as saying that the festival *produced* such myths or that these myths were necessarily the central focus of what must have been a massive complex of mythic recitals and ritual performances (1966; see also Kirk 1970:chap. 1).

Similar restraint must be used in conjunction with other theories spawned by the school, such as the claims of those around Alfred Jeremias (1864–1935) that all mythology arose out of ceremonies having to do with the solar zodiac. The danger is that of ascribing a single origin to as complex a phenomenon as the occurrence of myths and rituals: to find astrological references in myths and rituals, for instance, does not mean that astrology is the sole source of either one.

Or to show that there may be mythological stories that can be allegorically equated with alchemy—as did Antoine Pernety (1716–1801)—does not mean that their primary intent is alchemical. Pernety tried to demonstrate that mythology was nothing more than an elaborate linguistic system designed by Egyptian alchemists to conceal their ideas from the common people. R. P. Knight (1750–1824) developed a similar mono-answer: he thought that all mythic images and figures ultimately derived from reflection on the human genitals. Knight's example shows the absurdity of deriving every mythologem from *one* source or occasion, but such an approach recurs frequently in the history of myth studies. The ritual-dominant school's main failing is its obsession with proving that all mythology ultimately reflects origins within particular ritualistic contexts. By overemphasizing ritual, the school ignores what is often a subtle interdependence between myths and rituals; and it ignores the fact that either myth or ritual may be "dominant" within specific religious contexts even within only one society.

The ritual-dominant school has been important in literary criticism, as will be discussed in Chapter 6, and it led for a time to the suggestion that authors merely repeated a supposed pattern of events transformed into modern dress: "The myth and ritual approach seems to suggest that the artist is no more than the torpid holder of the pen which the myth and ritual pattern in some arcane fashion guides" (Weisinger 1968:137). But more sympathetic acceptance of the school's principles has produced many excellent accounts of the mythological patterning underlying great literary works of art (see Vickery 1966; and Burrows, Lapides, and Shawcross). In the hands of Northrop Frye, such an approach has been developed into a very sensitive tool for analyzing mythic seasonal patterns in correlation with types of literary texts; such "mythological criticism" is no longer dependent upon the findings of the ritual-dominant school, but much of its initial inception was due to the school's influence (see Frye 1957, 1963; and see Chapter 6).

Today there is widespread recognition of the complexity of the ways myths and rituals may be interrelated: there are indeed instances where myths provide an *aition,* an explanation for the origin of the ritual, but generally the relationship between related myths and rituals is not so explicit. The myth may explain the underlying perspective or general orientation of the ritual—and not necessarily in a "realistic" manner. For example, the Greek stories about Prometheus arranging which parts of the sacrificial animal should be presented to the gods (and getting tricked in turn: the gods get the parts corresponding to immortality, the humans merely the mortal, corruptible parts), or the child-god Hermes setting out a sacrifice for the twelve Olympians, among whom he cleverly includes himself (in the Homeric Hymn to Hermes): these reflect many actual details of Greek ritual sacrificial practice, but neither account simply mirrors any specific sacrifice.

It would also be misleading to follow the ritual-dominant school's opposition between the spoken and the enacted to the point of assuming that rites are somehow *pure action, wordless,* sheer choreography of movement—or likewise that mythic recitations are *purely verbal,* for no experienced performer will omit dramaturgistic body movements, impressive sounds and pauses, and carefully ritualized cadences of performance. And few rituals omit etiological or explanatory elements during their performances: "We do xxx because it was first done by yyy," or "Leave this ritual with a reminder of your mortality, of the briefness of life."

Mythic accounts alongside rituals may relate the wider cultural contexts: the Navajo chanter, for instance, may not learn the underlying mythic account until years after he has successfully mastered a complex healing ritual. Myths may provide the long-range social history from which a rite represents only a momentary snapshot, a specific occasion; hence mythic accounts, in setting out ideal details of initial performances, may vary considerably from the ways a rite is actually performed—but this variation also may be reflected in the spoken part of the ritual performance itself: "We no longer do zzz in this ceremony, but our ancestors did."

The myth versus ritual distinction is simply not very helpful in treating the ritual performance texts themselves, and in fact verbal texts may come to dominate the actual ritual performances, as can be seen in many formal religious rituals today. As happens so frequently in modern scholarship, the power of a dualistic opposition (myth *or* ritual) has ruled an entire discipline. But especially when studying several cultures simultaneously, dualistic oppositions are very misleading; in this instance the opposition led to the ignoring of more subtle differences and asked the scholar to label oppositionally (mythically *or* ritually dominated society) what should have been approached with a much larger set of differentiating features. We are not yet able to chart the entire range of ways a particular society operates with its mythic and ritualistic performances: we need a continuous-range typology that will allow for examples where myths and rituals are almost indistinguishable or where mythemes, ritemes, and public symbols interpenetrate within a complex whole that is further complicated by the wide range of skills of the performer-participants.

Contemporary Emphasis upon the Priority of Ritual

In contemporary anthropological studies, variants of the ritual-dominant approach are found in the work of Anthony F. C. Wallace and Victor Turner. Wallace states unequivocally: "Myth, in the most general sense, is the theory of ritual, which explains the nature of the powers, prescribes the ritual, accounts for its successes and failures. Together, they are religion." Wallace considers ritual to have an instrumental priority: "the goals of religion are to be achieved by performing rituals; myths are merely extremely valuable, and regularly employed, auxiliary equipment." Both mythology and folklore "function . . . to rationalize ritual," and "in the last analysis, a myth can be defined as a transformation of a ritual," leading Wallace to classify myths according to the ways they mirror or transform rituals (1966a:107, 104, 243–44).

It is difficult to argue against Wallace's view that "the primary function of religion is ritual" (102), if we have in mind religious ceremonies rather than theology or meditative reflection. But elevating this principle to explain the entire set of complex interrelations between myths and rituals seems strained. Myths are understood *only* as rationalizing, only as justifying and sustaining ritual performances, and we lose sight entirely of the use of myth for entertainment, for sustaining more general social values that are not directly tied to specific rituals, and for elaborating abstractly or graphically what a culture considers to be the meaning and purpose of human existence. The strong point in Wallace's approach—his identification of ritual as the acting out of religious beliefs—becomes overwhelmingly dominant and forces mythology into a purely secondary status that logically would require a ritualistic prototype for every myth. Such a conflation of myths and rituals is precisely what the myth-and-ritual school was arguing all along.

Anthropologist Nancy D. Munn, author of an excellent study of religious iconography (1973b), has developed her interest in ritual symbols in an analysis of their social functioning (1973a). Ritual symbols serve as vehicles for messages; they co-imply social relationships between members of a community and therefore may be considered as a sort of currency of social interaction. With Durkheim, Munn comprehends the ritual symbol as a junction box ("switching point") between the external moral constraints of the social order and the participant's internal feelings and imaginative projections. She goes beyond Durkheim in specifying, by means of semantic analysis, how it is that ritual symbols provide condensations of meanings. As vehicles or instruments, such symbols can provide possible restructurings of an individual's self-image, as in a curing ceremony where there is often a symbolic reordering of the patient into a more satisfactory relationship to her or his context than was true before the ritual.

Munn regards ritual as a societal control system, linking the individual to the community by a symbolic mobilization of powerful forces inherent in the transpersonal values of the community. Munn's analysis seems perfectly apt for the external analyst seeking to understand just why or how rituals receive so much attention within a social group: they enable us to find out who we are by comparisons with community values that have adaptive capabilities. But her analysis is of the sort that a practitioner of a ritual gesture doubtless would find abstract and rationalizing in the extreme; nor does it encompass activities such as ways of walking down a crowded street (decorum) or the ritualistic enactments of *anti*communal values that sometimes may be found in contemporary drama.

Our ability to analyze rituals, remarks Ronald Grimes (1982a:117), is about as rudimentary as is our ability to interpret dreams. Grimes's own project has been an attempt to provide a much wider range of purview (ranging from ritualization to decorum to ceremony, liturgy, magic, and celebration; see Grimes 1982a:chap. 3), and we will return to his important methodological insights later in this chapter. At this point, however, I want to recognize one major insight of his *Beginnings in Ritual Studies* (1982a), namely the observation that seems obvious yet has not been emphasized previously, that not all "ritologists" or students of rites have approached ritualistic phenomena with the same ends in view. Adapting Grimes's list of theoretical options, we have at present at least the following represented within contemporary studies:

1. Formulating indigenous interpretations, emic categories, of ritual behaviors (D. Tedlock, G. Witherspoon).
2. Recognition of etic biases, those awkward perspectives not adequately resolved by the "participant-observer" model (R. Grimes, B. Myerhoff).
3. Describing a ritual's phenomenological characteristics—themes or processes (M. Eliade, V. Turner, A. Van Gennep) or forms (K. Burke).
4. Identifying underlying symbolic structures (C. Geertz, V. Turner, B. Babcock, N. Munn) or gestural grammars (E. Hall, R. Birdwhistell, E. Goffman), metalanguages (G. Bateson), types of linguistic expression (J. Austin, R. Bauman, W. Wheelock), or logics (E. Cassirer, S. Langer), or deep structures (C. Lévi-Strauss, E. Leach).
5. Considering social functions (V. Turner, M. Douglas, R. Firth, H. Mol, S. Moore) or roles (E. Goffman, R. Schechner, P. Slater).
6. Relating rituals to archetypal prototyes (the neo-Jungians), developmental stages (E. Erikson), or games and strategies (J. Huizinga, R. Callois, L. Kliever).
7. Exploration of ecological ramifications (R. Rappaport, A. Hultkrantz) or biogenetic causation (E. d'Aquili, C. Laughlin, J. Huxley).
8. Study of historical origins and situations of rituals (R. Girard, M. Detienne).

9. Imaginatively reparticipating earlier ritual contexts as a hermeneutical device for comprehending them (P. Ricoeur, H.-G. Gadamer).

Doubtless other options could be charted here; my concern is not with inclusiveness of all perspectives but with indicating that the status of ritual studies (I'm not fond of Grimes's term "ritology") is at present nascent and confusing. Much as I have argued earlier that myth studies need to be practiced only with the widest possible operational framework, so must ritual studies.

Until that desideratum can be reached, however, we have to work with the best of the possibilities that are presently at hand; and both Grimes (1976a, 1982a) and I have found Victor Turner's ritual studies to be of great importance. In the following subsections of this chapter I focus upon Turner's series of books and articles at much greater length than has been possible for other theorists in this book. Then we turn to the problems arising when the close fit between symbol and social value is weakened or destroyed—represented in our context by the growth of an antiritualism; additional discussion of ritual in Chapter 4 will focus upon biological aspects.

Victor Turner's Ritual Studies

One of the most comprehensive and significant contemporary approaches to religious ritual has been developed by Victor Turner, who was associated with the Institute for Advanced Study at Princeton, the University of Chicago, and the University of Virginia.[3] The author of a number of impressive studies himself, Turner also oversaw the Symbol, Myth, and Ritual series for Cornell University Press. The scope of Turner's works is both extensive and wide ranging, and in drawing together some of his materials on the study of ritual here, we must pass over equally impressive and extensive materials on social interaction and on symbology (the study of symbolic expression and meaning). This approach is justified at least partly, however, by the fact that for Turner symbols are to be defined primarily in terms of ritual: "The symbol is the smallest unit of ritual which still retains the specific properties of ritual behavior; it is the ultimate unit of specific structure in a ritual context" (1967:19). And correspondingly, Turner refers to ritual as "an aggregation of symbols" (1968a:2).

Primarily concerned with developing a sophisticated anthropological approach, Turner was clearly a scholar in the best of the humanistic tradition that correlates analysis of other cultures with analysis of one's own culture. I will try to reflect this aspect, especially in describing Turner's development of the significance of the midphase of ritual (the liminal phase) for the evocation and nurturance of cultural creativity. First, however, I outline some of the methodological guidelines Turner has provided and, following that, some of his findings concerning the relationships between societies and their rituals.

The Means of Analysis

Having mentioned Turner's definition of symbol as "the smallest unit of ritual," I already have touched upon a crucial feature of his methodology, which works from discrete ritual symbols (storage units, building blocks, "molecules" of ritual; later Grimes will suggest a different focus upon "the ritological micro-units" [1982a:88]) to their incorporation in ritual systems—and then to the incorporation of such systems in the whole social complex being studied. Such an approach is self-consciously opposed to an approach that first would construct an abstract cosmology or mythological belief system and then would seek to organize ritual symbols within that framework (Turner 1969b:74). Turner stresses the "common diachronic profile or processual form" in rituals, that is, the sequence of ritual acts in social contexts (13); hence he treats ritual symbols not as static, absolute objectifications but as "social and cultural systems, shedding and gathering meaning over time and altering in form" (1974b:54).[4]

This emphasis upon the social dynamics of the ritual context led Turner to utilize a *dramatic* analogy. Social dramas include the playing out of roles, the use of rhetoric, audience reactions, performances according to rules, and narrative movement toward a crisis and then its resolution: "Ritual provides a stage on which roles are enacted and the conflicts of the secular drama reflected in symbol, mime, and precept" (1968a:274–75; "social dramas"—as "units of aharmonic or disharmonic process, arising in conflict situations"—are divided into four phases and the pattern is discussed in 1974a:37–42 and 78–79; see also 1982b:69, 92, 106). The analogy between ritual and drama also is augmented by developments in field theory, especially by the concept of social arena (1974a:129–36). Both drama and arena models of ritual action develop Turner's emphasis upon social process (see V. Turner 1977b; and K. Turner 1981); when using such models, "It is not the successiveness of isolated facts but the successiveness of connected facts, the successiveness of bundles or systems of relations, that engages our attention" (V. Turner 1974a:132). Hence the *sequence* of a series of ritual acts or a series of rituals is focal, as opposed to isolated ritual moments or symbols treated apart from the performance contexts. Tracking the stages of *breach* with customary rules and frames of reference, the *crisis* initiated by this breach, the *redress* of normative rules by authorities of the society, and finally the *reintegration-reconciliation* or the *schism,* the *"consensual recognition of irremedial breach,* usually followed by the spatial separation of the parties" (1982b:92), the analyst has a means of studying many types of social dramas, not all of which bear the formal traits by which we usually classify "ritual acts."

Turner provides a healthy corrective to an approach to myth and ritual that would focus only upon texts or upon micro-observations of a ritual in progress: he works toward a full-context appreciation that includes the intrasocietal dynamics of the actors and the audience. "Meaning" of ritual elements is assigned at many different points in the ritual process, and the student of a ritual must cast the analytical net as widely as possible: balancing explicit and implied meanings, gathering meanings stressed in one rite in such a way as to clarify something that is unclear in a second rite, judging between real and ideal interpretations, observing functions of ritual units in terms of differing actors and observers, and realizing that different levels of meaning may be stressed in any one performance. Essentially, then, Turner develops a sympathetic hermeneutic or theory of interpretation of the ritual process, a hermeneutic that can be fully operational only for living societies (see 1974a:153, 159; 1967:27, 43, 46; 1969a; 1969b:41; 1968a:2, 7); the model will need special adaptation for the study of cultures where the observer is limited to written records (Mircea Eliade, deploring the dependence of traditional myth studies upon Greek myths, reminds us that "we do not know a single Greek myth within its ritual context," in Beane and Doty:19, cf. 17). The emphasis upon the processual nature of rituals represents stress upon both the importance of the total social context and the sequence of ritual acts.

That sequence is the structure of the ritual, and Turner often found his clues to interpretation of ritual meanings in the ways the sequences develop within particular rituals, representing "deeper" foundational structures: "Underlying the observable structure of a ritual may be detected its 'telic structure,' its design as a system of ends and means" (1968:3). This system is primarily a system of social relations, a patterning of human interaction, and hence ritual and ritual symbolism provide important clues to underlying social values. This relation between ritual and society will be explored in the next two subsections; but first we must note further some of Turner's proposals for classifying rituals and analyzing their dynamics.

Turner does not attempt to classify all rituals, but rather he stresses a few types, especially those centered on important crises in human development. Much of his analysis has been generated from his amplifications of Arnold Van Gennep's 1909 *Les Rites de Passage*.[5] Van Gennep (1873–1957) analyzed three phases in the "passage" of an individual through rituals dealing with life crises: *separation* (stepping out of secular time or space, as entering a temple), *transition* or margin (an ambiguous area and period, the focal phase of adjustment to a new social role), and *incorporation* or reaggregation (the return of an individual to a social context, now in a new status). In parallel terminology, these three phases were called, playing on the Latin *limen* (threshold), the *preliminal*, the *liminal*, and the *postliminal* phases. (We will see later that Turner emphasizes the second of these.)

Initiatory rituals especially interested Van Gennep, and likewise they interest Victor Turner (cf. 1967:chap. 4, "Betwixt and Between: The Liminal Period in Rites de Passage"), who contrasts them with seasonal or calendrical rituals in terms of how they affect the persons experiencing them: "initiatory passage rites tend to 'put people down' while some seasonal rites tend to 'set people up'; that is, initiations humble people before permanently elevating them, while some seasonal rites (whose residues are carnivals and festivals) elevate those of low status transiently before returning them to their permanent humbleness" (1974b:57). Funeral ceremonies can be linked with initiatory rites as life-crisis rituals, rituals that "not only concern the individuals on whom they are centered, but also mark changes in the relationships of all the people connected with them" (1967:7–8).

Another group of rituals is named by Turner "rituals of affliction," and it has to do (among the African Ndembu, the society Turner has studied most intensively) with propitiating or exorcising ancestors' shades or spirits blamed for afflicting illness or misfortune (1967:9, 282). Those for whom the rituals are effective are healed and restored to proper functioning—which may be successful hunting or sexual reproduction.

Turner also distinguishes "corrective" from "redressive" rituals (1967:270); examples of the former, like circumcision, represent responses to cumulative mass social needs (for guiding the maturation process, for education, and so forth), rather than redressing a specific individual's problems. Finally, Turner distinguishes revelatory from divinatory rituals, and he distinguishes both of these from the life-crisis rituals: "In the former, the cognitive aspect, that concerned with feelings and desires, is clearly dominant" (1968a:44).

Generally speaking, rituals deal with recurrent situations, with the typical rather than the specific and individual (1968a:238), and Turner has not attempted to account for all the ways rituals may function or to chart all the ways specific ritualistic acts may be present in an individual's life. He has tried to take account of the range of rituals the anthropologist may encounter, especially those rituals richly textured by symbolism. And he is very much aware of the caution needed by the analyst in view of the fact that each performance will contain elements unique to that performance: "I am prepared to assert that no performance of a given cult ritual ever precisely resembles another" (1975a:41). Because no two performances are ever exactly the same, the analyst will need to observe a number of performances in order to determine the minimal units that recur most frequently; then she or he will be able to appreciate pattern-breaking occurrences when they take place and perhaps will learn something of the significance of the "ideal" performance pattern by noting the elements that are considered to break the ideal sequence. It is the *performance* or *enactment,* rather than the formal rules or frames, that should receive analytical attention: in any given instance "the ritual process transcends its frame" (1982b:79; for a more inclusive view of "performance," see Tambiah).

Turner anticipates the recent distinction between external theoretical and native experiential (etic and emic) approaches when he contrasts "real" and "ideal" patterns; precisely at the points where the ideal prototype is not evidenced in the real, where there is an element that strikes the educated observer as irrelevant, insights into the total pattern may be revealed (cf. my discussion of Freilich's "non-sense" in myths in Chapter 2). Often, for instance, conflict between the ideal structure of the ritual and the actual living out of social customs and norms may lay bare the societally permissible limits of behavior (V. Turner 1967:273), as we will discover below with respect to the trickster and the clown.

Conflicts in rituals come not only at the level of the observer's distinctions, however, but are featured within many rituals themselves, and in fact Turner speaks of the way rituals "condense" such social polarities: "what is distributed through many fields and situations of secular life is condensed into a few symbolic actions and objects" (1967:285). So we may have both auspicious and inauspicious aspects of a ritual symbol present simultaneously: for example, the name of one Ndembu ritual, Isoma, refers negatively to "slipping" while climbing a tree or to children slipping out of the womb prematurely—the inauspicious, the problematic—and positively to the healing ritual itself, in which the harmful cause of the problem is made "to slip out" from the patient (1969b:25).

Turner emphasizes this "semantic bipolarity" of ritual symbols (69); again an exact knowledge of the performance context is necessary to determine which particular connotation is intended: "the same symbols have varying significance in different contexts" (53). (An example from the historical development of primitive Christianity: the term *nomos,* "law," may refer to the deity's provision of universal norms for behavior, reaching back to Adam, or it may be used negatively, as sometimes in Paul's writings, to refer to the oppressive weight of custom that is to be overcome by the Christian experience of communal love.) And implicit goals may sometimes—as "infantile and archaic impulses"—run opposite to explicit ritual goals: Turner gives as his example the hostilities between the older and the younger generation that surface in the Mukanda (or circumcision rite) (1967:276), hostilities such as those Bruno Bettelheim explored in a famous paper on "Symbolic Wounds" (in Bettelheim 1954; see also V. Turner 1967:29–30, 99).

We may refer to "the ritual paradox" (V. Turner 1975a:184): it is often precisely by reversing the ordinary connotations of words or things by metaphor or symbolic extension that rituals perform their tasks. Wisdom and innocence, life and death, plenitude and scarcity: these oppositions may appear, as the result of a ritual process, to be much less sharply polar than they appear in day-to-day living (1977c:37). Indeed, Turner suggests that the most important phase of ritual is the in-between or liminal period, where the going definitions of reality are questioned, where there are few restraints upon reformulating and recombining accepted terms and customs, and where cultural creativity is therefore at its most intense (this concept will be developed in the concluding part of this section).

Rituals Reflect Social Structures

Turner seeks to develop a metacommunicative model of the relationship between symbol and rite on the one hand and of the social realities on the other. This model projects a tensive relationship between the reality and the symbol in which the two are more sharply distinguished than in the understanding that rites or symbols simply mirror the social reality. Hence Turner's model should provide "an alternate notion to that of those anthropologists who still work . . . with the [sociofunctionalist] paradigm of Radcliffe-Brown and regard religious symbols as reflecting or expressing social structure and promoting social integration" (1974a:52). Turner is aware of the constructive and critical role of the metacommunicative forms, and his position is an advance on those who treated myth and ritual from a purely sociofunctional or ritual-dominant point of view or in terms of psychological reaction-formation. These approaches "treat social action as an 'epi-phenomenon,' while I try to give it 'ontological' status" (1974a:52; Turner refers to Durkheim and Auguste Comte in the same paragraph).

Turner does follow Durkheim and others in understanding rituals as ciphering social structures, and I will demonstrate that in the next paragraph; but he stresses that rituals have a determinate influence in shaping social relationships and indeed social "reality" while remaining reflexive toward that reality rather than merely reflecting it. Hence rituals can serve as metacommunicative forms that provide models for behavior; they may comment upon the realities of actual behavior; and they provide "switchpoints of social action" when change comes about:

> Thus if we are to begin to understand how ritual makes people tick, it is not enough merely to consider the symbolic molecules of ritual as informational storage-units. They are these and more, and in the "more" we move into the field of social dynamics where ritual both maintains the traditional forms of culture and becomes at times of major crisis an instrument for adjusting new norms and values to perennially potent symbolic forms and discarding old ones from the ideological pole of crucial symbols. (1975b:80)

Turner's characterization of ritual as "quintessential custom" (1967:285; 1968a:23) is particularly revealing of his own stance: ritual "is the concentration of custom, its refined extract as it were. . . . It is distilled from custom, not directly from interactions" (1968a:23). Ritual symbolic actions "refer to or imply social relationships" (1975a:172); "a ritual is an epitome of the wider and spontaneous social process in which it is embodied" (1968a:273). And Turner cites approvingly a statement by Monica Wilson: "Rituals reveal values at their deepest level . . . it is the values of the group that are revealed. I see in the study of rituals the key to an understanding of the essential constitution of human societies" (cited in V. Turner 1969b:6; I have abbreviated Wilson's statement more than Turner does). Rituals articulate social values, and that necessarily means current values, for all the obscure or irrelevant items that may be carried along: "The ritual system is not a meaningless inheritance from a dead past, but something that meets contemporary needs. The form of the ritual is consistent with the form of the society. And the conflicts of the society are the same as those dramatized and symbolized in its ritual" (1968a:238–39).

Social structure tends to mask itself, to become unconscious simply because "it is there." On the other hand ritual may unmask this structure, leading to "direct apprehension of reality" (1975a:16) by pointing to the very impulses and conflicts that constitute social interactions, the negative and socially destructive impulses that primarily are mentioned only in the context of proscribing them. Rituals and myths may well disclose—in their contents, or in the sequence of ritual phases (1968a:3)—what it is that primarily bothers a society, what are the problems that threaten its cohesion: "Indeed, one often finds in human cultures that structural contradictions, asymmetries, and anomalies are overlaid by layers of myth, ritual, and symbol, which stress the axiomatic value of key structural principles with regard to the very situations where these appear to be most inoperative" (1969b:47).

The context of this statement is a study of the "Paradoxes of Twinship in Ndembu Ritual" (1969b:chap. 2): it is often the abnormal—in this case twins, which present a strain on Ndembu child-rearing patterns—that, in being provided for, raises into prominence the normal, the usual or desired. "The paradox that what is good (in theory) is bad (in practice) becomes the mobilizing point of a ritual that stresses the overall unity of the group, surmounting its contradictions" (1969b:49); "Cognitively, nothing underlines regularity so well as absurdity or paradox" (176). Precisely what breaks the normative pattern, and hence creates occasion for social disunity, becomes an occasion for reiterating the normative, that which unifies and coheres the social unity: "An event, such as twinning, that falls outside the orthodox classifications of society is, paradoxically, made the ritual occasion for an exhibition of values that relate to the community as a whole, as a homogeneous, unstructured unity that transcends its differentiations and contradictions" (92).

Social cohesion is sought by ritual means: humans perform rituals not only to celebrate an already present or guaranteed unity, but they also—or perhaps primarily—perform them to regain such unity when it is lost or threatened. Some rituals therefore appear both to reflect the social order (lack of social cohesion) and to represent attempts to modify it (cultivation of social cohesion). Both functions are interlocked, and Geertz's "model of and model for" distinction is again helpful on the plane of analysis, although the ritual performers may not recognize or be willing to admit that the distinction holds. (For example, politicians at a rally seeking support of a candidate would be loath to proclaim in public that their candidate was in need of greater support.)

Rituals Influence Social Relationships

If we accept Turner's premise that "Ritual is a periodic restatement of the terms in which men of a particular culture must interact if there is to be any kind of a coherent social life" (1968a:6), it is clear that rituals influence societal patterns directly, and here I will explicate some of the ways this influence occurs.

Turner assigns to ritual an instrumental role in conforming the individual to societal expectations, especially in terms of redirecting natural impulses into appropriate social behaviors: "To make a human being obey social norms, violence must be done to his natural impulses" (1968a:236). This sublimation (1974a:56), to use the term associated with Freudian theory, has to do with control of aggression and hostilities toward others (1969a, 1969b:93), with social cohesion and group-bond formation (1969a), and with the canalization of raw, undirected energies into socially constructed channels ("The raw energies of conflict are domesticated into the service of social order" [1967:39]). Such redirection is especially necessary with respect to social relationships involving sex and overt hostility that threaten to shatter the sought-for unity and cohesion:

> What we are confronted with in the [Ndembu] twinship rites is in fact a domestication of those wild impulses, sexual and aggressive, which Ndembu believe are shared by men and animals. The raw energies released in overt symbolisms of sexuality and hostility between the sexes are channeled toward master symbols representative of structural order, and values and virtues on which that order depends. Every opposition is overcome or transcended in a recovered unity, a unity that, moreover, is reinforced by the very potencies that endanger it. One aspect of ritual is shown by these rites to be a means of putting at the service of the social order the very forces of disorder that inhere in man's mammalian constitution. Biology and structure are put in right relation by the activation of an ordered succession of symbols, which have the twin functions of communication and efficacy. (1969b:93)

"Biology and structure"—or, we might say, the emotionally charged and the socially, structurally, virtuous. Hence: "Ritual adapts and periodically readapts the biopsychical individual to the basic conditions and axiomatic values of human social life" (1967:43); or ritual may be described as "a mechanism that periodically converts the obligatory into the desirable" (30). In adapting the individual to patterns of agreed-upon social coexistence, rituals emphasize the sentiments of " 'human-kindness,' a sense of the generic social bond between all members of society—even in some cases transcending tribal or national boundaries—regardless of their subgroup affiliations or incumbency of structural positions" (1969b:116).

Especially by identifying and anticipating social cleavages, ritual provides for or restores equitable relationships among group members (cf.

1969b:177). Such a regulation of relationships is quite clear in rituals wherein a leader undergoes public humiliation before assuming her or his position, or where leaders and followers periodically exchange master:servant roles: "Rituals of status reversal, either placed at strategic points in the annual circle [that is, in a calendrical sequence] or generated by disasters conceived of as being the result of grave social sins, are thought of as bringing social structure and communitas [the ideal concept of social equability] into right mutual relation once again" (1969b:178; cf. 101, 107) So too the leaders may appreciate a periodic release from the structural requirements of their positions (200) and an opportunity to experience the world once again from outside the confines of the leader's chair.

Rituals have, further, what Turner calls "expressive" and "creative" functions. Rituals are expressive insofar as they portray "in symbolic form certain key values and cultural orientations" (1968a:6). As a form of instruction, rituals pass on to the new generation the learned experiences of the older generation. And as a type of communication, they teach the language of the society, they invest ordinary artifacts and terms with their relative importance in the worldview of the particular society. This latter also may be regarded as the creative function, insofar as ritual is one of the social agencies that *names* things, and that means giving them social reality: ritual "actually creates, or re-creates, the categories through which men perceive reality—the axioms underlying the structures of society and the laws of the natural and moral orders" (7; see the elaboration of this point by Berger and Luckmann; Belsey; Fiske and Hartley).

But rituals do more than merely inform: they also elicit behaviors. Turner frequently speaks of the *orectic* function of rituals in this case, using a philosophical term referring to the stimulation of appetite or desire, but used by him with reference to the ways rituals impel members of a society to act in a particular manner (1974a:56). By eliciting emotion and expressing and mobilizing desire, ritual symbols add the orectic dimension to their cognitive function (1967:54); such symbols attain their motivating powers by fusing emotionally derived impulses to social values inculcated in the education process (29–30). Hence, as we have seen, Turner can speak of "biology and structure" being aligned into an effective coordination of knowledge and its application (1969b:93); and "emotional, mainly physiological, referents may well lend their qualities to the ethical and normative referents so as to make what is obligatory desirable" (1968a:44). Traditional knowledge, passed on through the storehouse of ritual information, therefore becomes powerful knowledge, knowledge that is given along with the necessary orectic stimulation to act it out: "there is undoubtable transformative capacity in a well-performed ritual, implying an ingress of power into the initial situation" (1982b:79–80).

The Trickster and the Liminal/Liminoid

Trickster figures appear in many cultures: Hermes in Greek myth, who slips from his cradle to trick his brother Apollo out of his fine cattle, or various North American figures, who share with Hermes the elements of trickery and humor and who likewise manage to bring cultural benefits (control of fire, music, commerce) almost as by-products of their fooling around (orientations to the trickster figure in Radin 1956; Ricketts 1966; Doty n.d.). Turner notes the kinship between trickster figures, neophytes in the liminal phase of rituals, and court jesters, dwarfs, and clowns. All these figures appear in a status of marginality: they "(1) fall in the interstices of social structure, (2) are on its margins, or (3) occupy its lowest rungs" (1969b:125—applied to a more diverse group). Medieval jesters or jokers, for instance, represented the poor or deformed classes and had a "structurally inferior or 'marginal'" position; they symbolized what David Hume termed the "sentiment for humanity." In a highly stratified society jesters were marked as the inferior group (V. Turner 1969b:110–11). In opposition to the authorities and power of controlled consensus in the social *structure,* these figures represent for Turner the ideal pattern of social interaction he calls *communitas.*

Communitas constantly is sidetracked by the growth of social structures, and its reappearance may so threaten the social structure that a revolutionary movement comes about (see 1969b:chaps. 3 and 4; 1974a:chaps. 5–7; 1978a). And in rigidly structural societies, it is primarily advocated or evoked during liminal phases or by persons such as clowns or tricksters whose social status is likewise marginal: "Communitas breaks in through the interstices of structure, in liminality; at the edges of structure, in marginality; and from beneath structure, in inferiority" (1969b:128).

The importance of such persons as clowns and tricksters is stressed by Turner in a way that highlights the creativity of such figures, as well as that of anyone undergoing the release from structure in the liminal phases that Turner calls antistructure (a similar argument is advanced in many studies of creativity theory; cf. Koestler). It is especially in the freedom of liminality that new metaphors are born, revisions of the social structure are first attempted, and creative insights are developed and nurtured. "Liminality is the realm of primitive hypothesis, where there is a certain freedom to juggle with the factors of existence" (V. Turner 1967:106); "Liminality is the domain of the 'interesting,' or of 'uncommon sense'" (1977b:68); it represents "a limitless freedom, a symbolic freedom of action which is denied to the norm-bound incumbent of a status in a social structure. . . . Liminality is pure potency, where anything can happen, . . . where the elements of culture and society are released from their customary configurations and recombined in bizarre and terrifying images" (1968b:577).

Monstrous beings—animal-headed gods, for instance, or masked figures (1977c:38)—often figure in initiation rites and provide an example of these "bizarre and terrifying images." They are not intended only to terrify initiates and thereby make them conform to the social norms of the social group, but they indeed may cipher in the most graphic and perceptual manner "the different factors of reality" as conceived in the initiate's social order (1967:105; 1977b:69). The initiate learns the received traditions and precisely by encountering them in such highly dramatized forms is encouraged to evaluate them and to consider them as available for new combinations and patterns. (Think of the particular life stances that may bond a group of fraternity or sorority initiates: they often represent a recombination or a selective new interpretation of the older members' rules and customs.)

In fact, with respect to the subject matter of this book, liminality is preponderantly the phase of social experience in which new myths and rituals are engendered:

> Liminality, marginality, and structural inferiority are conditions in which are frequently generated myths, symbols, rituals, philosophical systems, and works of art. These cultural forms provide men with a set of templates or models which are, at one level, periodical reclassifications of reality and man's relationship to society, nature, and culture. But they are more than classifications, since they incite men to action as well as to thought. (1969b:128–29; cf. 1977a:39)

Again we have Turner's emphasis upon the motivating fusion of human biological impulses with social norms—or, as he phrases it at one point, the fusion of nature and spirit. Myths represent the story of such processes having occurred, and hence "In myths we see nature and spirit at their shaping work—and this is the liminal moment in and out of time" (1968b:581).

It is one thing to point to liminal experiences as "the seedbeds of cultural creativity" (1974b:60), a notion that Grimes suggests leads

Turner "to stand the anthropology of ritual on its head" (Grimes 1982a:150), but it is quite something else to demonstrate how liminality is represented in our own societies, where rituals are much less highly structured, and certainly less obligatory in most instances, than in many less specialized societies. One problem with the vast majority of studies of ritual and myth has been their lack of reflexivity toward their own contemporary societies: the most significant achievements in recent years have been the attempts of experimental communes to model their communal life—often unsuccessfully—on the structures of some earlier, even primitive, social pattern.

One of Victor Turner's major contributions may well turn out to be his attempt to bridge the gaps between contemporary Western societies and societies more usually studied by anthropologists and myth analysts. He has done this by working toward a recognition of the liminal sector of our own culture, which he now refers to as the *liminoid* and which he understands to be something quite different from liminality in rituals of earlier or less technologically advanced societies.

Turner criticizes those who fail to differentiate "between symbolic systems and genres which have developed before and after the Industrial Revolution" (1974b:62), and he attempts such differentiation in terms of the concepts of work and leisure. I cannot repeat here his argument, which develops further Johan Huizinga's treatment of religion as "play" and subsequent approaches to religious ritual as "sacred play" (see Huizinga; Miller 1970a; Kliever 1981; and Neale). Essentially the *liminal,* which continues to exist in modern culture in attenuated forms, is an integral aspect of the social order, developed apart from the central economic and political processes though integrated with them; it is most often obligatory for members of a tightly cohesive social group, and it concerns mass-collective roles and values. *Liminoid* activities, on the other hand, are more characteristically individual activities taking place at the margins and interstices of the main cultural processes; they "are plural, fragmentary, and experimental in character," and they are closer to individual than to collective concerns (V. Turner 1974b:84–86; cf. 1978a:287).

If in other societies the crucial experience of communitas was and is to be found in the liminal phase of rituals that continue to hold their vital social center, in our own society such experience may still be found in the arts and in sports, in the liminoid activities and pursuits that fill our leisure time. Turner only began to develop this analysis to demonstrate the presence of specific liminoid activities in modern societies (1977c, 1978a, 1978b, 1984), but he laid an impressive framework for such analysis, and recent articles in anthropology have begun to expand and to challenge aspects of his proposals (cf. Abrahams and Bauman; and Abrahams).

At the same time, I wonder if Turner's emphasis upon the liminoid or liminal doesn't avoid dealing with the fact that the experience of most persons familiarized to a repeated ritual form (attending a service of worship, for example) is not characteristically "liminal" or "liminoid" but something more adequately characterized as "continuing in the middle of the same old thing." The major problem for most ongoing ritual observance today is engendering new emphases and performances in a manner that will be adequately appealing to ritual participants who have found "the same old thing" boring or moribund. Years ago A. M. Hocart was alert to the problem of maintaining the vitality of ritual forms:

> As a matter of fact, ritual is not a disease, though it may become diseased just like science or art. The trouble is that we may talk of ritual very much as if it were a thing in itself, an unchanging entity which can be defined like mass or elements. In reality, the word merely describes chains of action which can vary infinitely. They are in a perpetual state of flux, so that . . . ritual may become the negation of ritual. (64–65)

Clearly Turner's proposals concerning the transformation of the liminal into the liminoid have a great deal to do with the "problem" of the lack of ritual in contemporary societies, what Turner himself terms "deritualization" (1969a, 1968a:22). Ritual in the usual formal sense can be viable only in a community possessing strong communal bonds (1967, 1968a:2); given the lack of such bonds today, many commentators have predicted the complete dying off of ritual in the future or have redefined the classical concepts to make them applicable to civil religion or to other ritualistic aspects of modern life (see Bellah 1970, 1975; Cherry; and Warner).

But Turner, like Hocart, sees that the breakdown of ritual need not always be a negative matter: it can lead to new experiences of communitas and new social forms. "My guess at the moment," he writes, "is that during the present transitional period of history, when many institutionalized social forms and modes of thought are in question, a reactivation of many cultural forms associated traditionally with normative communitas is occurring" (1974a:172; cf. 250–51). New social forms—and new meanings to cultural forms (1974b:72–73)—arose in other societies from liminal experiences that were *regenerative* of communitas (1982b:84): there is no reason to suspect that today's liminoid experiences will not be similarly productive (see 1984:22; here and generally in his late writings Turner stressed the important function of social reflexivity in rituals: they provide occasions for the society to view itself critically).

Contemporary Antiritualism and the Postmodern

Anyone who attempts to analyze contemporary society using a model like Turner's confronts the problem of the prevalent antiritualistic attitude that is so widespread today. It is difficult to advocate a healthy respect for rituals, in the sense that Turner finds a link between communitas and ritual, when one first must deal with a mind-set that denies that rituals ever can be considered positively, when rituals are considered to represent only a negative deadweight from the past, or when the self-reflexivity of our postmodern culture intrudes its suspicions of any activities that are held to represent absolutes.

The adjective "ritualistic" covers a whole range of phenomena, of course, but it is used negatively so often today that it may be difficult to recapture positive meanings. Used negatively, it has come to refer to that which is not free, that which constricts human development or forces individuals into submission to group norms and customs that are out of date almost as rapidly as they are formalized. Contemporary antiritualism is an important element in modern consciousness; "Ritual itself has become foreign to us" (Grimes 1982a:intro.).

Such a viewpoint is widespread in theories of childrearing, in popular reactions to transitional rituals such as weddings and graduations, and even in scholarly analyses of "the current scene." It has been produced by many sources in the development of the human psyche. Margaret Mead points to one source, the fact "that Americans are conditioned to accept and expect a high degree of irregularity in their lives" (1973:98). Americans, and certainly many other peoples today, have now an "expectation of continuous change" that is reinforced by the way we regard any sort of repetition as stultifying, if not dangerous. Mead points to the adolescents who were bored with television coverage of the moon landings ("I used to be interested in trips to the moon when I was young, but I have heard and seen those moon shots ever since I can remember"); and she notes that people telephoned television stations during the funeral of Robert Kennedy, following as it did the televised funerals of John F. Kennedy and Martin Luther King, Jr., with requests that the daily serials be restored to the air because they were bored with the funerals and in the soap operas "something new at least will be happening" (99).

Mead also observes that many of us have come to equate ritual with formality, which is greatly distrusted (at least in popularizing accounts) in the framework of the participatory democracy and capitalism of the past century. Having been conditioned to irregularity and "newness," it is difficult to avoid equating ritual with "something superficial, meaningless, empty, phony, lacking in depth and sincerity" (97), precisely because it is formalistic and repetitious, and the contemporary existential person has been programmed to respond only to the momentary and transient, the "newest and best."

The "newest and best," of course, is something that we might hear or read daily in advertisements. Advertising has become an important locus of ritual in contemporary life; it is a peculiar type of ritualistic activity that bases its promises on the emotional needs, hopes, aspirations, and desires of the target audiences. As repetitious activity, as activity that takes place before vast audiences, as activity that both reflects and molds social values, advertising is truly ritualistic. Nonetheless it operates under the "newest and best" rubric that assures that its communicative terms and images are constantly changing, and thus it often takes an effort of conscious distancing on the part of the participant-observer to recognize it *as* a form of ritual.

Critics such as Brian Wicker have not been slow to point out that "advertising today is a strictly 'religious' activity, and the advertising agents are the high priests of the modern mysteries" (19–20; see also J. Berger). "Religious" as Wicker uses it refers to the inculcation of values and ideals; and advertisers are "priests" in the sense that it is their ritual actions that guide the "adherents" of a "religious" consumer society. Wicker writes of the advertiser-priests:

> Their work has the essential character of *priestcraft,* in the pejorative sense of that term. They are a cultivated, sought-after elite caste within commercialized society. Their spells enable us to enter into magical dreamworlds of exotic experience . . . but thereby they only help society as a whole to remain exactly where it always was. Their claim to have access to secret knowledge is characteristic of all priesthoods; their research files on the opinions and attitudes of the public . . . confirm the claim. (20)

"Advertising, then," Wicker suggests, "is the supreme instance of modern society's thirst for ritual." Precisely by its market research and its elaborate profiles of what people desire, it attempts to reinforce these wants and thereby to provide the greatest marketability for its clients' products—which thereby firmly support the status quo. Wicker does not discuss the deliberate creation of "wants" except to note that advertising plays upon the false hopes and illusions of a society, urging the acquisition of ever more belongings, whether or not they have anything to do, in the long run, with genuine human values.

The real irony, however, is that this urging is done precisely in the name of the "newest and best," that is, in a ritualized recourse to a stock philosophy of values that is just as binding, just as restrictive, ultimately, as any ritual pattern of the past. If ritual arises at the point where the society has something to express by ritual means, it expresses such values in a way that makes them seem self-evident, beyond question. And that is exactly the way advertising functions—imagine public acknowledgments that the most recent is so far from the "best" that indeed it may be its obverse, so that people ought to avoid the new in favor of the traditional! And all this in the name of progress and avoidance of ritualism. Surely a population seldom has been so blind to the true state of affairs.

But precisely by our lip service to the most modern, to the newest and best, we reinforce the antiritualism I already have mentioned. That is, while in theory, in our political slogans and advertisers' hyperboles, we are free from the past in a unique way, in fact we are as conservative as ever, in seeking the most universal common human denominator that will sell the most merchandise.

The underlying model of such a situation is that of progress, evolutionary progress toward the best of all possible worlds. The model is rooted in eighteenth- and nineteenth-century concepts of the perfectibility of humankind, and its impact has been felt throughout modern consciousness. In anthropology and theology—especially Protestant varieties (Bird:19)—it led directly to a negative view of ritualistic religions as opposed to idealistic or theological religions. So, for instance, the Hebrew prophets or the religion of Jesus and Paul was considered a superior advance over earlier "priestly" advocates. In general, ritualism was considered a trait of primitiveness, superseded eventually by belief in abstract ethical idealism. This developmental view was widely accepted, and consequently few recent studies of ritual have not had to justify giving serious attention to what has become stereotyped as relevant only to premodern or primitive or less well-developed societies (see especially Douglas 1966:chap. 1; in that book, and in Douglas 1970, the author is working to restore the rightful place of ritual in anthropological studies and in comparative religion).

The antiritualism we have been surveying is one result of the concept of evolutionary progress. It is especially allied with the contemporary supposition that the "hard sciences" represent the only fully adequate locus of human enterprise. This view has led to the situation summarized by Aidan Kavanagh:

> Until recently the consensus of the Western intellectual community was
> fairly solid in its assumption that ritual not only had little or nothing to do
> with the development of the individual person, but that it was inimical to
> such development—a primitive retardation to intellectual growth in a
> modern world, a delusion of order in a relative universe, a too simple
> reading of data presented by science. Ritual was thus regarded as activity
> suitable for those enterprises most peripheral to *real* human existence,
> enterprises such as the religious, the military, and, to some extent, the
> political in its purely ceremonial aspects. (146)

I will show in the next chapter how human society is essentially ritualistic society, how rituals both constitute and symbolize social realities.
The primary points to be made here are that:

1. Antiritualism itself may be pursued to the point where it becomes a
   ritual.
2. Contemporary societies are not less ritualistic than earlier societies—
   although their spokespersons have learned that we can be swayed by
   appeals to turn away from the past, away from "ritualistic" antiquity,
   and hence the ritualisms may not be recognized immediately (they
   may be couched in terms of appeal to "old-fashioned" values).
3. The contemporary turn against ritual is primarily a turn against formalistic group ceremonials, what Frederick Bird, citing Erik Erikson,
   calls "dead ritualisms" (25). What is not as often recognized is that
   precisely the sectors that appear to be most antiritualistic may in fact
   have substituted new ritualisms (compare the ritual passing of a jug of
   wine or a marijuana "joint" around the circle of intimate friends, or
   the stereotyped confession of "what's really bugging you" in encounter groups).
4. Rituals, as a form of social interaction, will be suspect when social
   interaction itself is troubled (Douglas 1970:144) or when the cosmologies reflected by rituals have ossified (Tambiah:165)—leading us
   to suspect that antiritualism will continue for some time in the contemporary postmodern world.

Polymorphic Ritual

One of the most telling observations in recent methodological discussions about ritual (for example, Grimes 1982a, Wheelock, and others) is
that most ritual studies have been dominated by a Western Christian
model of "The Ritual," namely the formal service of Christian worship,

in particular in its expression in the Roman Catholic mass. They have been dominated to the extent that the term "ritual" is almost useless for those critics who wish to analyze less formal types of ritual behaviors or behaviors practiced by groups in ways that could not be further in style from the ecclesiastical performances of Christianity.

While some writers simply have ignored the problem and have done whatever analysis they intended to do under the name of "ritual studies," it seems that the time is ripe to move toward greater care in classification; I am impressed with the ways Ronald Grimes and Frederick Bird have set out typological models for classifying rituals. Each of them finds a chart presentation helpful (Bird:29–30; Grimes 1982a:50; see also Grimes 1984:134); neither excludes the other, and in fact they are complementary, for they come at the classifications from different directions.

Bird classifies "types of ritual forms," although I think his use of the word "forms" is misleading: he is interested in the relation of the types of rituals to their "manifest ritual objectives" and their "latent social functions." His types of rituals include: taboo, purification rites (a: cleansings, exorcisms, expulsions; b: confession), spiritual exercises (a: ascetic; b: mystical), rites of passage (a: life cycle; b: seasonal; c: initiations), worship, shamanistic rituals, and finally etiquettes.

Grimes classifies in a much more comprehensive framework because he is looking for "modes of ritual sensibility" not types of rituals— indeed his classifications are presented as he moves toward a detailed definitional discussion in the following chapter of his book, and the orientation toward types of ritual is replaced by a progression of ritualizing moves from ritualization to decorum (Bird's "etiquette") to ceremony, liturgy, magic, and celebration. Each mode is then further classified in terms of its frame of reference (political, expressive, and so forth), dominant mood (from ambivalence to festive), "voice" (exclamatory to subjunctive), basic activity (from embodying to playing), and finally its motivation (compelled to spontaneous).

While Bird seems to focus primarily upon the types of rituals and the ways these function within particular social or ritual periodic calendars, Grimes's perspective is more global: he does not have a place for (or does not discuss) the rituals traditionally studied, such as healings or therapeutic rites, or initiations. That may not be a problem, for there are those who would argue, as does Victor Turner, that contemporary ritualistic behaviors of a liminoid nature cannot be classified within the systems that have been devised for ritual materials from premodern societies. (Bruce Lincoln argues just the opposite, the continuity of forms, as demonstrated in gifts given at graduations or in the convention of the scholarly footnote, which according to Lincoln ritualistically perpetuates the traditional veneration of one's ancestors [1977].)

Grimes's work is the first major work on ritual studies to proceed from the assumption that ritual is a polymorphic entity; he begins not with formal definitions of what rituals may or may not be but with an orientation toward the stylistics of ritual actions, toward what people do in ritualistic activities rather than toward a program of liturgical rubrics. Style is "the total outcome of conscious and unconscious, intellectual and emotional, bodily and attitudinal aspects of a participant-observer" (1982a:2). His book treats some of the various "styles" that can be observed in Zen Buddhist sitting meditation and ritual and in the Catholic mass, and it continues with four chapters that delve into some types of contemporary theater (Jerzy Grotowski's "Poor" Theatre and the Actors' Lab Public Exploration Projects) in which Grimes has been a scholar-initiate. That initiation leads him to draw parallels between processes underlying enactment of traditional rites, the field study of ritual, and the rehearsal and actor training process in some types of theater:

> discovering life in inert objects, orienting abstract spaces into founded places, responding to another's movement, repeating actions without loss of meaning, finding evocative sounds, observing without falsely objectifying, criticizing without judgmentalism, absorbing meanings below the threshold of language and reflection, listening to one's environment, allowing symbols to rise and recede rhythmically, anticipating consequences of symbolic acts, and knowing how the context of a gesture or position of a symbol alters its meaning. (1982a:17)

What I think he might have added to the list would be the importance of the embodiment of meanings, the giving-body-to aspects of ritual to which he is continually sensitive elsewhere; he is certainly attentive to the embodiment aspect when he discusses his own definition of ritual, for he can speak of "the ritualizing moment" as "a non-discursive, bodily way of knowing," and he proposes that "Ritual studies proceeds best if we attend first to a ritual's least verbalizable qualities, its 'choreography' and 'musicality,' and then to its 'meaning' or 'function'" (61).[6]

The emphasis upon the bodily anticipates aspects of my next chapter, but it also indicates within Grimes's own proposals that he has overcome the bias toward ritual texts that has plagued studies of (at least) Western rituals. "Words are not necessarily primary" (1982a:87), nor do "rituals nor their symbols necessarily have 'meaning,' a metaphor borrowed with only partial success from linguistics" (60). Borrowing not from linguistics but from language philosophy, Wheelock has sought to get beyond the perspectives that would suggest that ritual is either "just speechless action" or "concretized thought," and he proposes that ritual "involves an inseparable combination of articulate speech and purposeful action" (49–50).

Wheelock observes the "choppiness of liturgical texts in comparison with most other religious writing" (50) as well as its interaction with nonverbal symbol systems and the immediate environment of the ritual actors. He notes that, within usual speech-act theory, "practically every utterance of a ritual is superfluous" (56), that such utterances "convey little or no information" (58), and that the purpose of a ritual utterance seldom can be to communicate materials, because "Ritual language is frequently couched in metaphorical phrases and relies on an understanding of the symbolic connotations of objects in the ritual context to which it makes reference" (56). He proposes that the primary purpose of ritual language is to situate rather than to inform: "In general, then, ritual utterances serve both to engender a particular state of affairs, and at the same time express recognition of its reality. Text and context become manifest simultaneously" (58). Hence "the information content of the ritual message has usually been already mastered by the participants. The 'message' of the ritual is less an idea to be taught and more a reality to be repeatedly experienced" (66).

That might almost be Grimes speaking: Grimes, who stressed that "monotony and repetition . . . are necessary conditions for receiving a [ritualistic] gesture" (1982a:190), or the Grimes who has noted that "Rituals typically have phases but seldom anything like a plot" (58). "Ritual actions . . . curve with indirection or ambivalence; they have high evocative power but low entertainment value" (58): "Ambivalence is the heart of a ritualizing attitude" (63), and "whatever is achieved ritually begins to erode in the very moment of its success" (231).

Rituals, with phases, are therefore from Grimes's perspective "events; they have lifespans. . . . They are not artifacts" (57). We begin to comprehend Grimes's appreciation of Victor Turner's work on the phasic and creative aspects of the liminal: rituals "transpire," they breathe and fluctuate; they are performed in "animations," soul givings. And they do so in human bodies who perform them, who become ensouled in ritual acts. Those bodies, and even nonhuman bodies, will engage us in the next chapter.

A New Ritual Consciousness

One of the ways contemporary ritual sensitivities are finding focus first came to my attention when the person I live with and a number of other women began a long series of meetings and rituals centered around the theme of recovery of the Goddess. That activity led eventually to publication of a journal, *Lady-Unique-Inclination-of-the-Night,* and to other publications by the journal's founding editor, Kay F. Turner (K. Turner 1981, and 1978, earlier published in *Heresies: A Feminist Publication on Art and Politics*). In the years since that group began meeting in our living room (about 1971), there have been a number of indications that many women today are finding ritualistic means of recovering what they consider to be their spiritual heritage (Spretnak 1982 provides a good introduction to the major figures in the movement).

Kay Turner has developed insights from contemporary anthropological studies that demonstrate that "Women are anomalies in many cultures and have no cultural recourse for demonstrating the reality of female power" (1978:221); "The performance of ritual in most societies, 'primitive' and 'civilized,' is a simultaneous acknowledgment of men's warrant to create and define culture and, by exclusion, a sign to women to keep in their place, a place . . . outside culture and without the symbolic or real attributes of power" (221). She suggests that women have found new ritual forms (of which she gives several examples, 222–25) as a means of reconstituting the woman's role or consciousness: "For women, the ritual setting is often a place for naming individual powers and sharing the affirmation of those powers with the group or simply internalizing them through private ritual procedure" (230); but of special interest to such practitioners, Turner suggests, is "the way ritual upholds and celebrates the validity of feeling as a mode of revelation, communication and transvaluation" (226).

For such women ritual is not limited to reconstitution of past models, although the search for the "real" history of women's contributions may accompany the new ritualism—indeed, may even be built into rituals, as can be seen in the inclusion of hundreds of women's names in the ceramic tile floor that is such an important part of Judy Chicago's composite art installation *The Dinner Party* (documented in Chicago 1979). Turner suggests that one of the most important ritual modes for feminists is a visionary mode, a mode of presenting possible directions and self-definitions, and hence she joins Victor Turner in stressing the creative aspect of ritual performances: "In authentic ritual experience something, an ability to break through the present, is available which can lead to discovery and creativity. Ritual is a potent source of invention because the participants feel the extreme intensity, sometimes the ecstasy, of openness to possibility and revelation" (K. Turner 1978:227).

Kay Turner also mentions the way women's rituals may serve to convey information (in particular the images and stories of goddesses) that has been "unavailable to women and actually suppressed for hundreds of years" (227). Ritual is a means of recognizing life's progressions, its transformations as one moves through various roles and statuses; and in a study of a Brooklyn community's Good Friday procession devoted to the Virgin of Sorrows, Turner suggests ways such processions use "performed, cyclic movement to model the transformation of secular individuals into sacred members of the community" (1981:71). That study relates recent analysis of processual ritual movements (as by Victor Turner 1974a) to the feminist concept of "networking," a process that women constantly have represented, namely in connecting domains that we usually think of as discontinuous: "Networking refers to the power (covert, unnamed, and diffuse as it may be) that women have in facilitating relationship by means of their mediations. Networking refers to a horizontal, earth-bound spreading-out and crossing of boundaries that insures the life-flow of relationship between structurally opposed social domains" (K. Turner 1981:79).

A procession such as Kay Turner analyzes in Brooklyn can be related to Victor Turner's analysis of antistructural movement, or to what Barbara Babcock and others have studied as social inversion: it is in the crossing of horizontal and vertical movements in the Virgin of Sorrows procession that the ritual enactments shared by the women and men of the Brooklyn community can lead to a momentary unification of distinct contexts and relations (K. Turner 1981:87–88).

A graphic report on one self-consciously created women's ritual, from the 1978 conference at the University of California, Santa Cruz, with the theme "The Great Goddess Re-Emerging," comes from its leader, Hallie Iglehart. Iglehart led the participants in a ritual act of interweaving themselves with a skein of scarlet yarn; each person cut off the portion with which she was bound and carried it away from the conference as a reminder of the ritual. Iglehart, like Kay Turner, speaks of the renewed possibilities women may find for reconnecting with "spontaneous creative psychic power and the cycles of nature" (28), with the "powerful community-creating resource" (31) that contemporary rituals may provide. (Other contemporary women's rituals also are described in *Lady-Unique* 4, 1979; women's rituals in non-Western cultures are described in parts 3 and 6 of Falk and Gross, and in Lincoln 1981a.)

Other voices within recent discussions of women's religiosity, including ritualisms, have called for a revival of "feminist witchcraft," or Wicca (Budapest; Starhawk; discussed by Noel), a movement that has led both to the establishment of formal covens and to a more generalized

Wicca-oriented resurgence of festivals at the New Moon and for other occasions. Here, at least, antiritualism means anti-traditional-male-ritualism; clearly a new women's ritualistic self-consciousness has been established, and it gives the lie to the frequent complaint that "ritual is dead," at least in such contexts as I have described.

How Rituals Serve Society

In spite of the discussion that has led me to suggest that the polymorphous nature of "ritual" means that we ought to speak of ritualistic gestures or movement or action types rather than of set patterns, unchangingly repeated; and somewhat in parallel to the section in Chapter 2 entitled "How Myths Serve Society," we can draw together here some of the ways ritual studies have indicated that rituals serve functional needs within societies. (Some of the functions listed anticipate the discussions in the next chapter.)

1. Rituals may convey or reinforce personal identity or status, establishing new social rankings or marking social recognition by the members of the ritual community.
2. Hence rituals may provide a measure of cohesiveness between group members, whose interrelations are clarified by the etiquettes of ritual acts and situations.
3. Rituals may convey societal values through reiteration ("preaching") or exemplary dramas, admonishing the nonconformist to exhibit group values.
4. Within a complex social setting, rituals may provide a sense of continuity—with other spatially separated groups engaged in the same acts (the Brotherhood of Mine Workers) or with communities temporally distanced, in the past or the future (the members of the Church Universal).
5. Symbolic condensation may be evident in shorthand references to other rituals or values, in isolation of particular meanings for particular ritual situations ("bread" in the Eucharist), mnemonic devices, graphic designs on ritual paraphernalia, or in the architectural significance of the ritual arena (cf. Griaule's classic discussion of the symbolic significance of the granary's shape).
6. Ritual activities may relax socially tense situations by redirecting the focus of group energies or by providing social role compensations (the janitor who has glory as Grand Worthy Chipmunk). They may

cloak some social factors or expose others by semantic manipulations and condensations (Ortner; Lincoln 1977; Fiske and Hartley).

7. Rituals may convey or reinforce systems of meaning held in common by members: morals, political or religious values, educational aspirations; as well as agreed-upon (although perhaps implicit) significances granted to the natural order (seasons of the year, for instance) or to moments in the human life cycle (birth, initiation, marriage, and so forth). Customs may become formalized through ritual recognition; enforcement seems to depend more upon a sense of propriety and "shouldness" than because one expects immediate results (obviously magical rituals represent a special case in this respect, although everyone is familiar with the pressure to perform certain ritualistic activities, especially those involving membership in class-determined groups, in order to gain social recognition or status—which essentially reflects belief in a magical efficacy of participation).

8. Rituals may provide for a graphic and physical means of expression to supplement rational abstractions; they may allow dramatic enactment of feelings (singing, dancing) where discursive speaking would be awkward or would need augmentation. Or they may provide distancing from painful emotions by providing a formal and regulated frame for their expression (see Scheff); they may provide occasions for obtaining the relief provided by "play" activities.

9. Rituals may provide transitions between statuses, events, periods, and types of activities (Scheff:112 discusses the practice of saying grace before meals as an interaction ritual that brings a variety of persons engaged in different activities—adults working, children engaging in sports, persons preparing food—into a new configuration).

10. Rituals may mobilize segments of the community for action outside the ritual sphere for warfare, teaching, hunting, and so forth. They may assure the persons sent out that the community remaining behind will continue its expressed dedication and concern at a later date: "we'll never forget you"; "we'll be praying for you."

11. Rituals may regularize types of ceremonial behavior that are discovered to be useful elsewhere (as in the marketplace, the law court, a professional context). Rituals unlock communal energies that otherwise might remain dormant (Bird:23) by providing focuses for symbolic concentrations ("Mothers Against the War") and "disciplined rehearsal of right attitudes" supported by the community (Tambiah:126).

12. Ritual performances are often enjoyable! While this aspect fre-

quently is ignored in formal ritual studies, enjoyment is surely the primary reason one attends a ritualistic performance in the theater or other dramatistic format. While Schechner and others see the "entertainment" function as recent, I suspect it is ingredient throughout the range of ritual behaviors; that is not to say that every ritual moment or performance is enjoyable for all performers, but to note the somewhat intangible aspect that any observer or participant feels naively.

The future of ritual studies promises to be full of developments, especially inasmuch as we are seeing only the beginnings of adequate methodologies and typologies. Victor Turner's many insights will continue to have great appeal, I suspect, but they doubtless will be tempered by the need to distinguish a wider range of ritual activities than Turner has. I return to his distinctions between the liminal and the liminoid in another chapter, because that distinction seems to include the necessary redefinition of revered scholarly maxims about the separateness of "the sacred and the profane"; other questions have been placed from the perspective of nonhuman ethological research and the influence of strictly biological factors. It is to issues such as these that we turn now in Chapter 4.

The Cosmological Human Body: Biogenetic and Cultural Factors

4

Neither nature nor man will ever be understood, though certainly physical nature—and perhaps physical man, too—may in the meantime be very skillfully *manipulated*, until we accept that nature is the reflected image of man's conscious and unconscious self. We must remember that the human body is itself a part of nature. As long as the historical fallacy of born literalness holds sway, Freud's half-truth that many images have a bodily significance will be swallowed, without leading, as it should, to the reflection that this is only possible because the body itself has an imaginal significance. I think it also follows that the mind of man is not, as Coleridge put it, "a lazy onlooker" on an external world but itself a structural component of the world it co[n]templates.

Owen Barfield, *Rediscovery of Meaning*

THE HUMAN BODY IS ITSELF AN IMPORTANT means of communicating. Its postures, its inborn responses to stimuli, its moods and beauties, its positions in social intercourse: all these may be used in the communicative process, and all are utilized in myths and rituals. A ritual, as a formal social action, is an event that utilizes aural and kinesic patterns to express or communicate shared values and to inculcate or elicit them. It is more sensuously immediate than most myths, except as myths are actualized in performance contexts.

We turn here to the bodily dimensions of myths and rituals, to the ways the human body and the human social experience both reflect and share the mythic-ritualistic experience, becoming central items in cosmologies, which are formal expressions of the ordering experienced in the universe. The question of inherited patterns becomes especially relevant as we seek to understand both the local, individual instance, and the universal, underlying patterns that reach throughout the aeons of human history and prehistory.

Biofunctional, Biogenetic Approaches

Joseph Campbell, in the first of the four volumes of his comprehensive mythography, *The Masks of God,* makes the important point that the study of mythology must include not only the specific or *local* manifestations of myth and ritual within particular cultures—the historical dimensions, the particular or ethnic—but also the *universal* aspects that go beyond the historically determined. The universal aspects are determined by one's corporate culture as a human being, and they include the influences of our biological makeup, which I will designate here the biofunctional or biogenetic factors. (We may refer to a biogenetic approach if we wish to emphasize the influences of biological, somatic origins of cultural expression, or to a biofunctional approach if we wish to emphasize the ways biological factors function in human culture and society.) It is such an inclusive biological-cultural framework that is most relevant to the study of myth and ritual, although recent studies have had even more specific focus: considering which particular half of the brain is associated with which type of thinking, emotional or rational, and considering which parts of the cortex expand over time when thinking activities are repeatedly engaged.

This chapter moves through several issues having to do with the particular ways the human somatic and social experiences are reflected by or influenced by mythic and ritualistic expression. We begin with the tension between the local and the universal, already mentioned, and then move to the question prominent in recent ethological discussions: to what extent do human rituals originate in animal (nonhuman) behavior? (In Chapter 7 that question will be broadened to include biogenetic structuralism and the sorts of neurophysiological findings that promise widened horizons for a broad, strongly interdisciplinary study of humankind.) The human body itself often provides the basic forms for expressing cosmology, and some would argue that the body also provides the basis for codings of ritual colors; others argue parallels between primary human social experiences and mythic and ritual patterns.

Here we will follow Victor Turner and Mary Douglas in referring to the ways the human body is an important source of ritual symbolism, and the ways, as W. Richard Comstock puts it, "The body itself, with its various postures and stances, is itself a vehicle of symbolic communication" (35–36). The role of particular human biocultural patterns, such as prolonged infancy and hence extended dependence upon human parents, may be said to contribute to a proclivity for particular mythic or ritualistic sensitivities; we will look at the role of the family as well as at the societal functions of ritualism. Finally, we can highlight briefly the "ludic" or play approach to ritual, treating it as one of the types of social expression in ritual.

The Local and the Universal

Following Campbell's point that mythography must include both the local and the universal factors that are influential in the formation of any mythological or ritualistic pattern, we can let his distinction guide our discussion of one issue long debated in philosophical anthropology, namely whether culture or biology ("nature") is the determinative source of human characteristics. Campbell's point is that neither is exclusively determinative and that in fact "universals are never experienced in a pure state, abstracted from their locally conditioned ethnic applications" (1975:11; see also Geertz 1973:pt. 2).

Nonetheless, analogies with nonhuman animal species have been used to suggest that inborn patterns may precondition mythological and religious awareness, and Campbell began his tetralogy with attention to the role of inborn patterns: the first two chapters of *Primitive Mythology* (1959) are entitled "The Enigma of the Inherited Image" and "The Imprints of Experience." Campbell also devoted a chapter to "Bios and Mythos" in a later book (1969:chap. 2).

Animal studies have shown that newly born animals display instinctual behaviors that are inborn or biogenetic as opposed to learned. For instance, newly hatched chicks will run for cover when a model of a hawk is drawn over the coop but not when a model of another type of "safe" bird is used or if the hawk is drawn across backwards. Ethologists speak of "innate releasing mechanisms" as producing these effects, a concept not dissimilar to that of the *engrams* to which Carl Jung referred: memory deposits in the human psyche that lead to certain responses in given situations (recent studies refer especially to "imprinting" and the reactions to the first moving object registered by the infant; see S. J. Diamond:chap. 2). These are passed along through the history of the human psyche, Jung suggested, from the collective unconscious (or "objective psyche") of humankind. Certain *archetypes* precipitate out in symbols and representations that reappear again and again in human history, and they represent the "crystalline structure" that leads to mythic contents and configurations.

Earlier than Campbell and Jung, Adolf Bastian (1826–1905) differentiated between the elementary ideas (*Elementargedanke*) that are worldwide in provenance and the ethnic ideas (*Völkergedanke*) that are responsible for the actual, local manifestations of the universal forms. From this background, Campbell derived his leading concept for the study of mythology:

> We may therefore think of any myth or rite either as a clue to what may be permanent or universal in human nature (in which case our emphasis will be psychological, or perhaps even metaphysical), or, on the other hand, as a function of the local scene, the landscape, the history, and the sociology of the folk concerned (in which case our approach will be ethnological or historical. (1959:461)

Campbell's entire mythographic program balances these two views and shows how myths and rituals work in both directions at once "to render an experience of the ineffable through the local and concrete, and thus, paradoxically, to amplify the force and appeal of the local forms even while carrying the mind beyond them" (462; cf. 1975:11).

I turn to Joseph Campbell to initiate this discussion of the biogenetic approach to myth and ritual because his discussion of biological factors in mythological formulations is especially clear, rather than because this is the primary contribution of his analysis. (Indeed Campbell is much more important as an eclectic. His work is useful here also because Campbell avoids the evolutionary-development fallacy—from an inferior to a superior social level—that still plagues attempts to relate biological nature and religion.)[1]

The theme of "the local and the universal" often has been approached in terms of culture versus humankind, but this is an old dichotomy that Clifford Geertz has now adequately laid to rest (1973:chaps. 2 and 3; the dichotomy often is phrased in the biological, experimental-psychological, and ethological sciences as the distinction between heredity and learning or between innate and learned behavior). Geertz shows that in the long time span of human evolution humankind's biological nature was itself shaped by cultural factors—to the extent that humankind as we know it is not in tension with culture but is inconceivable without it. Or as we might say, *humankind means culture, the local means the universal*;humankind has created itself in such a way that "there is no such thing as a human nature independent of culture" (49):

> Between the cultural pattern, the body, and the brain, a positive feedback system was created in which each shaped the progress of the other, a system in which the interaction among increasing tool use, the changing anatomy of the hand, and the expanding representation of the thumb on the cortex is only one of the more graphic examples. By submitting himself to governance by symbolically mediated programs for producing artifacts, organizing social life, or expressing emotions, man determined, if unwittingly, the culminating stages of his own biological destiny. Quite literally, though inadvertently, he created himself. . . .
>
> The apparent fact that the final stages of the biological evolution of man occurred after the initial stages of the growth of culture implies that "basic," "pure," or "unconditioned," human nature, in the sense of the innate constitution of man, is so functionally incomplete as to be unworkable. Tools, hunting, family organization, and, later, art, religion, and "science" molded man somatically; and they are, therefore, necessary not merely to his survival but to his existential realization.
>
> The application of this revised view of human evolution leads to the hypothesis that cultural resources are ingredient, not accessory, to human thought. (48, 82–83)

"Culture" is essentially "human"—it is manifested in the social order as in the life of the individual; these are not dichotomous but integrally related entities. Their interrelation is accomplished, among other ways, by ritual, and hence, as we have seen, Evan M. Zuesse proposes that ritual has a mesocosmic position, relating as it does the microcosm of the self and the macrocosm of human culture:

> In regard to both space and time we can distinguish two levels which interact in ritual, the microcosmic and the macrocosmic: just as the human being is born, matures, grows old, and dies so does the year, but just as the year renews itself (or the moon revives) so does man. Just as

man has four limbs and a head (or umbilicus) so does the world space, whose four cardinal points receive orientation from the vault of heaven or the omphalos. Of course, not every culture has these correspondences, but the deeper motivation we find everywhere to establish links between the body and the world, anchoring points that make the world a cosmos. These links are the *ritual mesocosm*, interweaving Self and Other through the medium of the body. (1975:522; the idea and the term were expressed earlier by Campbell 1959:150)

Zuesse identifies two interacting orientations or vectors, "one internal to the field which embraces the actors and their immediate sensory world, and the other cosmic or transcendent in reference," and these two orientations interact with one another in a continual tension and interpenetration. Ritual, then, may be said to be an important means of organization of the self: "The sheer Otherness of things is brought into relationship with the centered Self and is domesticated" (Zuesse 1975:527). Ritual provides a means of relating the personal and the transpersonal, a making-personal that which transcends individual human experience; it is one of the ways by which the expressly biological and the expressly cultural may be integrated.

In this way ritual does not merely represent ideas. It does not merely illustrate mythological abstractions but is an immediate acting out that bridges and unifies the somatic and ideational, the bodily and the mythic. W. Richard Comstock suggests that "it is a serious mistake to think of the ritual as the symbolic dramatic enactment of a meaning already clearly expressed in some kind of ideational mode. On the contrary, the ritual may give a depth of significance and vital power to the religious intention which the accompanying myth itself needs for the full apprehension of its meaning" (36). The insight of the ritual-dominant school that myths should not be treated in abstraction from their ritual contexts needs to be reaffirmed, assuming that we can utilize this insight without being forced to accept the whole theoretical framework of that school: myth and ritual can, in such a view, be seen as complementary, perhaps as necessarily complementary, and we ignore the performance contexts, the somatic realizations of myths in ritual form, only at a very real peril of mistaking the whole for a particular part. Zuesse's treatment of ritual as mesocosm has the advantage of emphasizing its instrumental function and avoids the correlation Myth is to Ritual as Macrocosm is to Microcosm. Rather, we can see the rite as the enacted performance of macrocosmic values in a mesocosmic fashion that realizes the microcosmic potentials of the individual within his or her social group (see Munn 1973a).

Ethological Questions

It would take us too far afield to confront exhaustively recent ethological studies such as those of Konrad Lorenz, Robert Ardrey, and others. Here our focus will be upon questions raised in the comparative study of animal behavior and ethology where there has been emphasis upon the "ritual" behavior of lower primates. And I put ritual in quotation marks here in light of recent criticism that such use with respect to nonhuman animal behaviors tends to undervalue the distinctiveness of human rituals. For instance, Margaret Mead notes: "Ethologists . . . speak of the courtship ritual among birds, and use the term for such given, instinctive types of behavior that occur in wild animals. Such rituals are always inter-creature, and while this similarity to human ritual is important, we should not carry it too far or we lose sight of the peculiarity of human rituals" (1973:89).[2]

Parallels between lower-primate and human behavior patterns do not suggest at this point that the student of mythology will find in nonhuman animal behavior a "key" to human mythology. A recent summary of research concludes that the differences between human and animal societies are far greater than the similarities and that animal social patterns are only useful for comparison when human counterparts are independently established (S. J. Diamond:156; cf. Burkert 1979:45). However, parallels between human and nonhuman ritual patterns might suggest some limited continuities in, for instance, preconditioning toward group membership. It may be that nonhuman studies at least can alert us to formulaic examples of human expression that otherwise would not have been noticed. For example, learning among experimental animals has been shown to be greatly facilitated when animals were trained in groups rather than individually (S. J. Diamond:108–09).

Continuities must be understood, therefore, as including private or individual expression as well as nonhuman group expression, and it is often the case that nonhuman experiments can pretest situations that will lead to better understanding of certain human behaviors. A positive view of the possibilities for comparing animal and human rituals is presented by Anthony Wallace, who has developed a comprehensive approach that encompasses both societal (allo-communicative) and individual (auto-communicative) dimensions:

> In summary . . . we can say that among many of the lower mammals and birds, evolutionary processes have produced patterns of behavior that can fairly be denoted by the term "ritual." In common with human ritual, these behaviors are repetitive, stereotyped, and complex; they can be

either solitary or social; and they function to arouse or reduce drive, not by direct mechanical interaction with the environment, but by auto- and allo-communication. Social rituals (allo-communicative) arouse in the participants a state of readiness and an intention to perform the consummatory action, whether it be sexual or aggressive or the establishment of a relationship such as dominance-submission or mutual territorial rights. Solitary rituals (auto-communicative) seem useful principally in reducing anxiety in situations of ambiguity with respect to learning or discrimination. And, frequently, ritual behavior in animals incorporates regressive features, in the sense that one component or another is ontogenetically early, having been appropriate in the immature state as a signal for nurturance. (1966a:223–24)

Wallace clearly presents a maximal view of the similarities between human and nonhuman behaviors: "we are saying that a ritual is a common form of animal behavior, which serves a necessary function even in lower orders, and that comparable rituals (both religious and secular) can be observed in man, serving him in the same way" (224).

Such a view is biofunctional, in its stress upon the functionality of rituals, in a way that sounds very much like earlier sociofunctionalist statements of the ways myth and ritual serve societies. So Raymond Firth noted: "What ritual has done is to provide routinization and canalization for . . . tensions. These are not left for random expression, but are assigned their time and place for explicit mention and acting-out" (1967:23). Indeed some sort of functionalism would seem to underlie any comparison of human and nonhuman behaviors: inasmuch as we cannot inquire of nonhuman animals what is the significance they find in their ritualized behaviors, we are limited to analysis of how such behaviors seem to benefit them. It is clear that rituals serve as a form of communication in both animal groups, human and nonhuman; but the question consistently put to the ethologists (as by Margaret Mead, cited above) concerns whether it is appropriate to draw from the biological functions in nonhuman life forms implications about the significance of ritual in humans, who indeed can specify the significance of their rituals as an element in worldview and ordering of a meaningful cosmos.

My own perspective is that studies of nonhuman ritualization help us to understand the phenomenon of ritualization as such, but we should be quite careful of transferring such information to human behavior directly. The factors of emotional and rational signification, and of complex language and memory, which I take to be uniquely human, must be seen as at least complicating the transferral of such information, if not even invalidating it at important points (many of the factors involved are becoming particularly focused around issues of "artificial intelligence": see many of the selections in Hofstadter and Dennett).

The Cosmological Human Body

The dust jacket of Mary Douglas's *Natural Symbols: Explorations in Cosmology* (1970) includes a representation of da Vinci's famous Canon of Proportions, the drawing of a male nude with outstretched arms and legs within a square and a circle. The drawing was one of many Renaissance attempts to establish the geometrical proportions of the ideal human body, and it reflects the influence of social constructs upon artistic style. The drawing is appropriate to the contents of the book because Douglas argues that "there is a strong tendency to replicate the social situation in symbolic form by drawing richly on bodily symbols in every possible dimension" (vii) and that "The human body is the most readily available image of a [social] system" (xii).

Arguing against the traditional "compensation" hypothesis, according to which religious activities are held to compensate for lack of social adaptation, Douglas favors a "replication" hypothesis. In replication, religious symbols and rites are not just secondarily expressive, *reflecting* the social order, but are themselves also powerful in structuring and influencing the social order (xiv). Douglas's argument was stated in an earlier book: "So far from using bodily magic as an escape, cultures which frankly develop bodily symbolism may be seen to use it to confront experience with its inevitable pains and losses" (1966:20).

In *Purity and Danger* (1966), Douglas had anticipated the theme of *Natural Symbols* (1970), noting, for instance, that for the Dinka:

> The body is a model which can stand for any bounded system. Its boundaries can represent any boundaries which are threatened or precarious. The body is a complex structure. The functions of its different parts and their relation afford a source of symbols for other complex structures. We cannot possibly interpret rituals concerning excreta, breast milk, saliva and the rest unless we are prepared to see in the body a symbol of society, and to see the powers and dangers credited to social structure reproduced in small on the human body. (1966:115)

And in the last chapter of *Purity and Danger*, Douglas states that she had tried to demonstrate in the book that "The body . . . provides a basic schema for all symbolism" (164).

Douglas's position is presented in a statement that compares the social and the physical bodies:

> The social body constrains the way the physical body is perceived. The physical experience of the body, always modified by the social categories through which it is known, sustains a particular view of society. There is a continual exchange of meanings between the two kinds of bodily experi-

ence so that each reinforces the categories of the other. As a result of this interaction the body itself is a highly restricted medium of expression. The forms it adopts in movement and repose express social pressures in manifold ways. The care that is given to it, in grooming, feeding and therapy, the theories about what it needs in the way of sleep and exercise, about the stages it should go through, the pains it can stand, its span of life, all the cultural categories in which it is perceived, must correlate closely with the categories in which society is seen insofar as these also draw upon the same culturally processed idea of the body. (65)

Developing concepts proposed by Basil Bernstein, Douglas compares the "restricted code" of the human body with the "elaborated code" of the social structure. The first is "deeply enmeshed in the immediate social structure" (23), whereas the second concerns the expression of ideas, and may dominate the restricted codes acted out by individuals. (The distinction, worked out by Bernstein for the social structuring of speech and adapted for analysis of individual and social expression, is not unlike the distinction between the local and the universal with which this chapter began: the elaborated code challenges its users to reflect upon the values of the social process, whereas the restricted code "allows a person to receive his identity as part of his immediate social world; personal and social integration are achieved together" [Douglas 1970:157–58]). Ritual itself is understood in this system as a "restricted code," "which is used economically to convey information and to sustain a particular social form. It is a system of control as well as a system of communication. Similarly ritual creates solidarity and religious ideas have their punitive applications" (55).

Arguing that there will be various restricted codes within various segments of a society, and varying among societies, Douglas suggests that this variation may explain how it is that ritualism is still lively within certain subgroups but has been rejected in others—or, more exactly, how it is that certain restricted speech codes get switched. Here she makes a point about antiritualism I made in Chapter 3: "We find that the apparent anti-ritualism of today is the adoption of one set of religious symbols in place of another. It is like a switch between restricted speech codes" (166). She notes that contemporary antiritualism protests only against rites of differentiation, while it honors rites of enthusiasm, and she makes the point that "the secular world," a favorite term in much twentieth-century theology, is not a modern development but one that will recur whenever certain sociological conditions are present—in her terms, whenever group boundaries are weak and ego-focused grid is stong (139; studies exploring the grid/group analytic are in Douglas 1982).

Working from images of pollution and then of bodily images, Douglas develops the view that rituals are indicative of larger social matrices and that the analyst is able to infer the normative, regulative aspects of the social order by observing anomalies and interstices between classificatory categories in ritual usage (see Ellen's essay on semiotics and body-part classifications). Liminal and marginal situations within a culture are the places where the danger of pollution is most likely to be felt, for instance (Douglas 1970:chap. 6); and a category such as pollution will develop primarily where the social structure is clearly defined (113) and where social sanctions are otherwise only weakly stated (162). A condition such as witchcraft beliefs will flourish where there is role-pattern ambiguity (107, 111).

One strength of Douglas's approach, developed from this initial emphasis upon ritual correlates of the human body, is her correlation of types of social structure with recurrent patterns in the history of ideas; this approach is similar to the recent "field" and "trajectory" approaches to the study of late-Hellenistic religions and already has been used for analytical studies in the treatment of Judaism and Christianity.[3] While the so-called high religions often have been considered as too highly developed to reward analysis by the methodologies of the anthropology of religion, that situation is changing today, and we may expect some genuine advances in understanding both the origins (see Gager) and the contemporary forms of the major world religions. Nancy D. Munn, for instance, points to rituals surrounding the American celebration of Christmas as a richly textured object of study (1973a:607, referring to Barnett, which I have not seen); and Gregor T. Goethals argues that American television provides common myths and a sacred dimension provided earlier by religion.

Biogenetic Colors

An article by Victor Turner, "Color Classification in Ndembu Ritual: A Problem in Primitive Classification" (reprinted in 1967:59–92), treats the ways in which white, red, and black function as symbolic valences in Ndembu ritual settings and in the Ndembu value system. Struck by the ways in which these colors seem primary to the Ndembu of Africa, Turner then briefly traces the occurrence of the three colors in color symbolisms of other world cultures (as does Vlahos:19–32). The article seems as if it will develop in the direction of a structuralist approach, for Turner notes the way the colors white:red themselves form an important dyad, then are associated with black to form a white::black::red triad. Turner does not mention Claude Lévi-Strauss in the article's bibliography, but one is reminded of Lévi-Strauss's emphasis upon a third term mediating the features of a previous mythological dyad in such a way as to incorporate common features of each member of the dyad (this concept will be discussed in Chapter 7).

The part of the essay that brings it into the scope of this chapter, however, is at the very end, where Turner states that he is going "to throw caution to the winds for the sake of stimulating controversy" (88). Then Turner develops what I have been calling the biogenetic approach, and he does so in a very strong way. He argues: that the three colors, white, black, and red, "are the three colors representing products of the human body whose emission, spilling, or production is associated with a heightening of emotion"; that the production of these substances is associated with more than normal "power" of some sort; and that these colors therefore come to represent the suprahuman, conceived as "the sacred over against the profane" (88–89).

Turner's oblique reference to the study of classification by Durkheim and Mauss, and especially to Durkheim's thesis that human social order becomes deified ("society is god"), made in the subtitle of the article, becomes clear at this point, for Turner then develops the concept that the three colors also reflect "experiences of social relationships" (89). Instead of following Durkheim in suggesting that humans first were grouped and could then think of themselves in social, corporal, terms, Turner argues that "the human organism and its crucial experiences [hence the *individual,* rather than the *society,* as Durkheim argued] are the *fons et origo* of all classifications" (90).

Arguing from an analysis of the three primary symbolic colors to their associations with societal values and relationships, Turner suggests that the primary biological experiences of the individual, and then of the individual-in-family and individual-in-society, have a direct and determinant relationship with sociocultural realities, that "in other words, culture, the superorganic, has an intimate connection with the organic in its early stages" (89). Turner's conclusion brings together his argument:

> The point I am trying to make here is that the three colors white-red-black for the simpler societies are not merely differences in the visual perception of parts of the spectrum: they are abridgments or condensations of whole realms of *psychobiological experience* involving reason and all the senses and concerned with primary group relationships. It is only by subsequent abstraction from these configurations that the other modes of social classification employed by mankind arose. (91, my emphasis)

Turner can speak quite critically of Jung and Lévi-Strauss, who, he thinks, do not take seriously enough the "formative role" of culture in mythic and ritualistic symbolism; but it is clear both in the *The Forest of Symbols* (1967) and in his article on "Myth and Symbol" (1968b:579) that for Turner "culture" does not means just "social structure" (indeed, as a British-trained anthropologist, he insists on the distinction). Rather, culture includes the psychological and the biological: Turner suggests taking more seriously the "cultural dynamics of ritual as our point of departure" and if we do so we will find "a crucial anchoring of ideas and symbols in the human body and in its somatic processes" (579–80).

Likewise, Evan Zuesse refers to somatic anchoring when he speaks of "the 'Prestige of the Body' in ritual": "Ritual so affirms the body gesture that it becomes the vehicle for conveying and embodying the highest symbolic truths" (1975:518). Or, as Zuesse can suggest in summary: "Every gesture . . . is a revelation of a way of being located in the universe; each gesture points out a universe, too, and makes spaces in it for human life. In a word, ritual is body-language" (519). A similar emphasis is found in an article by Ronald Grimes, which makes an initial probe toward a phenomenology of "masking" as a kind of ritual gesture and which elaborates our need for "detailed microkinesic studies of religious body motion" (1975:508; one first-rate microkinesic analysis is Firth 1972).

Grimes shows that masks may:

1. Fix or concretize the qualities of a person or power, as in death masks or masks for dramas.
2. Conceal identity, providing concealment for the enforcer of social controls or for the person temporarily released from social controls, as in periodic ceremonies such as Mardi Gras.
3. Serve as the embodiment of some person or power, as in the danced ritual or in personalized facial gestures.
4. Provide a means of heightened expression, as in the use of cosmetics in drama or in daily life.

There is a self-consciousness about masking the body, a self-consciousness that reflects an awareness of the boundaries between Self and Other and the ways in which the Other may be acted out in a controlled illusion that makes present its specific inner powers. The four aspects that Grimes identifies are not mutually exclusive but represent modulations on a scale from the greatest concretion to the greatest expressivity:

> Concretion reaches its peak in religious ritual; concealment, in ceremonies of civil enforcement; embodiment, in interpersonal encounter;

and expression, in drama. These are neither better nor worse than one another, nor is one form higher or lower than the other. They are simply different moments in a process or different levels of a single performance. (1975:515; for further discussion on masking, see J. C. Crocker; and Crumrine and Halpin)

The essays by Grimes and Zuesse—which appeared in the same issue of the *Journal of the American Academy of Religion*—both articulate the dynamic quality of ritual action, the *present-actuality* of the ritual act, in which bodily stances portray the shared worldview of a community. Grimes probably would agree with Zuesse that rituals are in themselves already *interpretation*: as events happening in and of themselves, the ritual meanings are not so much talked about as directly experienced. Meanings are enacted by their performers because the enactments themselves have significance and are expressive, not because (although this may accompany the performance) they are in need of exposition. So Zuesse writes: "Ritual is difficult to interpret precisely because it is so *present,* so fulfilled in itself, that it can dispense with further interpretation or native exegesis (and often does). Ritual as such is the most satisfactory statement of what it means, and it resists representation in more abstract, verbal guise" (1975:517).

Carefully avoiding the trap of the ritual-dominant approach that would argue the priority of ritual, Zuesse advocates an approach that delicately balances the respective spheres of myth and ritual:

Myth is complementary, but it cannot replace the meanings of ritual. Ritual gestures forth the world as meaningful and ordered. It establishes a deep primary order which precedes the world that can be spoken, and out of which the word proceeds, to which it returns. In this sense myth is a secondary meditation on the world first seized in ordered symbolic action, that is, in ritual. (518)

We are speaking, in this instance, of rituals from the point of view and immediate emic apperception of the participant; we already have presented an introduction to Victor Turner's sophisticated methods of eliciting ritual meanings in societies where the observer is not "at home" (Chapter 3).

Significant interpenetrations of analytical approaches—those *emic* ones expressed within the culture, or the *etic* ones created by analysts— must be devised for study of societies where myths and rituals are fully operative. We may find it helpful to utilize a "field" approach, or a performantial or dramatic model, or we may correlate an ethnoscience model with that of descriptive ethnology. Whatever the methodologies, however, I consider the recent emphasis upon the cosmological symbolism of the human body exemplified here in the work of Mary Douglas and Victor Turner as the most appropriate focus for such study. Beginning with the human body, known by each of us as our essentially most primary experience, and giving meaning in human culture (as in effect an extension of our somatic constitution), indigen and observer alike share the most important basic data conceivable, our somatic-cultural existence. We turn now to the "cultural" half of that construct, exploring in a brief and entirely preliminary manner some of the ways social experiences both reflect and mold the human somatic makeup.

The Human Social Experience

Primary experiences in human culture and in human encounters with the natural world have contributed richly to the thematic contours of myth and ritual. Many of the factors just discussed in terms of the cosmological human body are relevant here because the individual modeling of the body has its corporate dimension as well, and so we have "the body politic" or, in early Christianity, "the church as the corpus of Christ."

Joseph Campbell points to several specific social themes that develop out of the life cycle of the human being: the contrast between darkness and light, or the experience of weight/gravity as leading to polarities between light versus dark, above versus below; or the apperception of the moon and the stars, in their regular coming and going, contributing to ideas of death and resurrection. Then there are male versus female polarities that become dynamic factors when they are lived out in social roles; and finally the human life cycle itself, contributing mythic metaphors of birth, growth, prime, decline, and death (four aspects of the life cycle—birth, puberty/adolescence, marriage, and death—are described in Fried and Fried in tandem with the ritual occasions to which they give rise in eight culture areas).

Out of such a plethora of possible topics, we discuss only three here: the probable influence of the infant experience of suckling, the role of gender differences, and the patterning of the family as the first locus of social status differentiation (A. Lee:173–205 surveys types of familial and nonsibling group settings as prototypes of later social forms, but he does not discuss myth or ritual aspects). This subsection concludes with attention to polarities and paradoxes and how they may be thematized in myths and rituals.

Bliss at the Mother's Breast

Some recent feminist critiques of scientific analysis have suggested that it was primarily a male obsession that led to focus upon the breasts as the distinguishing trait of the zoological class to which we belong— that of the Mammalia. Be that as it may, it is clear that the bliss experienced at the mother's breast represents an extremely primary and significant human experience. Negatively it can have an impact in the infant's fear of losing the mother, being separated from the breast, or in the later image of the cannibal or devouring mother, which may be a development from the weaning period when the mother first "denies" the child milk/food. Positively, of course, the same primary experience doubtless is reflected in the many images of heaven or paradise as places where everything is provided for one, especially food.[4]

Images of the child at the mother's breast appear and reappear throughout mythic iconography. The very term "nurturing" comes from a Latin root indicating nursing or suckling, and myths present a spectrum of related imagery ranging from the "withered dugs" of old hags, to the plump breasts of virgins in hero myths, to the conception of mining or farming as manipulations of the breasts of "Mother" Earth. Here, then, a common and almost universal human experience provides the biofunctional source for mythic expression of primal human relatedness, a theme that has been found viable enough yet today to provide the plot for a speculative fiction story ("The Wound," by Howard Fast), in which atomic bombs are used for deep mining of natural gas and oil. The wife of the geological consultant to the project protests this outrage upon Mother Earth's breast—and when the explosion occurs and millions of gallons of what appears to be red oil are produced, the red substance turns out to be blood from a now unclosable wound.

Gender Differentiation

Erik H. Erikson's work with play therapy is one of the classic studies of male versus female differentiation in terms of its impact upon social roles. Erikson's work led him to suggest that there are different modes of approaching the physical world that vary according to the sex of the subject. When Erikson gave 150 boys and 150 girls, aged ten to twelve, a selection of objects, including wooden blocks, toys, and so forth, and asked them to use the objects to construct scenes, a marked difference was found in the way the two sexes presented space and spatial relations.

Girls typically constructed a scene to tell a story about a house interior, enclosed with the blocks; people typically appeared *within* the enclosures, which were low and occasionally featured an elaborate doorway. Intrusions from outside were accepted with "an element of humor and pleasurable excitement." Boys' play scenes were frequently houses with walls and facades, with protrusions or towers; and the emphasis was upon *exterior* spaces with more movement than in the girls' constructions. Interest in high structures was accompanied by the danger of collapse or downfall, and ruins and accidents were frequent.

Erikson was very cautious in moving from his observations to his conclusions—a fact overlooked by the many negative reactions to the experiment—although he did suggest that:

> sexual differences in the organization of a play space seem to parallel the morphology of genital differentiation itself: in the male, an external organ, erectable and intrusive in character . . . ; in the female, internal organs, with vestibular access, leading to statically expectant ova. (Data and quotations are from Erikson 1968:268–71)

Feminist literature, especially, has criticized strongly both the bases and the conclusions of Erikson's research; a common counterclaim to Erikson's emphasis upon biogenetic factors is that bio*cultural* socialization factors are impressed upon the child at such an early age that it is ultimately impossible to differentiate biogenetic characteristics of males and females. On the other hand, striking confirmation of Erikson's findings by Phoebe Cramer and others are reported by Robert May.

Many mythic and ritualistic patterns concern coming to grips with male versus female differentiation—a series of volumes would be needed to catalog them all. I cannot extend this discussion at this point, but it shold be noted that increasingly emphasis is placed in our society upon the personality characteristics *common* to both sexes. So, for instance, Margaret Mead, writing of possible personal and social orientations in the year 2000, suggests as one alternative that: "There would be a growing disregard for sex as a basic mode of differentiation" (1967:872).

We are left, in such a situation, with a startling lack of mythic alternatives: androgyny and hermaphroditism, for instance, are in current vogue (see Singer), but few mythic models can be found for a social situation in which traditional male or female role models are not dominant. Phenomena such as the "glitter rock" of popular musicians in the 1970s represent attempts to work out newer ritualistic means of living through such a new situation, with all its confusing lack of role models and sexual statuses. Science fiction projections often indicate sensitive imaginings of possible futures, and both Ursula LeGuin's *The Left Hand of Darkness* (1969) and Robert A. Heinlein's *Time Enough for Love: The Lives of Lazarus Long* (1973) provide imaginings of future societies in which traditional sex-role differentiation has been left behind. The latter novel seems more typical of traditional male fantasy, in that extended "families" with extensive sexual sharing across marital boundaries are the new unit of genetic organization—according to patterns established in the "Howard family" that are kept pure through genetic manipulation over several millennia.

In LeGuin's novel, persons are truly biologically androgynous: sex differentiation occurs only during the period of sexual heat, and male or female characteristics develop temporarily in response to a coupling situation, that is, the person becomes sexually male or female in response to a partner who becomes the complementary sex for the period of estrus.

Neither novel—and they are only two random choices from a wealth of possible examples (see Clear et al.; and Mason, Greenberg, and Warrick)—provides a fully viable model for contemporary life, nor do they intend to do so. But both illustrate the ways possible social structuration can be imagined around models of sexual differentiation that are strikingly different from those that have structured the vast majority of myth-and-ritual patterns to which we are accustomed. (See Herdt 1981 for careful documentation of a society in New Guinea where male roles are standardized within a cosmological homosexual model—then when marriage takes place, a heterosexual model is internalized apparently without excessive social conflict.)

The Family and the Clan

Experiences in the interactions of the family are another primary setting for mythic and ritualistic themes. Even something as basic as initiation rites may be related to the "second birth" trauma of being forced to learn a secondary, social, mode of centering the self in the social world. Joseph Campbell, reflecting on this phenomenon, suggests that rooted in this central experience is the division of the world into categories of those who know and those who do not, that is, specializations of leadership and followership, the development of priesthoods and ruling dynasties, and so forth (1959:chap. 2).

Other work by Erik Erikson (1966, summarized by Kavanagh:54–55) has emphasized familial interactions, especially the recognition and interaction rituals that occur between parent and child, as patterns that may strongly influence the receptiveness of the youth and adult to ritual. Erikson points to the interlocking contingency between familial rituals of nurturance and social rituals such as adolescent initiations. He provides documentation for the frequently noted difficulties of modern youth to adjust to society when the transitional, initiatory rituals no longer function adequately.

The period of transition at adolescence has contributed a major theme to American fiction as the "coming of age" motif. In William C. Faulkner's "The Bear" or Stephen Crane's *The Red Badge of Courage* or, more recently, Philip Roth's *Portnoy's Complaint,* the transition into adult status has been probed both as a local manifestation of uniquely American social dynamics and as a reflection of universal tensions and anxieties between the generations. Poor Ouranos has been castrated over and over again by all his children; and the coming-of-age rite itself seems to be one of these inevitable psychological needs that surfaces in every generation. Recent studies indicate that schizophrenic "trips" are extremely close in pattern to the travels of the shaman, the healer, or the hero on his journey to the underworld and back with a boon (Campbell 1972:chap. 10, "Schizophrenia—The Inward Journey"; and Perry 1974). Perhaps some forms of schizophrenia function as modern, truncated initiation rites—but if that might be so, it is a frightening thought, for ours would seem to be a culture that no longer provides sympathetic, trained guides for the initiatory "trip" but defers to medicated bracketing of the experience.

Leaving our youth stranded between the worlds, the statuses in which life is lived out, is schizophrenia, which occurs most often among adolescents as the modern initiation ritual. Perhaps we need to be reminded that we cannot become mythically and ritually whole persons by chopping off important rites of passage, that if we do so the psyche shatters. We turn our modern backs upon the full gestures of archaic and modern ritual only to pay awesome penalties.

A line from Ovid's story about Hermaphroditus (*Metamorphoses,* bk. 4) stresses the child's divine parentage from Hermes and Aphrodite: Ovid suggests that Hermaphroditus's "pretty face showed who his parents were." That tracking of parentage was of special interest in Greco-Roman mythology, of course, but it is a typical interest in all mythical materials—on a par with the Greek interest in the "first finders" or inventors of artifacts and customs. To name the parents was to name much about the child's personality, interests, and behavior; the Greeks and Romans, no less than we, were convinced that the accident of birth counted at least as much as subsequent biohistorical situation.

But I think one theme in mythological studies that has not been regarded nearly as highly, but is as important, is the tracking of the children as mythological figures. I have often found it clarifies the nature of a deity to see what types of children the myth traditions ascribe to him or her. Likewise the manner of birth seems important: I am presently collecting instances of irregular births of Greek mythical characters, because this mythologem seems to indicate something about subsequent importance of the figures. The sorts of questions that must be asked include *why* the tradition includes such pairings of irregular births as that of Typhon and Hephaistos, both born to the Hera the Virgin, without father—were they merely stories meant to counter the tradition of Athene's birth directly from the head of Zeus? Or we ask about the curiously mixed stories around the birth of Dionysos—Zeus finally has to incubate the fetus in his own genital area. Or we ask about the "deceitful" births from misplaced semen: the first Kentauros that resulted from Ixion's embrace of the cloud that Zeus formed into the shape of Hera, or Erichthonios, born of Hephaistos's seed spilled on the ground after he had tried to overcome Athene by force, or the traditions that have Aphrodite born from Ouranos's phallus, in parallel to the births of the Furies and the Giants from his testicles that fell upon Earth (Gaia).

Doubtless there are here statements about competition in establishing a family line, a race; there are gender-competition issues surfacing as well as cult etiologies—and the creative play of a mythological tradition that was less prone to the one-to-one allegorical correlations that have become the norm in the West. The immediate family, the extended clan, the tribe, and then the people or nation: there is no way to indicate all the mythic and ritual patterns connected with these biocultural loci within the scope of a book such as this one. Clearly, however, "the family of humankind" provides the primary occasions for a great many personal and social tensions and complexities that may be highlighted and/or resolved in myths and rituals.

Dualities, Polarities, and Their Mediation

One of the recurrent emphases in modern mythography is the suggested role of myths in resolving or mediating opposing values within societies. That emphasis provides a useful introduction here to the function of myths and rituals in providing biocultural means of resolving some of the tensions produced within the biogenetic frameworks we have been examining. Myths and rituals do indeed provide means for working out resolutions of social and biological tensions, and they do so largely by cultivating the symbolic resources of humankind. Through mythic education one learns to identify the "powers" that surround one and to assemble a storehouse of responses to their presence or absence through an effective ritual repertory. In such a sense, "Ritual is a statement in metaphoric terms about the paradoxes of human existence"; it is essentially communication (C. Crocker:47, 49; but recall my qualifications of this function in Chapter 3), and it is a mode of fictionally acting out, as myth is a mode of fictionally imaging, the innermost transpersonal and intrapersonal experiences (Kliever 1972), particularly those that are complex and/or dualistic.

It is striking how many myths, especially, reflect societal polarities: rich:poor, servant:king, hero:monster, chaos:order, male:female, older:younger, light:darkness, destructive:constructive, socially approved:socially disapproved, gods:humans . . . and the list could be greatly extended (see Watts 1963). It is also striking how many rituals provide concretizing (or "somaticizing") of these polarities: just as an example, think of the shift of the Christian liturgical colors at Lent and Easter—the somber purple of death and sorrow being transformed on Easter Sunday into the joyous bright white symbolizing resurrection; or think of the dramatic transition from outsider to insider in a traditional initiation rite.

It is not my intention to develop only a sociofunctionalist position in which myth and ritual are appreciated almost exclusively for their constructive roles in providing the societal glue that binds societies and enables them to adjust to the polarities of personal existence. Of course myths and rituals do have such a function, and that is not denied here. But I would like to move beyond such a position by emphasizing that myths and rituals do that *and more*. Specifically they not only provide functional resolutions of such problems but they also are creative insofar as they are a communicative means through which persons find meaningful systems of symbols for identifying their experiences. Myths and rituals carry the traditional societal assessments of values assigned to this or that experience; and they provide an important means of living through one's life experiences when they become resources for identifying, labeling, and relating to the forces experienced as active within one's environment.

Myth and ritual are indeed communication media, then, vitally important ways by which "reality" is perceived as an entity projected from implicit social consensus. We perceive polarities and dualities because we have learned so to perceive them, something that is immediately clear once we grasp the ways something like "dirt" is seen as a culturally relative category.[5]

Symbols add material form to values and abstractions; they provide the necessary concretizing and materializing by which communications are possible, and which subsequently become what is considered proper and moral (or improper and immoral). Subsequently these values are thought of as "factual reality" or "common sense," as "the way things ought to be," and then become the usually unconscious normative framework for behavior and belief. It is because they are usually unconscious and prereflective that the social analyst may be met with a great deal of resistance when eliciting "why" such and such a custom is thought to be so proper. The analyst, or within the culture the religionist, who seeks a more rational understanding threatens the going order of things, the "factual" structure of reality, whenever he or she brings into consciousness the apparent arbitrariness of the mythic and ritualistic symbols that have been at work.[6]

Such a role also may be performed by the clown or trickster figure, who is likewise resented for highlighting the contradictions in status roles or symbolic expressions in a culture. By mocking pretensions to absolute perfection or by using humor to illuminate social disparities, the jester inadvertently may poke holes in the fabric of assumed factuality and cause an awareness of polarities and contradictions that most people would rather leave at pre- or unconscious levels of awareness. Today, of course, we no longer cause the jester who goes too far in this direction to be executed outright, but even our supposedly rational culture is not slow to provide strict sanctions (Lenny Bruce) or to find ways of suppressing those whose wit is too acerbic and probing (the television program, "The Smothers Brothers"). The comedienne Lily Tomlin, for instance, has noted how angry she was at viewing a biting social satire she had recorded for television—the show's director had insisted that taped laughter be played during the segment "so that people wouldn't take it too seriously."

We turn now to the "ludic liminality" in which such probing of societal polarities and dualities—many of them growing out of the human social experiences we have been examining—is not only taken seriously but is evoked and honored.

Ludic Liminality

The concept of liminality was introduced when we discussed the ways Victor Turner developed Van Gennep's tripartite division of rituals. The "ludic" of the section title here refers to *homo ludens,* the human as the player, as Johan Huizinga, a Dutch historian of culture, sought to label humankind: *homo ludens* instead of *homo faber,* the human as maker in the sense of technological mastery (ix). Huizinga's phrase has caught on, so that today there are frequent references to "the ludic dimension," although both Huizinga and Josef Pieper's subsequent *Leisure: The Basis of Culture* (1952) treated play or leisure not as merely one dimension but as the underlying substance of culture. The concept of ludic liminality points to leisure and play as places for exploratory search for the metaphors that advance human creativity, and it points to ritual as play (because rituals are constructed the same ways play activities are: delimited arenas for the activities, marked and regulated schedules, rules and statuses applicable only in the ritual/game, and so forth).

There also has been emphasis, in cultural criticism as in sociology, upon games theory, leading to elaborate studies of strategy and projective mapping (as in "The World Game") used to study alternatives for future deployment of military or natural resources; games theory has led to several types of educational experimentation and to a theory of mathematical models initially developed by Oskar Morgenstern. Another sphere in which this emphasis upon play has been useful is in literary criticism, where it has provided a means of structural analysis of the inner dynamics of the literary work (see Ehrmann 1971). As a focus in studies of religion, play theory has been useful for analysis and interpretation of the religious rite, the liturgy, a special interest of Pieper. More recently David L. Miller has written *Gods and Games: Toward a Theology of Play* (1970), a work that advocates a mythological-aesthetic playfulness and a comic seriousness in modern fiction and in religion.[7]

The concept of ludic liminality needs, perhaps, to be defended against the suppositions that play now must be made ultimately serious—and hence technological, and subsequently made into antiplay—or that it is only to be seen as the leftover time/space after one's "work" is completed. Play theorists have not been entirely satisfactory in avoiding these extremes: Pieper, for instance, seems to conceive of leisure primarily as a metonym for philosophy, and Huizinga's emphasis upon the "agonistic" or contesting aspects of play seems to leave little room for what we are likely to call today "spacing out," regarded here as a legitimate exercise in reflectively establishing the necessarily limited boundaries of self-worth and personality.

Perhaps the primary problem has been that play and leisure have been treated too much as if they were antipodal to work; Victor Turner's category of "the liminoid" reflects the significance of the historical change brought about by the Industrial Revolution: contemporary liminoid experiences are lived out in something of a continuum with work (1974b). The liminoid is, for instance, purely voluntary and optional—

as the liminal ritual is not—and it is not something restricted to a privileged sector of the society. And of course today there are many confused cases where one may be hard put to label the activity "work" or "play": is it work when in the evening or on vacation I read professional journals that I enjoy because of their play of ideas? or when I read novels that I may discuss in a classroom at a later date?

Better ways of understanding myths and rituals as occasions for creative reflection and metaphor making need to be developed. As ludic, and as liminal, myths and rituals transpire for most of us on the margins of everyday/secular/work-consciousness. They take place in the gaps between obligatory acts, sanctions, and product-oriented technologies. As gap fillers they complete movements from status to status and from place to place. But their very betwixt-and-between position means that in them a person can have a certain distance from the compulsory. He or she can enter imaginatively into realms other than the workaday and can play out alternate possibilities that otherwise would be impossible.

The health of a people may be read off from how they play, and that means here: from how they participate in their myths and rituals, exploring their leads toward understanding the universe, heeding their alternate explanations of reality, and giving metaphoric shapes to social and individual experiences. The culture that fails to take its mythographic task seriously stands in danger of finding itself overwhelmed by cheap pseudomyths. The culture that fails to educate its citizens toward rich experiences of leisure time activity (and I mean image work, imagination, aesthetic appreciation, not just sports and hobbies) stands to lose valuable resources for its own renewal.

It is in this framework that I believe Victor Turner's emphasis upon the positive rather than the negative aspects of the modern experience must be taken quite seriously. Ritual, Turner suggests, is precisely the site within which new ways of modeling and framing social realities may emerge—specifically within those "liminoid" rites that have come to characterize our own historical situation. We tend to focus upon the restrictive, repetitive nature of rituals, but Turner sees as well that the formality and repetition allow a sort of freedom that can provide channels for creative impulses to find expression and articulation. Hence Turner's indication that he sees "the liminoid as an advance in the history of human freedom" (1977a:54). We need not think only of *traditional* rituals in this case but must begin to reconsider the weight of recent feeling against any "ritualistic" experience, as we seek somehow to survive the pressures of a civilization that seems less and less "connected" for all of us.

The Psychological Approaches

5

A psychological approach means what it says: a *way* through the psyche into myth, a connection with myth that proceeds via the soul, including especially its bizarre fantasy and its suffering (psychopathology), an unwrapping and leading out of the soul into mythical significance and vice versa. For only when the psyche realizes itself as enacting mythemes can it "understand" myth, so that a psychological exegesis of myth begins with the exegesis of oneself, soul-making. And from the other side: only when myth is led back into the soul, only when myth has *psychological significance* does it become a living reality, necessary for life, rather than a literary, philosophical or religious artifice.

James Hillman, "An Essay on Pan"

IT OFTEN SEEMS AS IF THE FIRST HALF OF THE twentieth century ought to be called the Era of Psychology, given the widespread interest in all matters psychological. This period saw developments ranging from experimental psychology of the laboratory to psychoanalysis, and few aspects of human culture were exempt from one or another type of psychological scrutiny. It would be a rewarding project to catalog the many analyses of myths and rituals and mythological themes in the academic and popular journals of the field, but my scope must be much more limited here.[1] I focus primarily upon Sigmund Freud and Carl Jung, noting some of the directions in which Freudian and Jungian followers have taken the masters' thought further.

Freud and Mythology

Sigmund Freud's psychoanalytical insights concerning the human personality and the nature of human culture have influenced the study of myths and rituals profoundly. I will try to indicate some of the contours of Freudian perspectives here with respect to Freud's own work—notably in *The Interpretation of Dreams* (1965)—and afterwards with respect to those who are identified explicitly as Freudians (Otto Rank, Géza Róheim, Karl Abraham) and others who utilize a Freudian approach only along the way. But in between I want to suggest that a mythological analysis of Freud's approach in itself is rewarding. For that purpose "mythological" is used to indicate the presence of a comprehensive and inclusive worldview incorporating deities of primal forces (here: instincts, Eros, Thanatos, Ananke) and providing a particular hermeneutics or symbological mapping that buttresses the worldview by providing an overarching framework and coding for individual components.[2]

Two of Freud's contributions to mythography are discussed: the first has to do with the layering of meanings by which humankind is immersed in reality—this leads us toward hermeneutics or interpretation of dreams and myths. The second contribution has been no less global and involves the untimate origins of myth and religion.

Manifest Contents versus Latent Contents

The Interpretation of Dreams (Die Traumdeutung) first appeared in 1900 and went through eight German editions by 1930. Some parts of the work seem unnecessary today, for we no longer have to justify devoting serious scientific attention to dreams, as Freud did. Many of the actual interpretations strike the modern reader as arbitary and strained, but of course we are all now perforce *post*-Freudians, and something of the Freudian viewpoint has been accepted throughout our culture. Furthermore even orthodox Freudians accept revisions to the "topography" of the human mind mapped in this early work (especially in its seventh chapter). And finally it is sometimes very difficult to sustain interest in so many of Freud's own dreams!

Nonetheless we are interested in the impact of the early editions of the work (the first English translation, by A. A. Brill, appeared in 1913; see V. Turner 1978b for just one account of the impact of this work) and especially the impact of the work's differentiation between "manifest dream-content" and "latent dream-thoughts." It was this distinction— typical of what I call a hermeneutics of deceit, which proposes to show us that a second hidden meaning lies beneath the surface level of expression—that caught the attention of a generation dismayed with the outward course of events (such as the political turmoil of Europe) and made *Interpretation* a crucial document in the process of unveiling "deceits" in cultural artifacts of all types: dreams, stories, myths, rituals, and works of art. Henceforth even the most highly regarded work of art might be analyzed not only as a moment in the history of artistic expression but also as a product reflecting the artist's personal life history, including his or her neuroses and sexual problems (see also Freud's *Psychopathology of Everyday Life* [1960]). Having once been exposed to such a negative hermeneutics, there can be no going back to naive belief or uncritical acceptance of tradition.

While I would not credit Freud with accomplishing such a revolution in thought singlehandedly, I would argue that the Freudian/post-Freudian critique is now an essential aspect of the contemporary worldview. Keeping the "naive" aspect in view, Paul Ricoeur distinguishes, for instance, between the "first naiveté" that dismisses myth and symbol because of their supposed incongruity with science, and a "second naiveté" that permits us to heed the meanings of the myths and symbols without taking them literally (1973:92; 1974a:29). The Freudian/post-Freudian/Marxist developments in hermeneutics now call for expansion of a more systematic and sensitive symbology such as we see Freud only approaching.

Freud argued that dreams represent an inner psychic human function by which unacceptable impulses such as incest, the drive for absolute power, or hostility toward one's kin are reworked into more acceptable behaviors.[3] The dream reworkings then will not lead to the sorts of anxiety that lead to neurosis or, in the case of dreams, to disruption of sleep. The whole process of dream formation was therefore to be understood as veiling, covering up, transforming that which the dreamer's consciousness would find unacceptable. Or dreams may project successful fulfillment of unacceptable desires and give them such transfigured forms of expression that, again, they will not cause the "dream censor" to awaken the dreamer. (Most of the unacceptable issues represented, for Freud, unresolved childhood traumas, and hence psychoanalytical therapy focuses upon a recovery or "anamnesis" in which these traumas can be relived and hence resolved.)

The dream itself was not what it appeared to be but represented some earlier trauma that had been resolved unsatisfactorily—that is the point (Freud 1965:585, 592). The unresolved traumas were primarily problems having to do with sexual frustrations (431), we may add, as in the "Oedipus complex" (the son, desiring to sleep with the mother, wishes the father were dead or removed) that Freud increasingly saw as foundational to many aspects of civilization.[4] It is not to our purpose to discuss further the psychic dynamics Freud understood to be reflected in the dream production of the individual; we do need, however, to look a bit further at the types of mechanisms he saw operative in the transformations of the latent thoughts into the manifest contents, for these mechanisms themselves have been discovered in social artifacts as well, and Freudian analysis detects them in myth formation, in the expressions of religious ritual, and in artistic products generally. (The structuralists to whom we turn in Chapter 7 similarly practice a hermeneutics of deceit: the surface level of expression is understood as ciphering the latent or "deep" content that generates it.)

The two basic mechanisms of "the dream work" (the process by which latent thoughts are transformed into manifest content) are: *Condensation*—compression of extensive contents into "brief, meagre, and laconic" expression or fragments; and *Displacement*—transference of psychic intensities, so that the highly freighted items actually may refer to matters of little real concern, and vice versa. These two "are the governing factors to whose activity we may in essence ascribe the form assumed by dreams" (343).

The third basic transformative mechanism emphasized by Freud is *Visual Representability* and refers to the predominance of dream thoughts that can be expressed visibly—this is the the *symbolic* mechanism, which according to Freud "is not peculiar to dreams, but is characteristic of unconscious ideation, in particular among the people, and it is to be found in folklore and in popular myths, legends, linguistic idioms, proverbial wisdom and current jokes, to a more complete extent than in dreams" (386). Freud is careful to note that the therapist must practice "a combined technique, which on the one hand rests on the dreamer's associations and on the other hand fills the gaps from the interpreter's knowledge of symbols" (388). And he states in the same paragraph that "the correct interpretation can only be arrived at on each occasion from the context." A store of dream symbols interpreted in context eventually might be compiled, and it would obviate, Freud thought, purely arbitrary assignments of meaning.

It is easy to overlook these qualifications, however, when Freud then proceeds to correlate ladders with sexual intercourse (cf. the English euphemism "mounting") or "all complicated machinery and apparatus occurring in dreams" with the male genitals (390–91)—we could give many additional examples that strike the contemporary reader as extremely arbitrary and as overly determined by Freud's emphasis upon sexuality.[5]

The fourth major mechanism is *Secondary Revision,* by which Freud refers to the psyche's rounding off or reinterpreting dream contents into a version more acceptable to the dreamer; it is often the agency by which the dream is given smooth contours within the dream itself, as when the sense in the dream is: "but after all this is only a dream and hence does not need to be taken seriously." Hence Freud compares this fourth mechanism to daydreaming, in which we are in conscious control of the process of image formation.

Other aspects of the dream work are discussed by Freud, and I mention some of them because of their relevance to the whole pattern of the hermeneutics he develops: *Unification*—linking of dream elements on the basis of some quality common to them, which may be a displaced or a wished-for commonality; *Reversal*—turning something in the dream into its opposite; *Distortion*—the general term for what happens in the dream work, it is compared by Freud to postal censorship. Instead of cutting out snippets, as would a mail censor, however, the dreamer has "replaced them by an incomprehensible" or transfigured content (176, n. 2); and hence we especially find *counterwish* dreams, such as sadism represented by masochism. Another aspect is *Linking*—dreams of a series, like dreams of a single night, usually can be shown to have some common element in the associations of the patient, even though they seem to be concerned with quite different topics; and such sequential dreams therefore are to be considered as expressions of the same issue.

It should not be difficult to imagine ways these mechanisms and aspects can be applied to materials other than dreams of the individual: we need only think of collections of fairy tales, or of texts of religious rituals, to have a textual corpus in which these transformations can be illustrated. The analysis can follow Freudian psychoanalytical theory (and so the bishop's crosier is a penis, the house in the story of Hansel and Gretel is the vagina, and so forth), or it can utilize the transformation patterns as insights into the construction and variation of folk materials more generally. However we utilize Freud's interpretation patterns, it is clear that he was one of the most typical representatives of the twentieth-century hermeneutics of deceit that has taught us to be conscious of the fact that construction and variation of dreams, and of psychic and cultural materials generally, possess regularities and patterns of alteration, transformation, and expression by means of stating the opposite to what is expected, or by metaphorical linking.

According to Freud, myths are probably "distorted vestiges of the wish-phantasies of whole nations—the age-long dreams of young humanity" (in Nelson:53) and hence we may think of myths as *cultural dreams,* if you will. In this perspective myths and rituals can be approached the way the individual's dreams can—given the restriction, of course, that the associations with specific images are much harder to establish in the case of entire cultures, and especially those chronologically or spatially distant from our own.

The Primal Horde, Civilization, and Religion

I have just suggested that Freud's hermeneutics directed to the interpretation of dream contents had wide-reaching consequences. The second area in which his work is important for mythography also has stimulated widespread discussion, especially as it has provided interface work between psychology and anthropology and between psychology and the study of history (the former is represented by Hunt 1967, the latter generally by the work of Erik Erikson and in the journal *Psychohistory*).

This area has to do with etiology, as did his dream interpretation, but in this case the origins sought are not the originating traumas in the individual's childhood but rather the origins of myth, of religion, and ultimately of civilization itself. To be sure, Freud's theses concerning these origins are rejected almost universally today by cultural anthropologists and historians, and theologians strongly oppose his suggestions concerning religious origins and sustaining concerns (see Küng for a temperate and receptive reaction by a contemporary theologian). But it cannot be denied that Freud's proposals have stimulated a great deal of analytical study that might not have been evoked without the forcefulness of his models. I will discuss: Freud's concept of the primal horde and its consequences; the origins of civilization in guilt; and the place of religion as that which one must transcend.

Developing what he calls "the Darwinian concept of the primal horde," Freud sketches a picture of the earliest social grouping in which a dominant primal father excluded the sons from sexual access to the females in the group.[6] Eventually frustrated to the point of rebellion, the sons ("cannibalistic savages") killed the father and symbolically ingested his powers by eating his body. Totemism, and especially totemistic feasts, represent the sons' subsequent admiration and longing for the killed father; this mechanism of dealing with the guilt produced by the parricide, as well as the necessity of regulating subsequent interactions among the brothers, is referred to by Freud as "perhaps mankind's first celebration," and its repetition and commemoration the first beginnings of civilization, of "social organization, moral restrictions and religion" (1918:182–83; cf. 205 and the summaries of the argument in Freud's last book, 1939:102, 107, 167–71; a typical statement: "this totemism may be regarded as the earliest appearance of religion in the history of mankind," 105).

Working from analogy, as he so frequently did when he discussed social matters such as religion, Freud developed the probability of the primal horde theory on the basis of its similarity to what he had learned from working with neurotic patients:

> I have never doubted that religious phenomena are to be understood only on the model of the neurotic symptoms of the individual . . . as a return of long-forgotten important happenings in the primeval history of the human family, that they owe their obsessive character to that very origin and therefore derive their effect on mankind from the historical truth they contain. (1939:71)

The primal horde theory was the social equivalent to the individual's Oedipal complex (1918:185; cf. 202); and as the reaction to the Oedipal situation is to elevate the injured father, so "All later religions prove to be attempts to solve the same problem"(187). The primary deity—except in interludes of matriarchy—therefore will be a male deity figured with the characteristics of the personal/primal Father:

> Psychoanalytic investigation of the individual teaches with especial emphasis that god is in every case modelled after the father and that our personal relation to god is dependent upon our relation to our physical father, fluctuating and changing with him, and that god at bottom is nothing but an exalted father (190; cf. 1961b:42, "the primal father was

the original image of god, the model on which later generations have shaped the figure of god").

The success of Judaism, according to Freud, was its ability to confess to having killed the Father (who, in Freud's unique theory, was one of the two contrasting figures later assimilated under the name of Moses). Christianity—which at first seems superior to Judaism in its unequivocal confession of original guilt, now expiated by the death of the Son—ultimately turns into a religion of the *Son,* who is totemistically consumed in the Eucharist. Actually, however, Christianity represents "a new setting aside of the father, a repetition of the crime that must be expiated" (1918:199), and hence is less psychologically satisfying to Freud than Judaism (Rubenstein argues a very different conclusion from the same Freudian basis: Christianity's emphasis upon the Eucharist is psychologically significant).

The basic pattern of the religious believer is to be compared psychologically with the basic pattern of the obsessive neurotic: "In view of these similarities and analogies [previously listed in the essay] one might venture to regard obsessional neurosis as a pathological counterpart of the formation of a religion, and to describe that neurosis as an individual religiosity and religion as a universal obsessional neurosis" (Freud 1959:126–27). In the essay from which this quotation is taken, Freud suggests that both religion and obsessive neurosis stem from repression of vital instincts in such a way as to give rise to a ritualized mode of behavior. Religious ceremonies are rationalized to cloak the repression, just as the patient will rationalize her or his obsessive behavior.

Rejecting the religious toleration exemplified by G. E. Lessing's Nathan the Wise—which evidently attracted him in the period before his marriage (Rainey:chap. 3)—Freud finally suggests that the psychologically mature person will be able to understand the thoroughly illusory nature of religion. Working again from analogy, Freud suggests that religion is "the universal obsessional neurosis of humanity; like the obsessional neurosis of children, it arose out of the Oedipus complex, out of the relation to the father" (1961b:43). And as the patient comes to replace obsessional neurotic patterns by greater application of logos, intelligence, so Western civilization is now in a stage of development where it should be able to replace the effects of religious repression "by the results of the rational operation of the intellect" (44; cf. 53, where Freud is optimistic that "mankind will surmount this neurotic phase [in which religions have been strong], just as so many children grow out of their similar neurosis").

Science is the opposite of religion, resting not on the wish-fulfillment illusions of religion but on the results of empirical evidence or the conscious effort of thought; and it is under the rulership of science that "our god *Logos*" will prevail and that religion's illusions are replaced by the "education to reality" in which one realizes that he or she is thrown completely upon his or her own resources and must work out his or her own adjustments to Ananke (necessity) without childish recourse to a projected religiosity that provides nonreflective dogmatic solutions (1961b:54–55, 49–50; on the Enlightenment aspects of Freud's position in this respect, see Roazen:chap. 6, pt. 4). (We have come to realize since Freud's own time that perspectives emphasizing the primacy of the rational faculties ultimately may be counterproductive if the emotive/feeling side of humankind is thereby suppressed. Freud's viewpoint here falls within the confident trust in science of the late nineteenth and early twentieth centuries—a confidence that is questioned increasingly today, when we have had a full experience of the negative and destructive possibilities "science" can contribute.)

I do not need to present further Freud's critique of religion at this point, because this book is focused more narrowly on myth and ritual. Freud's view of the repression of instincts through civilization and religion is an important perspective for us, however, because it has been one very influential aspect of the approach that sees religion—and hence two of religion's components, myth and ritual—as representing something akin to a psychological childishness that must be transcended in maturity. If Müller saw mythology as a disease of language (see Chapter 2), Freud may be perceived as characterizing it as a disease of the psyche that may be "treated" by appropriate psychological methods.

A Mythological Reading of Freud

It is sometimes instructive to reverse our usual approach to a topic in order to gain insights that otherwise remain hidden. In this case I propose a brief reading of Freud's mythology—not Freud's approach to mythology, but aspects of his approach that in themselves appear to function mythologically. Our range of view must be restricted: a study of all the features of Freud's system that could be analyzed in this fashion would require a monograph in itself. I mainly want to argue that Freud's object as a mythologist has become his belief; that is, that the method of analysis Freud chose led him to construct his own mythological value orientation from the materials he studied and the methodologies he developed.

In this way I agree with Christine Downing's observation concerning the necessary involvement of the mythographer in her or his material; Downing observes: "Myth study is *never* disinterested, objective; perhaps Freud's main contribution is this insight. The analysis of myths, of primitive thought, is always in part self-analysis, *and* self-analysis is always also self-creation, therapy" (1975a:4). Therapy (Greek: *therapeia*) is more literally an attendance upon, a carrying of another's projections (Nagy:292), but in a medical context, the carrying is for healing, and so we have self-analysis as self-healing, but Downing's point well expresses the judgment of this section: Freud's "self-healing" was shaped at least partly by his involvement in the study of nonmodern mythologies. My more immediate aim is to indicate some of the ways in which aspects of Freud's approach bear comparison with more traditionally identified mythological systems.

It is impressive to see a conceptual system develop, and such development is especially apparent in the work of Freud and Jung, for which we have available annotated or edited editions (*SE,* the *Standard Edition* for Freud; *CW,* the *Collected Works* for Jung) that enable us to see developments and realignments of thought taking place over a long span of time. Comparative studies (such as those by Lilliane Frey-Rohn or Henri Ellenberger) or monographic studies focusing on a particular aspect (such as those of Ricoeur or Downing) are further helpful in exposing the under-contours of such systems—a sort of analysis of analytical theory.

With respect to Freud, I think it especially instructive to consider the under-contours shaped by the increasing reference to the mythological entities Eros and Thanatos. The frequently used term Eros is for Freud the life principle, the principle of erotic energies, but less specifically, of energies directed toward relatedness in general (for instance 1961b:69); it appears throughout the Freudian corpus. Thanatos, "death" in Greek, appears by contrast only a few times, although Freud's later writings demonstrate increasingly his own concern with Thanatos, understood as that powerful force resisting love, life, expansion. (Ananke, "necessity," also appears frequently in the later writings as Freud turned his attention to the possibilities that a "therapized" civilization might attain: it would function according to the reality principle.)

I cannot provide documentation here, but it is an extremely fruitful exercise to read the *Standard Edition* of Freud's writings with a sensitivity to the *mythological* function of these two "drives" or thrusts of energy. Again and again one comes across them, or theoretically cognate terms, at crucial points in the development of Freud's thinking about human psychological behaviors, reflections on the tensions between the individual and civilization, and in materials concerned with the origins of religion. Eros and Thanatos become shorthand symbols for representing whole conceptual fields—and that is precisely one characteristic of an operating mythological orientation.

The high evaluation of myth stressed throughout this book must be kept in mind at this point, for I by no means wish to suggest that Freud's mythological use of these terms is a weakness or inferiority in his work, but rather I wish to note the applicability of a mythographic approach to the comprehension of such an important modern figure as Freud. Myth as it is being used here is similar to what might be called modal concepts or scientific paradigms or (in literature or music) leitmotivs; in each case we have to do with terms that gather up important connections within a modeled universe or worldview (so Ricoeur 1970:63, "the final part of the theory [of instincts] marks the return of psychoanalysis to a sort of mythological philosophy, the emblems of which are the figures of Eros, Thanatos, and Ananke").

Etiological Bias

Frued's work is also "mythological" at the points where he emphasizes the childhood (or early cultural) origins of later neuroses—their etiologies. As I already have suggested, one of the most striking features of Mircea Eliade's treatment of myths of nonmodern and non-Western cultures is his focus upon their great concern with etiology, that is, their concern to identify the origins of things, whether tools or totems. Persons in these cultures are especially interested in locating beginnings of things in *the* time of origins—*in illo tempore,* as Eliade terms it, in the primal period of world ordering and world creation (Beane and Doty: §§ 11 12, 18–20, 48–52, 70, 83). And it is not material artifacts alone that are "placed" by etiological grounding in the primal times, but also religious myths (which supposedly were first told to The Ancestors then) and rites (which were first performed then). By ritual retelling of the Creative Acts (*gesta*), the society believes it can make present once again the powerfully creative dynamics of that primal period and so recharge the energies of the present.

This is but a brief overview of Eliade's proposals, which have been widely accepted for a particular type of etiological myths. The essential aspects are: making present the energies originally available in the "childhood" of the culture, understanding interrelations between artifacts or societal forces by placing them within the original schema of creation, and conceptualizing the present times as being dependent upon the primal times.

I have set out these aspects in a manner calculated to evoke a nod of recognition from anyone who knows something of Freud's concept of the psychoanalytical process, for there are marked coincidences—something Eliade apparently recognizes when he gives illustrations from Freudian analysis in his writings on mythical etiology (Beane and Doty: §§ 31–32; cf. Downing 1975b:10, "There is a parallel here to the retrogression into chaos which in initiation myths precedes rebirth. In the erotic encounter of the therapeutic hour the patient finds himself back in primordial times, in the timespace of recreation"). My point should be obvious: in seeking to ground neuroses and other psychological matters of the contemporary patient in childhood traumas, and arguing that their negative, disabling consequences may be neutralized through psychoanalytical retrieval and reliving of these traumas, Freud proposes a therapy that is strikingly congruent, in its concern for etiology, with the picture Eliade paints of non-Western and nonmodern humankind.

At times Freud seems almost fanatically concerned with *first* occurrences, with the archaic or primal situations that "produced" religion, civilization, and totemism. One of his very last writings, *Moses and Monotheism* (1939), for instance, demonstrates Freud's need to ground religion in a particular historical situation.

I always think of Hesiod's *Theogony* when reading Freud on the primal family situation: if anything, Hesiod seems less concerned than Freud to set up primal determinants for contemporary situations. Freud's etiological mechanism reflects the late-nineteenth-century emphasis upon physical mechanism, and most studies of Freud are quick to point out the "topographical" characteristics of his system: each psychic function such as ego, id, and so forth, has to be mapped and located in a particular psychic "place," and every psychological occurrence has its origins in some other place or time than the present. Hence previous-day experiences, physiological factors (such as needing to urinate at night), or neurotic repressions were considered to have determined the dream contents, and the killing of the first patriarchal leader by the primal horde was regarded as the ultimate source of guilt, of overvaluation of the Father, and of sexual anxiety, as in the Oedipus/Electra complex. Everything must truly be something else: we have seen the importance of this hermeneutical principle above, and it remains here to suggest additional ways in which Freud's hermeneutics itself functions mythologically.

Mythological Interpretation

The title of this subsection is to be understood as referring to "Freud's interpretation theory as a mythological construct," not to "Freud's interpretation *of* mythology," which is a different matter and is open to criticism of a different sort. It is the "as if" on which I wish to focus here: dream contents are figured within the dreamer's psyche as if they were the real issues. But as we have seen, Freud refused to believe the apparent straightforward character of these contents, referring instead to the underlying latent thoughts that had been symbolically transformed.

Here the mythological parallel is to the way a mythological system transforms and modifies materials foreign to it, materials that are assimilated to the central worldview of the system by being reshaped to fit. So a place for the white explorer was found within indigenous Middle and North American mythologies—the white person must be the long-lost brother, or from a race of gods mentioned in the primal narratives. In either case—that of Freud's reinterpretation or that of the shaping of new external factors to fit an already existing mythological lexicon—the mythologically coherent universe provides the semantic fabric for assuring its adherents that change is only apparent, that the eternal recurrence of all things has not been threatened.

It would not be fair to insist upon the parallel in Freud's case, insofar as his basic theory is modified and altered throughout the course of his career. If anything, he is less topographic-mechanistic in the later writings and is increasingly receptive to a more symbolic approach,[7] but the substantial "as if" retelling remains absolute in terms of reshaping case material to fit Freud's own projected understanding of the patient's neuroses. It is this absoluteness that leads to the arbitrary interpretations of dream images cited above, and I find these interpretations just as deterministic and arbitrary as are any examples one might give of rigidity in forcing events into the matrix of a particular society's religion or mythological system. My own preference for Carl Jung's analytical or archetypal psychology largely rests upon Jung's much greater flexibility in dealing with dream images and symbols.

Jung was especially convinced that the particular chronological context of the dreamer's life might be more essential to the dream's interpretation or amplification than a previously established interpretation coming from the therapist's training and experience. He stressed that the analysand was not to be forced by the analyst to accept interpretations that did not feel appropriate.[8] In this sense Jung—in spite of his extensive concern with mythological and symbolic imagery and his personal desire to revivify the power of Christian materials—was less tied to a mythological worldview than was Freud, although secondary and popular studies sometimes have made it seem as if he were as arbitrary in relating particular symbols to particular psychological states. Before looking directly at Jung's mythography, and that of some of his followers, we will turn to Freud's direct and immediate influence.

Post-Freudian Mythography

Two features of Freud's influence upon mythography are especially striking: on the one hand Freudian theories were engaged by some of the major anthropologists of this century, such as A. L. Kroeber and Clyde Kluckhohn.[9] On the other hand, there are only a few workers who, as followers of Freud, could be cited as having represented an explicitly Freudian point of view. Among these Otto Rank, Géza Róheim, and Karl Abraham stand out—excluding for the present the great number of scholars who utilized Freudian insights in the fields of literature and the arts.

Rank completed *The Myth of the Birth of the Hero* (1959) in 1909, when he was a young (twenty-five-year-old) follower of Freud, and the master makes reference to Rank's book in a number of writings after that date. It antedates, therefore, the later painful break between the two men and represents the classical psychoanalytical point of view rather than the more inclusive approach Rank was to develop later. The essay is one of those that manages to be tremendously informative, no matter with what interests one approaches it and whether or not one wishes to agree with classical Freudian positions represented in it.

Arguing that hero myths in general "are structures of the human faculty of imagination" and that specifically they are romanticized versions of the mythmakers' own childhood experiences (10), Rank gives brief sketches of mythical heroes who have associated with them sagalike accounts of their development and careers. The sketches all emphasize the *birth* of the hero, and Rank relates these stories to childhood fantasies of revenge and retaliation against the father or the parents, and hence he understands them as helping to legitimate the termination of the period when one overvalues the father/parents. Ending this overvaluing is crucial to maturation. By identifying the hero with the personal ego, one credits oneself with "heroic" qualities and hence can complete the revolt against the father's domination.

Rank's work dealt with a small group of mythological heroes and was self-consciously restricted in scope.[10] One of the most direct mappings of the Freudian system onto the wider study of myths and rituals, and indeed onto anthropology as a whole, was made by the Hungarian scholar, Géza Róheim (bibliography in La Barre 1961:400–402; and Zinser:145–46). An anthropologist who carried out comprehensive fieldwork in Australia, Róheim was concerned to identify the Freudian motifs in the actual mythological materials and in the tribal rituals he observed or about which he read. Again and again in his writings we read about infantile fantasies being projected onto the adult world, about penile and vaginal symbolism, about Oedipal tensions acted out in rites of initiation, and about society itself considered as being merely a defensive reaction to childhood frustrations, to the dangers of libidinal acting out. One sample will suffice:

> Society is formed by people "clutching" or introjecting each other as substitute parental imago's, as part-realizations of their own neurotic systems or on the basis of identifications as sharing the same anxieties and ways of dealing with these anxieties. The paraphernalia and variations of our culture have been produced by a balancing system between object erotic and narcissistic tendencies super-added to group-neurosis formation. (1971:108)

Cultural elements such as myths and rites are to be understood as being based upon the same sorts of psychological mechanisms that underlie the various types of personal neuroses, and Róheim notes approvingly Freud's threefold comparison of paranoia to philosophy, compulsion neurosis to religion, and hysteria to art (29).

This way of loading anthropological materials with analyses derived from personal psychology often gives Róheim's writings a strongly arbitrary quality (see particularly 1945 and 1950; I have similar reservations about the work of Helene Deutsch): one frequently has the sense that the myths he discusses must have more to offer than adult resolutions of childhood misconceptions. But Róheim was an important figure in showing that the psychoanalytical interpretations were often *possible* interpretations of the native data, and that was a significant contribution. I know of no one who so thoroughly demonstrated the possibilities of the Freudian hermeneutic for approaching material from cultures not our own, and I think it may have been necessary to have such a demonstration of total immersion in the Freudian perspective for us to realize both the contributions and the limitations of this perspective for anthropological analysis.

Alan Dundes, a professional folklorist, has given sustained attention to psychoanalytic interpretation, arguing that too many studies of complex texts remain monocultural and overly restricted by utilizing only one methodology (such as the folklorist's comparative evaluation of folklore variants). His essay, "Earth-Diver: Creation of the Mythopoeic Male" (1962), shows strong regard for the contributions that Freudian-influenced methods can make to analysis of myths, although Dundes remains critical of those who restrict their interpretations to any one arbitrary analysis. Such methods may, for instance, illuminate the reasons behind variations in similar myths or tales that occur within differing cultural contexts: changes may reflect psychodynamics that are present in different strengths in the different cultures. Hence the *present-day* functions of the folk material can be evaluated, shifting the analyst's emphasis away from concern with cosmogonic myths and other myths of origins to the psychodynamics of the group that continues to retell the stories.

Dundes explores the widespread variations of the earth-diver mythologem, the story of a primordial figure who dove into the primeval waters and surfaced with a bit of mud from the bottom in its claws; the mud then magically expanded upon the surface of the waters to become the earth. Even the dove in the story of Noah may represent a variant of this myth type, which Dundes relates in Freudian terms to anal creativity, and to the correlation in several cultures between gold or money ("filthy lucre") and feces.

We are saved from the dreadful one-to-one equation of Freudian psychoanalytical terms with terms of the tale we will encounter shortly with respect to Jack and the Beanstalk. Dundes is satisfied to draw from his research the suggestion that "what is important is the possibility of a theory of universal symbolism which can be verified by empirical observation." It is important, he feels, to realize that some myths may have universally shared features, and others may not, as well as that some myths may directly reflect unconscious, but others conscious, cultural materials. This is clearly a *post*-Freudian perspective in that Freud's monolithic hermeneutic has been augmented substantially by recognition of the importance of alternative analytical perspectives (see also Dundes 1975 and 1980, which contain several of his analyses; and see Carroll's critique of Dundes 1962a).

Earlier Edmund R. Leach explored the ramifications of psychoanalytical theory for anthropological research in an extensive article on "Magical Hair" (1958). Leach was interested to find that the apparently intuitive interpretations of the psychoanalysts could correspond so closely to the results of detailed ethnographic analyses. He reviews the manifold ways in which body hair (length, mode of cutting, private versus public showing, and so forth) may be employed as a ritual symbol, in an attempt to clarify the psychological power of ritual symbols to arouse emotion and to serve as societal models. (More recently, Raymond Firth has explored the public symbolism of hair in 1973:chap. 8.)

Like Dundes, Leach found that psychological and sociological or anthropological analyses need not be entirely congruent in order to enrich each other: "They are separate aspects which illuminate quite different aspects of a single general problem (1958:161). Leach does take issue with the Freudians' suggestion that important public symbols should be considered as originating from "sublimated libido," especially from the individual's projection of such psychic elements onto ritual objects. Rather, Leach would argue, important ritual symbols are psychologically powerful because they arise out of being socially valued, out of their focus in ritual situation. The crucial statement is found in a remark about the opposition between the sacred and the profane:

> The psychoanalyst's thesis implies a causal nexus—sacred things are sacred *because* they are secret and taboo. The anthropologist argues the other way about: Sacred objects are taboo because they are sacred—that is because they are full of dangerous potency, including sexual potency. The hidden element, the secrecy, is not, for the anthropologist, a crucial part of the pattern. . . . In the anthropologist's view, ritually powerful human hair is full of magical potency not because it is hair but because of the ritual context of its source, e.g., murder, incest, mourning, etc. It is the ritual situation which makes the hair "powerful," not the hair which makes the ritual powerful. (159)

The works of Dundes and Leach provide examples of the recent post-Freudian use of Freudian insights; we have seen that in each case such insights were considered most helpful when they were treated as just one of the insights that might contribute to interpretation of myths and rituals. An explicit demonstration of such a multifaceted approach is found in an article by Elli Köngäs Maranda, in which five different approaches to the same myth are briefly charted—the psychoanalytical among them (Snyder:chap. 6 also surveys psychological approaches). Maranda's essay demonstrated visibly what seems to be the most useful role of psychoanalytical theory today: as one of the many component disciplines that may aid in interpretation. We are a long way from the sort of mapping of Freudian categories onto units of a tale represented by this interpretation of Jack and the Beanstalk by William H. Desmonde:

> We may interpret Jack psychoanalytically as an oral dependent. Incapable of competing successfully in the market, he returned home, the tale tells, feeling depressed and inferior, and went to bed without any supper. We may regard the remainder of the story as an incestuous masturbation fantasy or dream, of a regressive nature.
> The miraculous stalk growing from the beans is the erect phallus, and the little old lady with the fairy wand is the phallic mother-image. The imprisoned father indicates Jack's Oedipal hostility, while the cannibalistic ogre is the same father in a threatening aspect. Treasures are incestuous representations. Pursued by the menacing ogre for his thefts, Jack castrates himself: the beanstalk shrivels at the first touch of the hatchet, and

> the threatening father-image disappears. (108–09; Dundes 1965b provides comparative readings of the folk tale as well as helpful bibliography on the use of psychoanalytic insights for the study of folklore)

Dundes, who selected this example for his reader, *The Study of Folklore* (1965), amply shows the problems with such an approach—merely treating the tale variants, for instance, provides an important check upon the arbitrariness of Desmonde's interpretation. It was precisely this type of arbitrary overinterpretation that has led to a reaction against Freudian interpretation in recent decades, such as Sontag's indication that it frequently "indicates a dissatisfaction (conscious or unconscious) with the work, a wish to replace it by something else" (10). Indeed it is precisely this sort of arbitrary retelling of the original materials that has led (by reaction) to some of the more creative expositions in recent literary theory and to emphasis once again upon the actual performance setting of the material, to interpretive stress upon its societal function within the ongoing life of the transmitting community.

Freudian interpretation of mythological and ritual materials was especially important for its contributions toward a ritual and mythological symbology, for its stimulus to development of more sensitive approaches to the inner meaning of ritual and mythological symbols. And it repeatedly raised the question of the possible universality of human cultural products—an issue I discussed at the beginning of Chapter 4 and that will appear in different guise with respect to structuralism in Chapter 7. Carl Jung and his followers developed and expanded this aspect of Freud's heritage to the point where Jungian psychology often is referred to as Archetypal Psychology, and it is to the development of that school that we now turn.

Jungian Archetypes and Amplifications

Freud's own training included instruction in the classical languages—and hence in classical mythology—typical of the secondary education of his day and social class (cf. Rainey; Glenn:226; Jones 1961; Bettelheim 1982); his personal collection of objects from classical antiquity, and the references in his writings to Greek and Latin mythology, demonstrate that this training led to lifelong interests. Most of Freud's biographies include portraits of him at his desk, surrounded with small statuettes from antiquity. Nevertheless, it was the Swiss psychiatrist Carl Gustav Jung (1875–1961) who developed a stronger and more inclusive approach to mythology as a whole, by no means restricted to Greek and

Latin materials. Freud seldom treated particular myths in much detail: perhaps that is due to his generally negative view of religion, as sketched earlier, and to his fundamental determination to work from those patterns in his own patients' psychodynamic materials that exemplified his own theories.

Jung developed "analytical," "archetypal," or "depth" psychology as a field in which the mythological dimensions of the materials presented by his patients would be of great importance.[11] He agreed with Freud that the logic of myths and the logic of dreams display great similarity. But Jung differed at the point of Freud's insistence upon the "primitive" nature of these logics: "The conclusion that the myth-makers thought in much the same way as we still think in dreams is almost self-evident. . . . But one must certainly put a large question-mark after the assertion that myths spring from the 'infantile' psychic life of the race. They are on the contrary the most mature product of that young humanity" (*CW* 5:24). Maturity here seems to refer to the characteristic tendency of mythical thinking to press beyond immediate or historical human causation; elsewhere Jung refers to "the age of myths, which did not explain everything in terms of man and his limited capacities but sought the deeper cause in the psyche and its autonomous powers" (*CW* 10:187).

Freud had given indications that he also considered some sort of a universal human substratum responsible for the production of concrete images: "the archaic heritage of mankind includes not only dispositions, but also ideational contents, memory traces of the experiences of former generations" (1939:127). Jung greatly developed the concept of the archaic heritage as a means of dealing with the suprapersonal elements that arose in his patients' dreams. In fact, one might say that Jung turned to the study of mythology and iconography out of his frustration in working with purely personal associations. He recognized that themes in fairy tales, graphic representations, and mythology (which must include more than merely "accounts of the gods" in this instance, but also ancient and medieval theology, philosophy, alchemical meditation, and non-Western religious thought) could provide clues to personal meaning for his patients, clues that otherwise might emerge only very slowly if at all. Modern self-consciousness and historical and scientific thinking systematically have excluded and reduced the networks of relationship and explicit societal attention to the values, significance, and meaningfulness of existence. Often such values and meanings now can be recovered, Jung suggested, only by careful critical study of myths, fairy tales, legends, visual imagery, and poetry. In dreams and in many poetic works, "there are numberless interconnections to which one can find parallels only in mythological associations of ideas" (*CW*, vol. 9, pt.

1; cited from Jung and Kerényi:71); exploring the associations may enable us to reach beyond purely personal materials into older and deeper cultural wisdom.

Even conscious fantasies may contain materials no longer (or not yet) recognized as mythological; and "great art till now has always derived its fruitfulness from myth" (*CW* 5:31–32; cf. *CW* 10:303). Hence Jungian analytical psychology has been very influential in the arts, and Jungian analysis works specifically toward the goal of enriching the analysand's creativity, first through the path of a more productive comprehension of one's dreams, and then through a process known as "active imagination" whereby the unconscious images are consciously meditated upon and refined (see Hannah; and Humbert).

Jung's attitude toward dreams was generally more positive than was Freud's, and that means both a greater prospective role for dreams and a higher evaluation of myths. (Mahoney provides a useful compendium of Jung's materials on dreams.) Jung saw dreams not as symptoms of sickness, derived from unresolved problems in the dreamer's infantile stages, hangovers from the past, as it were, but teleologically or projectively, that is, as pointing the way toward a potential future wholeness. For Jung the dream may present a vision or image of meaning that has to be taken very seriously not in terms of personal problems so much as in terms of what the dream says toward the future life of the dreamer, toward his or her "vocation": as David L. Miller summarizes, "A dream is not a mirror reflecting personal sickness . . . but . . . a magic mirror, projecting man's vocation for personal meaning" (1970b:32).

Materials disclosed in dreams are not regarded by Jungians as purely personal, as items restricted to one's own personal agenda, but rather dreams and imaginal materials may have consequences for human society as a whole. Such materials are shared in the psychic depths and the mythical imagery of people everywhere: "The dream is a little hidden door in the innermost and most secret recesses of the psyche, opening into that cosmic night which was psyche long before there was any ego-consciousness, and which will remain psyche no matter how far our ego-consciousness extends" (*CW* 10:144–45; also cited in Jaffé:382). The dreamer shares with other dreamers, with mythmakers, and with artists a universally experienced world of images and symbols.

Jung therefore suggests that dreams and myths reveal the structure of the human psyche or soul. Recurring images and symbols are "collective representations"; considered as coming from the universal substrate of humankind, they form the "collective unconscious" or the "objective psyche" in contrast to the personal or subjective unconscious or preconscious Freud emphasized. Jung was so convinced of the reality of these recurrent images and symbols that he suggested that if all the world's traditions suddenly were destroyed, the whole of mythology and the whole of religion would start all over again with the next generation—not, of course, in the same format and contours, but as the forms of energy ("libido") passing through every imaginable transformation in mythologies. Hence Jung can refer to "myths and symbols which can arise autochthonously," that is, independently, of themselves, "in every corner of the earth and yet are identical, because they are fashioned out of the same worldwide human unconscious, whose contents are infinitely less variable than are races and individuals" (CW 10:120–21).

Myths and dream images represent projections from the unconscious rather than conscious inventions; the similarities in the human unconscious provide similar mythological motifs, and correspondingly, myths and symbols provide representations of typical psychic phenomena. Nor are humans dependent upon cultural contexts for transmission of mythological themes: a mythologem (a mythical image or theme) can arise anywhere, at any time. And hence the investigation or *amplification* of any individual's unconscious imagery may be developed by referring to any other apparently similar pattern, wherever it occurs. Readers of Jung's writings will know just how extensively his analytical practice followed this principle: for example, an American woman's fantasies provided the occasion for the elaborate and richly illustrated *Symbols of Transformation* (CW 5), the book that led to his break with Freud and in which the amplificatory material ranges from ancient alchemy to Longfellow's "Hiawatha."

The universal substrate of humankind, the objective psyche, may be thought of as a sort of ultimate psychic energy that leads certain images and symbols to resurface at different times and places. Jung used the phrase "primordial image"—and later, the "archetype"—to refer to the "tendency to form representations of a motif." There is a certain numinosity about archetypal images, recognized when personal feelings are particularly engaged by a dream or mythic image, and the personal analysis will work with the "complexes" of images, representations, and the types of relationships evoked by them.

The archetypes themselves remain essentially transpersonal and transhistorical; we know them (examples would be The Mother, The Divine Child, The Trickster, The Spirit) only by their specific appearances in particular cultural manifestations. Jung compared the archetypes to the structuring force in a chemical solution: we cannot "see" either the archetype or the axial pattern of the precipitated crystal itself, but we can see how the force has "shown" itself in either case. The imminent force "constellates" a dream or mythical symbol in the one case, the formation of crystals in the other; hence in Marie-Louise von Franz's formulation, the archetypes are "dynamic units of psychic energy" (1974:155).

The mythologems and the myths themselves reveal the structure and the contents of the soul or psyche, especially the unconscious psyche, and they form a vast interlocking system that one must never regard "literally" but only symbolically. It is a system in which the various units may interchange roles, giving any individual symbol an equivocal possibility of meaning, determined by a particular dreamer's associated meanings. And it is a system in which imaginal relationships and chains of images develop.

Psychic *compensation,* a mechanism Jung identified in dreams, may be at work: the conscious situation may be taken further than seems realistic, or weakness may find strength, and so forth. Myths therefore provide a means of attaining individual identity and personhood, for they can show the limits and the possibilities of human development. Mythical structures are those that appeared in the past; analogous dream structures may operate for the individual today.

Jung was impressed with the modern possibility of developing a science of mythology along the lines of a science of the psyche he saw developing. While he can be quite devastating about the way "science" itself has mythological overtones, especially insofar as it accepts as material reality that which is actually psychic and imaginal in its origins, a "science of mythology" presumably would parallel his method of working with personal unconscious contents. It would be characterized primarily by the "amplification" that leads to a contemporary reconnection of consciousness with the archetypal sources of energies.[12] His hermeneutic leads him to ask what force or deity it might be that is trying to work through the unconscious materials, and it leads him to seek to revitalize such Western traditions as Christianity by a process of penetration to the levels of energy or power (the "libidinal" levels) of their mythologies.

Hence in contrast to Freud's negative views, myth is regarded by Jung as an integral part of all religions and a supreme achievement of humankind. Religious myths provide links with the transpersonal, the eternal, and are to be left behind only when more meaningful statements of the resources and the significances of human existence are found. In the meantime, the most we can hope for is reconnection with the energy systems represented in past myths in such a way as to lead to a personal affirmation of *one's own* mythic system and hence to a meaningful personal universe. The mode of expression will be full of imagery, for "Myth is the primordial language natural to [the] psychic process, and no intellectual formulation comes anywhere near the richness and expressiveness of mythic imagery. Such processes are concerned with the primordial images,and these are best and most succinctly reproduced by figurative language" (CW 12:25).

Eric Gould, to whose important *Mythical Intentions* (1981) I will return several times in this book, has responded quite positively to Jung's reflections on myth and archetype, even though he ultimately finds the Jungian position helpless in bridging the gap between a hypothesized level of archetypal existence (the "primordial wonder-world" of Jung's writings) and the actual productions of the graphic or literary artist. Gould treats Jung's system more seriously than most who reject it (such as those listed in J. White 1972:104, n. 62); he seems quite aware that the Jungian archetypes do not have to be taken as *prescribing* effects in contemporary artworks. And he comes close to the way of using the concept of archetypes I have always found most helpful, namely as a post facto means of identifying, clarifying, and organizing patterns of human expression, rather than as Platonic-cosmological determinants.[13]

Gould notes, however (44–45), that even the mere recurrence of motifs—in semiotic terms, the signifiers—is hardly as important as the persistence of our attributions of interpretations, meanings (the signifieds). The recurrence of assigned meanings tends to reduce the open-endedness of symbol and metaphor, and while Jung's analytical position was defended by emphasizing the individual client's *personal context,* Jungian mythographic applications are much more likely to sound curiously monotheistic in literary or artistic analysis that refers to *the* Hero Archetype or the like.

Gould and Jack Carloye both note that Jung tends to refer to "images" frequently but never deals comprehensively or adequately with human language—that human activity that is both the expression of and the interpretation of the archetype. The Jungian enterprise remains essentialist, positing a fullness of meaning "back there" in the collective unconscious, suggesting that something or some Being yet ties everything together in a divine realm of total and perfect meaning, which for Jung would be the transcendent coincidence of all oppositions. Yet such a linguistic a priori is hardly conceivable without the corrective recognition that an archetypal representation must be in itself already a movement within language—expressed metaphorically, in a limit-aware context but yet open-endedly symbolic (cf. Gould:33–34): language describes what is *not* present, the *lack* presupposed by our speaking anything at all, rather than an essence or a presence that can never be spoken or expressed absolutely outside a system of relationships (Jacques Derrida's "differance"; Gould [37] finds René Girard's existentialist narrowing to "sacred violence" no less "archetypalist" than Jung's own work, and I have similar hesitations about Walter Burkert's otherwise very impressive *Homo necans* [1983]).

The use of the term "archetype" can be retained, if given a grounding within a wider semiotics and semantics of mythicity and discourse: archetypes are signs for a necessary exteriority of speech in which we recognize the impossibility of language speaking fully or ultimately. Archetypes are significances shared by speaker and listener (artist and observer) who inhabit the same language world, who continually seek (and historically have sought) to bridge the ontological gap between event and meaning by metonyms that constantly slip into metaphors: "The archetype carries a necessary exteriority whose interpretive challenge must be met—as metonymy becomes metaphor—or else we lapse into a superstitious worship of the hidden side of its meaning" (Gould:69), into Jung's "essentialist" Platonism that Gould criticizes and that may be the reason for Jung's repeated emphasis upon the unconscious and the archetype of the Self. If, following Freud, and Freud read in a Freudian way by Lacan, we conceive the unconscious as a part of the linguistic setting of human experience—as the unknown, the lack or desire to supply what is not present—archetypal expressions become supremely interpretive attempts to temporize, to exist meaningfully before the awesome Nonbeing of Heidegger and the existentialists. We see that "the gap between the subject and his desire is distinctly homologous to the gap between the thing and its name: ironically, both are produced by a repression which is language itself" (Gould:73–74; see also Bär).

The archetype of the self in this sense indeed may be "a universal" but not a numinous universal so much as a process by which personal attempts to bridge the ontological gap remain open-ended and self-consciously limited. "So the universal may well be only that which is always open to interpretation" (Gould:85). Perhaps this explanation casts light on the situation I have noticed among many readers of Jung (especially the compelling *Memories, Dreams, Reflections*—see Jaffé 1963): these readers are almost overwhelmed with Jung's own self-awareness of numinous forces impinging upon his personal life history, but they seldom experience similar situations as bearing "numinous" overtones. Their own need to compel a meaningful sign reflects their own hermeneutical experience, the construction of idiosyncratic semantic fields. As one wag put it, "Maybe *you* have met the Great Mother, but *I've* met the Great Father."

Works produced by Jung's followers have taken his emphasis upon figurative language very seriously. Many of their works, such as those of

Erich Neumann or of Edward F. Edinger, provide a rich store of illustrations complementing and completing the texts. Neumann's *The Great Mother* (1963), his *The Origins and History of Consciousness* (1954), and his *Amor and Psyche* (1956) provide a mine of information on mythological subjects, interpreted according to principles developed from Jung's own writings. And *Man and His Symbols* (Jung and von Franz 1964), the popular presentation of the Jungian approach that was in production when Jung died and to which Jung himself contributed the initial chapter, is likewise a sensitive interweaving of iconography, mythology, and psychological commentary (a unity destroyed by the abbreviated paperback version).

Except for British works by Charles Aldrich and by John Layard, detailed expositions of ethnological and ritual materials comparable to those found among the early Freudians have not been developed within the Jungian school, in spite of Jung's explicit suggestion that "many dreams present images and associations that are analogous to primitive ideas, myths, and rites" (Brenneman's brief study makes some intriguing initial moves; and S. Moon and Sanders each provide model Jungian studies of Navajo materials).

Many literary studies have used Jungian analytical categories (notably the Shadow, or dark, suppressed side of the personality, and the Anima/Animus, the contra-sexual component of the unconscious, male for females, female for males) as a means of exposing the dynamics of works of poetry and fiction (Bodkin's 1934 study retains analytic power in this regard). Many of these studies have been merely allegorical, correlating Jungian categories with literary characters (Duràn—but many other examples could be given): we are informed that the hero's wraithlike lover who is drawing him into intrigues and mischief represents his Anima-projection, or that the Jesus figura has so much power because it is a manifestation of the archetype of the Divine Son. The best of these studies avoid the slavish correlation of Jungian categories and literary figures; and in fact I think the most successful influence of Jungian modes may be represented by works that entirely avoid explicit mention of the categories. Even in sophisticated studies, however, where the Jungian model of the self is helpful in elucidating some of the dynamics of modernist and postmodernist literature (I will cite Spivey as an example), it is astonishing to see how the critics' knowledge of Jung's work comes almost exclusively from secondary sources or compendia of Jung's writings. I suspect that there is a great deal to be gained by a close reading of Jung's massive corpus of writings, focused upon its implications for literary amplification, but to my knowledge such a project remains to be completed.

The only substantial published analytical materials include Jung's Visions and Dream Seminars (Jung 1976; McGuire 1984) and Marie-Louise von Franz's interlocking commentaries on fairy tale themes (see for example von Franz 1972a and 1972b). The von Franz studies are from training programs for analysts at the Jung Institute in Zurich and reflect the practical contexts and uses of Jungian thought in analytical work; von Franz also has published quite sophisticated and technical studies, such as her work on depth psychology and modern physics (1974).

There is in the Jungian system a strong emphasis upon individuation, the process by which selfhood is attained by an individual. The transpersonal or archetypal Self is thought to be manifested through an individual, and there is a strong bias toward the attainment of an integrated and creative individuality. But subsequently the sociological applications of Jungian theory have been minimal. Likewise, there have been few studies relating social patterns of earlier societies to contemporary problems, such as can be seen, for example, in the Freudian overtones of Rank's *The Myth of the Birth of the Hero* (1959).[14]

One compelling application of ancient myth-and-ritual patterns to work with adolescent schizophrenics has been developed by Jungian analyst John Weir Perry (1974). Perry argues that schizophrenia may be approached as an extreme case in which a human psyche betrays a problematic relation to the ego, based on a fragmented or warped experiencing of *eros* (understood as relational abilities) in the association between the child and its mother. Taking seriously schizophrenics' "delusions," Perry recognized in them a common pattern that also can be found in ancient myth and ritual concerned with the kingship of the society. The delusions, in light of this pattern, reflect not so much loss of contact with daily reality as the cultural situation of modern society that has forced the lone individual to bear the weight of the cycle of death and rebirth, enthronement and sacred marriage, once carried symbolically by the king on behalf of the entire country.

Pursuing cultural analogies as did Erich Neumann earlier, but in a uniquely American and contemporary idiom, Perry proposes a means of working along with (rather than "treating") schizophrenics within healing communities. Here their psychic experiences and images are listened to and responded to very seriously—and related, at least intellectually, both to the experiences of religious mystics and to the chemically induced psychotic experiences of those who have taken psychedelic drugs.

It would be hard to find any figure in contemporary psychology, except for Perry's mentor, Jung, who is so cognizant of the parallels between mythic and ritualistic humankind of the past and today's democratic individualism. Perry sees our whole culture now acting out individual-by-individual the patterns once communally experienced—the yearly enthronement ritual was the symbolic re-creation of the entire universe. And Perry suggests that the schizophrenic adolescent can be regarded not as someone who must be tranquilized and silenced but as someone exhibiting an extreme case of an experience we must all confront at some point or another, an experience for which patterns from antiquity may provide models of therapy. Diabasis, a community for working with schizophrenics established by Perry in the San Francisco area, seeks to provide a model of a receptive community in which the fragmented relationships between parent and child can be healed and the individual guided through her or his psychotic experience into an effective mode of behavior that will be considered healthy in modern society.

James Hillman, the most independent of the neo-Jungians, has engaged ancient mythology in a series of articles and monographs and in several books.[15] Hillman has given considerable attention to what he calls, in a book of that title, *The Myth of Analysis* (1972): the analysand learns to tell a coherent personal myth, on the basis of careful fantasy work that in its formation is partly imaged from classical mythology. Great attention to and care for language and a far-reaching retrieve of the meanings of classical imagery are evident in a later work, *Re-Visioning Psychology* (1975). There Hillman works toward a "polytheistic psychology" in which the stories of the gods and goddesses are canvassed as recourses for understanding elemental situations of the human psyche. And *The Dream and the Underworld* (1979) emphasizes further the importance of psychological imagery that goes against literal and "daylight" realities.

To discuss Hillman's works extensively would take us further in the direction of contemporary psychological theory than I wish to go here. They provide a fascinating perspective on the ways a Jungian perspective may be developed and extended—even against Jung himself. Hillman has learned both to project a mythical psychology and to revision classical mythical images in ways that often make them newly powerful for today (Bedford provides a compressed catalog); I regard Hillman's work as being among the most truly creative approaches to mythology presently available, and much of the mode of reseeing the classical approaches to mythography found in this book derive from what I have learned from it.

The Jungian enterprise often is criticized as not being empirical, as not being able to prove its theses within the increasingly externally and data-oriented branches of modern psychology. But I suspect it is an approach not subject to such standards of judgment. There is a sense in which it either works to illuminate a personal or social worldview or it does not. The Jungian emphasis upon individual development and maturation produces an inherent tension between personal acceptance of its insights and broader scientific criteria for truth. By positing transpersonal, essentially eternal, archetypal powers, it leaves itself open to questions about their topography and verification. But verification of such factors is out of the question, except as one accepts the similarity of materials from many sources (a problem yet unresolved in any of the social sciences) or the meaningfulness of an archetypal approach to myths or to one's own life-myth as sufficient "proof."

If any psychological-philosophical position that vests its ultimate "essence" in transpersonal, eternal Being can be considered viable today in our "postmodern" world, I think the Jungian position remains more adequate than most traditional theisms. Recent suggestions that the contemporary "decentered" person cannot remain within such a "logocentric" perspective will be discussed later in this book. Certainly if Jung's emphasis upon individuation is read as merely another of the developmental models of growth into a unified selfhood, it fails to provide a sufficiently flexible perspective for the phenomenon of a succession of selves that has been suggested. See for instance Lifton, who analyzes the "Protean" personality, or A. Lee who emphasizes the variabilities of social roles to which we must adjust daily, or the frequent references within humanistic (or transpersonal) psychology to a contemporary necessity to change our models of selfhood.

One less sweeping test of the adequacy of a methodology for mythography, however, would be the power of the Jungian analytic to illuminate mythology and iconography, and for my work it often fulfills this promise. Validity of such an approach is established when it "takes us into the heart of that of which it is an interpretation" (Geertz 1973:18); and, as Geertz puts it, "You either grasp an interpretation or you do not, see the point of it or you do not, accept it or you do not." (24)

Jung's approach need not be considered as the sole interpretation of a particular mythic account—that would be contrary to the mythographic principles I am developing throughout this book. The elucidations of Jung, and those of his followers, especially Hillman, clarify many interconnections and similarities in intellectual and artistic history, and that seems a sufficiently significant achievement to earn it a place in a multidisciplined mythography. More as a training of the myth analyst's sensitivities than as a specific mapping of Jungian analytical terms and frameworks onto individual mythologems, the Jungian and neo-Jungian contributions have been significant and promise to remain so.

Psychosociology

An example of what Jungians call synchronicity—the apparently chance concurrence of related events—happened the day I finished writing the last part of the preceding subsection of this book and turned to a book by Philip Slater that I had not finished previously. Slater's *Microcosm* (1966) utilizes Erich Neumann's Jungian insights about the mythological Great Mother and about the development of consciousness in its analysis of contemporary therapy and interaction groups. That I had not realized; but more striking was the fact that Slater develops a critique of the Jungian posture, identifying almost the same problems I have mentioned and concluding much as I did:

> We must not lose sight of the advantages yielded by such specialization. It is this very unconcern with the concrete origin of their symbols that gives [Jungian theorists] such great skill at establishing symbolic connections. And this skill must certainly be granted, *for no group has so thoroughly and illuminatingly explored the network of symbolic connections underlying mythology and religious systems.* (1966:236–37, my emphasis)

No one who knows Slater's research would think of him as "a Jungian"; he has developed a sensitive tool for probing ancient culture and mythology that deserves its own name. In designating his approach as psychosociology, I hope to characterize Slater's essentially sociological perspective, which is, however, deeply informed by psychoanalytical theory.

His work *The Glory of Hera: Greek Mythology and the Greek Family* (1968), reviewed somewhat testily by many classicists, is closer to orthodox Freudianism than to Jung. Subsequent articles have developed the underlying perspectives of *The Glory of Hera*, namely that the familial, and the sexual, relationships of Greek men and women were psychodynamically determined by the particular sociological contours of ancient Greek society (1977:chap. 8; 1974; an earlier fusionist approach, termed psychoecology, was developed by Court).

Struck by the ways in which Greek women were presented in myths, Slater identifies an ambivalence between mother and son that derived from a vicious circle. Greek women, separated from close daily contact with their husbands, treated their sons both as substitute husbands and as substitute gratifiers, who were to succeed in the world outside the home as they could not. Slater suggests that the result of this ambivalence was the cultivation of a narcissistic masculine homosexuality that contributed to a personal vanity that could be expressed only through extreme contests such as warfare; it also contributed to a postadolescent fear of women.

John Peradotto summarizes the responses to the mother:son ambivalence Slater has traced in Greek myths:

> sexual dominance in the figure of Zeus, "masculine antisepsis" in Apollo, the matricide of Orestes, the "self-emasculation" of Hephaestus, "identification with the aggressor" in Dionysus, "maternal desexualization" in the story of Perseus, and finally the character of Heracles whose checkered career illustrates every possible response to maternal threat. (29; the quoted phrases are derived from chapter titles in Slater 1968)

This is quite a list, but it provides some indications as to why Slater's analyses are stronger and more satisfying than older psychological analyses of mythology. Whether or not one agrees with Slater's analysis of the Greek familial situation, it is clear that he provides intriguing possible ways of understanding the psychodynamics of Greek society as well as the mythical stories they influenced.

Sarah B. Pomeroy disagrees with Slater's analysis of the segregated and unhappy role of the Athenian wife, and she thinks fathers and children were more intimately related than Slater suggests. But she finds his work "useful for the analysis of the male playwright's creative imagination," and she reminds us that "The mythology about women is created by men and, in a culture dominated by men, it may have little to do with flesh-and-blood women" (1975:96; Pomeroy, in her "Selected Bibliography on Women in Antiquity" [1973], is apparently the only critic to refer to Slater in the entire issue of *Arethusa* devoted to Women in Antiquity; other more recent critics from within classics are Foley 1975; and Arthur).

Slater has a knack for the pithy aphorism and pregnant summation, such as the remark about myth being like a political platform, cited in Chapter 1. His striking reflections on the myths he treats make *The Glory of Hera* an important and insightful volume. And I often find his work extremely helpful in identifying and interrelating the emotions that the mythical actors convey. It is one thing to have been taught about *hybris* (overweening pride) as a vague philosophical concept, and another to read Slater's comments that "the Greek concern with limits [that is, as reflected in the concern with *hybris*] derives from a sense of the insatiability of these needs" . . . "To achieve revenge and arouse envy were the twin delicacies of everyday life" (1968:40). And with respect to Dionysian ritual, Slater can quip: "Over and above any intrinsic beauty or edification in the ritual, Bacchic ceremonies must have served as something of a tranquilizer" (216).

Readers of Slater's *The Pursuit of Loneliness* (1976), knowing his strong concern for contemporary society, will not be surprised that the last part of *The Glory of Hera* is concerned with cultural pathology. Slater argues "that the motivational basis of our own society is simply an advanced stage of the same disease that dominated Greek life" (1968:453). And Slater's summarization of parts of *The Glory of Hera* in chapter 8 ("The Family in Ancient Greece") of his more recent *Footholds* (1977) is followed by a report on subsequent research he has done on "Traits of Warlike Cultures" (chapter 9) and then on "Civilization, Narcissism, and Sexual Repression" (chapter 10). Clearly the psychosocial analysis of Greek myth in the earlier work and his continuing interest in contemporary American family patterns have provided him with a fruitful combination.[16] Mythographic analysts could learn from Slater something about combining separate disciplines into an approach that is more effective than any single component, but the possibility remains, unfortunately, more promise than actuality, although much of the work of the group of scholars working with Jean-Pierre Vernant (discussed in Chapter 7) has produced additional instances of a sophisticated combination of ancient history, sociology, structuralism, and psychoanalysis.

Psychoanthropology

The term I am using for this subsection is not one many anthropologists whose methodologies are influenced by psychology would be likely to recognize. In fact the majority of "straight" anthropologists probably would respond to it with an off-handed rejection or would find it a label appropriate only to Róheim or other Freudian-influenced anthropologists whose studies were never widely influential among the disciplines of academic anthropology.

Several signs of a renewed interest in psychology on the part of anthropologists lead me to suggest that the term may become useful: I refer to the work of George Devereux (who prefers the term "ethnopsychoanalysis") as well as to a volume of essays edited by Ioan Lewis (*Symbols and Sentiments* [1977]) that is intended explicitly to bring together around the study of symbols "work in social anthropology, history, psychoanalysis, and psychotherapy" and "to elicit the *emotional* as well as cognitive meaning of symbols in a variety of settings" (vii). The essays in the Lewis volume range widely across several cultures, but all of them include psychological and psychoanalytical insights as part of the perspective of the writers. Several essays are explicit attempts to derive additional insights by using psychological insights or by revising traditional views of psychology (for example, "Is Freudian Symbolism a Myth?" by Charles Rycroft); others develop new ways of working from the older "culture and personality" approach—an approach widely discussed in the essays in *The Making of Psychological Anthropology* (1978), an intriguing volume edited by George D. Spindler.

The Spindler volume is of historical as well as methodological value in that it includes in almost every essay the author's personal autobiographical reflections on how she or he has been related to one or another aspect of psychoanthropology. The older specialists represented in the first part of the volume share in general a conceptual structure, Spindler suggests, "derived from neo-Freudianism, Gestalt, and social learning theory"; the younger writers tend to be more at home with symbolic anthropology, altered states of consciousness, and cognitive anthropology, and they focus more frequently on microstudies than on global constructs such as "culture and personality," which was the earlier rallying point.

Spindler himself provides a quick outline of the reception and subsequent rejection of psychology by anthropologists (7–21), concluding that "psychologizing is central to cultural anthropology, even to anthropologists who are not explicitly psychologically oriented" (21). Some of the issues Spindler considers to be lasting problems for a psychological anthropology are directly relevant to psychological approaches to myths and rituals: he notes the dangers of psychological reductionism, the tendency to be influenced by the cultural determinism of the observer's own culture, the lack of attention to the relationship between the individual and the overall cultural matrix, and the problems created by the interfacing relationships between investigator and subject (the "participant observer" dilemma that Bohannan first voiced so poignantly in her novel, *Return to Laughter* [1954]).

The work of the Eastern European George Devereux seems very little known in this country, although it may well be the extreme breadth of his work that has made him a slightly familiar name in several disciplines (classics, ethnology, psychiatry, education, history) rather than well known in only one. He provides an extended survey of his eleven books (1978a:19), and essays published from 1943 to 1975 now published in *Ethnopsychoanalysis* (1978) are likewise helpful in gaining an overview.

Devereux has critically analyzed the subject:observer relationship in ethnology and the behavioral sciences in general; his *From Anxiety to Method* (1967) recognizes the anxiety that behavioral data often evoke among scientists, anxiety they in turn deal with by countertransferences that become methodologies. Few other analysts of the social sciences, with the possible exceptions of Michel Foucault and Thomas Kuhn, have been as clear about the role of the scientist's *own* involvement in the process of scientific study. Much like Slater, Devereux focuses upon the relation of the individual psyche and the societal context: he argues against the logic of treating schizophrenia as an organic problem, for instance, viewing it instead as "the ethnic psychosis of occidental cultures" (378).

The sort of complementarity of disciplines that Devereux advocates seems to me to be of great value for future interdisciplinary work: neither of any two disciplines involved ought to try to mingle with the other, nor can the two perspectives simply be conflated. But put side by side, in tandem, as it were, sociocultural and psychoanalytic studies may well mutually illuminate an ethnic context, sometimes by the act of mutual critical self reflection of the one discipline upon the other. What is considered operant motivation in sociological discourse, for instance, may be what is considered instrumental motivation in psychological discourse—a sort of free-associative use of the other discipline's categories that may expose more contours of the subject than otherwise would have been visible, and neither discipline is required to conform to the theoretical framing conceptions of the other (see Hook:intro., in a book that was dedicated to Devereux and includes appreciations of his work).

The Psychological Functions of Myths and Rituals

Rather than presenting a section on "how myths and rituals serve society"—as I have done in Chapters 2 and 3, but oriented here toward psychological factors--I will conclude this chapter with a brief consideration of some of the ways psychologically oriented studies of myths and rituals may add to approaches that are oriented primarily to social-functional or other dimensions. How to focus my conclusion is a problem closely related to the question of defining the "psyche" in psychology at all: a close look at most academic psychology today leads one to wonder about the disappearance of the soul/psyche in the discipline supposedly devoted to its study (Hillman 1972b and 1979, and Bettelheim 1982 are instructive in the historical development of this situation).

Behaviors, emotions, realities: I identify these three terms as central to understanding myths and rituals psychologically, not in distinction to other ways of understanding but as the features psychology can illuminate most helpfully. Of course, behaviors can be understood in terms of how they function, in terms of who demands this rather than another behavior in a given social situation. But they also can be understood in terms of how they are evoked and stimulated—and psychology is especially well equipped to provide this type of information. Behaviors may well be tracked in terms of personal and social histories, in terms of the types of responses (behaviors) persons most frequently make when confronted with one or another stimulus; the stimuli may be overt or covert—but then Freud has taught us that the behaviors likewise may be either overt or covert, and questions about deep-cultural, social, or individual motivations have refracted themselves differently in the whole great panoply of human worldviews.

Behaviors may result from or lead to emotional states. Rituals clearly facilitate expression of certain emotions. They may diffuse overpowering feelings such as grief or separation (see Scheff), or they may provide indirect expression for emotions that are blocked by social constraints or personal psychohistory. (Freud's vast influence upon our intellectual life is not exhausted by reference to what he led us to ask about indirect—symbolic, metonymic, metaphoric—expression, but it certainly was among the most powerful pressures toward symbolic studies in the history of human expression; see Victor Turner's account of the impact of Freud's "*style* of thinking and working" upon his own development of symbolic anthropology [1978b].)

Myths (indirectly) or rituals (directly) may provide for a redirecting of emotional valences, either providing for communal expressive acts that are eutropic for the whole group rather than individual expressive acts that are dystropic, or providing forms of expression that facilitate communal expressions of joy, fear, and hatred—or even, according to René Girard, of the ultimate human drives toward violence themselves. [17]

Myths in particular function as reflections of the society's decisions about what is real and what is not; they identify the levels of reality (spirits, co-humans, beasts; day-reality or dreams), and they reiterate modes of proper relation to these realities as modes that may be enacted in ritual forms. Myths and legends and fairy tales may set up models of prototypical or correct behavioral reponses in given situations, hence connecting the past with the present. They may give ordered form to ideals of what human behavior might be, or they may deplore models of inappropriate behavior. In this way they relate transcendent aspects to a seemingly local/individual instance/situation: and hence such materials provide a means of relating the wondrous and the grotesque, often naming as images or personifications those feelings or emotions that otherwise would remain idiosyncratic or amorphous (see Webster).

The psychological function of myths and rituals can be referred to as a coding and switching mechanism that enables one to coordinate familial and personal backgrounds and capabilities with societal and transcendental factors. Myths and rituals seem particularly concerned with the "psyche" of psychology, with the soul-dimension of human experience, the dimension that asks about meaning and significance in terms of a wide "humanism" not exhausted by data and statistical averages (those curious creations of the American 1930s—see Susman:18) nor reducible to any particular specification of this or that codification or behavioral norms—although religions characteristically develop both myths and rituals into constituent components of ethical systems and liturgical norms.

Providing systems of recognizing one's universe in terms shared by one's progenitors and peers, myths and rituals share with highly developed artistic endeavors certain aesthetic values and capabilities for idealizing who one wishes to be, for projecting the possible selves one might become (either negatively, as roles to be avoided, or positively, in terms of models for self-development). Hence they function as agencies for release of emotional charges but also as agencies for learning the "something more" about human cultural desires and possibilities not often given full expression in the brilliant rationalism of our contemporary scientific worldview. Traditional materials such as myths, rituals, and folktales "occasion and mediate a transcendent contemplation of the world, the better to return with altered experience to the mundane and particular situation from which one took one's departure" (Jackson:97). That modern return to mythical forms, suggested Ellmann and Feidelson twenty years ago,

> is in part an attempt to reconstitute the value-laden natural environment that physical science has tended to discredit. At the same time, it is a repossession of a cultural heritage. Though history itself has produced the increasingly rational, disinherited mind of modern man, history may also be invoked as a non-rational mythical memory, a man-made record of men's intuitive conceptions of themselves. These mythical forms are still available because in another sense they are outside of history, residing in a timeless world below the threshold of consciousness. Myths are public and communicable, but they express subliminal mental patterns that come close to the compulsive drives of the unconscious. (617)

While it is true that our generation has been fascinated with the phallogocentric nature of the unconscious (fascination derives from *fascinus,* a bewitching amulet in the form of a phallus), more than one of our logocentrisms, our assumptions that "something out there" can be expressed directly in words have been shattered recently. I am not so sure but that the sway of our recourse to the unconscious may itself be attenuating, not so much due to the social-scientific turn to behavior as to our general-scientific refusal to ascribe positive valences to the unknowns that surround us.

If my approach throughout this book has been consistently "functionalist," in one or another way (although not in the reductive socio-functionalist manner reviewed in Chapter 2), this doubtless reflects my own secular or nondeistic orientation. Myths and rituals may disguise or reveal reality, as the society defines it; but I do not think myths and rituals ultimately are comprehended merely on the basis of an acting out of unconscious drives or of a great vague store of unconscious submental drives. There is great wisdom in Heinrich Dörrie's reminder (115) that myth in the classical world was not a function of the unconscious but precisely of the conscious aspect of culture. Myth was specifically a tool of *paideia,* that broadly inclusive transmission of culture the Greeks incorporated in all their social institutions, not just "education" (see Jaeger's brilliant and thorough exposition).

Our love of those hermeneutics of deceit that claim to uncover hidden meanings in everything; our implicit assumptions (due, of course, largely to Freud and Marx) that every social activity cloaks underlying psychic or social forces; and our naive trust in the exhaustiveness of modern science, which attempts to explain *everything*—these have left us predisposed to ascribe a "cause," any "reasonable cause," to more, perhaps, of the human experience than is possible. Psychological approaches no less than any others need to be proofed rigorously with the pragmatic yeast-test that asks about specific historical contexts of explanations and does not, at the same time, shirk questions of ontological sufficiency. My judgment is that most of the psychological leads I have discussed in this chapter remain just that: leads, segments of a comprehensive mythographic approach, but not satisfactory methods in and of themselves.

Myth Criticism in Literary Analysis

6

Myth is in one sense simply a body of knowledge consisting of collections of myths, of detailed knowledge of myths, and of investigation into the narrative, linguistic, and historical particulars of these myths. In another sense, myth is assumed to be a creative process, a mode of the imagination usually directed toward art or literature. And in a third sense, myth is seen, by the romantics especially, to have a religious quality; myth becomes a way of redeeming modern man and restoring him to his early simplicity—his original and primeval union with God and nature.

Burton Feldman and Robert D. Richardson,
The Rise of Modern Mythology

MOST OF THE CHAPTERS IN THIS BOOK COULD BE expanded into separate monographs, and that is certainly the case with respect to literary criticism focused on myth texts, criticism that has viewed fiction, poetry, and drama as portraying mythological patterns, and an analytic that is itself an elaborate myth, namely the impressive contributions of Northrop Frye.

My first task will be to develop a perspective on the development of myth-lit-crit, as it sometimes is abbreviated, and that perspective will provide occasion for sketching the many different meanings "mythological criticism" may convey. Some methods, for example, concentrate upon myth as the content of literature, and others treat myth as a sort of worldview, reflected within the structure and figuration of the literary work.

This chapter is intended more to provide an overview of a range of critical approaches within literary study than to document actual procedures used or to argue what myth-lit-crit "ought" to be. And I want to note that a critic who emphasizes mythological analysis within a department of comparative or English literature, say, would not necessarily appreciate being labeled a mythological literary critic; but for the purposes of this book, I shall pretend that there are "schools" of myth-lit-crit that can be differentiated and compared.

The chapter ends with discussion of some approaches that apply a critical view of mythological or ritualistic elements within contemporary society. Because we are dealing primarily with materials recorded or reported in such ways that they become "literature" almost by the fact of publication, there must be a certain arbitrariness to the topics selected for attention here and in Chapters 7 and 8. The critical mode of structuralism discussed in Chapter 7 has been deeply influential in literary criticism and especially in myth-lit-crit; and the critical mode of semiotics discussed in Chapter 8 likewise has touched literary criticism very deeply. Sections on "Transformation and Transmission of Mythic Materials" and on "Universalizing Fairy Tales and Myths," both in Chapter 8, are quite explicitly literary matters.

But the sequence of topics in this book frequently reflects a necessity to balance chapter lengths and relatively equal treatments of topics, and hence the reader may be alerted here once again to the fact that no single chapter in this book is intended to stand independently and that the mode of mythography argued here is a multiphasic, polyperspectival mode that depends upon a constant overlayering and comparison of approaches.

The Literary Importance of *The Golden Bough*

Self-conscious literary-critical analysis using reference to mythological and ritual patterns as its touchstone is very much an inheritance from what John B. Vickery has termed the literary impact of Sir James Frazer's *The Golden Bough*. It was Frazer's thirteen-volume work—itself an elaborately conceived literary enterprise—that brought about a literary-critical approach based on the awareness of mythic prototypes, archetypes, and mythic remnants in literature. Vickery provides a brief history of the wider nineteenth-century intellectual context in which Frazer's volumes were written (1973:chap. 1). Vickery's analysis leads one to feel that something like *The Golden Bough* was almost inherently necessary within its epoch, and we can appreciate how important it was that most of the proto-anthropologists of the nineteenth century were excellent literary stylists. Comparisons with Darwin and Freud, or with Durkheim, give us an indication of the ways in which the shaping of his materials into their unique literary format enabled Frazer's vast compilation to reach a much more widespread audience than contemporary ethnological materials ever achieve. (Hyman:427 notes that the successors of Frazer, as well as those of Darwin, Freud, and Marx, all write prose accessible only to scientific specialists. There is also the factor of the vastly expanded ethnographic context today, with literally thousands of studies, in contrast to the nineteenth-century situation, where *most* literate Europeans were soon familiar with Frazer's enterprise.)

Frazer's influence was not the sole component of a developing mythological criticism, of course—and it is important to view Frazer within the even broader context of nineteenth-century attention to mythology portrayed for instance in part 3 of Feldman and Richardson, *The Rise of Modern Mythology: 1680–1860* (1972). But clearly for the primarily British and American developments of mythological literary criticism I shall be reviewing, *The Golden Bough* provided the fountainhead. We also must take into consideration the later works of the philosophers Ernst Cassirer and Susanne K. Langer, who provided a broader theoretical grounding than Frazer's works did; but before turning to them, I will indicate briefly some of Frazer's specific impact.

Vickery (1973:chap. 3) patiently has tracked initial reactions to *The Golden Bough* through an impressive array of the disciplines of the humanities and social sciences, including psychology, anthropology and ethnography, classical studies, the history of religions, sociology, ethics, philosophy, and historical studies. Frazer's volumes were discussed in general journals and periodicals read by persons across the span of intellectual interests. It is with Frazer's influence in the study of literature, however, that Vickery primarily is concerned, and it is in this sphere that Vickery finds Frazer to have been "as fully seminal a mind as Freud or Marx" (105).

Frazer's own literary sophistication included structural techniques of composition, the use of rhetorical strategies for the rendering of the ironic and elegiac, artistic impersonality, and a cyclical mode of literary presentation that conveys an almost ritualistic quality.[1] *The Golden Bough,* as a matter of fact, is itself an enormous mythic cycle whose very careful artistic ordering was not destroyed even by Frazer's vacillations and changes in its various editions. Vickery calls it "less a compendium of facts than a gigantic romance of quest couched in the form of objective research." The work could be termed "a displaced quest romance," and Vickery suggests that "the myth underlying *The Golden Bough*—the myth beneath the myths, as it were—is that of Theseus and the Minotaur" (1973:128, 136, 135).[2]

But beyond its own literary qualities, which indeed left impressions upon much twentieth-century poetry and fiction, the several volumes of *The Golden Bough* and the subsequent one-volume abridgment had a wider influence upon both literature and literary criticism in terms of its contents (specific influences in modern poetry and fiction are traced in Vickery 1970). The care with which the work marshaled its array of cross-cultural behaviors, its insistence that mythic and ritualistic patterns have insinuated themselves into all aspects of daily life, and its intense preoccupation with the relativistic sanctioning of human acts within particular ethnological contexts, all provoked wider recognition of transpersonal factors in social behavior. In contrast to a positivist individualism that threatened to reduce biography to biology and culture to commerce, the work contributed to another strand of turn-of-the-century thought, namely the developing cultural pluralism that became so important in later reflections on the constitution of human culture.[3] Ironically enough, Frazer's influence upon twentieth-century anthropology—he claimed to be working primarily in social anthropology—has been less than impressive, perhaps because of what Edmund Leach calls his "remarkable intellectual isolation" and his repetitiveness (1961:374, 373, and 375, where Leach, in his bitter review, suggests that approximately 95 percent of Frazer's materials were simply reworkings of other scholars' findings).

One schema proposed by Frazer was especially attractive: he suggested that after prehistoric cultural specialization generated the role of the religious technician or magician, it further generated that of the priestly office, and finally that of the ultimate power-wielder, the king. This schema was an influential model in later attempts to explain social development as being a matter of progressive differentiation of social organization, combined with an increasing secularization of the social order (Goody 1977:20–21 gives examples and notes Durkheim's reactions).

Myth-and-Ritual Criticism

A second major contribution to twentieth-century literary criticism was that of the ritual-dominant school. Many similarities exist between this school and Frazer's approach, upon which it is largely dependent and with which it was approximately contemporary. As a direction within literary criticism, however, the myth-and-ritual approach is precisely what first comes to mind when the topic of mythological literary criticism is introduced in professional literary circles.

We seldom have an opportunity to study a volume of essays by one author that encompasses both his acceptance and application of a literary-critical method—in this case the myth-and-ritual approach—and his subsequent modifications and reservations about it. Herbert Weisinger, known especially for applying mythological criticism to Shakespearean literature, provides just such an opportunity in his *The Agony and the Triumph: Papers on the Use and Abuse of Myth* (1964; cf. Weisinger 1966; Moorman provides another example). The ritual-dominant pattern centering around the divine king's death and rebirth in his successor, and the rhythmic sequencing of seasonal rituals and personal-societal development transitions—all these rites, Weisinger suggests,

> repeat, each in its own way, the deep-rooted and abiding circle of death and rebirth. Not only do these rituals symbolize the passage from death to life, from one way of life to another, but they are the actual means of achieving the change-over; they mark the transition by which, through the processes of separation, regeneration, and the return on a higher level, both the individual and the community are assured their victory over the forces of chaos which are thereby kept under control. The purpose of these rituals is by enaction to bring about a just order of existence. . . . In the myth and ritual pattern, then, man has devised a mighty weapon by which he keeps at bay, and sometimes even seems to conquer, the hostile forces which endlessly threaten to overpower him. (1964:97–98)

The Hebraic-Christian adaptation of the pattern stresses the "dialectical leap from out of the endless circle onto a different and higher stage of understanding. But the crucial moment in this transformation of the myth and ritual pattern comes when man, by himself, undertakes on his own to make the leap . . . by making the leap, he makes himself" (98), and Weisinger finds here the seedbed of tragedy. "Tragedy therefore occurs when the accepted order of things is fundamentally questioned only to be the more triumphantly reaffirmed" (103); and such patterns can be sighted clearly in Shakespearean tragedies, most powerfully in the earlier and least effectively in the later plays.

Ritual-dominant analysis has provided Weisinger and others with an effective tool for comprehending the inner dynamics of the Shakespearean materials. However, the same critic remains committed to "ruthless self-criticism" and admits that there are ways in which the pattern may shout down the actual performance by an author.

Leslie A. Fiedler provides an example of another type of myth critic, one for whom the mythic is not as restricted to the particular ritual-dominant pattern of the king's fate and the seasons but represents more generally the ruling idea and image in a literary work. Fiedler uses the term Archetype to refer to the dominant thematic image in a work of literature, not in the Jungian sense to the generative archetypal matrix. Fiedler's Archetype can be a "technical or structural myth," "a plot configuration or a technical device with an archetypal meaning quite independent of any individual's conscious exploitation of it" (47). Literature is formed when Archetype and Signature are united by an author; Signature refers to "the joint product of 'rules' and 'conventions,' of the expectations of a community and the idiosyncratic responses of the individual poet, who adds a personal idiom or voice to a received style" (319).

Fiedler's distinction is a helpful one, but I find somewhat more accurate John J. White's use of the concept of *prefiguration* to designate the ruling, thematic aspects. Medieval literature could refer to typological signification in ways we no longer can; but in either case, the critic seeks to disclose an earlier figuration (motif, theme, image—corresponding roughly to Jung's archetypal image, not the archetype but the embodiment of its shaping force) whose analogic structuring provides a helpful way to appreciate the contours of its later antitype. White is especially helpful in warning against the proclivity of mythological literary criticism so to concentrate attention on the prefiguration as to slight the author's own unique reshapings (the stylistic results of what Fiedler calls Signature).

The danger is not unlike that of the early structuralist literary crit-icism that Claude Lévi-Strauss suggests is too often

> limited to a play of mirrors, in which it becomes impossible to distinguish the object from the symbolic image in the subject's consciousness. The work studied and the analyst's thought reflect each other, and we are deprived of any sense of sorting out what is simply received from the one and what the other puts into it. One thus becomes locked into a reciprocal relativism, which can be subjectively attractive but which does not seem to refer to any type of external evidence. (1976:275)

The most careful attempt to avoid such solipsism is to be found in William Righter's brief but excellent *Myth and Literature* (1975). Righter appreciates the way mythological literary criticism exposes the far-reaching resonances often found in literary works: "To see the myth beneath the surface of literature is to plunge one deeply into the human condition, and so to see the very way in which literature intensifies, concentrates, and reveals the human depths" (51). But Righter is very critical of the "vagueness" with which mythological literary critics have referred to the prefigurative mythologies. He notes the danger of the romantic recourse to allegorical suprasignification; and he cautions that the manner in which we present "ancient myths" often represents our contextualization of them within our own social consciousness, apart from their original contexts (55–56, 80). Righter's caution that "Far from containing any ready intelligibility they are remote, complex, mys-terious and opaque. Whatever clear-cut and accessible meaning they have is one that we have invented for them" (80) seems extreme, but it is an important caution. I would add to it that we must beware of taking a late compendium of myths from an earlier period—such as Apol-lodoros's *Library* or Ovid's *Metamorphoses*—as representative of the function or significance of those myths from the earlier culture that are being reworked.

The dangers become evident—the mythological literary critic may do the same violence to the actual authorial expression as may the Freudian critic or any critic who seeks to impose a prefiguration upon a text: "The opposite to the inviolable text is the notion of an inner text or sub-text that must be found beneath the surface of whatever words an author may have chosen to leave us, a text which liberates all of the finder's art" (Righter:65). The irony is deliberate: "the finder's art," not that of the author.

Similar criticism is voiced by René Wellek, for years considered the dean of American literary criticism, in a quotation that also provides us with an appreciation of myth-lit-crit's appropriate focus upon content and theme as opposed to the emphasis upon poetic mechanism practiced by the earlier New Critics:

> In the United States myth criticism may be described as the most successful attempt to replace the New Criticism. It allows, to put it bluntly, the discussion of subject matter, of folklore, of themes and content that were slighted by the New Critics. The dangers of the method are obvious: the boundary lines between art and myth and even art and religion are obliterated. An irrationalistic mysticism reduces all poetry to a conveyor of a few myths: rebirth and purification. After decoding each work of art in these terms, one is left with a feeling of futility and monotony. (360–61)

Part of the problem may be stated in yet another way, with respect to variations from critic to critic of the way the critical terminology has been used. "Myth," "mythic," "mythical," and "mythological" have been utilized very much as the individual critic has desired, and often nonreflectively (J. White 1972 demonstrates that the confusion exists in criticism in English, French, and German). Doubtless an analytic mutually influenced by a number of nonliterary disciplines almost necessarily will entail such terminological confusion during its inception. But in surveying several recent textbooks intended to clarify myth-lit-crit, I find that the problem is still quite prevalent.

It is not my assignment to clarify these concepts for use in literary criticism, however, and I turn instead to mention of the influence of the mythicosymbolist writings of Ernst Cassirer and Susanne K. Langer upon literary criticism, and then to the monomythic theories of Campbell, Frye, and Graves.

Mythicosymbolism and Monomythicism

However it be defined, contemporary literary interest in myth indicates an emphasis upon content in addition to literary form, quite in contrast to the Aristotelian *mythos,* which referred essentially to the formal sequence of thematic units (*topoi*) or to what subsequently was called plot (see the brief but helpful discussion by Scholes and Kellogg:26–28). Attention to myths or mythic prefigurations provided a means of broadening the scope of literary analysis, or rather of recognizing the broadly humanistic aspects of literary criticism that go beside and beyond formal literary analysis.

The works of Ernst Cassirer and of Susanne K. Langer, who expanded

Cassirer's position on myth into a general aesthetics, were influential in the 1950s and 1960s largely because they provided a philosophical means by which to relate symbolic form and symbolic—mythic—content. Cassirer, for example, suggested that the primal human experiencing of the cosmos and its articulation were inseparable. Discursive logic and creative imagination subsequently came to be differentiated, but, in the primary realm of mythic conception, distinctions between subject and object, between logic and metaphor, do not apply. The language-ing act expresses the union; it does not (primally) merely talk "about" an experience, but it "is" that experience:

> Whatever has been fixed by a name, henceforth is not only real, but is Reality. The potential between "symbol" and "meaning" is resolved; in place of a more or less adequate "expression," we find a relation of identity, of complete congruence between "image" and "object," between the name and the thing. (Cassirer 1946:32; overview and critique of Cassirer in Verene, with bibliog.; in Montagu; and in Langer 1949)

It was to be in the "intuitive creative forms of myth" (Cassirer 1946:34) that the original conceptions of language were to be found: "all verbal structures appear as *also* mythical entities, endowed with certain mythical powers . . . the Word, in fact, becomes a sort of primary force, in which all being and doing originate" (45). Language, art, and myth form the differentiated "triad of independent modes of spiritual creativity"; and the way back to the regeneration of primal creativity is "achieved as language becomes an avenue of artistic expression" (98).

Langer's *Philosophy in a New Key* (1941) portrayed the excitement Cassirer's work provided when it led to the understanding that all the humanistic disciplines collaborate, ultimately, upon the symbolic dimension of human existence (cf. 1953; on Cassirer, Langer, and Wilbur M. Urban, see Wimsatt and Brooks:699–708). The works of Cassirer and Langer were highly stimulating to the literary critics, whose work suddenly appeared to represent the elucidation and appreciation of a primary mode of human symbolizing, and to the artist, whose works were elevated, considered now not as the surplus fantasy products of an otherwise economically productive humankind but as the elemental productions of a trained creativity that might directly express fundamental human experiences. It would not be an exaggeration to regard many of the best midcentury graphics and literary works as attempting to give form and voice to a primal creativeness that was felt to have been buried by the predominance of the supreme "discursive logic," modern science.

The mythicosymbolist position remained somewhat too vague with respect to the actual primal or contemporary shapings of the resulting metaphoric expressions. We turn to the more specifically delineated monomyths of Joseph Campbell, Robert Graves, and Northrop Frye, whose works can be seen in this context as attempts to carry forward the recovery of primal power, but in the context of specific literary shapings of a more delimited range of mythical frameworks.

Campbell's writings are referred to frequently in mythological literary criticism, but the manner of reference suggests that his works have had importance more as resources for comprehending a wide range of mythological perspectives than as contributions to a methodological posture. Exceptions would be his statements about the types of myths I reviewed in Chapter 1, his Freudian and Jungian leanings, and the analytical section on the "monomyth" of the hero, in *The Hero with a Thousand Faces* (1968b:30–36; Leeming provides a collection of myth texts illustrating Campbell's pattern). Campbell was a member of the Sarah Lawrence College literature faculty, and his interests in the formal literary qualities of his materials are especially well demonstrated in his early *A Skeleton Key to Finnegans Wake* (Campbell and Robinson) and in volume 4 of the Masks of God (*Creative Mythology,* 1968a).

Campbell's more recent work, *The Mythic Image* (1975), presents a sort of monomythicism of its own, finding in Kundalini yoga a master key to religious meaning. But the most important type of mono-mythicism associated with this mythographer's name is surely his account of the *separation-initiation-return* pattern of the career of the classical hero, what Campbell refers to as "the nuclear unit of the monomyth" (1968b:30): "A hero ventures forth from the world of common day into a region of supernatural wonder: fabulous forces are there encountered and a decisive victory is won: the hero comes back from this mysterious adventure with the power to bestow boons on his fellow man." Campbell thus presents a simple, easily graphed cycle, with great analytical power—as he exemplifies with many accounts of heroic figures from a wide range of cultures, East and West. Campbell's cycle has been an analytical tool for literally hundreds of secondary studies, for it takes analysis of the heroic pattern much further than Raglan's or Rank's statistical accountings of the motif. Few modern studies have had quite as wide an influence.

One of the most compelling accounts of a monomythic pattern from more recent scholarship is the account of "the American monomyth" written by Robert Jewett and John Lawrence (1977a). An exceptionally acute reading of contemporary American mass-media values and themes, the work argues that there has been a marked shift from the classical monomyth of the hero analyzed by Campbell, a shift attributed to the American historical experience and to religious popularism.

The American monomyth is, in fact, a secularizing of Judeo-Christian redemption dramas, and the heroic figure becomes a replacement for the Christ figure of traditional Christianity. This hero (or some feminine transforms such as Heidi and Mary Poppins in their American man-ifestations) is motivated by selflessness, not by the quest for self of the classical pattern; he operates outside the traditional context of the estab-lished social community, and he is a frontiersman-defender of a hypo-thetical Eden that surfaces most directly in the stereotype of the typical Midwestern small town.

The sexuality of this American monomythic hero is "segmented," which means basically that he never engages in sexually fulfilling ac-tivities, or at best he simply gratifies needy and clamorous women (à la *Playboy*'s sexual ethic, which Jewett and Lawrence analyze very skillfully by contrasting the expressed "philosophy" of the magazine with its ico-nic photography). Certainly this hero seldom has the satisfaction of the *hieros gamos,* the sacred marriage of the successful classical hero that symbolizes his bringing together successfully the natural and the social order. But the American hero is an outsider, and he leaves the communi-ty after helping it repel "outside agitators"; he appears magically as a fantasy projection of cool and clever purity who knows how to use violence properly on the side of the American Way, but who is never crushed by Evil nor sullied by the empty beer bottles and dirty diapers of ordinary life.

There is in fact a great deal of pathology in this model, one fed by a growing distrust of the City and the Government (three recent presi-dents of the nation have referred to our capital city as a seedbed of evil and monstrous depravity [Jewett and Lawrence 1977a:221 and notes]) and fed by a refusal to trust participatory democracy any further than the town school board. The outsider:insider motif (civilized:barbarian, as discussed in my notes on the "primitive," Doty 1981a) is a simplistic way of dealing with the complex imbrications of a modern technological society, but the American monomyth repeatedly has supported ad-herence to the most chiliastic of modern apocalyptic movements, move-ments that hold out little hope for betterment of the present situation, vesting all hopes in a cataclysmic return to a restored American Eden. The monomyth has these features: "A community in a harmonious paradise is threatened by evil: normal institutions fail to contend with this threat: a selfless superhero emerges to renounce temptations and carry out the redemptive task: aided by fate, his decisive victory restores the community to its paradisal condition: the superhero then recedes into obscurity" (Jewett and Lawrence 1977b:xx).

Jewett and Lawrence amply document the features of this pattern as conveyed by popular films, comic strips, and novels; the work is an excellent account of mythic materials functioning in contemporary society (the authors' "technomythic critical theory" will be discussed in a later chapter). Several related essays have applied their theses to additional materials (1968, 1976, 1977b, 1979) and a revision of *The American Monomyth* is in production; I would also call attention to Jewett 1973 and 1979, which are equally valuable in terms of analyzing the depth of religious dimensions within contemporary society.

Robert Plant Armstrong has argued for a "mythoform" that he considers the "ground" and "anterior condition to specific myths and cultural expressions. It operates behind particular relationships to the world, anterior to time and space" (96–97) but as the "vital, operative principle of culture" and the "generative principle of culture" (126), in a manner quite similar to Jung's archetypes (102–10). However, Jung, like Susanne K. Langer, was determined by the exclusively European aesthetic and worldview (as Armstrong shows by contrast in an exposition of Yoruba materials), which lead to an emphasis upon creative individuality and dialectic separation rather than an additive repetition of well-known forms (148).

Certainly more monomythical in perspective than Campbell, Jewett and Lawrence, or Armstrong, the mythographic works of the poet and novelist Robert Graves center around his conception of the White Goddess of Birth, Love, and Death. His "historical grammar of poetic myth" emphasizes northern European materials stemming from an early matrilineal culture held to predate the Greeks and reflecting directly "grave records of ancient religious customs or events" (1966). *The Greek Myths* (1960), Graves's massive compendium, is our most inclusive English-language handbook and remains valuable due to his exhaustive compilation of variants—the work is a modern-day parallel to the *Library* of Apollodoros—and to his clear organization and index. The compiler's own historiographic perspectives come through in the commentaries: the Greek materials are recoded into what Graves considers the earlier historical strata of goddess worship organized into yearly cycles. The perspective has not found wide acceptance, and one tires rather quickly of reading about a supposed subservience to the Goddess of nearly every Greek male deity as temporary king, and of his standby "tanist." Graves's own ritual-dominant positions are clear in his introduction: "True myth may be defined as the reduction to narrative shorthand of ritual mime performed on public festivals." "If some myths are baffling at first sight," Graves suggests, this is due to iconotrophy, the resulting condition when "the mythographer has accidentally or deliberately misinterpreted a sacred picture or a dramatic rite" (1960:12, 21).

Graves's influence is hard to calculate, although I find the *The White Goddess* is widely known among persons interested in fields we today lump together as "the occult." Far greater self-consciously literary-critical attention has been given to Frye's mythological archetypology, and it is to his monomythicism that I now turn.

Northrop Frye's Myth

The complexity of Frye's *Anatomy of Criticism* (1957) makes difficult any attempt to portray the full dimensions of his mythical or archetypal criticism. His schemata for such criticism are most elaborated in that book, but the book encompasses much more than an approach to mythical aspects of literature. The proposals made there with respect to genre criticism, for instance, are in themselves an important contribution to literary criticism. There is the further problem that the many applications of Frye's typology do not necessarily reflect Frye's own intentions. In fact Frye carefully disclaims any intention to found a "school" of myth criticism, and one suspects that the frequent use of his typology reflects more a desperation on the part of those seeking to compile useful materials for myth-and-literature anthologies than Frye's own confidence that he has found the master monomyth.[4]

Frye has suggested that there are four basic ways in which literature may be imaged and developed, and it is this central pattern that has been so influential. A summary from a book of essays published after his *Anatomy of Criticism* will illustrate the unifying system: "Myth seizes on the fundamental element of design offered by nature—the cycle, as we have it daily in the sun and yearly in the seasons—and assimilates it to the human cycle of life, death, and . . . rebirth" (1963:32). Such a natural cycle provides forms for literary works; it structures them, or Frye can say it is their archetype, adding yet another reference for this word: "The myth is the central informing power that gives archetypal significance to the ritual and archetypal narrative to the oracle. Hence the myth *is* the archetype, though it might be convenient to say myth only when referring to narrative, and archetype when speaking of significance" (1963:15).

Very much as Cassirer could state that myth and language were coterminous, Frye can speak of myth and narrative being so: "because myths are stories, what they 'mean' is inside them, in the implications of their incidents" (32); and insofar as mythology is a "total structure," it is "the matrix of literature" (33):

> The structural principles of a mythology[,] built up from analogy and identity, become in due course the structural principles of literature. The absorption of the natural cycle into mythology provides myth with two of these structures[:] the rising movement that we find in myths of spring or the dawn, of birth, marriage and resurrection, and the falling movement in myths of death, metamorphosis, or sacrifice.The movements reappear as the structural principles of comedy and tragedy in literature. Again, the dialectic in myth that projects a paradise of heaven above our world and a hell or place of shades below it reappears in literature as the idealized world of pastoral and romance and the absurd, suffering, or frustrated world of irony and satire. (33–34)

Four basic patterns may be derived; Frye develops these in the third essay in *Anatomy of Criticism* and has continued to refine his typology (see especially 1970:chaps. 12 and 13; and see 1976). The brief table in "The Archetypes of Literature" will serve to summarize the phases here (1963:16).

1. The dawn, spring and birth phase. Myths of the birth of the hero, of revival and resurrection, of creation and (because the four phases are a cycle) of the defeat of the powers of darkness, winter and death. Subordinate characters: the father and the mother. The archetype of romance and of most dithyrambic and rhapsodic poetry.
2. The zenith, summer, and marriage or triumph phase. Myths of apotheosis, of the sacred marriage, and of entering into Paradise. Subordinate characters: the companion and the bride. The archetype of comedy, pastoral and idyll.
3. The sunset, autumn and death phase. Myths of fall, of the dying god, of violent death and sacrifice and of the isolation of the hero. Subordinate characters: the traitor and the siren. The archetype of tragedy and elegy.
4. The darkness, winter and dissolution phase. Myths of the triumph of these powers; myths of floods and the return of chaos, of the defeat of the hero, and Götterdämmerung myths. Subordinate characters: the ogre and the witch. The archetype of satire.

Frye's analytic has been subjected to such extensive criticism that it seems purposeless to take that approach here (see for example Krieger;

Feder 1980). Much as I suggested that Freud's analytic is treated rewardingly as mythology, however, a similar approach may be suggested here.[5] Frye has attempted a vast typology of genres for the correlation and interrelation of world literature. His underlying monomyth of the seasons (not entirely dissimilar to T. H. Gaster's approach in *Thespis*, discussed in Chapter 3) is apparently mythic insofar as it functions to provide a totalistic explanation of literary production. I am not as negatively disposed toward the enterprise as are most contemporary critics, perhaps because I find it salutory to begin the literary-critical activity with some such classificatory framework, especially one that encompasses correlation between literary genres and mythological contents and structures. Any myth as such may be used to generate a too rigid stratification of reality. The most useful way to avoid such strictures is to recognize them and then to proceed to the Signature of the particular literary work at hand. Schemata such as Frye's provide possible ways of explicating the interrelations of our literary traditions, but they cannot function as an exhaustive noetic straitjacket, if for no other reason than because the literary work remains imaginal as well as intellectual, and if its own rightful aesthetic autonomy is fully honored, it will always demand to be understood, finally, on its own terms. As one of the "codes" underlying a text, the mythic is one of the cultural semantic structuring constraints, but the text itself is not nearly comprehended when that code has been clarified.

Mythological literary criticism is no longer a widely influential school of criticism. When it was, it seems to have been tied to the suggestion that the presence of a mythological motif necessarily means that earlier instances of that theme represent the best resource for understanding the later work. It remains, however, a lively component of a complex and robust criticism that is aware of possible prefigurative aspects in a literary work, and it does not hesitate to explore the ways those prefigurations may have enriched the author's expression or the reader's comprehension of it. I would suggest that the following relationships between myths and literary works may prevail:

1. A myth, or mythic themes, images, and characters, may prefigure the development of a later author's writing; here the focus will be upon tracing the ways the actual myth/themes/and so forth are found in the later work, whether directly or by transformation. (Cf. Thomas Mann's use of the figure of Hermes.)
2. Mythic themes, figures, or stories may have a more indirect influence upon the later work, suggesting the names of particular characters,

for instance, names that trail long wakes of associations but are not further related to the prototypes whose names they carry. (Cf. John Barth's *Chimera.*)

3. The plot pattern of a myth or legend (here I follow the usual distinction by which legend refers to a mythic story about a historical person or event) may be influential in the shaping of the plot of a later work. As an interior shaping device, the pattern may or may not be explicitly identified as mythical, that is, as referring to any specific mythological system. (Cf. the many fictional transforms of the Christ figura.)

4. Later works may retell mythological stories, or myths, or legends, explicitly intending the later work to be a contemporary adaptation of the earlier. (Cf. Mary Renault's novels retelling legends about Theseus and Alexander.) (For summaries, see Feder 1980:53; Strelka:vii; J. White 1980:72.)

John Vickery's recent *Myths and Texts* (1983) is the most comprehensive and subtle treatment of the ways various mythic plots, themes, and names surface in modern authors, especially D. H. Lawrence and James Joyce.

Mythic Figures in Literature

In addition to surveys of mythic figures and themes across a whole range of literature, a number of monographs have traced just one figure.[6] Psychological interest in the figures of Narkissos and Oidipous (Latinized: Narcissus and Oedipus) has led to more studies of these two figures than any others, and full bibliography for each doubtless would run to hundreds of pages. My focus here is upon analyses of mythic figures as literary themes, and I will mention only works with that specific focus.

Narkissos found a splendid chronicler in Louise Vinge, whose work on the classical sources gives original language versions with translations and then extends into the influence of the figure down into the early nineteenth century. Contemporary analysts of culture suggest that the psychological phenomenon of narcissism is the major psychopathology of the present, although already in 1956 Grace Stuart found it to be a major problem, and Paul Zweig traces the pain of "I-saying" and the image of the mirroring of the self in sources as diverse as ancient Gnosticism, medieval lyrics, Kierkegaard, and de Toqueville. The figure in literature has been prominent especially in Europe, in realizations by Wilde, Valéry, Gide, Rilke, Hesse, Dostoevski, Spitteler, Kafka, Mann, and Musil. Some of these authors have written more than one work with a Narkissos theme.

Both Sigmund Freud and Claude Lévi-Strauss focused upon the figure of Oidipous, and both the psychoanalyst's treatment and the anthropologist's have alerted literary critics to this theme. One of the most comprehensive treatments, including dramatic texts along with analytical essays, is Kallich, MacLeisch, and Schoenbohm, *Oedipus: Myth and Drama* (1968). Freud's chance viewing of a classical play and his subsequent use of the Oidipous figure for his own hypothetical construct has been criticized as inaccurate to Sophokles (see among others, Dörrie 1980:114–15; and Vernant and Vidal-Naquet 1981:chap. 4), but then Terence Turner (1969) is no less critical of Lévi-Strauss's structural analysis of the mytheme. (Additional bibliography: R. Smith:155–56.)

Both Herakles and Odysseus have exerted powerful literary influences, well chronicled in each case by G. K. Galinsky and W. B. Stanford. Galinsky emphasizes the extreme complexity of the classical representations of Herakles and suggests that it was precisely this complexity, and a related lack of an orthodox or canonical account of Herakles' exploits, that allowed the mythic figure to be variously conceived and realized in literature. Stanford devotes more of his study to classical accounts, and subsequently much less to modern realizations of Odysseus, but his insights on Homer make his study very profitable. His remarks on Joyce and Kazantzakis are brief but acute. A subsequent volume (Stanford and Luce) includes the Odysseus/Ulysses/Ulixes figure in the plastic and graphic arts.

Patricia Merivale's study of the changing literary faces of Pan stresses the tensions inherent in this figure: she contrasts the benevolent and the sinister Pan figures and argues that Pan is a crucial factor in the thought-world of D. H. Lawrence. James Hillman expands the image of Pan, not by tracking literary realizations, but by correlating the figure with a wide range of psychological factors.

The last three chapters of *The Quest for Theseus* (1970, edited by Anne G. Ward) include treatments of later literary realizations of Theseus, although strangely enough Mary Renault's popular but influential works receive slight attention. A wide-ranging collection of essays on Orpheus edited by John Warden is full of insights and is exceedingly well written. Although there have been several studies now of goddess figures (Friedrich; Downing 1981; Spretnak 1978; Stone), we lack studies of female mythic models that trace the models in modern literature the way male heroes and gods have been traced (the best bibliography of works tracing influences and motifs from the classics remains Highet:550–55; Simpson is also valuable).

Literary Criticism of Native American Materials

One large body of mythological materials, those of the Native North American peoples, is only now beginning to receive critical attention comparable to that long granted to figures from European and Ancient Near Eastern antiquity. As long ago as 1911, the great linguist Franz Boas complained that interpretations of the mythology, religion, and social culture of Native American peoples were being made by ethnologists who proposed "to elucidate the innermost thoughts and feelings of a people without so much as a smattering of knowledge of their language" (in Holder:56). Boas compared the situation to study of Eastern culture by someone who could neither speak nor read Chinese or Japanese, or to the study of antiquity by someone with no facility in the classical languages: that person's observations would carry little authority. Seventy years later we are not much advanced in terms of specialists in the fifty-four families of Amerindigen languages, and thousands of surviving native speakers have died. This is an astonishing situation whereby the dominant culture has ignored the mythological richness of an entire continent and has continued to treat the beginnings of the land's literary traditions only from the perspectives of the transplanted European materials of "New England."

A few ethnologists and literary specialists have learned Amerindigen languages sufficiently to be able to recognize native categories of expression (Paul Radin; Dennis Tedlock for the Zuni; Barre Toelken and Gary Witherspoon for the Navajo), and some Native North Americans have become prominent interpreters of their own native materials (Alfonso Ortiz, N. Scott Momaday). But the concept of an anthology of Amerindigen literature in which native speakers edit the materials of their own ancient and modern culture seems only now to have become a reality, in an issue of *Sun Tracks: An American Indian Literary Series* published at the University of Arizona and reissued in 1980 as *The South Corner of Time*, edited by Larry Evers and others. Here each tribal literature is introduced by a phonetic alphabet, and many of the selections are bilingual. The main editor's brief bibliographic recommendations are excellent, but it is striking how few technical literary studies are available.

Karl Kroeber has introduced and edited a small collection of essays that focus on linguistic and literary-critical interpretations. The essays (by Kroeber, Jarold Ramsey, Tacheeni Scott, Dennis Tedlock, Barre Toelken, and Dell Hymes) stress the stylistic sophistication of the texts analyzed and prove that it is our unfamiliarity with Amerindigen literary conventions that has led us to assume that much of North American native mythology was naive and simple: "It is our scholarship, not Indian literature, which is 'primitive' or undeveloped" (K. Kroeber 1981:9); in a later essay D. Tedlock notes that materials earlier classed as "primitive" may now well be classed as "poetic" (1983:71). Other essays in the volume edited by Kroeber demonstrate the sorts of criticism that may be accessible to someone who does not have full linguistic competence, but Barre Toelken, in publishing his third successive version of a set of Navajo materials (Toelken and Scott 1981) provides a healthy caution to the critic who feels she or he finally "has it right."

Abraham Chapman's introduction to his reader, *Literature of the American Indians* (1975), observes that although we now could cull from various sources many thousands of volumes of Native North American literature, "*native American* literature" has meant, in almost every treatment of British and American literature, the literature produced by the Christian Europeans who settled primarily along the northeastern seaboard. Chapman's book samples a wide range of literary criticism of North American Indian literature, mostly written early in this century, and includes both negative and positive analyses of such recent works as Hyemeyohsts Storm's *Seven Arrows* and Jerome Rothenberg's "total translations" (the introduction and first chapter of Astrov would have been a valuable addition; and now see Witherspoon). Elémira Zolla provides a literary history of the various images of the American Indian in non-Indian literature, with one chapter on "Indian Literature" as such (see also Keiser, somewhat dated but still useful). Texts and essays in *Alcheringa: Ethnopoetics* (an excellent periodical that survived from 1970–80) and in scattered literary journals augment literary-critical treatment of Amerindigen materials, but a turn toward the indigenous mythological materials treated with full literary-critical expertise is just beginning (see especially Rothenberg 1969 and 1972; Tedlock 1980 and 1983; and Bierhorst 1974, 1975, and 1976 are excellent).

The publication in 1983 of *Smoothing the Ground: Essays on Native American Oral Literature* (Swann), and brief notes and bibliographies in SAIL (*Studies in American Indian Literatures,* edited by Karl Kroeber at Columbia University) indicate that Native American literature, including its mythological materials considered properly *as* literature, is beginning to receive wider and more sustained critical attention. Krupat's 1982 essay in *Critical Inquiry,* besides developing a Marxian analysis of the "mode of production of the text," raises many important issues about Native American "literature" that have surfaced in the poststructuralist, deconstructionist, circles I will discuss in the next two chapters.

Mythicity and the Modern/Postmodern

Recent essays within literary criticism, as exemplified for instance in the collection edited by Strelka in 1980, play through most of the methods and themes of myth-lit-crit we have seen above. There is perhaps more critical distance—ritual-dominant essays are now lacking, and wider mythological issues take their place: Haskell Block writes about "the myth of the artist," or specific classical authors are described in terms of their shaping by mythological themes (Adolf on Rilke, Dresden on Mann, Weinberg on Mallarmé). Lillian Feder notes that the work of Elizabeth Sewell broadens her own earlier studies (see Feder 1980, referring to Feder 1971) and that modern poetic exploration of mythical figures has become largely a comparison of the psychological and symbolic expressions of the earlier cultural mythologies with the expressions and needs of the present. And John J. White expands his earlier (1972) work on prefiguration by referring to recent reader-response criticism, following Stanley Fish; in this way he is able to demonstrate the sorts of prefigural expectations James Joyce may have utilized and to argue that Roland Barthes's *S/Z* (1974) is "the most elaborate model for exploring the impact of prefigurations upon the reading process to date" (1980:83). Finally I may mention the first chapter of Frank Lentricchia's *After the New Criticism* (1980), which is devoted to a finely developed criticism of the mythographic work of Northrop Frye, relating it to philosophical and poetic issues both in literary New Criticism and in post-Saussurean analysis as a whole.

Generally, however, there have been few recent book-length studies informed by mythological literary criticism, making Eric Gould's *Mythical Intentions in Modern Literature* (1981) all the more noteworthy. An extremely dense work, demanding absolute concentration as Gould constructs his arguments from across a wide range of contemporary criticism (literary, psychological, historical, and philosophical), the book illustrates its principles in just three writers, James Joyce, D. H. Lawrence, and T. S. Eliot. Yet the work strikes me as one of the most significant studies yet to have dealt with mythological aspects of modern literature and, I would say, with postmodern literature as well. It sets out ways of refining a poetics that should be applicable not only across the range of literature but beyond (I shall return in Chapter 8 to some of the implications of *Mythical Intentions* for philosophical and religious issues).

Gould does not set forth from study of particular mythic patterns or myths, for he treats myth as "reasonable structure rather than repeatable motif" (181); he likewise avoids the snares of formalist or functionalist definitions, both of which have tended to become bogged down in diachronic historicisms and have left us with so many floating elements in a definition of myth that it "is now so encyclopedic a term that it means everything or nothing" (5). Myth is still immensely important in modern literature but in a "dissipated" form: "it is abstracted to a sophistication that only literature can handle" (134; in italics in original).

Gould's concentration is upon the nature of the mythic, or what he terms *mythicity,* upon "the ontological status of myth as part of a general theory of human expression" (3), and that will mean an intensely synchronic concentration upon what remains "essential" about the mythic today. The work concentrates as well upon the ways language is implicated in human expression, as it attempts to span that perennial gap between event/s and meaning/s. Mythic discourse (whether it appears in materials traditionally defined as mythic, or in modern/postmodern literature) represents one human project to close this ontological gap, and mythic expression seems essential when it aims at universal symbolic meanings that compromise the impossibility of closing the gap, functioning both as compromise or temporalization and as hypothesis. "It is the nature of language itself to be symbolic, and the nature of myth to be the rhetoric of that attempt" (14).

The vast significance of the Heideggerian negativity about essential Being comes to the fore constantly: it is the grounding of the sense of closure within language as a stopgap that needs constant interpretation and reinterpretation. Events and meanings are never coterminous: "We have no meaning without interpretive processes, given the perennial failure of verbal expression to be adequate to experience and to be an adequate naming of the world" (7); consequently "The nature of the mythic . . . must have something to do with semiotics and interpretation theory" (7). And that insight—the intimate interlocking between mythic expression and interpretation—leads Gould to discussion of contemporary semiotics, which "must appear to the historically minded as one aspect of the growth-into-consciousness through language which is part of the romantic revival of myth" (7).

As we have seen in an earlier chapter, Gould rejects the "essentialist theory of the archetypes" represented by Carl Jung because it leaves the primordial event/s somewhere back "behind language," somewhere uninterpretable and hence inexpressible. Gould is likewise critical of the "applied Jungianism" of Northrop Frye (25); both Jung and Frye ulti-

188 • Myth Criticism in Literary Analysis

mately develop only "a kind of impressionism of the unconscious . . . which takes too much for granted about the interpretive process" (28).

Gould wishes to retain "archetype" in critical discussion, not as an essentialist notion, but rather as a function of the open-endedness of discourse (55); it is "a sign open to repeated signification rather than a closed and objective fact," a "transactional fact" (125; cf. 64)—that is, "a representation of experience resulting itself from the quite distinct intent to make an interpretation of the world" (33). Hence archetype is part of a signifying system, not something that itself has an absolute subject or center (36, citing Derrida); we may speak of myth's "allegory of intent," "its exemplary function of intending-to-interpret" (34; cf. 212, "the motive for allegory is the motive for myth").

What is to be interpreted is the Other, that which is not present, that which is concealed; myth heightens the human linguistic experience by pointing to itself and to the paradox of language that attempts to close the meaning:event gap yet can never include fully the Other or the Nothing that is the predicate of what we do know or experience. Myth is "a working proposition, an unfolding of understanding which persuades us of its logic" (44)—or myth is a metaphoric mode of knowing and expressing that bridges the "outside" and the "inside" of my experience in such a way as to give temporary voice to a meaning that can serve as a semantical structure as well as a semiotic organizing principle. Mythic narratives represent "exemplary versions of how that [ontological] gap *might* be filled" (54) just as metaphor seeks to be a totalizing metonym even while it remains a trope that is at best a temporizing adjustment device.

The archetype remains a proleptic device: it provides an externalized mode of expression or interpretation for the interior meanings we have found, and the mythic discourse expresses the potentiality of language to bring forth into the everyday the interior meanings we have found useful in living with the ontological gap. Hence Gould has derived the nature of myth from the conditions of interpretation and the archetypal motif can be seen as "a triggering device for interpretation which will lead us to some understanding of the absent element in knowledge" (69).

That absent element—traditionally, "the unconscious"—comes around as the object for the subject's desire; in Lacan's terms, the unconscious is that discourse that has escaped from the subject's conscious control. Language itself is similarly an indication of a lack, a way of closing the gap between desire and object or between a sign and its referent, and substitution of one sign for another within a system of differences becomes the basis for the meanings that sustain us from period to period. Myth "is not allowed to be a translinguistic fact" in Gould's enterprise but has its essential feature in "an exhilarating play of nihilation and authenticity" because of its nature as a linguistic fact, as the site within which our self-constructions take place before the possibility of naming that Other, the Nothingness, that is created by language itself (Gould:86, summary statement).

Gould suggests that "insofar as we rely on fictions to make sense of our world, and indeed, on the inadequacies of language to explain the inexplicable" (11), mythicity is as alive for contemporary persons as for the pretechnological societies idealized by many students of myth. Literature and myth exist on a sort of continuum, "by virtue of their function as language: myth tends to a literary sense of narrative form, and fictions aspire to the status of myth" (11). Attention to the key figures for Gould's study, Joyce, Lawrence, and Eliot, clarifies the parallels between the ontological functions of modern literature and traditional mythological functioning: "mythicity is no less modern than it is ancient . . . it is preserved in the gap which has always occasioned it, through our attempts symbolically to represent and give meaning to our place in the world through discourse. Insofar as literature preserves the fullness of that intent, then it preserves mythicity" (12). The traditional-mythic and the contemporary-literary constitute a pairing that Gould makes upon a very different basis than traditional myth-lit-crit has preferred; but it is a pairing that suggests not that "fiction is no longer mythic" so much as that fiction (literature in general) functions for us the way mythological narratives have functioned for traditional societies.

We will see in the final chapter of this book that such a view has a great deal of importance for definitions of the sacred as well: I would argue, and I believe Gould would join me, that the best way to approach religious language is along a continuum of fictive expression that stretches from the metaphoric nature of all linguistic naming all the way to the scientific datum—the "fact" that is etymologically related to the "creative" author's "fiction" (both ultimately from *facere,* to construct or make).

What Gould does not do is to confuse myth and fiction: "The meaning of a fiction is always *potentially* mythic" (113, my emphasis); but the adverb is to be stressed—"it would be simple-minded . . . to say that all fictions are necessarily myths even if all myths are fictions" (113). "There would seem to be no absolute means of differentiating the narrative structure of myths and fictions" (115), a statement that resolves for me a conflict of long standing about the "narrative" nature of myths (see Chapter 1) and that summarizes Gould's negative response to Lévi-Strauss's suggestion about the entropic fall of the fictional plot in contemporary literature (95) as well as his acceptance of the analysis of Roland Barthes, who pointed out the ways in which received mythic terms and forms can themselves be revisioned, can become new signifiers in new realizations of their potential meanings (118–24).

If the aim of myth is that of literature— "to go on in some way forever giving meaning further meaning" (130)—then we also must attend to the role of the reader (a function analyzed in this country especially by Norman Holland and Stanley Fish; abroad and here, the works of German theorists Hans-Robert Jauss and Wolfgang Iser have been influential), inasmuch as "the reader . . . is after all myth-making in his reading as much as the writer in his writing" (Gould:142): the reader seeks to bring the text to a close also, the reader seeks to vest the particular text with mythic meaning that will close, for a time, the ontological gap, just what the metaphorician-writer sought (or the mythic economy sought) in the text's production.

Mythicity, as Gould develops the concept, giving a name for what seems self-evident only after it has been named by someone, is like any other condition for the narrative expression and experience: it is "born of the competition between the participants in the interpretive event, each caught in a metaphorical world seeking stability" (62). We have merely an endless series of homologies, a substitution of one objective signifier as the subject for *another* signifier (77–78): so that the meaning, as the personal subject (in Lacanian thought) is found only paradoxically, only in the Other, and "our fate is transacted in the *potential* spaces of language" (86).

Our search for a lost origin within writing is an impossible search for a nonlinguistic or prelinguistic essence that would have no meaning, no dialectical relation to a speaking subject. And modern literature portrays nothing if not the dialectical tensions between emptiness and fullness, the "constantly self-transforming sets of signs" that Gould finds in Joyce and Eliot, signs that "reveal the urge to discover reasonable and progressive form" (132). Joyce's logic of the pun, the epiphany, and the multilayered plot are reflections of myth's insistence "that reality is not static but a changing systematic" (12), and the works of Lawrence and Eliot disclose very hermeneutical attempts to replace the numinous within literary expression—demonstrating quite clearly their own mythical intentions.

As others have spoken of myth speaking through the mythmaker (most notably Lévi-Strauss, quoted in Chapter 7), Gould can speak of myth as revealing "logic making itself apparent" in plot; to speak of archetypal aspects of a novel is then to speak of the ways in which the novelist has been constrained into the transformational modes of mythic thought. If the logic that makes itself apparent in Joyce (and in other contemporary writers as well) resembles very little the traditional diachronic-developmental logics of the recent Western tradition, the reason may well lie in the fact that the writer (Joyce in this case) anticipated much of the "deconstructive" logic of our own day. If "the modern novel chooses to move away from a naturalistic empiricism and a mimetic responsibility to concentrate" upon these new deconstructive logics, we must not see this as "a sign of aridity in the modern imagination. Rather, it is the inevitable and necessary step for myth in an analytic age" (143; for a very incisive summary of the ways classic realism represents "the old order," see Belsey). Such decentered or deconstructed views of the world are not necessarily nihilistic but are above all playful and exploitative of the potentiality of linguistic expression in ways in which Joyce has tutored us all. Gould can even speak in another context of "the therapeutic of sheer inventiveness" (189), echoing an emphasis upon the ludic that has surfaced repeatedly within contemporary critical theory.

Structuralism and Structural Patterns of Myths and Rituals

7

Order is, at one and the same time, that which is given in
things as their inner law, the hidden network that
determines the way they confront one another, and also
that which has no existence except in the grid created by
a glance, an examination, a language; and it is only in the
blank spaces of this grid that order manifests itself in
depth as though already there, waiting in silence for the
moment of its expression.

Michel Foucault, *The Order of Things*

THIS CHAPTER BRINGS US TO ONE OF THE MOST recent approaches to myths and rituals, the structuralist approach associated especially with Claude Lévi-Strauss. My discussion will focus upon the concepts of "structure" the movement uses, relating them to analysts who came before the movement chronologically but whose methods were related in crucial ways to what the structuralists are doing. Instead of summarizing one of Lévi-Strauss's typical myth analyses (something that has been done many times, in introductions to structuralism), I stress some of the overall conceptual matters that have become evident during the years structuralism has been so important.

Structuralists working at the level of sequential movement of narratives are discussed before the modified structuralist methods of French scholars Marcel Detienne, Jean-Pierre Vernant, and Pierre Vidal-Naquet. Finally the chapter introduces biogenetic structuralism, an analytic that promises a broadly interdisciplinary collaboration between scientists working in the disciplines of biology, neurology, and psychology and those working in disciplines more traditionally concerned with the nature and culture of humankind, such as anthropology and sociology.

The Concepts of "Structure" and Structuralism

There is a certain irony in the choice of "structure" as the key term for the most recent methodology for study of myths and rituals. It is difficult indeed to speak of any myths or rituals *without* discussing something of their structure at some point: either structure as the elements that compose the myths or rituals, considered element by element, or as the structuration that differentiates one performance from another. It would be difficult to reach back to a point in mythographic history where these factors were not recognized and discussed. Most of the classical mythographic approaches we have looked at were "structuralist" in orientation if we mean by this simply that they were interested in the ways myths and rituals were divided into sections or elements and were variously related to their originating contexts.[1]

Frazer's *The Golden Bough,* for instance, might be called structuralist insofar as he compares structures of mythic or ritualistic elements common to diverse cultural backgrounds. Van Gennep differentiated structural phases of ritual performance. And we will review Eliade's *Patterns in Comparative Religion* (1958) as a typical pre- or protostructuralist attempt to reach beyond in-depth study of one or more religions to comparative features that can be cross-culturally evaluated (usually from the point of view called "the phenomenology of religion," although I agree with Ninian Smart [19–20] that it more properly ought to be referred to as typology, thematic comparison, or morphology).

However, most of these approaches dealt primarily with what present-day structuralists refer to as only the "manifest structure," the "surface manifestation" or the "superficial transform" of the more significant underlying structures. Generally the Freudian and Marxist hermeneutics of deceit has modulated into the structuralist distinction between the "deep" underlying structures and the "surface" manifestations (the "manifest" as opposed to the "latent" in Freud's terminology).

The crucial modifications of these concepts come at the point of the relevance of the actual cultural settings of the materials (the question of "history") and at the point of reference to "meaning" or "message." The argument whether or not structuralism denies or affirms history is now extensive and will not be entered here except to note that structuralism is a complex method of interpretation that has many aspects and phases. To expect that "history" would be valued the same throughout the various phases is somewhat like demanding that the whole cultural history of the development of mathematics be learned along with the multiplication tables.[2] It may be something that would be admirable, but any discipline encompasses both mechanical phases that simply have to be mastered—and a large number of structuralist studies are still working at this level—and then the more subtle mastery of an inclusive hermeneutics that integrates the elementary tools with the ongoing history for the purposes of interpretation.

By shifting emphasis from the "message" to the "medium," however, structuralism indeed has differentiated itself from earlier methodologies. Again any particular instance may be quite misleading; we can only grasp something of the ways the perspective is meaningful if we have in view a number of different studies. Generally speaking, the emphasis upon the medium—the ways myths or rituals are conveyed, for instance—comes not as a replacement for traditional emphasis upon content and values but as a complement to it. This bears reiteration because I have encountered persons who think the method remains entirely concerned with coding formal elements onto particular classification grids and is not the least concerned with the meaning of the elements to the culture producing them.

What does distinguish structuralist approaches is an emphasis upon *origins* of the cultural distinctions that produce meanings to participants in the culture. A *pattern* of distinguishing between cultural artifacts, for instance, may disclose fundamental values and orientations within a culture that can be learned from comparing the ways the culture consistently codes artifacts; such a coding otherwise would be obscure if the analyst only studied the explicitly named oppositions in a particular myth or body of myths (cf. Scholte:696: "The structuralist hopes to determine the characteristics of the 'place' where meaning is made and coded; he is not so much concerned with the message or meaning itself").

Therefore structuralists claim to be able to extrapolate meanings and values from the ways in which artifacts (and words, myths, meanings, and so forth) are counterpoised consistently within a particular culture. "Structure" means more than merely arrangement, but today it includes the interrelation of parts and especially "the hidden infrastructural logic" (Scholte:652). Structure has reference to the whole entity as seen, say, both by an outside observer and by an inside observer, and to the ways in which the parts are influenced by the context of the whole (for reflections on structuralist "structure," see Lane:intro., 19–39; Pouwer; and see the index to Rossi:484).

To discern the structures, however, a delicate means of analysis and coding is required; any hermeneutics of deceit requires that such a secondary mapping of the constituent elements be performed. This sort of translation into some other terminology or symbols is essentially the process by which one culture interprets another, converting "their" perspectives into "they would think this way if they were we"; and hence structuralism represents one more hermeneutical device for understanding another culture that is distanced from us in space or in time. (This definition does not exclude structuralist analysis of contemporary cultures, for there is always a necessary distancing of the artifact from the recipient or observer.)

The key to development of this particular hermeneutics historically has been the modern study of linguistic structures and languages—in brief, modern linguistics (see Hawkes; Pettit). Linguists distinguish, for instance, between two aspects in a language, the "deep" and the "surface" structures. The deep structure is the underlying principle (at times approaching the Platonic ideal-forms, at other times the energizing dynamics of the Jungian archetypes) that generates surface (or periphrastic) structures—the actual linguistic forms one hears or reads when listening to or reading the language. Although many different uses of linguistics have been components of different structuralist approaches, this fundamental distinction is usually present, along with tree diagrams of possible choices, derived from the classification of acoustic (phonemic) units according to a continuous series of choices between two closely related possibilities—the sounds b/v, for instance, or d/t—termed "binary oppositions." (I will demonstrate later how this distinction operates, for example, in Claude Lévi-Strauss's approach to myths; and I discuss other heritages from linguistics in the third part of this chapter.)

After introducing one further key notion we will have the necessary framework for introducing structuralist analysis proper. That final key notion is the concept of transformation, which is the process by which units at one level of a given structure are modified as they are expressed at another level. Transformation also is understood in the more usual way in terms of changes between any two interacting systems. The relation between transformation in the structuralist usage and the concept of structure as a totalistic, "Gestalt" framework is well expressed by Jean Piaget, whose brief and technical *Structuralism* (1970) was translated before many English-speaking persons had notions of what the structuralist approach was all about:

> As a first approximation, we may say that a structure is a system of transformations. Inasmuch as it is a system and not a mere collection of elements and their properties, these transformations involve laws: the structure is preserved or enriched by the interplay of its transformation laws, which never yield results external to the system nor employ elements that are external to it. In short, the notion of structure is comprised of three key ideas: the idea of wholeness, the idea of transformation, and the idea of self-regulation. (1970b:5)

Piaget's statement sounds much like modern systems analysis, and I think the parallel is a helpful one. Systems theory places greater emphasis upon the "flow" of materials through the structure, however, whereas structuralism seems more concerned to chart the abstract logics by means of which the structure is composed. Readers familiar with recent trends in the psychology of perception doubtless will be reminded also of some of the basic principles of Gestalt psychology; Piaget reviews the similarities, suggesting that structuralism provides an important means of correcting and developing Gestaltist principles.

Protostructuralist Structuralists

Having mentioned Sir James Frazer as a candidate for classification as a prestructuralist structuralist—operating, to be sure, with an earlier concept of "structure"—it would not be difficult to approach similarly many of the nineteenth- and twentieth-century students of religion and mythology. Here, however, I take only one such example, that of the work of Mircea Eliade, finding some justification for using the label "structuralist" with respect to Eliade in Lévi-Strauss's citation of Plutarch as "a precursor of the structural analysis of myths" (1981:45, n. 4).

I am not at all sure Eliade would be happy with the label of structuralist. He prefers the term historian of religion, and he has not, to my knowledge, engaged the practice or the theoretical framework of structuralism in writing. But he is typical of what we may at least call protostructuralists in developing as a methodology for the analysis of religious phenomena a comparative model that perhaps is best seen in his books treating a wide range of cultural examples clustered around particular themes: his *Yoga* (1969), or *Shamanism* (1964), for instance, or even more explicitly, a very early work, whose title is clearly indicative for our purposes, *Patterns in Comparative Religion* (1958).

The whole question of structuring a phenomenological study of religious spirit has been debated among religionists for some time, and even to use the adjective "phenomenological," as I have just done, would raise eyebrows among some partisans. Eliade and others at the University of Chicago have kept methodological issues alive in this country, and debates at various international congresses have provoked quite a remarkable intensity with respect to the appropriate methods for the analysis of religion (Sharpe traces some of the issues surfacing in the international meetings; see also Segal; Penner and Yonan).

Eliade's *Patterns* tracked what he termed the "morphology of the sacred," as manifested in the sky, the sun, the moon, water, stones, the earth, vegetation and agriculture, and so on, showing how each natural object has evoked corresponding types of worship. The volume ends with special attention to sacred places and the nature of sacred times, the morphology and function of myths, and the structure of symbols.

Each chapter of the book provides a wide range of examples, culled from Eliade's wide reading in the literature of anthropology and religious studies, and each chapter concludes with helpful bibliographic references. The comparative emphasis is upon similarities and dissimilarities in the religious thematics of various cultures, and the conclusions and recapitulations in each chapter sketch features that are common in the development of the particular type of deity or religious phenomenon.

Almost anyone who dares to demonstrate comparatively the similarities and dissimilarities between the appropriations of a similar theme in different cultures tends to be criticized by those who specialize in just one culture, and that indeed has happened with respect to Eliade's contributions. Structuralist anthropologists continue to criticize similarly global proposals by their own peers, however, and it might be argued that structuralism itself, practiced and developed especially by anthropologists, has the inherent problem of working comparatively with materials that have not yet been completely understood in their individual particularity.

Eliade has been especially criticized for being "Jungian" in orientation, although a careful reading of Eliade's works will disclose very few direct references to Jung's works. The criticism seems to arise more from "tarring with the same brush" than from careful explication and comparison. Certainly the two are alike, however, in seeking not just additional data for collection systems but rather significant appropriations of symbols to guide the search for more meaningful human existence (see Beane:462–65 in Beane and Doty); each also suggests that Christianity's symbols, if appropriately revoiced, are among the richest treasures available. Both Jung and Eliade recognize that almost insurmountable problems occur in such a contemporary revoicing, and hence they suggest parallel resources from other cultures.

Comparative viewing of cultural products in several cultures leads Eliade to focus on their commonality or disparateness, as a means of showing which features are or are not cultural homologues having the same functions. He can suggest, to give only one example, that whereas education in our society is the formal result of schooling and books in general, in other societies (and especially earlier ones) education was transmitted primarily by the recitation of myths and their enactment in rituals (1960:chap. 9).

But neither Jung's massive collections of comparative data, nor Eliade's, nor other thematic collections of anthropological, mythological, or religious custom, or of folktale and literary thematics, have stressed the inner logics of the ways the themes were developed, transformed, or interrelated as emphatically as have the explicitly structuralist studies in the 1970s and 1980s. Impatience with modes of collecting information, despair about satisfactory methodologies for comparing the results, and the desire to introduce more scientific and abstract models into the collection and comparison system are certainly some of the pressures that led to interest in and development of a structuralist method that promises an almost mathematical means of working with comparative materials. But before I can discuss the extent to which structuralist methods lead to the extreme of computerization of structures, and to specific methods of studying texts in cultural frameworks, I need to review briefly the contributions of the "founding father" of anthropological structuralism, Claude Lévi-Strauss, and indicate how his initial contributions have been extended and modified.

Lévi-Strauss: The Myth and the Mythed

My approach with respect to the work of Claude Lévi-Strauss will be similar to that used in approaching the work of Freud and Jung—again we are faced with a large volume of relevant materials, covering many aspects of myth and ritual, and again the implications of the work carry well beyond mythology alone. Instead of documenting each point, I will select some of the most important overall aspects, summarizing and drawing together diverse items in terms of their eventual significance for the study of myths and rituals. (The Selected Introductory Bibliography includes materials on structuralism and suggests a program for reading Lévi-Strauss.)

Two primary focal points are used here, first the method of myth analysis developed by Lévi-Strauss, and second the broader question of the nature of myth and what that suggests about the human mind creating myths. We will see that these focuses are somewhat interdependent in Lévi-Strauss's work, and both are necessary to support his striking claim that he can show "not how men think in myths, but how myths operate in men's minds without their being aware of the fact" (1969:12).

The quotation should alert us to a different approach to content than that to which we are accustomed. Lévi-Strauss does not stress content or meaning but rather "the system of axioms and postulates defining the best possible code, capable of conferring a common significance on unconscious formulations which are the work of minds, societies, and civilizations" (12). System, structure: meanings not to be discovered on the level of apparent significance in terms of the actual language of the myths but in their structuring in relation to one another and to other social systems. Hence this is structuralism proper, with its emphasis upon logical structures and whole Gestalts rather than upon the poetical expression or the social functionality of the material—it is especially not the Durkheim-Malinowski sort of sociofunctionalism viewing myths and rituals as merely expressing or guiding particular social institutions.

Perhaps Lévi-Strauss's analytical method may best be described as a process of decomposition and recomposition: mythological narratives are "decomposed" by identifying and charting their most elementary constituent units, termed "mythemes" (on the analogy with the smallest units of spoken language, phonemes). Lévi-Strauss notes that these units are not usually high-sounding religious themes but are often bits and pieces from many everyday sectors of the society. We are asked to recognize that the mythmaker works much as does the maker of a collage or a fix-it person (*bricoleur*), using whatever happens along to create by organizing and structuring the bits and pieces into coherent wholes.

The mythmaker assembles these units into meaningful wholes according to structures that are deeply imbedded within the cultural framework of meaning available at a particular period. We experience the resulting mythical statements as a series of wholes, having harmonies and dissonances similar to the materials related in a musical composition—a comparison of which Lévi-Strauss is especially fond in the first and fourth volumes of Mythologiques. Only careful formal analysis can distinguish the harmonies or the particular scores played by different groups of instruments; and only careful myth analysis can elicit similar awareness of the mythical harmonies, solos, and the like.

The structures into which the bits and pieces are assembled reach down to cultural bedrock at many points, although any particular mythical figure may have to be decomposed many times by the analyst before we recognize the ultimate cultural value or problem being represented. The ultimate values are, for Lévi-Strauss, primarily those that have the character of binary oppositions, that is, those that are expressible only in terms of contrasts that are completely polar. Examples would be: life:death, male:female, good:bad, human:superhuman, and mortal:immortal.

These oppositions represent the primary conflicts of human existence.[3] In fact they are so primary as to be incapable of being resolved, for they are ultimately versions of Hamlet's "to be or not to be" (1981:694). Instead of living with such insoluble dilemmas, however, the human mind finds structures that enable the oppositions to be lived through by bridging them with mediations, what I would call "third terms." The central conflicts are fictionalized; they are resolved and transcended by replacing them with ever more removed secondary oppositions that have also a third, intermediate term: hot:cold-*warm,* for instance, or raw:boiled-*broiled.* The structural patterns for which the analyst looks, therefore, are the patterns by which the materials in the actual corpus of myths being studied have resolved an earlier insoluble dilemma; we are normally to work from the later resolution of an issue back to its primary opposition.[4]

Having completed such an operation with a number of myths in a particular set, we will have analyzed all the variants in that set and should be able to spotlight the continuities between variants, the transformations of the mythemic units, and the "broad mythemes" or master categories that can subsume the parts. Such a procedure represents a spiraling interpretative pattern insofar as the interpreter's understanding of all the units in the system is being revised continually as he or she takes in additional materials, in this case other mythemes and variants. Theoretically the analyst may begin at a point near either end of the spectrum of the primary or secondary transformation levels and then may track the transformations in either direction; we can speak of mythic systems rotating to the right or left (1981:108; note the curious parallels here to Hart's revising the traditional concept of the hermeneutical *circle* of interpretation to a *spiral* [Hart:chap. 2]).

And not only should each myth in a mythset clarify the others within the set, but eventually the mythographer ought to be able to include all possible mythological sets! Although the four volumes of Lévi-Strauss's Mythologiques (Introduction to a Science of Mythology) analyze more than 800 particular myths and as many variants, it seems certain that Lévi-Strauss is not as concerned to develop a method for the careful analysis of particular mythological narratives as he is to work out an understanding of The Mythical in general, what he calls "the quintessential mythic formula" (1981:564). He is not as interested in individual stories as in all of mythology, and in *all principles of structuration,* or what other structuralists have referred to as the constraints of the mythical structures themselves.

The italicized phrase in the last sentence is important: Lévi-Strauss includes within the purview of his approach not only mythical stories but also artistic designs (as in facial and body tatooing), classification in naming objects such as plants and animals, and many other types of cultural activities and artifacts. In fact he refers to a logic or science "of the concrete," stressing that empirical categories or natural articles can serve as conceptual tools when working out abstract propositions, such as propositions dealing with the fundamental oppositions enumerated above. The inherent structures operate at various levels within particular myths or systems of social organization (such as geographic, technoeconomical, sociological, and cosmological levels), and any level may be operationally or functionally more important within one particular society than in another or at different times within a particular society.

On each of the various levels, the same message is (redundantly) expressed in such a way that the central oppositions eventually are given full articulation. And the levels themselves may demonstrate a mutual interrelation, for they all are concerned to express the same message, though in each case it will be phrased in the frame of reference appropriate to the particular level. A statement about the directions north:south, therefore, may be making the same distinction as the categories raw:cooked in a related myth.

With such an emphasis upon systems and structurational patterns, Lévi-Strauss is not particularly concerned with the ways the myths are voiced, their aesthetic dimensions, or what we customarily call their content or significance to the persons articulating and preserving the myths. In fact Lévi-Strauss's analysis only secondarily concerns the content of the myths, their meanings to the cultures in which they are transmitted; but it is not to native informants that one turns to discover such significances but rather to the principles of logical operations.

"Truth" in myth therefore has reference to the adequacy of its expression to convey the essential cultural standards, to reflect the structuring polarities that have shaped a particular group. It is the position of the materials within the innate structures of the society that is important, not the intrinsic value of the materials. Therefore "truth" in myth refers not so much to the valuational "right or wrong?" as to the way the analyst can decide whether or not a particular variant that appears to be contrary to a broad mytheme is actually germane to it, or whether it is an external influence.

To be sure, variants may represent successive attempts to resolve a continuing problem, but they also may represent the influence of an external social group, or the degeneration of the material in terms of its ability to express the fundamental cultural oppositions. Hence Lévi-Strauss's dynamic model which I quoted in Chapter 1:

> A mythic system can only be grasped in a process of becoming; not as something inert and stable but in a process of perpetual transformation. This would mean that there are always several kinds of myths simultaneously present in the system, some of them primary (in respect of the moment at which the observation is made) and some of them derivative. (1973:534; most myths originate, Lévi-Strauss suggests, from materials presented to the system by neighboring societies [1971b:573])

Any particular myth actualizes only part of the total mythological structure of a culture, which may appear additionally elsewhere in its cultural creations (its organizations of artifacts, its table manners, its astrology, and so forth); and any one mythological text or related artifact may reveal several levels or systems at work simultaneously. Again we see that individual elements are not particularly important in themselves but only as they form part of a system: "no feature is significant in itself" (1981:559). It is not the particular aesthetic "thickness" of a narrative that is important; nor is it the individual creativeness of the mythmaker that matters. Rather myths signify the human mind that is making myths—the details from *natural* order providing the materials, the way natural sounds provide the materials for speech. But *culture* is structure, system, and Lévi-Strauss's reference to "myths thinking themselves through humans" is to be understood as the transpersonal mythic structure being unconsciously but logically imposed upon the human environment. Such a position leads Lévi-Strauss to the following statement, which actually brings together many parts of his work:

> I never had, and still do not have, the perception of feeling my personal identity. I appear to myself as the place where something is going on, but there is no "I", no "me". Each of us is a kind of crossroads where things happen. The crossroads is purely passive; something happens there. A different thing, equally valid, happens elsewhere. There is no choice, it is just a matter of choice. (1978a:3–4; see Lévi-Strauss's discussion of the authorial "we" and the contemporary problematic of the self, in 1981:625–26)

Hence myths do not represent "facts" pure and simple, but they demonstrate a dialectical organization of facts—so that the social institutions portrayed in a myth, for instance, may be quite the opposite of what is the case in social reality. Myths represent a way to speculate about the possible contours of the social order, a way to show up the shortcomings and tensions of reality or the limitations of any other mode of social existence. And this is the case regardless of the conscious explanation of the matter, for anthropologists and linguists concur in the observation that conscious models often obscure rather than clarify the actual reasoning for an act. Myths use a "metalanguage" (rather than "paralanguage" in ritual); or they use language "hyper-structurally"; hence:

> the particular ritual sometimes adds a function to praxis, and sometimes supplants it: gesture and objects occur in loco verbi, as substitutions for words. Each connotes a global aspect, a system of ideas and of representations; when they are used, ritual condenses under concrete and unified forms procedural elements that would otherwise remain unrelated. . . . Ritual substitutes for gestures and things a corresponding analytical expression. . . . The gestures performed, the objects manipulated, are as much the medium as is the ritual, insofar as they all supplant the use of words. (1971b:600, my translation)

I have not described the complex algebraic and geometric systems utilized by Lévi-Strauss, although his own studies, and those of analysts following his methodology, are full of such. One model common to many structuralists that should be mentioned, however, is the matrix formed by syntagmatic and paradigmatic (or synchronic—at a given time, and diachronic—across time, or even cross-culturally) mythemes. Simply put, the matrix formation involves charting the mythemes horizontally across a series of columns, using a separate entry for each element of a particular version of a myth (hence following the "syntagm" that occurs in one particular synchronic or "empirical" version).

Coding a series of myth variants in this manner, on the same chart, it is possible to read the resulting columns vertically as well as horizontally. The vertical columns represent the "paradigm" or "deep structure" of the material—that is, the essential, regular features of the motif that are common, with variations, to each motifeme. The vertical columns may be said to represent the diachronic (or metaempirical) aspect of the myth because they will demonstrate the variations over a period of time. (Attention to a *particular* text of whatever nature, by whatever method, is synchronic or syntagmatic, whereas genre criticism of a body of texts, or comparative motif criticism, is paradigmatic or diachronic. A particular text that presents a number of actors or situations, however, may need to be analyzed with both dimensions in mind. The complexity of mapping narrative moves in multistoried narratives will be engaged in the next section.) Those who criticize Lévi-Strauss's lack of regard for "history" are arguing that he concentrates too exclusively upon the syntagmatic as opposed to the paradigmatic or that he does not sufficiently honor the historic significance of the syntagmatic sequence within its social matrix.

The benefits of structuralist analysis are not yet completely apparent. It is clear, for instance, that the methodology does expose tensions and underlying patterns in myths and rites that seem accessible only through such a process of decomposition and coding: hence Lévi-Strauss's suggestion that the method can work like a newly discovered photographic developer upon an old negative, disclosing dimensions not previously developed, may be accurate. In addition the method can provide helpful ways of dealing with a textual corpus in which later intrusions (editorial changes, for example, or revisions, or additions) can be recognized by their deviation from the characteristic paradigms of the original author. And finally the method contributes significantly to the question of contemporary translations of antique materials: substitution of contemporary terms or narrative moves may be regulated by showing which terms or moves in our society have or do not have the same paradigmatic functions they had in the society producing the text or ritual.

Criticisms of Lévi-Strauss's approach to mythology are numerous and can be indicated only briefly here (see Scholte; Munz 1973; Kirk 1970:chap. 2):

- he imposes logics, he does not discover them
- he does not take into account the randomness of a particular nar-

rator's performance context, in which variants are introduced merely as a device of narration to hold the audience's attention
- such analysis may overlook elements that are not important to the analytical matrix but which have a great deal of importance elsewhere in the society (this is a variation of the earlier criticism of Stith Thompson's motif index of folktales)
- he ignores conscious literary intervention in the process of passing on the mythological or ritual traditions, shaping them for various uses in the society; the sorts of algorithmic systems he devises are themselves shaped by writing so substantively that they are of questionable analytic propriety for preliterary groups (see especially Goody 1977:105)
- he does not deal satisfactorily with privileged or "master" myths
- he does not treat sufficiently emic variations, that is, the ways myths and rituals are thought to have explanatory value within the socicties where they are shaped and transmitted
- he overvalues the heuristic values of categories derived from linguistics, and in fact he improperly carries over qualities of the elementary phoneme to the category of mytheme (see Carloye; Pettit)
- he lacks the sort of formal semantical rules that more recent scholarship demands, or at least he seems unaware of them, so that they come into the analytical schema sub rosa, as "codes."

Often the resistance to Lévi-Strauss exposes a basic difference in approaching matters of the mind, and in deriving models for analysis, that reflects differences between the French intellectual tradition and the more empirical Anglo-American tradition. To a certain extent this difference boils down to a preference for induction rather than deduction, but in other respects it simply reflects ignorance of the wider philosophical and literary frameworks in which Lévi-Strauss formulates his proposals (useful for sketching this framework are Gardner; Boon; and Jameson 1972).

I share Schneidau's qualifications of Lévi-Strauss's work (along with those of any number of other critics), but I also share Schneidau's belief that "Lévi-Strauss's work forces us to respect the profound otherness of myth, and not to treat it as either *archē* or *telos* of literature" (1976:274), a perspective that returns us to the whole myths, rather than the archetypalists' perspective of disjointed variants and motifs.

To enter into the extensive number of criticisms of Lévi-Strauss's enterprise would take us too far afield at this point—especially because any discussion of the criticisms would necessitate engaging the many aspects of speculative and applied ethnography where the name Lévi-Strauss is also a very important one. I have tried to limit the discussion to his development of a particular approach to mythology, and I turn now to other structuralist options that are being developed to replace or to augment those of Lévi-Strauss.

Sequential and Semiotic Structuralists

One feature of my presentation of Lévi-Strauss's approach to mythology will have caught some readers' attention: I deliberately tried to emphasize that Lévi-Strauss is concerned primarily with the mythical structures of a society rather than with clarification or appreciation of the actual narratives themselves in terms of their aesthetic/poetic dimensions or in terms of their immediate semantic significance within the societies producing the myths or rituals. Precisely these dimensions have been pursued by other scholars before Lévi-Strauss and subsequently. Often "structuralist analysis" today refers primarily to narratological analysis and poetics, or to semiology and semantics, and it is these structuralist developments that are of relevance within much of the academic study of literature and literary criticism and within ethnology and symbology (surveys: Scholes; Culler 1975 and 1981; Via).

Our beginning point must be to develop the understanding that the "mythical structure" analyzed by Lévi-Strauss's methods represents but one of the various deep structures at work in a literary text. And in fact, much of the analysis being done today under the structuralist rubric hardly mentions the mythical structure upon which our attention has been focused. In this section, therefore, we look briefly at types of structuralist analysis aimed at the narrative, aesthetic, and semiological structures of a text—I say "briefly" in light of the rather astonishing length of some of the studies. In the presence of masses of analytical material, it is sometimes forgotten that this stage of analysis is still programmatic and may have to be scrapped entirely. But there are surely some agreed-upon features, and it is to them that we direct our attention. The major features may be categorized as an emphasis upon the shape of the narrative ("narrativity" or "narratological features"), changing recently to study of the semiotic and symbolic constraints a narrative exhibits.

The narratological emphasis mostly concerns the ways mythemes are to be segregated and then regrouped—already a concern of Lévi-Strauss, as we saw above. The key figure is that of Vladimir Propp, a Russian folklorist whose important work of 1928, *Morphology of the Folktale,* was given an effective English translation only in 1968 (see also

Propp 1966 and 1972). Propp argued that the surface language (characterizations, descriptions of locales, and so forth) in folktales might change extensively within a folktale corpus but that "underneath" (here is the frequently recurring spatial metaphor again) the surface details, certain basic "moves" occur that are not dependent upon particular characterizations in the story. (For example, "lack" or "loss" can be a move—actually Propp used the term "function"—connected with a small child *or* a mighty king.)

By using a simple system of substitutions for syntagmatic elements, Propp developed a means of describing folktale plots algebraically, and Alan Dundes in the United States, Heda Jason in Israel, and Erhardt Güttgemanns in Germany have revised the basic Proppian coding system extensively. But Propp did not develop the paradigmatic element that Lévi-Strauss and subsequent structuralists have emphasized. Alternative frameworks for coding stories—notably those of the French literary analysts Algirdas Julien Greimas and Roland Barthes—have become a common feature of contemporary structural analysis of literature.

Emphasis frequently is placed upon the flow of movements through the story as a result of sequential binary decisions about possible actions—a sort of narrative flow pattern, if you will—rather than upon the details of composition themselves. Once again we have to recall that the structuralist thinks in terms of various constraints of language and of logical expression impressing themselves upon an author, not in terms of authorial intent. An author may be totally unaware of the ways the unconscious structural constraints work through his or her materials, and in fact too much awareness may be damaging to the aesthetic wholeness of the work. (We need only refer to literary works intended to illustrate Freudian ideas to remember how contrived they now seem.)

Literary analysis may be directed primarily toward *the surface expression* of mythological content (see Greimas) rather than as with Lévi-Strauss toward the structure of the mythological content. There is weight to a colleague's suggestion that we need to obtain much greater sophistication in dealing with the forms of expression before we can adequately understand the "deep" oppositions themselves (Petersen:172); and it should be noted that one of the most frequent complaints against early structuralist studies was that they were unsatisfactory as models for working with units of material larger than the simple sentence.

Dependence upon linguistics was greatly reduced when it was realized that words and simple sentences could be analyzed according to linguistic *semiotics* (correlating signifiers and signifieds) but not paragraphs and entire discourses, which required also the use of *semantics* (analyzing how the signifiers are related to one another to convey meanings). Semiotics was invaluable in understanding how the smallest literary units were expressions of deep structures in the speaker's resources; but semantics—and hence emphasis upon the narrativity of the utterance—was necessary to deal with the more complex combination of signs (words) and simple expressions into meaningful discourses.

A. J. Greimas, in particular, has worked with the development of a structuralist semantics for materials that can be recognized as being meaningful narrative (and coded in his system, therefore, with the value "narrativity"). The discourse is thought of as an empty semantic structure until it is invested with semantic features that express a particular meaning; at the present, research centers upon finding the appropriate discourse subunits (the favorite term for the smallest units of semantic meaning seems to be "lexies") that can be understood as carrying the significant elements of the discourse. Once this coding has been achieved, it is possible to speak of many statements in terms of satisfying a limited number of "canonical narrative functions" (such as arrival:departure, departure:return, domination:submission) or of investing the "actantial model" (a device for indicating who does what in a particular narrative: a Sender acts upon an Object intended for a Receiver, and so forth).

Roland Barthes, in an extended lexie-by-lexie analysis (in *S/Z* [1974]) of Balzac's story "Sarrasine," assigns hermeneutic, semantic, symbolic, proairetic (actions), and cultural or reference codes to particular statements in Balzac's story, but he also speaks of the ironic code (44), the artistic code (55), the code of statuary (73), the codes of signification and of execution (80), the rhetorical code (129), and the codes of passion and the novel (139), or the code of institutions (which he refers to as "the principle of reality" [185]): all in all the codes are not clearly distinguished, and subsequent studies using the *S/Z* model have had to stipulate the analysts' particular ways of using Barthes's terms, or their own.[5]

I have used some of the technical terms currently being developed for narratological and semiological analysis primarily to give some indication of the type of analytical precision that is being developed. If coding schemata are agreed upon, it should be possible to describe a narrative analytically by describing it in such terms, which remain the same possibilities in all materials having the quality "narrativity." I know from my own experience that agreement among analysts is still something to be desired rather than something obtained. We have, for instance, experienced considerable argument about how the slots in the actantial model should be filled. But the future holds the promise that use of such

delicate analytical models will provide crucial insights as to how "mythical" narratives are constructed or whether the semantic point of a narrative is to provide an example of behavior, to stimulate discussion, or to
provoke rejection of its own claims.

A proverb, for example, may function differently in different
cultures; in some parts of Africa it may serve to establish legal prece-
dents in a lawsuit. So the question of the relationship of the literary
material to the society in which it is produced is then reintroduced, as is
the question of cross-cultural comparisons I mentioned in the first part
of this chapter. For if there is a scientific basis for comparing discourse
types, we should be able to recognize how particular types function
wherever they appear, or at least we should have a basis for understanding how the same types of materials can function differently within
different cultural contexts.

Perhaps the most important contribution of semiological studies has
been their insistence upon the context in which literary works appear—
their "intertextual constructs," to use the technical term. "The work is a
product not of a biographically defined individual about whom information could be accumulated, but of writing itself," as Culler puts it
(1981:38). Along with the characteristic emphasis upon the role of the
Literary Tradition itself being a creative constituent in any literary work
(which we already have noted several times with respect to mythological
traditions), this emphasis is therefore constructive—showing where the
actual terms or signifiers of a metaphor or literary work derive—and
deconstructive—showing how a particular work is innovative in reworking the traditional meanings into a new meaning that stands in a
dialectical relationship with the past expressions. A whole "semiotics of
reading" follows (Culler 1981:52–62 summarizes the work of Holland,
Jauss, and Todorov), and indeed the whole scope of literary history begins to be seen in new contexts, as a tracing of the meaningful segments
received from the tradition but now revoiced and reheard in terms of a
dialectical tension with whatever "meanings" have been predominant
within the formal constraints of "great literature." "Literature" itself
begins to be seen differently, from this perspective, and the recent deconstructionist movement has been most insistent about the uses of its
analyses for probing philosophical and other traditionally "nonliterary"
texts.

It is perhaps not surprising that much of the structuralist (narratological and semiological) literary analysis to date has worked with
biblical texts and mythological materials.[6] These are materials for which
contemporary reappropriation is especially necessary if they are to survive; and if a valid hermeneutics can be developed from an elaborated

and refined narratological and semiological model, one of the long-lasting problems of the analysis of myth and ritual will have been resolved, namely how to give voice to materials from antiquity or from cultures other than our own in ways that fully respect their original dimensions and yet remain understandable in our own terms.

Precisely this issue is met head-on by a direction in French mythographic scholarship that is beginning to be known in the United States. I refer to works by Jean-Pierre Vernant, Pierre Vidal-Naquet, Marcel Detienne, and others (for bibliography, see Nagy; Gordon). Although these scholars share several methodological principles—they are all second-generation structuralists, quite critical of Lévi-Strauss, and informed by technical scholarship in the Greek and Roman classics as Lévi-Strauss was not—they represent to date not so much a formal school as an influence. The scholars named have shared the writing of several studies, and they refer to one another constantly. They work collaboratively with others in the Centre de Recherches Comparées sur les Sociétés Anciennes, in Paris, where research topics are undertaken by a multidisciplinary working team (*équipe;* the most consistently collaborative study to date focuses upon Greek sacrifice: Detienne et al. 1979).

Among their emphases are the following:

- the role of symbol has been much too restrictively understood and studied: it is a typical form of mythic expression that does not intend to code social features mechanistically;
- the search for origins or the "most primitive" layer of a tradition, and the suggestion of a primitive level of human cognition we have now surpassed, are misleading;
- myth ought not to be treated reductionistically, as if it were a language saying one thing that has to be decoded so that it says the same thing in our own language;
- while it is helpful and necessary to pick out primary mythic and literary elements (what I could term "systematic analysis" of all the social, aesthetic, and psychological components), the "communal framework of reference, the background which made the very structures . . . intelligible," is also crucial (Vernant and Vidal-Naquet 1981:vii);
- and cross-cultural thematic studies are less valuable than studies that track interwoven meanings of a mythic symbol within a particular culture.

Perhaps the best example of the last-named emphasis is Detienne's *The Gardens of Adonis* (1977), where the author presents a comprehensive mapping of associations between mythical stories and figures, all *within* Greco-Roman culture. Vernant's essays in Gordon's *Myth, Religion, and Society* (1981) are especially clear examples of what preliminary structural analysis and attention to the various codes of mythic narratives can disclose; we see for example that Prometheus's subterfuge by which (in Hesiod) he "cheats" the gods out of the better portion of the sacrifice actually represents a "cheat" of another sort: humans are left with meat, ephemeral food, as opposed to the immortal foods retained by the gods (14–15; see also Vernant's portrayal of the double-meaning language characteristic of Greek tragedy, in Vernant and Vidal-Naquet 1981).

Generally in agreement with structuralist analyses, but not as cluttered with elaborate coding frameworks, the works of this group of scholars stress the following analytical tasks (expressed by Detienne in Gordon:108, in an essay referring to Lévi-Strauss's American studies): construction of a grammar of the way of thinking expressed in the myths; grouping the myths by means of exhaustive analysis of their ethnographic contexts; analyzing the semantic fields of the materials in which the mythic materials appear; and relating the linguistic structures to the mythological structures of the texts.

Vernant and his colleagues represent not only a poststructuralist approach but also a post-Freudian one, although in each case "neo" may be substituted for "post." For example, Detienne makes explicit the necessity to focus not only upon the explicit and normative values represented in a myth but also its unexpressed aspects: "To discover the complete horizon of a society's symbolic values, it is also necessary to map out its transgressions, interrogate its deviants, discern phenomena of rejection and refusal, and circumscribe the silent mouths that unlock upon underlying knowledge and the implicit" (1979:ix).Perhaps no other direction in mythography has been so willing to face the "dark" side of mythological references, to explore the violence and agony as well as the nobility of mythic expression (see also Girard; Sagan; Burkert 1983). Not only the generic theme of violence, but in particular sacrifice, is now receiving close attention (for bibliography, see Svenbro; Hecht; see also Reverdin and Grange).

Works from these French scholars now are being translated into English, but I know of few direct influences upon English-speaking scholarship. Apart from the monographic studies of Detienne, I suspect that we shall have to wait for evaluative essays or for a volume of coordinated and selected essays (rather than the accumulated collected essays that have been published and that often are so involved with refuting parts of the French intellectual tradition that they are obscure in our own context) before we will be able to speak of an explicit school of mythography (the volume edited by Gordon is fairly inclusive; see its introduction by R. G. A. Buxton).

Biogenetic Structuralism

One of the striking features of Jean Piaget's structuralist work, as of this scholar's lifework as a whole, has been his continued emphasis upon the necessity for coordination of research designs and evaluation among technicians in several disciplines (see his introductory chapter in *Major Trends of Research in the Social and Human Sciences,* published separately as Piaget 1970a; Piaget 1970b is also still very helpful). In spite of Piaget's wide-ranging influence, however, few fully interdisciplinary structuralist projects have been developed. All the more striking are the contributions of Eugene d'Aquili, Charles Laughlin, and others in an approach to humankind, and especially human ritual, that carries the title biogenetic structuralism and incorporates materials from physical and cultural anthropology, cognitive psychology, neurophysiology, neurobiology, ethology, and psychiatry (Laughlin and d'Aquili; d'Aquili and Laughlin; d'Aquili et al.). To this list, gathered from *The Spectrum of Ritual* by d'Aquili et al., I would name the presence of the disciplines of philosophy, archaeology and ethnology, the sociology of knowledge, and the history of psychology and of science, as well as religious studies, linguistics, biology, and sociology. With so many academic disciplines expecting to be satisfied by the proponents of biogenetic structuralism, we must anticipate an extended period of refining all its details. Yet d'Aquili and Laughlin have prepared their case with thoroughness, and I suspect their proposals will interest many scientists whose work has not already led them to study myths and rituals.

D'Aquili and Laughlin have created a bridge between natural scientists and researchers in the humanities at the point of relating several aspects of the contemporary laboratory sciences to more speculative and philosophical analyses of the nature and function of myth and ritual. If biogenetic structuralism is accepted and developed further, we shall be able to speak more concretely and specifically about the ways myth and ritual both originate and function in the individual and in societies.

The approach is *structuralist,* but of an evolutionary and diachronic orientation rather than the semiotic and synchronic orientation represented by the materials I presented earlier in this chapter. And it is *biogenetic* insofar as it relates social phenomena to neurophysiological findings—going considerably beyond the popular treatments of right:left brain hemisphere characteristics. Biogenetic structuralism suggests that ritual and myth arise and are maintained because they have survival value (a similar argument for art is made by Alland); they represent cultural concretions of neurophysical events rooted in human evolution, tunings of the complex systems by which individual and society intermesh and interact. As forms of social communication (also emphasized by Leach 1976), rituals and myths are not merely developed from secondary cerebrations of the human intellect but are forms of acting out and explaining our physical and cognized reactions to our surrounding environments.

Biogenetic structuralism is interested in the cross-hatched areas where several types of research overlap: ethological studies of ritualized behavior in nonhuman animals, neurophysiological findings concerning relationships between developments in neural systems and the relative complexity of cultural patterns, and functional studies of what rituals accomplish, as well as how myths are related to rituals (as explanatory, supplementary, and so forth). The language of biogenetic structuralism is dominated by the technical terminology of the neurobiological sciences to the point where adequate summary here in the context of studies developed mostly in the humanities would necessitate a great amount of exposition. D'Aquili and the others associated with biogenetic structuralism are careful to relate their findings and hypotheses to several of the directions in mythography I have sketched here, and once some of the technical language is assimilated (scientific reference works are necessary for such terms as endocast, myelination, conspecifics, limbic system, trophotropic, pheromone, and so on), the basic proposals are readily comprehended.

In providing a large-scale model of analysis of human social performances of ritual, and of cognizing within mythologies, elucidated by the findings of neurobiological research, I suspect that biogenetic structuralism has established a new fundamental position in the study of myths and rituals (see d'Aquili). Such a position, informed by the many disciplines noted above, represents not a takeover of the "soft" sciences by the "hard" so much as an important synthesis and perspective that promises a more inclusive understanding of myths and rituals than we have ever known. What remains to be seen, however, is whether or not the traditional compartmentalization of scholarship will continue to defeat synthesizing and integrating models such as that presented by biogenetic structuralism.

Mythic Dimensions of Our Decentered Cosmos

8

The totality of meaning that is encountered in the mythological stories and acts is expressed by a thoroughgoing
interrelationship between the mythic figures. In their
functions, and occasionally also in their names, they
merge into one another. The creator-god becomes the first
ancestor, the earth, the sky; the culture hero turns into
God or the first ancestor, and vice versa. Metamorphosis
is thus a universal category of the mythological figures
that expresses the comprehensive reality of the mythic
dimension. The polarity of man's existence is mediated in
the unique meaning of being-there.
        Wilhelm Dupré, *Religion in Primitive Cultures*

What we have to deal with here is a major cultural shift
from a time-honored aesthetics of permanence, based on a
belief in an unchanging and transcendent ideal of beauty,
to an aesthetics of transitoriness and immanence, whose
central values are change and novelty.
        Matei Calinescu, *Faces of Modernity*

THE FOCUS IN THIS LAST CHAPTER CONTINUES to be upon methodological approaches to the study of myths and rituals, but the scope is somewhat narrower than in the preceding chapters because we will be concerned here with the most contemporary studies of myth and ritual. We will look at semiotic studies that expand upon the structuralism presented in Chapter 7 and at other ways of probing the impressive "afterlife" of myths, in such genres as fairy tales (hence continuing materials introduced in Chapter 6); and the theme of transformation and metamorphosis recurs frequently. We shall be entertaining questions about the role of myth as such in a cultural context (our own) that often is described as *decentered*—hence apparently just a situation where myth as a *centering* device ought to have little relevance. Finally, some of the themes of Chapter 5 return here, in terms of the psychological aspects of experiencing mythic patternings and the satisfactions of ritual; the literary-critical frame of Chapter 6 and themes of Chapters 1 and 2 are engaged once more when we look at some of the ways the "sacred" is being fictively expressed today.

Our task is partly that mythical task assigned in Babylonian epic to Marduk: in the classic epic, *Enuma elish,* Marduk is tested to see if he can rearticulate a fragmented body merely by "speaking it together." Something of the ancient respect for the power of words comes through in that story, as in the Egyptian tale where the hero obtains power by the drinking of a sentence—in fact he imbibes a whole book of magic soaked in beer (Cuthbertson:32).

That we are less impressed today by the power of language is reflected by the old saw "It's just a matter of words"; but on the other hand, most of us still regard as somewhat special the ability to speak several languages other than one's native tongue. And if on the one hand the career of poet or novelist could not be less secure than it is in our megacorporation society, we generally have great trust in politicians who film well, whose tone and manner of phrasing before the camera is, as surveys show repeatedly, more important than her or his previous training or political experience. (Such judgments often reflect differing evaluations from different segments of the population: when I first heard that Ronald Reagan would stand as a candidate for president, my response was "but he's an actor!"—meaning to express my disbelief that someone trained as an actor would have the administrative abilities required by the nation's highest office; but obviously a statistical majority of voters were swayed by Reagan's film career rather than his much briefer political career, about which little was actually known.)[1]

Social and Cultural Semiotics

The rise of semiotics as a classifying system for analysis of all sorts of social and cultural products (not just literature) is surely one of the striking features of scholarship in the 1960s and 1970s. Hardly one serious journal has not witnessed some variety of semiotic analysis, whether of literature, film (especially), sports, politics, or even foods. While it is tempting to see this "pop semiotics" as merely another flash-in-the pan fad, I suspect that it is more important and indeed that it may represent an inescapable stage in future cultural analyses. Not all semiotic analyses look alike, however, and the very mode of discourse varies greatly from one to another work. We begin here with reference to the earlier work of Roland Barthes, whose essays in the French version of *Mythologies* are available in two English translations (1972; 1979; see Coward and Ellis:chap. 2).

Barthes's earlier essays are valuable to anyone engaged in the interpretation of mythological elements of culture, including literature, and hence he usually is included among the literary structuralists reviewed in Chapter 7. *Mythologies* is essentially prestructuralist in Barthes's career, however, and it is indebted more generally to earlier linguistics than to the later narrative-analysis structuralist studies, many of which Barthes himself initiated with *S/Z* (1974) and his later writings.

Barthes's basic argument in the *Mythologies* essays, which were written as brief essays for periodicals, is that myths function to reduce the historicity of objects, to give them a tone of "nature," as when a detergent is advertised as cleaning "deeply." At first the metaphoric nature of the claim is striking—obviously we do not think primarily of cloth as being "deep"—but with repetition it seems only "natural" that particular soap powders should "reach deep down" to hidden filth. Or a travel guide (in this case the exhaustive Hachette World Guides, the "Guide Bleu," in contrast to the green or red Michelin series) may so emphasize the "interesting" or "entertaining" or "amusing" features of a locality that its historicalness is practically lost to view. (Viewers of American television documentaries or visitors to historical reconstructions will be familiar with a similar trivializing and "personalizing.")

Barthes is especially interested in the ways certain arbitrary signs may function to indicate carefully assigned meanings. So a commercial wrestling match is marked by a definite opposition between the good guy or gal and the bad guy or gal. Several distinguishing markers—color of boxing trunks, hairstyle, conspicuous bruises, and the like—as well as particular postures—such as offensiveness toward the referee—instantly convey who fulfills which role. Or popular magazines may provide clues to the readership they are trying to reach by the ways culinary articles are presented: those featuring pale gelatin glazes, for instance—distancing the natural condition of the food—see their readers as seeking to move upward socially; those featuring simple stews or pot roasts are directed toward a working-class readership.

One is often reminded of the persistent opposition between nature and culture (or nature and history) in French intellectual history (see for example Sahlins 1981; Augé). (The opposition has been engaged most recently in the works of Lévi-Strauss, and some of the essays in Barthes's *Mythologies* remind one of the traveler's observations in Lévi-Strauss's *Tristes Tropiques* [1974].) Apart from the concluding essay ("Myth Today"; see also "Change the Object Itself: Mythology Today," in Barthes 1977), which is something of a tour de force, Barthes addresses the issue most directly in a two-and-a-half-page essay on "Plastic." I can best convey a sense of the essay, and hence Barthes's attitude toward the dichotomy between nature and mythicized nature (that is, history), by quoting extensively from the last paragraph of that essay:

> The fashion for plastic highlights an evolution in the myth of "imitation" materials. . . . It is the first magical substance which consents to be prosaic. . . . for the first time, artifice aims at something common, not rare. And as an immediate consequence, the age-old function of nature is modified: it is no longer the Idea, the pure Substance to be regained or imitated: an artificial Matter, more bountiful than all the natural deposits, is about to replace her, and to determine the very invention of forms. . . . Plastic is wholly swallowed up in the fact of being used: ultimately, objects will be invented for the sole pleasure of using them. The hierarchy of substances is abolished: a single one replaces them all: the whole world *can* be plasticized, and even life itself since, we are told, they are beginning to make plastic aortas. (1972:98–99)

It is rare to find a sophisticated intellectual critique applied to the design of new cars, films, soap powders, margarine, and the like, but Barthes manages to avoid cuteness and to illustrate his basic premise that myth is a form, a way of signing meaning (and hence a semiotic system; to paraphrase Marshall McLuhan, the myth is both the message and the form in which the message is conveyed): "the form does not suppress the meaning, it only impoverishes it, it puts it at a distance, it holds it at one's disposal." Or, as suggested earlier, myth "transforms history into nature."

While Barthes's more recent works have moved in quite different directions, *Mythologies* sets an impressive model of an attempt to track the ways the mythological mind-set operates within the culture immediately before one, and I have seldom found a writer so able to apply an analytic so precisely and so succinctly. The elucidation of a literary work is clearly related to such an analysis of a culture, and one wonders if the best preparation for myth-lit-crit might not be assignments to treat something like contemporary advertising as a mythical universe. The question of metaphor and symbol must be addressed in such analysis, and my own students have shown me striking parallels with features of ancient myths in their analyses of contemporary materials such as rock music, political speeches, advertisements, and the like.

It would not be difficult to provide a list of works that have attempted the sort of analysis Barthes has successfully developed but that have not been nearly as rewarding.[2] Perhaps it is too much to expect that a satisfying analytic for contemporary materials can yet be devised, for we have not yet developed adequately comprehensive analytics for materials from antiquity (Klein's analysis of the Homeric Hymn to Hermes demonstrates just how many new insights can be gained from adaptations of Barthes's methods). But insofar as semiotic criticism has as its focus the analysis of materials that reflect particular cultural climates, its practitioners should find it important to include both sociological and psychological studies within their purview. Again we are reminded that our greatest single need is for a multiphasic mode of criticism whose various parts mutually inform each other.

While not explicitly semiotic in orientation, a successful multidisciplinary approach to thematic analysis is to be found in the essays edited by Barbara A. Babcock as *The Reversible World: Symbolic Inversion in Art and Society* (1978), a work that treats inversion in graphic expression and literature as well as in ritual and social behavior. The essays in the volume are concerned with "the ways in which symbolic forms, especially inverted ones" such as creative negations, symbolic inversions, and the roles of tricksters and clowns "affect the ways we perceive, group ourselves, and interact with others" (31), and they seem to me to be a model for the sort of team approach that is possible today.

A volume of essays edited by James J. Preston, on Goddess/Mother figures, is slightly less inclusive of perspective but also gains in analytical power by its groupings of studies oriented toward several different historical periods and geographical areas. Neither Babcock nor Preston includes the sorts of technical semiotic analyses oriented toward the classical discussions of de Saussure in Europe (where the preferred term is semiology), or C. S. Peirce in North America (where the preferred term is semiotics); and neither volume relies upon specialized semiotic vocabulary. I tend to agree with Dundes that "the scholarship of semiotics seems bloated with pompous terminology and littered with competing unintelligible abstract formulations which seem far removed from any close contact with empirical data" (1980:35), an agreement that doubtless has led me to emphasize here semiotic studies that stress application of the method rather than the analytical terminology.

A study of public ritual and drama in Santa Fe, New Mexico, by Ronald Grimes (1976b) helpfully combines religious studies, anthropology, and sociology. The book explores the roles of the interacting cultures (Hispanic, Catholic, Pueblo, Navajo, Protestant, civic, artistic, folkloric, and others) with reference to the unifying theme of the yearly Fiesta de Santa Fé. Grimes develops a history and critique of the fiesta that suggests that symbolic articulation is always selective articulation: one particular *entrada* of the Spanish conqueror DeVargas, for instance, a particularly bloodless coup, is celebrated in the fiesta, rather than the bloody one of two years later. Sensitive not only to what informants told him but also to their sociocultural backgrounds, Grimes was able to perceive the dynamics of the involvements of fiesta participants at many levels, few of which were overtly stated. The work sets a standard for analysis of public rituals that are still occurring regularly and in full view of the entire populace, supported by written texts yet subject to continued oral reinterpretation; Grimes might not wish to label his approach "semiotic" in a strict sense, yet his study seems to me to represent an exemplary semiotic analytic that does not depend upon complex labels and coding systems.

General surveys of semiotic approaches to modern media that may well be of value for mythographic analysis appear in two volumes of the British New Accents series, namely Hawkes, and Fiske and Hartley. Hawkes surveys the developments of contemporary semiotics in an exceptionally clear fashion and provides comprehensive bibliographies and suggestions for a sequence of readings (see also Pettit, who is primarily focused upon the background of semiotics in traditional linguistics).

Fiske and Hartley develop Barthes's concept of "second-order signs," with specific reference to the mythmakers of such signs and their function as connotative agents (41–47). A second-order sign is a development from a first-order sign where simple meanings are equated with signs explicitly; second-order signs are textually more complex and include "a whole range of cultural meanings that derive not from the sign itself, but from the way the society uses and values both the signifier and the signified" (41). The automobile, for example, carries in our social framework all sorts of connotations of virility and masculinity, doubly emphasized by the generally phallic shape of many modern sportscars and elaborated even further in a masculine-oriented society. Finally, third-order significance is attained when the automobile becomes a typifying sign for our own industrial, mechanized, and mobile society.

The language, contents, and iconographic materials of the novel, or of the evening news program, can be shown to be rich with specific signs indicating attitudes and values: the mythological universe (Barthes's third-order system, resulting from the first two orders of signs) will be graphed onto the most everyday stories and events in ways that can be analyzed to disclose their underlying roots.

Watching a David Niven comedy on commercial television recently, I was dismayed by the number of interruptions of the movie for advertisements, including "teasers" for the ten o'clock news program. After my initial anger at having the film broken after periods of seven, and then five, minutes, I applied some of the analysis being surveyed here, and I realized just how accurately the sequence of the telecast film did indeed reflect our contemporary values: we are constantly expected to switch attention from situation to situation, story to story; we are not encouraged to find much "meaning" in what is presented, for that task would take time that otherwise might be used to generate interest in yet another program (or activity or product). And the artistic coherence intended by the film's director is clearly second best to commercialized portrayals of upward social mobility (Berger et al., *Ways of Seeing* [1972], is especially perceptive on this aspect of contemporary advertising).

Semiotic attention to the actual advertisements themselves discloses yet further indicators of contemporary worldview and value systems: for example, Fiske and Hartley point out that the traditional standard of logical persuasion has been left far behind—or as they argue, has been replaced by an earlier stage of oral logic more familiar to non-technological societies: "television's meanings are arrived at through the devices of spoken discourse fused with visual images, rather than through the structures of formal logic" (112). The mode of oral logic is not cool, rational reasoning through a series of propositions, but it is rhetoric, which operates primarily by oppositions between pairs of contrasts (their brand versus ours) or asserts the value of something previously untried (the constant appeal to "the newest and best," a significance that most of us have come to realize usually means only that a new, more expensive form of packaging has been developed). Leymore's more technical study of modern British advertisements relies upon Lévi-Strauss's attention to binary oppositions (which Leymore develops as "Exhaustive Common Denominators") and statistical algebraics to demonstrate just how some of these oppositions actually are employed by advertisers.

We are always far from perfectly realized signs, and probably always will be, which may well be what saves us from some form of insanity. I am thinking of two contemporary stories that suggest that limits are important: Richard Grant's "Drode's Equations" (1981) concerns a fellow who discovers lost mathematical equations, but as he begins to understand them fully, he himself begins to transcend time, and disappears. And in Christopher Cherniak's "The Riddle of the Universe and Its Solution" (1981), the perfect symbol appears in the middle of a computer-generated readout. That symbol was something like "an abstract piece of information," so constructed that "any human who encountered this information lapsed into an apparently irreversible coma." Hofstadter and Dennett also refer to an Arthur Clarke story about a musical tune so catchy that it seizes control of the mind of anyone who hears it; Cherniak's story, with its reference to "the present logophobic atmosphere" in the universities, doubtless refers to the antilogocentrism of contemporary deconstructionism. A story by Stanislaw Lem concerning the virus that destroys all paper comes from the same mind-set.

In their study of the American monomyth pattern, Jewett and Lawrence (1977a) reject the "bubble-gum fallacy" that would treat popular entertainments as merely trivial and diversionary while denying that they may convey mythical materials or perspectives of any formative influence. They argue quite the opposite, that the features of "mythic massage" present mythical stories (and paradigms) in such ways that audiences uncritically accept their efficacy as realistic patterns for coping with current experience.

Mythic massage occurs within the explicit framework of the frequently repeated "myth of mythlessness," that is, the unexamined belief that scientific culture has transcended mythical forms of thought, and hence by implication modern materials cannot be mythical in any important manner. But actually mythic paradigms are fully regulative of the worldview presented, even when the form of the materials may be expressly antitraditional in nature (it is often pseudoempirical, with technological and surface-realistic details enhancing the supposed scientific veracity of the presentation; and it is often anti-intellectual, demonstrating a continued suspicion of education as an agent of change).

Among the ways mythic massage actually functions is the "Werther effect," in which audiences uncritically alter their behaviors to bring them in congruence with paradigmatic models—which may even be explicitly presented as models for emulation, what Jewett and Lawrence refer to as "Werther invitations." Examination of the actual sources for the popular entertainments (often this will mean the historical materials or the fictions used as the bases for film/television versions) according to the "technomythic critical theory" (simply their technical term for criticism, but emphasizing the role of sophisticated modern technology in the actual expression of the paradigmatic models) will disclose any number of awkward incongruences between the sources and the actual expressions; principles involved in the cooptation of the materials include mythic "alchemy," "cuing," "denial," and "selectivity."

The alchemy referred to is the transformation and adaptation of historical materials to fit the mythical paradigm, and it includes omissions, rearrangements, and new emphases of the original materials, shaping them to fit the monomythic framework; the cuing refers to the way in which "iconographic photography" often manages to convey aspects of the mythical paradigm without direct verbal articulation, by using visual and aural cues that may screen out many actual aspects of the original so that one responds only to those selected. Selectivity is related to cuing: repeatedly films presenting urban locales focus only upon the ugliest sections, or the villain is presented only in a negative light.

And finally mythic denial refers to something like Freud's neurotic defense mechanisms: essential components of the original story are denied verbally or symbolically, even though they actually continue to play a vital role—advertisements for the sequel to the movie *Walking Tall* completely reversed the pattern of attendance to the film when they focused not on the actual violence central to the film but upon Buford Pusser's embrace with his wife.

The "technomythic critical theory" of Jewett and Lawrence holds great promise for myth analysis, especially analysis of mythic aspects in contemporary popular entertainments—precisely the type of material experienced by the majority of the population, whose attention is going to be diverted to academic analyses such as those of Campbell or Eliade only rarely. And especially when myth is equated with the less-well-developed past, in such a way as to deny that mythic paradigms or values have any relevance today, we need such analyses that debunk and expose the latest emperor's deceitful suit of clothes. London and Weeks are clear about this moral task of myth study:

> All mythologies contain a vision of what we aspire to be and have within them the purgatory of destructive thoughts. Myth illumines and projects a light in the darkness of reality and the haze of misperception over the glow of truth. It is our task to distinguish between those myths that give us light and those that blind our vision. (xvii; Bidney 1967:296 notes that regarding myth as neutral is a danger to society)

Ariel Dorfman's scathing critiques of such standard Western fare as the Lone Ranger (but also the elephant Babar and other figures of children's literature) and above all his analysis of ten years of the *Reader's Digest* (under the rubric of "The Infantilization of the Adult Reader") show just how extensively persons in Third World nations are affected by the mythical standards exported by American popular media. Dorfman also demonstrates the links between the production of children's literature and the publications politics of his own native Chile. Again and again we Norte Americanos are reminded of the tendency of our vision to shadow out any focus upon the *producers* of the market economy, our inability to think past a sort of decayed individualism that is effectively irrelevant to the problems of most of the world, and our tendency to replace rationality with sentimentality, while denying historical settings and social contexts within our own continent and elsewhere. Something of a corrective is being developed (see Coward and Ellis; Jameson 1981), as a new generation of academics recovers a non-Stalinist Marxism that enables more sophisticated analyses of literary and artistic production as well as of transmission and transformation.

Transformation and Transmission of Mythic Materials

Although we shall be turning to Lévi-Strauss's structuralist algebra of transformations, it is not immediately self-evident that structuralist analysis would be the best place to go for assistance in understanding transformation and change within myths and mythic systems because its perception of structure has been predominantly static.

Pierre Maranda, summarizing "Structuralism in Cultural Anthropology" (1972b), to take only one non-Lévi-Straussian example, is quite emphatic about structuralism as "the study of those properties of a system which remain invariant under a given group of transformations" and in his affirmation that it discusses "a system whose properties can be mapped in terms of a constant set of related propositions" (330); cultures therefore are to be seen "as logical mechanisms for reducing the randomness of history" (330–31).

Maranda sees structuralism focusing upon the ways "societies preserve their identity over time," but he defines this focus as "the study of negentropic processes" (331), a definition that is in tension with his repeated emphasis upon *formal causes* or upon the cultural order as "a system whose properties can be mapped in terms of a constant set of related propositions" (330). From this perspective he sees Lévi-Strauss's charting of vast numbers of permutations of myths in South America as a process of (static) "mappings." Both transformational analysis (as adapted within structuralism) and the generative approach (adapted from generative grammarians) "are essentially a matter of mapping rules which reduce empirical diversity to cognitive manageability" (343).

Lévi-Strauss himself can speak of different levels of transformation—the semantic, the formal, and the etiological (1971a:12), and he suggests that a myth may be stable on one level but not on another. Hence Lévi-Strauss speaks of the "inherent constraint of mythical thought"—that "myth has no inertia." His view leads him to see the possibility of "a mythical typology which would renounce all external criteria. Instead, it would use a single internal and formal criterion, namely the 'degree of order' at which the myths of a region or a population. . . . cease the process of composition which proceeds from the indigeneous eth-nobotanical and ethnozoological base" (20).

If we can never follow myth tellers throughout every instance of their myth telling, we can consider their activities intellectually: "What Lévi-Strauss' work suggests is that although we cannot observe actual trans-formations in this way, we can try and reconstruct them experimentally: we can take intellectual transformations between related myths as hypo-thetical models for genetic transformations" (Sperber:42).

While Lévi-Strauss's oeuvre may be said to be founded, eventually, within the scene of Hamlet's question about being versus nonbeing, and while he may be said to be seeking ultimately "the perception of invar-iant forms within different contents" (D. Bell:23), nonetheless I think we must take the scholar at his own words when he states that he is pursuing a *transformational* method rather than a fluxional method (Lévi-Strauss 1976:18). He is interested in structures, in "the study of transformations through which similar properties are recognized in ap-parently different systems" (18) rather than in a merely derivative ("fluxional") sequencing of mythemes. Hence the informal statement of his position in an interview with John Hess: "My real problem was not to bring out the resemblances [among the many myths studied in the twenty-year production of Mythologiques] but to show that myths that were apparently very different were in fact the same" (Hess:2).

That "apparently . . . different . . . the same" becomes for Lévi-Strauss a hermeneutical tool: a curious example he has cited "would remain incomprehensible if we did not see it as the product of a system-atic inversion" (1981:326); or two congruent but not comprehended myths may be clarified by finding points within them that are linked in another group of myths (1973:120–21). We hear a good deal about inversions and reversals (for example, 1973:128; 1969:310; 1966:chap. 3), and we learn that different *aspects* of a mythic system may be realized or that different levels or codes may be emphasized in different transfor-mations (1981:388, 588–89). Strong as opposed to weak forms of myths exist (1981:591, and frequently); and "remnants" from an earlier version may continue to be present in much later strata (1981:338; cf. the discussion of "vestigial energy" in 1978b:17). And myths may "die" (1976:chap. 14) or "decline" into other forms (1981:603; the geological image of erosion is used, 594).

The whole structure of transformations is best represented as a spiraling process (1973:356, 395), and, typically applying such a guiding metaphor to his own endeavor, we are warned at the outset of Mythologiques that the spiral is the best image for the overall structure of that four-volume work (1969:4). Myths are to be treated not statically but *processually,* in the process of perpetual transformation (1973:354), and within any cultural system we may expect to find various stages of transformation of any particular myth.

But in spite of the two "constraints" in transformation resulting from the permissible grammar of previous versions or the strictures of foreign versions, or the constraint of the infrastructural requirements of the particular system (1981:628), "Properly speaking, there is never any original: every myth is by its very nature a translation, and derives from another myth belonging to a neighboring, but foreign, community, or from a previous myth belonging to the same community" (644).Hence transformation may be called "a sort of principle of conservation of mythic material" (1976:256), and the most one should expect is continued variation between the local and the universal form (1981:355).

Hence every myth is a transformation, and in theory there is no limitation to the possible number of transformations (1981:675), which may be one explanation for the often observed redundancy of myths (a quality of communications systems that compensates for inefficiency at the level of any single transmission; but see Lévi-Strauss 1973:127).

One fairly typical analysis of a transformation process may stand here for the hundreds Lévi-Strauss develops (1981:322):

[bad neighbors = bad weather]::[spatial enemy = "Sioux" = temporal enemy = "Frost"].

This formula may be read: "the category of *bad neighbors* may transform into or be transformed from the category of *bad weather;* that transformation is related to the way a *spatial enemy* may be transformed into a particular group such as the *Sioux* or into a *temporal enemy* such as would be symbolized by a mythological personalization such as *Frost.*" Such a transformational system may work from either extreme toward the middle, may reverse the sequences of transformations found in an adjacent society, or it may stress one side of a transformational equation so much that the implied equivalents are suppressed. A more systematic presentation of the types of transformations traced in the Mythologiques includes:

- a weakening of the polar opposites
- an inversion of the explicit etiological content
- the mutation of the hero
- a correlative inversion of the relations of kinship
- a mutation of family attitudes (1969:138–39); and we must also include larger contexts, as when
- a myth = a romantic tale, or
- a myth = a legendary/semihistorical tradition, or
- a myth = a politicized version (1976:266-67).

And as noted in Chapter 2, transformational variants may come about in order to deal with the nonsensical elements of mythic expression (Freilich 1975:220), just as the related theme of *translatio* in the Christian hagiographic traditions provided a means of removing the saint from the present "vale of tears" into another, more religiously congruent and "blessed" realm.

Likewise *metamorphosis* remains a feature of many types of literature, a feature by which, Rodney Needham suggests, "certain narratives represent the evasion of constraints" (59) in ways characteristic of the play of the human imagination when confronted with the ineluctable strictures of time and place. Hence, Needham argues, many features of mythic transformations are simply features of the human imagination as such (64)—an argument not far from Lévi-Strauss's declarations about the transcendental quality of myths as representing Mind in general.

Another feature of human imagination and thought in general is the parallel between transformation or metamorphosis and *syncretism,* the merging of variations or discrepancies into one colossally inclusive figure. An example from sixteenth-century France—a time of great conflict between the contemporary and the antique—will illustrate the way the syncretistic view can "have its cake and eat it too": There is a painting of Francis I presented as a fusion of Minerva, Mars, Diana, Cupid, and Mercury:

> the king is transformed into a monstrous hybrid, his bearded and be-helmeted head placed on a feminine body, his breast protected by the aegis [Athena's shield], and his feet equipped with wings. On his back he carries Diana's quiver and hunting horn; with his right arm . . . he brandishes

Minerva's sword, and in his left hand he carries Mercury's caduceus and Cupid's bow. (Panofsky and Panofsky:59, n. 9)

While the lack of semantic joins seems apparent in the Panofskys' description, it may not have been as evident to the court of Francis I, any more than the late Hellenistic period was aware of the (to us) awkwardness and incongruity of the many fusionist perspectives in much of its religious art (it was the rage to show Greek parallels with Egyptian and Near Eastern figures; some of the allegorical figures are literally crawling with miniature attributes that seem to have come forth from some great mythological bestiary).

There may be something unusual about the role of language in metamorphosis, and I am still puzzling over Massey's suggestion that literary metamorphosis represents a critique of public language (the protagonist who is transformed—and I think immediately of Kafka's figure in "The Metamorphosis"—ends up estranged, isolated, caught in a private world from which no communication with the ordinary world is still possible; the same problem with language is made evident in the figure of "the double" in literature [Massey:26–27]).

Such questioning of the role of language also enters into questions about the nature of irony, discussed seemingly endlessly and without much resolution, even in studies focused upon its psychic function or "deep" structural purposes. And so a modern term for transformative language such as Bertolt Brecht's estrangement-effect (*Verfremdungseffekt*) or Viktor Schlovsky's defamiliarization (*ostranenie;* see Stacy) may be useful for describing a phenomenon in the arts that is perhaps unusually frequent within the modern period, but such a term merely names a phenomenon that undergirds all aspects of communicative expression, even with respect to the phenomenon of masking discussed earlier in this book. Masking includes the disguising of appearances at least temporarily, and Stacy (17) reminds us that Ovid, the famous author of the *Metamorphoses,* was also the author of a text on the use of cosmetics for altering women's hair coloring and appearance.

Casey Fredericks also argues that the application of terms such as defamiliarization only to self-consciously literary materials is insufficient; he particularly highlights the "dislocations" of usual experienced reality within mythic narratives (40, citing Kirk 1970) but then takes the idea to its extreme: "A 'myth' may then be defined simply as a fiction whose entire narrative field is taken up with dislocation effects" (41); and "in myths we find dissolutions of antitheses normal to the real world" (41). From such a perspective Fredericks quite helpfully raises the participant-observer dilemma of learning how to recognize where a native account would be comprehended by the informant as nonordinary: "It may well be the case that myths represent a nonnaturalistic distorted world even for members of their own cultures and are no more to be considered realistic thought patterns and images than the 'white tornado' and 'helping hands' magic that appears in our TV fantasies could be considered our 'reality'" (46). Something such as the "garfinkeling" litmus test to which Pettit (62) and Jewett and Lawrence (1977a:49, 52) refer is needed to find the odd joins and elements within a system: the extent of "normal" or "realistic" frames can be discovered by systematic substitution of one nonusual act in a set situation—for example, assigning grades from M to R instead of from A to F, or lecturing with gloves on.

Universalizing Fairy Tales and Myths

One of the types of transformation is that between genres, in particular between those of fairy tale and myth.[3] David L. Miller argues against Marie-Louise von Franz that fairy tales represent a fusion of mythic elements and might be referred to as "collapsed myths" (1976:158; on the relation of nursery rhymes to myths of origins, see Moebius; and on the relation of folk to fairy tales, see Zipes). Miller contends that the fairy tale tends to rework mythic elements in allegoristic fashion, seeking to reduce the plurality of mythic characters and motives to a more simplified life story. Instead of von Franz's position that myths are degenerations of fairy tales (because they are "contaminated" by historical references and specific names), Miller argues that the leveling effect by which myths become tales is a result of the collapse of the mythic narrative, with the subsequent pluralizing of single heroines and deities into a plurality of deities (usually referred to merely as "the Bride" or "the Ogre") who no longer have the open-ended context of myth but become merely moralistic ciphers.

One of the most consistent positions in distinguishing myths from fairy tales is represented in Bruno Bettelheim's extensively Freudian *The Uses of Enchantment* (1976). The book argues strongly for giving children many stories in which they can proleptically and imaginatively play out serious psychosocial situations. Fairy tales provide imaginative compensations for real lacks, or they demonstrate ways of dealing with threatening or negative impulses in terms children are likely to be fantasizing anyway.

I often find Bettelheim's studies of fairy tales too excessively psychosexual in focus, and I wonder if the primary function of the tales may not be to provide means for dealing with issues neither parents nor children can efficiently and gracefully name as creating tensions between them. Such a view would see fairy tales as representing a language of accommodation, neither an adult mode nor a child's; I am curious about von Franz's suggestion that "until about the seventeenth century, it was the adult population that was interested in fairy tales. Their allocation to the nursery is a late development" (1972a:1).

Such a view would be close to Max Lüthi's judgment that the fairy tale represents an initiation (61; Bettelheim 1976:35, 278), and hence it can share the initiatory/liminal characteristics of lightness and freedom from the usual social constraints (Lüthi:77), an overcoming or transcending of time (by ignoring it!—44), fondness for the riddle (131), and a sublimation of material things (93) before the larger issues of cosmic meaning and the posited permanences of the religious sphere (25, 143).

But according to Bettelheim (1976:34) it is just the "gentle, indirect, undemanding" fairy tale that does *not* engage such universals, although Bettelheim does find that the fairy tale gives one hope for one's personal future, and he repeatedly stresses the *didactic* elements in the use of fairy tales for the child's imaginative education (161, 201; often this function results from allegories in the fairy tales—cf. 75 n.—but "the greatest merit of a fairy story is that it gives answers," 218; or it gives an "overt message," as in the story of Cinderella, 258).

What puzzles me in Bettelheim's treatment is his strongly negative animus against myth, which always comes out poorly when compared with fairy tale:

- Myths with their majestic manner of presentation present superhuman heroes making constant demands upon mere mortals with whom we cannot possible identify (26)—but can we identify any more easily with fairy tale figures possessing iron hands or headless torsos?
- Myths involve unique, grandiose events as compared with the everyday, ordinary encounters in fairy tales (37)—but are gingerbread houses, wolves that speak, or magical transformations of humans into beasts all that "ordinary"?
- Mythic endings are tragic or pessimistic, those of fairy tales happy or optimistic (37)—yet the Christian savior myth ends with transcendence of death, and "Cinderella," in many versions, with punishment of the greedy sisters.
- Myths are the stories of particular heroes whereas fairy tales tell the story of Everyone (40)—yet the "absolute uniqueness of this event"

in "The Frog King" negates Bettelheim's usual description of the generality of the tales (62); and the judgment ignores the vast number of myths about "The People, Our Ancestors."

- Myths give definitive, fairy tales suggestive answers to questions about the true nature of the world (45); hence fairy tales correspond to the child's "animistic" ways of thinking and experiencing—but are the Chaos personifications in the book of Job or at the beginning of Genesis any more "adult" or "less animistic"?
- Fairy tales involve perils equal to those in myths, but they are always "successfully overcome," leading to "higher integration" and " happiness" (198)—but if myths do not also function to foreshadow hopes and patterns to resolve crises, the whole emphasis of myths as providing part-resolutions for the not-finally-resolvable mysteries of life and death is entirely negated.

Many of Bettelheim's distinctions simply will not hold water, and I think one of the reasons is that his analysis is not sufficiently flexible to encompass the many *types* of myths *or* fairy tales (it seems similarly limited when utilized for tales other than European fairy tales). But the main reason why the analytic becomes skewed so that myth becomes primarily a straw target used to highlight his preferred fairy tales is that Bettelheim's psychological applications of tale materials determine his formal analysis: "Myths project an ideal personality acting on the basis of superego demands, while fairy tales depict an ego integration which allows for appropriate satisfaction of id desires," and hence "myths are useful in forming not the total personality, but only the superego" (41). Finally, the judgment that mythic heroes are good superego models but they "discourage the child in his fledgling strivings to achieve personality integration" (39) becomes for Bettelheim a sufficient basis to reject myths as such.

Fairy tales are not to be moralized, for they are self-sufficient, and they "offer figures onto which the child can externalize what goes on in his mind, in controllable ways" (64)—yet when Bettelheim refers to specific myths, such as that of Herakles/Hercules (34, 41, 313), he uses only Gustav Schwab's extensively moralized and allegorized retellings (corresponding to those of Thomas Bullfinch in anglophone areas).

And while I happen to agree with Bettelheim that one way of distinguishing the *fable* from either fairy tale or myth is that it states a moralism directly, leaving little to the imagination (42–43), to state that "The Three Little Pigs," contrasted by Bettelheim to fables, "teaches the nursery-age child in a most enjoyable and dramatic form that we must not be lazy and take things easy, for if we do, we may perish" (41–42) seems to undercut the very distinctions Bettelheim wishes to establish.

I do not deny that Bettelheim's serious treatment of fairy tales from a psychoanalytical viewpoint expands considerably our repertory of ways of approaching fairy tales, but it is done in a markedly less historically informed and less sophisticated fashion than that of von Franz or Hedwig von Beit (Bettelheim dispatches the Jungians in one passing reference, 36). Bettelheim's writings are important, and the book has been cited regularly (see Zipes's strong critique); hence I have given so much attention to this issue at this point. Ultimately, however, I find that Bettelheim overinterprets in an arbitrary fashion; there is justice to Stacy's comment (174) that Bettelheim, "like a Church Father hunting allegory in Scripture," "searches for sexual allusion in . . . familiar fairy tales."

Discussion of all the various forms of transformation of myths, and of generic changes in the shifting from myth to tale to epic, or even the range of metamorphosis and change within any one body of mythical materials such as the Greek, would be a book-length enterprise in itself, and one that should be highly rewarding. We have begun to understand some of the ways mythical materials are transmitted, especially as a new type of specialist in "oral literature" has appeared within our own century. Many of our long-cherished ideas should have been relinquished long ago, such as the idea that change in oral literature takes place only gradually: Frank Cushing's experiences in the nineteenth century among the Zuni of New Mexico should have put the lie to that idea—he introduced in 1886 a European tale about "The Cock and the Mouse," and he found when he returned only one year later that the story had grown fivefold in length as it had been assimilated to Zuni cultural contexts (recounted in Gill:46–47).

Similarly, we now have available studies that recount the change-over-time in a number of symbol complexes, such as Linenthal's account of the changes in ascribed meanings given to the Little Bighorn battlefield in Montana. In this case it is possible to track the transformations of the ascribed significances of the monument from those that emphasized General George Armstrong Custer's "noble campaign for the preservation of civilization" to those of the twentieth-century recognition of the destructiveness of white "civilizing" pressures upon Native American populations. "Until 1976 only voices of celebration and affirmation were publicly heard as some Americans honored those who 'conquered' the frontier and its inhabitants and ritually revivified the national virtues displayed on that June day," but subsequently there has been "a call to confront the dark side of the battle and the relentless ideology it represented" (Linenthal:279).

When the revisioning of psychology is now a relevant possibility—either in the Lacanian revisioning of Freud, or Hillman's revisioning of

Jung and archetypal psychology in general (Hillman 1975c)—or when Foucault and others ask us to reimagine the history of human sexuality or of penal and mental institutions, it is clear that the theme of transmission and transformation has become a dominant hermeneutical concern of the modern period.

"Many indeed are the shapes and changes of heavenly beings," remarks Euripides in *Helen,* but that remark is no less fitting for the shapes and changes in the ways of human analysis or even in the means of understanding something as fundamental as the human mind (as Hampden-Turner illustrates in his large catalog of approaches to the psyche, ranging from Chinese philosophy to Julian Jaynes to Martin Luther King). Transformation and transmission may even become forms of dismantling of the received traditions, in an enterprise that stretches within the modern period from Nietzsche through Derrida. And it is to that recent context of deconstructive thinking that we now turn our attention.

Decentered, Deconstructed Universes

No generation is exempt from the power of ruling metaphors to describe its temper. "Deconstruction" is one such metaphor that has contemporary power—notably as represented by Jacques Derrida and a host of critical theorists who just a decade ago were hardly recognized outside of highly specialized enclaves of critical theory. If we take one definition with which I believe many literary deconstructionists would agree, I think we will find that the movement trails a long line of related mid- and late-twentieth-century critical terms and outlooks (see M. C. Taylor 1983 for a good introductory survey). Jonathan Culler states that "to deconstruct a discourse is to show how it undermines the philosophy it asserts, or the hierarchical oppositions on which it relies, by identifying in the text the rhetorical operations that produce the supposed ground of argument, the key concept or premise" (1982:86).

It is pretty obvious here that deconstruction appears within the context of the hermeneutics of deceit or suspicion we have met earlier in this book; and because deconstruction as a movement is sometimes difficult to differentiate from movements known as *post*modernism, *post*structuralism, *anti*modernism, or *post*scriptive analysis, it is not possible to situate the movement fully without extensive contexting in terms of the various twentieth-century modes of analysis and criticism— an endeavor that has been initiated in this book but that would require much more space for comprehensive discussion (helpful introductions include: Culler 1982; M. C. Taylor 1982:67–105; Norris:introductory bibliog., 143–52).

My focus here will be only upon the ways contemporary critical theory and analysis have begun to clarify the decentering of our experienced, perceived, and ideologically conceived universe. I am concerned primarily with one aspect of the modern experience, namely that extensive shattering of a coherent worldview that began in the West at least by the time of the European Renaissance. I am sympathetic to Marshall Berman's suggestion that all the *post-* and *anti-* qualifiers are essentially irrelevant: the primary phenomenon with which we have to wrestle, and have had to wrestle since the Renaissance, is that of modernism itself.[4] A period such as our own that is strongly ruled by fads and progressive phases of analysis (a pernicious leftover from Social Darwinism, I sometimes suspect) follows a market economy of ideas and labels not unlike any other type of economics but one that may so promote "the newest and best" that we avoid dealing with the underlying decentering and fragmentation experienced in all modern cultures.

Sometimes, of course, we still seek final answers, anchors, determinate meanings; yet our everyday experience is much more accurately expressed in a brief poem by A. R. Ammons entitled "Things Change, the Shit Shifts" (5):

we are abandoned
here to found
our lives on gossamer
distinctions
where steel rusts
& rock cannot hold

But if there is a lack of anything other than "gossamer / distinctions," we still search, and fiction and poetry writers in particular continue to intrigue us with hints toward a collocation of meaning that may last beyond the immediate moment, what Charles Newman perceptively refers to as cultural (as well as economic) *inflation*.

I have been intrigued and somewhat dismayed to find even in recent speculative fiction writers the sense of giving up projected meanings— as expressed for instance in the comments of the character Lamarr in Alan Brennert's story "Stage Whisper": "Lately I wonder if all of us— writers, artists, the whole neurotic bunch—don't just confuse the issue [of what life *should* be], lead people to believe there's an order to life when there's nothin' of the sort" (152).

The traditional way of dealing with the experienced lack of order has been to assume that it must be yet present at some "deeper" level of the classical texts of the Western tradition—whether scriptural in the religious sense or in an aesthetic-artistic sense. Elaborate hermeneutical regulatory systems have been devised to safeguard the primacy of the text and the assumption that its *inner*-textuality somehow contains privileged meanings: consequently religious scriptures, for example, are held to be exempt from the "secular" types of literary criticism applied to any other texts. But today theorists confront us with the vast importance of texts' *intra*-textuality—and hence their relativity, with the fact that meanings are *given to* the texts *by the critic* who initiates the interpretive gestures by seeking to discover what is there; different critical postures produce different meanings.

In such straits Catherine Belsey reminds us that "In producing knowledge of the text criticism actively transforms what is given" (138), alerting us to the fact that it is not only Brennert's "writers, artists, the whole neurotic bunch" who have led us to believe that there is actually an "order" out there somewhere, but also critics and theologians who have promised to discover and disclose that centralizing order.

But if the text is actively transformed in the critical act, if the hermeneutical spiral itself is an inadequate metaphor for interpretive activity when it still gives privilege to an originating Something There, then even the "showing what's there" is suspect as an act not of discovering but of adding to, *supplementing,* as Derrida would have it, or filling in the blank spaces of "the grid created by a glance, an examination, a language." The object of analysis is itself differently objectified in particular ways by particular analysts.

Such a view of what happens within literature (both the writing and the criticism of it) brings with it a fundamental revision of our traditional notion of the Author—who, Foucault suggests, makes a "voluntary obliteration of the self" (1977:117) by creating a literary work that is now available as an object for various critics rather than a work that reveals the author's own purposes or selfhood. Nietzsche's concept of "effective history" contrasted with history as objective chronicle becomes an "affirmation of knowledge as perspective" (Foucault 1977: 156)—*not* an establishment of truth as an absolute, *not* as an uncovering of transcendent Truth or Order lying somehow concealed or embedded within the text.

The consequences for the formal mythographic work are considerable, as they are for all the sorts of disciplines that have claimed some authoritative knowledge about "classics of thought," "Western theology," "the humanities," or "great ideas." In some ways participants in the knowledge-technology industry (that is, the educational establishment, no matter at what level) have left to them a role more akin to Sokrates' method of evoking knowledge through a shifting of patterns within what one already knows, that is, a metaphysical revisioning through which the learner begins "to see" in new combinations and applications. "The philosophy of truth and identity, and the institutions and pedagogy which serve as its handmaidens" (writes Bouchard, introducing Foucault's 1977 *Language, Counter-Memory, Practice*:23) "will be replaced by the philosophy of difference, a philosophy which arises 'through the looking glass' and through a perspectival reversal into new sense." In that case mythography no less than any other hermeneutics would be recognized as a matter of knowing-power, of controlling the distribution of information (as Foucault and Derrida demonstrate in their quite different styles of expression: see Sheridan's critical summary of Foucault's treatment of the knowledge-as-power theme, and Derrida's several remarks concerning the politics of shaping a new college of philosophy for the French government).

Whether or not we wish to speak of "modernism" or "postmodernism" in this context, terms that seem primarily to have been developed within the context of North and South American literary discussions, it is clear that it is not only contemporary theory and criticism that reflect the new significance of *the signifier* (rather than the transcendental signified), but fiction as well; and I would argue (and have, in Doty 1975) that the very constitutive style of much contemporary literature itself reflects the decentering of our consciousness. Gerald Graff makes this point clearly: "Modernist fiction radically disrupts the linear flow of narrative, frustrates expectations about the unity and coherence of human 'character' and the cause-and-effect continuity of its 'development,' and calls into question, by means of ironic and ambiguous juxtapositions, the universalizable moral and philosophical 'meaning' of literary action" (306). Graff stresses the "tone of epistemological self-mockery" that dominated so many of the American fictions of the 1960s and 1970s, which he considers "a symptom of declining bourgeois values" (306). Central to this symptom is the decline of the realist perspective that had been entrenched so firmly in American and to a lesser extent European fiction.

Realism was doubtless the last flourishing of the "prose of the world" hermeneutics and prose theory, and when realism itself became a matter of self-consciousness guiding the literary work, when it became merely a convention, its innate conservative tendencies simply could not provide enough creative freedom for the artist. Or we might say it no longer provided a necessary tension between the artist and the social context: "Realism is plausible not because it reflects the world, but because it is constructed out of what is (discursively) familiar" (Belsey:47), yet the artist constructs and makes meanings not only out of the familiar but the unfamiliar also, that which strains at the meanings of the foreground in order to become the new background.

"Classic realism," in Belsey's summation (70), "is characterized by *illusionism,* narrative which leads to *closure,* and a *hierarchy of discourses* which establishes the 'truth' of the story." Postrealist critics, on the other hand:

> seek not the unity of the work, but the multiplicity and diversity of its possible meanings, its incompleteness, the omissions which it displays but cannot describe, and above all its contradictions. In its absences, and in the collisions between its divergent meanings, the text implicitly criticizes its own ideology; it contains within itself the critique of its own values. (109)

Most of these characteristics apply as well to fiction as to criticism; nor do I find much difference any longer between the writer of a text and the critic of a text with respect to the voice that has become increasingly familiar as the "deconstructive": "To deconstruct the text . . . is to open it, to release the possible positions of its intelligibility, including those which reveal the partiality . . . of the ideology inscribed in the text" (Belsey:109). To deconstruct the mythic text would similarly be to expose the structures by which it works, to lay out the possible alternative futures to which its gestures might lead, to show how its expression is molded and shaped by its cultural contexts—including the ways its mythemes and its language are grounded in its cultural worldview.

The opposite of this sort of deconstructionism would seem to be the type of perspective represented very powerfully in our own day by B. F. Skinner's *Beyond Freedom and Dignity*; that response is to search for a new centering and controlling principle for society, one perhaps rooted in presumably unchanging psychobiological realities and hence finally resistant to any essential change or transformation. Ted Spivey considers Skinner appropriately enough within the context of a longing "for the kind of stasis the Victorians sought after the revolutionary fervor of romanticism" (3)—but I would also point to the resurgence of dogmatic conservative ("fundamentalist") Christian movements that became so widespread in the United States during the 1970s.

But if the conservative Christian reaction to the decentralization of our culture represents one reaction, a reaction based on returning to a mythic frame and theological center that most of the contemporary world is no longer able to find intellectually stable, there are other types of conservatisms: for instance, returning to a model of standard educational requirements (the various standard-curriculum reforms) or, on the other hand, a self-conscious attempt to de-emphasize the liberal arts, as more commercially oriented curricula come to dominate a collegiate atmosphere where students are terrified of not having immediately marketable skills upon graduation.

There are mythic models functioning fully today no matter where one turns—I suspect that no culture has ever existed where that was not the case, although we have noted above the tendency to think of our own era as an era of "mythlessness" (see Jewett and Lawrence 1977a, on the contemporary functions of a "myth of mythlessness"). The alienation effect discussed earlier, the breakdown of most meaningful communal associations because of the rapidity and separation of our complex professional and social lives, the rush to live through a multiple series of self-identities that threaten to become obsolete before we have selected the right hairstyle: ours is a vastly decentered cosmos. Its "deconstruction" seems not so much a threat as a promise if it will tutor us in a more satisfying metaphoring of the whole complex of knowledge and its application—a sort of "athletics of the psyche" that might enable us to weather more satisfyingly this mad rush of alternative selves and worldviews that otherwise seem only disjunctively decentered and passionately *dys*constructed. (James Ogilvy's *Many Dimensional Man* [1977] strikes me as the single most impressive attempt to respond comprehensively to the new polycentrism of the "self.")

The reconnecting may well be a "religious" function—at least if the primary meaning of *religio* still has any validity: I mean "tying together," relating, framing various elements into a meaningful whole. But it may look little like any previous "religious" systems. In the last two sections of this book, I ask what sorts of theological resources are available for more holistic patterns in human expressivity. I find them in arguing that the sacred can best be regarded in terms of its fictiveness, its mythicity. After that section, several moral aspects of mythographic study are delineated and evaluated (in "Mythographic Moralities").

The Sacred as Fictive Mythicity

Those within the disciplines associated with contemporary theological reflection are usually quite aware of developments across the range of the humanities, and so it is not surprising that we hear increasingly within recent theological contexts of a "deconstructive" move precisely as powerful and disturbing as within, say, literary criticism or the analysis of historical movements. Some view deconstruction as the logical application of the 1960s' "death of god theology" to theological discourse. Perhaps we should also see it as the logical fruition of the movement toward an acceptance of the radically symbolic (and hence radically relative, radically fictive) hermeneutics that touched all twentieth-century disciplines in the liberal arts—a movement initially identified as well as supported by Ernst Cassirer and Susanne K. Langer.[5]

The key names of Nietzsche, Feuerbach, Hegel, and especially Heidegger are no less important for most of contemporary theology than they are (with the exception of Feuerbach, so far as I know) for deconstructionist Jacques Derrida. Those whose work is primarily within religious studies in Western universities find such contemporary deconstructive works as Richard Rorty's *Philosophy and the Mirror of Nature* (1979), or Foucault's brand of deconstructive history, as well as Derrida's treatments of literary and philosophical texts, not strange new influences from abroad so much as the logical culmination of hermeneutical moves already well established within liberal scholarship and theory.[6]

If there have been relatively few works produced under the explicit rubric of deconstruction (Altizer et al.; Detweiler; Kemp; and M. C. Taylor 1982), that may well indicate a disenchantment with so many short-lived fads within religious studies in recent years, or even—and I think this more likely—the matter of commercial publishers' near-total withdrawal from the "religion" market, due to their being capitalized primarily by profit-seeking corporations. Those few presses that remain interested in titles in religion are primarily subsidized houses, and they in turn are bound toward a conservative point of view by their own boards of directors, who represent the people-in-the-pews who could not be *less* interested in movements that threaten yet more decentering of their already fragile worldview.

Given the influential role of religious thinkers in earlier periods of American intellectual history, it is probably important to recognize the contemporary marginality of professional theologizing, what Charles Winquist names as its liminal position. Today even symbolic meaning, which almost any theological analysis of the functions of religion assumes to be absolutely crucial, "is often decorative at the periphery of the secular culture but it is not an enigma at its center" (Winquist 1983:301). Others also have noted that the aftermath of the earlier emphasis upon symbolism as a major component of religious expression has been a recognition of *the contextual nature of the symbol;* as M. C. Taylor tersely summarizes, "Meaning is contextual; context is semiophantic" (1982:49).

Hence the self-referentiality of the symbolic itself comes to the fore rather than the reference to the Absolute Other that is still presumed in most Western theology. But the deconstructionist's theme of the "death of the author/ity" becomes another version of "the death of the gods": "Language . . . not rooted in and does not point toward an extra-linguistic referent. . . . the death of God paves the way for the birth of the sign, the sign whose distinctive traits are its conventionality and its external relation to and thus arbitrary association with the signified" (M. C. Taylor 1982:91).

Part of the issue in contemporary discussions is the extent to which the modern person "really" experiences or lives out a symbolic/fictive worldview as opposed to more traditional truth claims and religious centers: Charles Hardwick considers the fictive or "polysymbolism" alternative only a question of deceit, of bad faith. Hardwick's judgments occur within a debate with Lonnie Kliever (1978, 1979), who is more receptive to living with a radically symbolic/fictive perspective. It would involve the second-level naiveté Paul Ricoeur has commended: analysis may lead one beyond the level of an initial naive acceptance of a text's authority to a second level where it no longer has the same authority yet still "means" symbolically, or perhaps we might say "authoritatively-as-symbolically."[7]

Janet Varner Gunn proposes another, more pragmatic test, in referring to the issue of "truth" in autobiography and myth:

> Truth lies in the story's *sufficiency:* in its capacity to make sense of experience told, shared, and even made newly possible for both the teller and the hearer of the story. Just as the authorship of autobiography is tacitly plural [the authorial "we"], so the truth of autobiography is to be found, not in the "facts" of the story itself, but in the relational space *between* the story and its reader. (142)

Such a view is similar to that of William Shepherd (to whose 1974 article on "being wrong religiously" both Hardwick and Kliever are responding; Shepherd in turn was strongly influenced by the thought of Norman O. Brown, having written a study guide to *Love's Body*). Shepherd's advocacy of a "polysymbolic religiosity" acknowledged that "Truth . . . in our context somehow lies in the interstices widely dividing the apparent stabilities of life" (80).

The issue quickly becomes the acceptance or avoidance of one or another type of transcendence model. John Hayward shows the essential rationalism behind several modern models, including those of David

Bidney's scientism and those of Henri Bergson and Cassirer upon which Bidney is dependent for his trust in rationality. Hayward notes that"One feature of the intellectual history of the West is that it has gradually 'demythologized' its discourse by converting mythical transcendence models (concrete narratives of gods and men) into abstract transcendence models (general principles underlying systems of thought). In this process, scraps of myth continue to remain, even in modern discourse" (207).For his own choice, Hayward ultimately opts for a dynamic, anthropocentric process model, "a humanism in a theistic setting" (217), which he brings together with "the Christian dying and rising imagery" (218), a choice that seems to me to do just what he thought ought to be avoided, namely mixing "scraps of myth" into his analytic.

Nonetheless, Hayward identifies some of what must be given up if we are to avoid totally a "doctrine of transcendence," and I would suggest that precisely what he says we must give up *has* been relinquished in much of the contemporary deconstructive orientation: "any image of a stable and orderly reality transcending human consciousness"; "history . . . would be stripped of all purpose and all progress"; "One would have to chase away the remnants of a myth of the soul (which says that one's individuality is sacred or worthy *in se*)"; and "one would also have to chase away a myth of the neighbor (which claims that what one encourages or prevents in others is equally subject to sacred considerations)" (212–13). There is a strangely proleptic quality about this list from 1968, and while I think many of its components strike us as initially "atheistic" or disturbing, the list is almost a summary of the philosophical residua that a deconstructive position would seek to rethink, if not purge.

The element of "ecstasy" Hayward wants to stress in the eventual reconstruction of a mythic ontology (217) also is emphasized in a more recent essay by Jack Carloye, who relates it to the "dreamlike quality" of myths (I would qualify: of *some* myths): the mythic gods and images have a built-in ambiguity of identity and can transform at will into fantastic forms—these are as well two characteristics of Carloye's definition of the *mythopoeic* experience (182). This opening to the mythopoeic is one I will follow later; for now I will indicate at least a certain impatience with his suggestion that the semantical rules of the mythopoesis are "based on a revelatory mystical experience" (188) as with his suggestion that "The need for myths is to replace the diverse empirical (common sense) explanations with a unifying worldview" (188). I would argue instead that myths attempt not to replace empirical explanations but to add to their lot, seeking to become privileged metonymic explanations rather than metaphoric/poetic approximations to the finding of ontological meaning.

Otherwise we are back before the "mirror of reality" that Rorty has shown to be shattered within the modern era, back at a time when the translinguistic fact of transcendence could be understood as originative of all empirical reality. Rather I agree with Gould's formulation that fiction and myth arise precisely from a refusal to accept that the world's reality is sufficient: "We need it [the real world] in more vicarious, even abstracted forms, *for it to be fully alive*" (138, my emphasis).

My reflections about the contemporary distrust of artistic realism earlier in this chapter may be recalled at this point: if the realist mode declined along with a (deconstructive) sense of its political aspects, its implicit distinctions between upper- and lower-class realities, it also became too much like the daily data obsession of our time. If fiction moves now to a more speculative tone, we might see that move as an attempt to point more vitally toward some *projected meanings* of the world that are more imaginatively fictive than the realistic claim merely *to reflect* the world mimetically.

Eric Gould's impressive *Mythical Intentions in Modern Literature* (1981) already has been cited a number of times in this book. Few scholarly analyses manage both to clarify so well complexities of the modern/postmodern uses of myth and to establish at the same time a new base of probing what the uses of myth may be, as a perennial aspect of literary expression.

But I also find Gould's emphasis upon the philosophical functions of the mythic as an element of consciousness, upon *mythicity*, to use his own term, to have wide-reaching consequences for all the modes of reflection that concern human expression and meaning but especially the modern forms of imaginative fiction. I will first recapitulate here some key elements of his exposition and critique that I have not developed earlier in this book, and then I will suggest some of the ways I see his work establishing guidelines for the future, in myth-lit-crit as in several other disciplines, including the philosophical and theological— however and wherever they may be taking shape today.

Gould works initially with the concept of the archetype, showing that (in contradistinction to Jungian essentialism, as discussed in Chapter 5) its significance lies more in its universality, its signifying as a moment of discovering meaningful pattern, than in its sacred origins (29). It is "a representation of experience resulting itself from the quite distinct intent to make an interpretation of the world" (33), hence a powerful sign at the heart of mythicity (it is this "powerful sign" aspect Winquist

1974:109 established as a necessity for grounding the personal story: I come to tell my own life story only by reference to the ruling master stories of my age).

For most of the span of Western culture the divine has ciphered the incapacity of language to bridge the ontological gap between an event and its meaning. Although it repeatedly comes to stand as an effective fiction for living in the anxiety produced by a recognition of that gap, produced by our discomfort at recognizing the arbitrariness of various religious traditions in naming the "event" with many different "meanings," the divine actually indicates little more than the impossibility of fully filling the ontological gap: "The fact that classical and totemistic myths have to refer to some version of translinguistic fact—to the Gods and Nature—proves not that there are Gods, but that our talents for interpreting our place in the world may be distinctly limited by the nature of language" (Gould:7).We live within a world where symbolic meanings may help—do help—yet are never fully able to bridge the ontological gap; fictions and religious myths both aspire to do the bridging work, yet both remain incomplete, insufficient. However, myths become tautologous, become the archetypal benchmarks that we forget are only temporary, whereas fictions tend to remain more provisional.

The relationship between the two is infinitely difficult to distinguish: "all fiction, however much it looks like reality, is a refusal to accept that the real world is ever quite enough" (138), but "The meaning of a fiction is always potentially mythic" (113). Myth follows a deconstructive rather than a syllogistic logic as it makes itself apparent in plot. "It is impossible to create a fiction without approaching the condition of myth, without attempting to be tautologous," Gould reminds us, or without the tacit attempt "to complete a meaning, . . . to continue a transformation and close an action." Fictions and myths inhabit a spectrum of imaginary discourse upon which we depend for the meanings we live by—but almost any religion demonstrates how its constructs soon obtain dogmatic-mythic authority. Only a form of symbolic criticism, in particular literary criticism, can "decide whether a fiction actually is mythic or not—and that is one of the demands of its unavoidable functions as a signifier of literature" (113).

If a fiction is a refusal to accept that the world's reality can ever be sufficiently expressed, however, the question facing the contemporary writer is whether or not it will ever attain the ontological status accorded to myth as a superior treatment of fact.[8]

The contemporary literary voices that attempt some possible connections between event and meaning serve primarily to enrich our comprehension of reality: James Joyce shows us that "reality is not static but a changing systematic . . . recoverable in Joyce's logic of the pun, the epiphany, and the multilayered plot" (Gould:12); D. H. Lawrence and T. S. Eliot (the other modern writers to whom Gould devotes most of his attention) "attempt to recover the numinous in literature in their belief in the logocracy of writing" (13).

Gould's treatment of the archetypal aspects of these authors is entirely different from the search for the essentialized Quest motif Northrop Frye's program would seem to foster. Gould focuses rather upon the statement, the archetype, *and* its network of interpretation-signification: once we have discerned an archetypal pattern, we have yet to analyze how a particular author incorporates it and gives it the unique shaping it has *within* the literary work (Leslie Fiedler's "signature").

Derrida establishes that there is no absolute, central origin or core to an archetype "back there" (in opposition to both Carl Jung and René Girard), and the hermeneutical emphases of F. D. E. Schleiermacher, Wilhelm D. Dilthey, and Rudolf B. Bultmann seem to have been essentially wrong in their various ways of emphasizing the individual self, apart from ongoing social and historical contexts of meanings (as we see both from Heidegger's and from Gadamer's subsequent development of interpretive method). We are left, then, with the insight of contemporary linguistics that meanings are made possible by systems of *differences,* by systematic choices between possible alternatives, not by individual willing or disclosures from an utterly transcendent author/ity. Hence we come to the understanding of poststructuralist hermeneutics that "There is in writing no lost origin to be sought after, no inherent monomyth to celebrate, but only the enigmatic myth of interpretation as play, dependent on concealed lack" (Gould:44).

We hear a good bit about "play" and "lack" in contemporary critical theory—and about "desire." But perhaps behind it all is the disappearance of the privileging of the individual self, a theme I already have suggested as a long-range consequence of the change in the contemporary worldview wrought by semiotics. Gould too has gathered a sense of the change: "the impact of linguistics on psychoanalytic theory in the last few years has been largely to demythologize the libido . . . even while it has remythologized desire as an *effect* of language itself."[9]

Gould finds in Eliot's *Four Quartets* "nothing if not a grand hermeneutic for poetry" (131) and in both Eliot and Joyce certain "signposts to the process of thought" (132)—signposts to the continued attempts to relate the poetic to the ontological, an attempt also preeminent in Wallace Stevens. In these writers (and Gould adds Lawrence) the use of myth has become utterly sophisticated—to such a level that only the conventions of fiction and poetry provide sufficiently flexible modes of signifying. Perhaps it is only in the fragmented nature of modernist and postmodernist art that the intent to interpret, to add mythic meaning to the everyday, may be fully gestured—especially because it is in the encounter with the modernist traces of language that the reader is so fully implicated, so fully engaged in a dialectical relationship with the work and with the finding of meanings.

Gould notes the avoidance of any substantive engagement of the question of "the numinous signifier and the validity of the supernatural" in contemporary critical-theory discussions (171); his chapter on "The Mythic and the Numinous" may, in fact, be the first substantive discussion of this issue in contemporary criticism outside strictly professional religion-and-literature seminars and publications.[10]

The answers to the question about the sacred will not be found in some archetypalist version of motif charting but in uncovering what it is that myths do in their sacred functioning: we must look more closely at the ways myths themselves implicate and imbricate the questionable realms between event and meaning, and we must look at the ways rituals complement myths as performed-enacted-fictions.

As a sort of science of the abstract-become-concrete, myth appropriates sense from the sacred, making it a realistic aspect of the nature/culture system (Gould:176–77; Barthes's emphasis upon myths "historicizing" nature is similar). Insofar as myths take on literary expression, they share with all narrative form the tendency "to communicate as a closed plot, a finite system offering its own coding in the midst of a world of negative knowledge and open-ended signs" (Gould:176), but because the user of a myth uses it in a symbolic rather than a literal fashion, myth must be treated "as an expanding contextual structure rather than a recurring motif" (177; I would refer back to M. C. Taylor's apothegm cited above, "context is semiophantic," and compare that with Gould's reference to "the highly suggestive paradox of myth: it is discourse resisting mere ideology," 256).

Hence "a theory of myth and the sacred is in part a theory of how the imagination creates fictions given the conditions of language" (178)—conditions according to which "the fate of literature is tied up with the fate of myth as language" (177) in providing some temporizing manner of dealing with the mysterious absence that "occasions our sense of awe at the arbitrary nature of meaning . . . above all a hermeneutical problem" (175).

It is not "reusable plot" that makes a myth mythic and that literature admires; rather, "the intention to go on in the business of making the world transform into further meaning" (180) is what is crucial to the represented "reality" of the mythic—a reality accepted in its symbolic and hence its signifying nature. In claiming to represent, to make present origins, myths make languages aware of their inability to signify ultimately.

Myths embody the hermeneutical circle by which they establish not "literal meanings" but patterns of relationships between things.[11] These relationships are not "out there" but are "within the story": myth like literature seeks to express the tentative seizure of meaning from any structure by embodying narrative, by aphorism, by an almost allegorical approximation. Mythic answers are always compromises generated by the semiotic function of their own terms; even cosmological claims are tensional fictions reflecting a semiological role in the structuring of the social and natural environments, a metaphoric role rather than a metonymic seizure of a transcendental signified.

The most sacred expressions are those that most fully express the *absence* of a meaning-present, the absence of God, the nonpresence of the Totally Other (a term familiar to Protestant theologians but used in contemporary critical theory in a very different way than its use by Karl Barth, for instance, to express the utter transcendence of the deity *apart from* language or human culture). Gould's own aphorism sums it up: "Myth is a metaphysics of absence implicit in every sign" (195, there partly in italics).

Mythographic Moralities

By definition moralities grow out of the habits (mores) of the society. If the society is changing rapidly, the moralities too will change, except to the extent that they trail a normative, proscriptive function from past eras. In concluding this book with a discussion of mythographic moralities, I want to attend to both aspects: the ways myths continue to be models *of* our society and models *for* our society. The question is again the implicit one that has followed much of the analysis of the entire book: it is the question of the functions of mythic materials within social contexts (but including within that "social" the intellectual, aesthetic, religious, psychological, and history-of-consciousness aspects that often are ignored in standard sociometric accounts).

The ways myths are studied, advocated, utilized, altered, set as models of self-development or social development; the many ways particular master myths build within a core of adherents or are exposed as partial articulations of meanings that cannot be fully expressed; the fostering of imaginal activities, the sorts of athletics of the psyche that may be our only hope in countering the deadliness of any particular attempt to claim exclusionary propriety over a culture: these are some of the matters of mythographic morality that have surfaced within the large panorama of this book.

The question of the "semiophantic context" returns to haunt those of us who work within the contemporary university whenever our society expresses its intolerance of Otherness and Difference. The danger of closure toward anything other than that with which one feels initially comfortable is more intensively present in a mass society where decisions about the contents of mass communications are made increasingly on the basis of market value or inoffensiveness to commercial advertisers rather than on the basis of values that traditionally have characterized our cultural achievements. But of course those "achievements" themselves are often questionable, for they have conveyed the drastic exclusion from participation that has hurt so many members of our society, or they have fostered a chauvinistic perspective that itself leads only to a narrowing down to the present situation or the present social level.

Myth studies do not promise easy answers. If anything, they provoke and tease and challenge our usual standards of values, our traditional determinations of success and happiness. It is when myth study can "facilitate or mediate a dialectic between subjective particularities and conventional or universal meanings" (Jackson:96), when "myth analysis becomes like . . . myth, continually transcending the conditions that foster it" (96), that it can be a discipline continually regenerative and recollective in ways that contribute to ultimate cultural significances.

The moralities of the mythographer's role cannot but reflect many of the moralities of the present, a time that no longer provides an assured context of meanings locked around an affirmation of absolute, timeless signification. Mythographic moralities will be no less easily determined than any other moralities; they will be no less indeterminate, while hovering around what has been, for both Western and Eastern (and Northern and Southern) civilizations since the beginning of human culture, a primal source, a moment that bridges meanings and events to provide at least a temporary benchmark at that point of continued revivification that is the human species' grappling with its own expression through language. As Frank McConnell suggests:

> We know what the myth *means*. . . . But of course the moment you think you know what a myth *means* you have lost contact with the myth itself. Because a myth, whatever else it might do, does not *mean* in that way. If anything, it is a kind of predisposition toward meaning, a verbal *prima materia* where narrative and order, drama and metaphysics, the aboriginally linguistic and the insuperably unspeakable all dance together in the

moment before all other moments of human utterance. Myth is not *about,* it *is* that precarious energy-exchange between self and other, language and silence, word and world which . . . is the explosive origin of speech. (285)

The "explosive origin of speech" can be controlled. It can be silenced by the deadly dedication to the present time and to the personal as representing the only producers of significance. And the politics of interpretation easily can reduce the potency of the "explosion" to significance-only-for-males or only-for-our-own-economic-class (as recent feminist and neo-Marxian criticism has very properly reminded us). The avoidance of a wide sense of civic responsibility may lead the "communities" in which rituals and myths are important sources of renewal to shrink drastically.

But I have also been impressed with the sensitivity toward our planet that myth study has evoked in more than one critic; the concluding paragraph of Claude Lévi-Strauss's *Table Manners* provides a moving example:

In the present century, when man is actively destroying countless living forms, after wiping out so many societies whose wealth and diversity had, from time immemorial, constituted the better part of his inheritance, it has probably never been more necessary to proclaim, as do the myths, that sound humanism does not begin with oneself, but puts the world before life, life before man, and respect for others before self-interest: and that no species, not even our own can take the fact of having been on this earth for one or two million years—since, in any case, man's stay here will one day come to an end—as an excuse for appropriating the world as if it were a thing and behaving on it with neither decency nor discretion. (1978b:508)

I am not particularly sanguine about the role of profound imaginative thought in our culture. We seem to be developing an insularity and a self-centered me-too-ism that bodes only retardation and sluggishness, as the complex future rushes toward us with ever-increasing velocity. The perspectives surveyed in this book represent tools for discovery of alternative modes of wisdom within the enormous heritage of rituals and myths from a vast display of human societies; my own "mythographic moralities" can be satisfied only by urging that we use these tools well, that we inculcate a richly textured discipline of the psyche that recognizes the mythic call to be something *more* than narrow individuals lost in the fragmentary "fun" and "relevance" of the contemporary moment.

There are no guarantees from an extracosmic Source, yet we go on fictionalizing the possibility of such Sources and living from out of our fictions, as fragmentary holding patterns within the sweep of universal history. The fourth century Saloustios touches upon the hesitancy with which even fictions such as my own book must maneuver (in his *Peri Theōn,* "About the Gods"; see Nock's edition):

> *Tousauta peri mythōn eipousin hēmin autoi te hoi theoi kai tōn grapsantōn tous mythous hai psychai hileōi genoito.* To those of us who have spoken in these ways about the myths, may the gods themselves, and also the spirits of those who wrote the myths, be kind.

Notes

Preface

1. The mythographic tradition might be said to have begun in the eighth century B.C.E. with Hesiod and "Homer"; it continued, one way or the other, in the sixth century B.C.E. with Pindar, Herakleitos, the Tragedians, Pherecydes, and Acusilaus. And then there was a long sequence of writers, some of them well known but most hardly recognized today: in the fourth century B.C.E.: Kallimachos, Asklepiades, Palaiphatos, Euhemeros; third century B.C.E.: Pseudo-Erastothenes, Ennios; second century B.C.E.: Apollodoros, Cicero; in the first century C.E.: Ovid, Plutarch, Virgil, Diodoros, Cornutus; second century C.E.: Apollonius, Hyginus, Lucian, Antonius Liberalis, Pausanias, Pseudo-Plutarch, the Aesopic traditions, Dionysius of Samos; fourth century C.E.: Servius; fifth century C.E.: Nonnos, Fulgentius; and finally, the medieval Vatican mythographers. To this listing we might add materials of various dates: the Greek Anthology, the Orphic Hymns, the Homeric Hymns, Greek literary papyri, and the scholia. See Rose 1930; Mary Grant (Hyginus); Nonnos; Frazer 1929 (Ovid, *Fasti*); Simpson (Apollodoros); Nock (Saloustios); R. J. White (Artemidoros); and Oldfather (Diodoros).

In some contexts the term mythography is taken to refer to one aspect of study I have found it impossible to treat adequately here, namely mythological iconography.

Chapter 1

1. On euhemerism, ancient and modern, see Ruthven:5–10; materials cited in his bibliog.:84–100; and D. C. Allen:chaps. 1 and 2.

An ancient mythographic movement similar to that of Euhemeros is found in the remnants of a work, *Katasterismoi,* attributed to the Alexandrian librarian Eratosthenes (ca. 275–194 B.C.E.). The work epitomizes Hellenistic interests in astrology, relating forty-four accounts of the metamorphoses of people into stars. Its only importance (inasmuch as the actual association of Greek mythological names with the constellations was not a development of early antiquity) is in the associations of myths and legends with astral lore, which preserve a number of legends that otherwise might have been lost. Olcott collected many myths and legends associated with the stars; more recently de Santillana and von Dechend have sought to demonstrate a universal, archaic, astrological-mythological system underlying most of Western mythology.

Allegorical and euhemeristic interpretations and retellings of myths in the Middle Ages are discussed by Seznec; D. C. Allen provides similar coverage for the Renaissance period. Feldman and Richardson provide an excellent account of eighteenth-century euhemerism and allegorizing; see also Cooke; and Galinsky:129. There have been a number of monographs studying the allegorical history of one figure (Cupid) or concept (the Greek *sophrosyne*).

2. The book by Cords and Gerster is perhaps typical of analyses tracing American stereotypes: most of these (including a series of studies published by the Bowling Green University Popular Press) seem to be subject to the same critique as my students' project, that is, they stress revisionist views of stereotypes and false historical models, but they seldom include attention to deep underlying mythical models.

3. Chase:106 refers to "paramyth": "A philosophical concept, a moral allegory, a symbol seized upon, cut off from the living whole—this is what I should call a *paramyth*. A paramyth differs from a myth because it is no longer closely involved in the aesthetic emotions, it can no longer furnish that peculiar mythical complication of brilliant excitement, of the terrific play of forces natural and human, of the upshot of the play, of reassurance, of reconciliation."

4. On definitions, see especially Honko; Kirk 1962. An earlier form of the definitional probe developed in most of the rest of this chapter was published as Doty 1981b and is republished by permission of the journal's editor, Robert P. Scharlemann.

5. Harris's (1976) rather than Durbin's views of the *etic-emic* distinction are followed here; Rappaport's terms (1968) are perhaps more functional: he distinguishes between operational and cognized environments. At any rate, Harris 1979:chap. 2 indicates the usefulness of the distinction in enabling the social sciences to move beyond the perennially problematic distinction between objective and subjective perspectives. V. Turner 1982b:65 points to the politics behind the distinction: Third World persons point to Euro-American etic categories (generally claimed to represent nomothetic cultural universals) as themselves more properly comprehended as merely Western emic categories.

6. Cf. Wiles:230, "Insistence on a very precise definition of myth usually turns out to be part of a Pyrrhic victory in which the author succeeds in proving the points he wants to make about myth by the simple process of making them true by definition." Part of the difficulty with definitions is that they must sufficiently comprehend both the uniquely local-temporal-ethnic referents and the transcultural; Ellul:24–25 is sensitive toward this dilemma. Cf. also Berndt and Berndt:98, "Myth, then, is *relative*. It has many faces. It changes through time,

and at any one time it can exist in different versions and convey different messages." A brief résumé of how different schools of myth interpretation would view the same myth is provided by E. K. Maranda; Snyder summarizes mythographic schools and demonstrates various approaches that might be used for his key myth.

While I am sympathetic to the argument of Leach 1982 that mythic "meaning" or "message" should be read out only from a set or corpus of myth accounts rather than from a single multiform, I find his restrictions (that we may call "myth" only what has been tape- or camera-recorded recently) quite incompatible with what I am surveying in this book. That he can cite only two examples of studies that satisfy his requirements for structural study of a mythic set within a single community (by persons whose doctoral work he supervised, C. Hugh-Jones and S. Hugh-Jones) suggests to me that his most recent approach is so exclusionary that it cannot be of much long-range use in myth criticism.

I would similarly question Leach's restrictions on the impossibility of studying myths without their ritual contexts: "not only is the ritual *incomprehensible* without a knowledge of the myth, but the details of the myth are *incomprehensible* without a knowledge of the ritual. The anthropologist's cine camera now becomes as important as his tape recorder" (1982:6, my emphasis). If Leach were less arbitrary and spoke of "ideal" situations, I would find his suggestions more acceptable: cf. ibid., "myth loses all meanings if it is taken out of context," and "all procedures of cross-cultural comparisons . . . are methodologically defective" (7).

7. An early account of such computer coding: P. Maranda 1967; see also Colby and Peacock; Dundes 1965a; and essays in Jason and Segal. One of the most informative accounts of the significance of structuralism for myth studies is P. Maranda 1972b.

8. Delcourt; Dover; Price; and Wyman provide examples of the ways iconography can correct and supplement information from literary texts. In cultures such as ancient Greece, plastic and graphic representations sometimes reveal that a particular mythic theme was much more widespread than we would ever guess from written records.

9. The anthropologist and his wife were more fully accepted into local society after they unwittingly participated in an illegal flight from prosecution for attending a cockfight: by their flight, they conformed to behaviors expected from "real people."

10. Ellul rightly suggests that the primal time most relevant to contemporary mythic formation is now a projected *future* time, not the past (40; cf. Dundes 1969), but often future projections are imagined as a perfection of primal situations—*Endzeit gleicht Urzeit*.

11. The ways the actual "speaking" is related to the cultural systems are now receiving closer attention; for a summary, see Bauman and Sherzer 1974. Tarn raises some interesting issues with respect to the experiential limits of such semiotics and with respect to the nature-culture relationship perceived through it. In Doty 1975, I have discussed some of the narrative conventions that reflect contemporary modes of personhood.

12. Hallowell 1966 has developed such a distinction for Ojibwa culture: the "other-than-human" is a "personal" category in which the Ojibwa world is experienced. Dawn, for instance, is an other-than-human person who can be influenced; and the other-than-human ancestors may have as much present-day reality as the actual family, due to continual reinforcement of their reality in myth repetitions and in shamanic performances, where they are given characteristic movements and tones of voice.

Hallowell likewise seeks to avoid the term supernatural: "The concept of the 'natural,' ambiguous as it often is when used in Western culture, is certainly not indigenous to Ojibwa thought. Consequently the use of the term 'supernatural' doubly distorts their outlook. Supernatural is an easily applied cliche but its descriptive accuracy, when introduced into the discussion of the cognitive orientation of non-Western peoples, is highly questionable" (the quotation is from 274–75, the discussion cited from those pages and 278–79).

Although a majority of earlier definitions of myth seems to include some form of "stories about the gods," this element is now increasingly rejected: see Dörrie:116—strongly resisting a "religious" interpretation of classical mythology; Waardenburg:57; and Oliver:76, who seeks to shift emphasis from defining myth as "stories about the gods" to asking "What are the stories of the gods *about?*" and suggesting that the primary concern of myths is that of expressing aspects of human relationships, whereas Gould:7, 13, argues that references to translinguistic facts (Gods, Nature) are indications of the inabilities of language to give full presence to extralinguistic realities.

13. Myerhoff 1974 portrays the interpretive impact that intense participatory experiencing—in this case through ritual ingestion of peyote—may have on the analyst; see also Myerhoff 1978 and V. Turner 1982b:89 on ethnodrama as a resource for the discipline of anthropology.

14. Here I must indicate some of my strong agreements with the approaches of the deconstructive critics, especially in the subtle studies of Jacques Derrida. We are being taught a great deal about subtexts and rewritings of one thinker by her or his successor, and I anticipate deconstructive analyses of myths and legends along the lines of the analyses of Hegel, Freud, Marx, and others now being published.

15. I also have not engaged the question of tacit mythic functioning, as when a group of listeners can complete the initial statement, "A penniless shoeshine boy set up his box by a railway station . . ." with "and by dint of persistent hard labor, became president of the transportation monopoly," without a single person in the group having ever heard of the Reverend Horatio Alger. It is likewise necessary to deal with the ways myths can be "believed" at the level of the "second naiveté" Paul Ricoeur discusses, that is, how a postcritical affirmation of the validity of a mythic system is possible.

I am indebted to rigorous critique of earlier versions of parts of this chapter at the Five-College Seminar on Religion, meeting at Smith College; another portion was presented at the New England regional meeting at Harvard University of the American Academy of Religion.

Chapter 2

1. Jarvie:35, n. 1, assigns the term functional to Malinowski's approach and the term structural-functional to the approach of Radcliffe-Brown. I use the term sociofunctional to indicate the importance of sociological theory in the work of this movement as well as to avoid the term structural, which now has different connotations than it had earlier—cf. for instance Levy with Piaget 1970b. Harris 1979:50 considers the sociofunctional approach "the most influential strategy [of research] in the social sciences in the United States and Great Britain during the period 1940 to 1965."

2. Brown traces the adoption and adaptation of the myths and legends about Hermes in various stages of Greek culture. A. G. Ward:chaps. 7 and 8 demonstrates the self-conscious adoption and adaptation of Theseus myths to justify and bolster the developing political role of Athens in the classical period. Seltman is good on the social reasons for the changing representations of Athene. Donlan traces the steps by which the native Roman origin myths were conformed to Greek models and sources.

3. See also Leach 1958 and a more recent treatment of the same topic by Firth 1973:chap. 8. Kluckhohn also moved in a broader disciplinary direction: 1968:46–60; and 1953.

4. Another role is noted by Firth 1973:chap. 10—a dissident group's unorthodox display of the national flag may lead to angry exchanges about the use of that symbol, the flag, rather than to discussion of the subject of the dissidents' protest. The role of ritual in creating and reinforcing social values is emphasized by Mol:233–37, 244–45. Leach 1976:45 emphasizes the use of rites "to transmit collective messages to ourselves," that is, to highlight and reinforce what I would call systems of corporate meaning.

5. R. E. Moore discusses three phases of myth in the way I am doing here; my model is influenced by his. He illustrates three phases of myth in the history of Christianity and demonstrates the presence of several competing stages of development of the mythological story, the "primitive," the dramatic, the liturgical (used as a script in services of worship), and the literary; this schema is linked with the ritual-dominant school discussed in Chapter 3.

Much earlier the Italian philosopher Giambattista Vico (1668–1744) described three cycles of human history: in the theological age, everything is viewed in terms of deities; in the heroic age, humans view themselves as children of deities—here we have emphasis upon the god-humans, heroes or savior figures; and finally there is the age in which absolute human autonomy is proclaimed. Vico traces these ages as recurring cycles in several cultures; his own sympathies were in each case with the first age, where he found "poetic" creativity, in contrast to "philosophical" reflection in the human age.

Larsen:33–45 develops five developmental patterns of relationships between humankind and the mythic imagination: Mythic Identity (possession), Mythic Orthodoxy (religion), Objective Phase (science), Suspended Engagement (meditation), and Mythic Engagement (dialogue, transformation, renewal). Larsen advocates the last pattern and argues that contemporary persons are involved with myth as completely as were persons in any earlier culture, but the traditional modes of relation to mythic consciousness have become moribund. Much of his book is directed toward evoking a more satisfying relationship to myth: "This book is intended as a simple instruction manual for owning and operating a mythic imagination in the present time" (8). A similar intention is pursued on an even more popular "how to" level in a number of "new consciousness" guides: see for example Samuels and Samuels; or Houston. Albert Cook tracks six large phases of mythic vitality as reflected in literary genres.

6. Denis de Rougement refers in this connection to "fallen myths"; Waardenburg refers to "tired" myths.

7. Guepín notes the ways details may be added to myths from a desire to increase their entertainment value. He also notes that details may have significance in secondary settings (as when a myth is used as part of a cultural ritual) or in a specific usage that was not part of the original signification.

Lévi-Strauss 1976:158 notes that the levels of analysis imposed by the outsider seeking to distinguish what is imaginary and what is real in a society's myths would not necessarily be the levels a native would distinguish within them. The works of Radin and of Reichard repeatedly have emphasized yet another factor, namely that narrative style and contents will vary among myth raconteurs within any given social group who are constrained by the expectations of particular audiences during particular seasons of the year; see for instance Reichard.

8. The most useful collections of emergence/origins/creation myths: Doria and Lenowitz; Eliade 1967:chap. 2; Brandon; Freund; Maclagan; Sproul; Long 1963; O'Brien and Major. Important studies include: James; Pettazzoni:24–36; von Franz 1972a; S. Moon; and S. Thompson:303–18.

The typology I use for classifying such myths is as follows:

(1) Creation by ordering chaos
(2) Emergence/evolution through a series/stages of worlds or underworlds
(3) Dividing/deconstructing/separating primordial unity/pair/twins
(4) Overcoming primordial creature/monster; conflict between primordial good/evil figures
(5) Creation from primal egg or containerlike item
(6) Monist creation: sacrifice; cosmological body; sun myths; hermaphrodite
(7) Creation through primal deity's sexual activities: masturbation, phallus-alone, parturition (both male and female), incest
(8) Earth-diver motif
(9) Trickster creator; accidents in creation; devolution and disappearance of deities
(10) Creation by divine word, thought, dream, fantasy; from the seven laughs of the deity; from numbers and letters; from the deity's vomit
(11) Creatio ex nihilo

9. I am particularly impressed by the demonstrations by Jean-Pierre Vernant (Vernant and Vidal-Naquet 1981) that a literary artist indeed may play upon the

various meanings words have at particular moments in social history. In fact, Vernant argues that the great tragedies of Athens do not "work" until the hearers gain a sense that the very language was experienced as that which carried multiple meanings simultaneously (such as the tensions between the traditional religious values of the past and the new laws of the polis). It is precisely because characters such as Oidipous and Antigone are caught between changing value systems and conceptions of the social universe that their portrayals have such power (on the figure of Antigone in several cultural epochs, see Steiner).

In one of my own essays (1980c), I have tried to show how the language web of the *Oresteia* is, similarly, not something "merely decorative or metaphoric" but creative of the linguistic space necessary to the expression of the dramatic tensions, which otherwise could not be expressed. Laurence Kahn demonstrates that a major work (the Homeric Hymn to Hermes) may present several meanings simultaneously overlapping one another: the very polysemy of the text's surface expression reflects the polyvalence of the conceptual orders expressed through it.

10. This point is relevant to the study of all so-called folk materials: myths often may be the special province not of the mass of persons in a society but of specially educated technicians—see P. G. Allen:112, Radin 1915. Guiart illustrates the role of the politics of the raconteur. Tambiah:159–60 documents very clearly one instance of ritual change, correlated with changes in administrators' status.

11. Myerhoff's 1978 study has shown the vast importance of Little Traditions in maintaining a level of minority religious consciousness within a larger assimilationist context: for the East European Jews living within cosmopolitan Los Angeles she studied, "Survival comes in cultural inflections" (257). See also Muchembled's distinctions between popular religiosity and that of the "elites."

12. The point is Slater's (1968:343, n. 3); a simple illustration: ten Raa notes that the African "Sandawe creator is at once of celestial origin and earth-bound, that he is supra-human yet mortal, aggressive yet productive, beneficial yet cheating, foreign yet Sandawe" (333).

13. The Cartesian dichotomy was already perceptively rejected in the context of myth studies by Wheelwright 1942; a more recent discussion of great sophistication and simplicity is Bly:introductory materials. Polanyi and Prosch are very good on seeing through the positivist blinders that ignore the personal-integrative role of the scientist.

Eric Gould refers to the "facts waiting to be discovered" theory as the "essentialist" position common to such different analysts as Carl Jung and René Girard. Gould's exposition of the contemporary decentralized and deconstructed self will be discussed in later chapters.

14. Cf. Lévi-Strauss 1976:172; van Baal 1981:163–64 stresses that the paradoxicality "of myths is at least as striking as their etiological character"; he is interested that so few mythographers have dealt adequately with the ways in which myths apparently contradict reality and reason. An exception, not noted

by van Baal, is Guepín; and A. Cook:184 emphasizes that myth "always" brings the unexpected.

15. See for example Gaster 1969, a work that revised James Frazer's *Folklore in the Old Testament* to point out the very large number of mythological and folklore themes that influenced the literature of the Hebrew bible. Many other works have been devoted to mythological lore of the Ancient Near East and ancient Israel, especially with respect to the Genesis story cycles. A more recent study by Rogerson traces the various schools of interpretation.

16. This distinction is based upon Ong. Rappaport 1979:129 notes that the Maring are perfectly aware of agricultural mechanics—our technological agriscience—but: "Of 'greater meaning' to them is the subsumption of material facts by cosmological oppositions and the elaboration of taboos and other rules on the foundation those oppositions provide."

Chapter 3

1. Harrison's distinctions telescope a whole range of linguistic issues concerning the "doing": Gregory Nagy, of Harvard University, is working with the interior literary evidence for differences between *poieō* (lyric and epic), *draō* (tragedic), and *prattō* (comedic). Kerényi 1967:96 notes that the term *deiknymena* ("thing shown") has been used in literature on the Eleusinian mysteries to refer to the actual highpoint of the rite; Kerényi does not approve of this technical usage, however, insofar as terms of "having been shown" could apply to the religion as a whole rather than to a specific aspect of one rite.

2. Gaster represents some strongly modified adaptations of the ritual-dominant approach; see his criticisms, 1954:187, 210–11.

3. I am grateful to Professor Turner for reading the original draft of this presentation of his views, which he found to be an "accurate translation" (personal correspondence). The section "Rituals Reflect Social Structures" includes some rephrasing of his position at his suggestion. An extensive bibliography of Turner's writings will be found in Grimes 1976a, reprinted in 1982a:289–91. Professor Turner died in December 1983.

4. Note Turner's approval of recent use of process theory in anthropology, 1967:112–13. He deplores "the concentration, until quite recently, on the elicitation and analysis of highly localized, fixed, and focused 'structures' and 'patterns' rather than on patterns and processes on a national or even international scale" (1974a:187). On the "flow" of ritual, see Grimes 1982c:274 and 1982a:chap. 4; and V. Turner 1977a.

5. Van Gennep; brief studies: T. Turner 1977; Belmont. Myerhoff 1982:115–17 gives an account of his significance in his historical context; selected bibliography in Belmont:160–65.

6. The point is well demonstrated in Grimes's phenomenological sketch of masking, 1982a:chap. 5, which looks at concretion, concealment, embodiment,

and expression; or in his review of the psychosomatic theories of Gotthard Booth in chap. 8.

Chapter 4

1. The most recent such attempt known to me is by Gallus, who argues that mythological thinking is but one developmental stage on the way to total scientific abstraction—this judgment is made even in spite of Gallus's expressed concern not to be thus understood! The article is very difficult to penetrate; it contains a wealth of material touching on biogenetic aspects, and it is perhaps most valuable for developing the view that myth or religion is a way of knowledge not to be confused with the scientific way of knowledge. Gallus also argues that religion fulfills needs of the total human personality—which has proved extremely recalcitrant to the most withering attempts at scientific mechanization—and hence that religion always will be a human necessity so far as personality, motivation, and emotions are concerned.

2. See V. Turner 1969a for a review of the issues, especially those raised by the work of Julian Huxley. The essays in Schechner and Schuman:pt. 1, Ethology, provide an introduction to some of the ethologists' extrapolations. Ellen discusses some of the problems with analytical or synthetic classification generally and specifically with respect to the human body understood as a signifying agent.

3. Although it would take us too far afield to develop Douglas's notion of "group and grid" for analyzing social structure vis-à-vis ritual/mythic consciousness, I cannot avoid noting that the fourfold charts she develops in *Natural Symbols* strike the person familiar with quaternity patterns in cross-cultural mythological materials as themselves bodylike in structure. Her grid/group distinction is developed in 1970:vii, 57, 97, and elsewhere; it is summarized in the excellent review-essay on Douglas by Isenberg and Owen, and is tested by a group of essayists in Douglas 1982.

The field or "trajectory" model is developed in Koester and Robinson, and the studies dependent upon the methodology in Douglas's *Purity and Danger* are: J. Z. Smith 1970; Neusner 1973 and 1975; and "The Rise and Function of the Holy Man in Late Antiquity" in P. Brown:103–52.

4. Cf. Manuel and Manuel:89, where the authors rather jokingly refer to a "collective gastronomic unconscious." The Manuels discuss an even earlier human experience, the intrauterine period, as a possible explanation for the frequent theme of utopias being presented as island communities: "The human fetus, too, is an island, and in their island paradises men have often expressed a longing for the protective fluid that once surrounded them. In most paradises the maternal symbols are compelling" (87; cf. 119).

5. In Tanzania, the fellow serving us tea remembered that Americans like their tea glasses cleaned before using them—so he very graciously pulled off his

undershirt and wiped each glass carefully! Sutherland's essay on the classification of clean:unclean among Gypsies demonstrates the culture-relative point very clearly.

6. Cf. Geertz 1973:129: "religion supports proper conduct by picturing a world in which such conduct is only common sense"; and 131: "The need for such a metaphysical grounding for values seems to vary quite widely in intensity from culture to culture and from individual to individual, but the tendency to desire some sort of factual basis for one's commitments seems practically universal; mere conventionalism satisfies few people in any culture."

Actually, in many cultures "We do XXX because the ancestors did it" *is* the sufficient or sole rationale, but Geertz's main point is valid. I reread this article ("Ethos, World View and the Analysis of Sacred Symbols," which originally appeared in *Antioch Review* in 1957) after these paragraphs first were written, and I realized how extensively I have internalized Geertz's perspective; a more immediate influence was Berger and Luckmann.

7. My own initial professional research was in the field of religion and leisure and is reflected in R. Lee. Both R. Lee and Miller 1970a provide overviews of the relevant literature; Ehrmann 1971:31–57 develops an astute critique of Huizinga's proposals and of the work of Roger Callois, who is represented in the Ehrmann volume (148–58) and whose 1961 work is an important supplement to Huizinga's work. J. Z. Smith 1978:206, 298–300, discusses the "play" between incongruities well expressed in myths, riddles, and jokes.

Chapter 5

1. Studies primarily influenced by classical Freudian psychoanalysis are canvassed by Caldwell. Earlier bibliographies are listed (117), and a motif index to Freud's references to mythology in the *Standard Edition* of his works is provided (132–34). Glenn's bibliography is of much more limited value.

2. Christine R. Downing, who is completing a book-length study of the uses of myth in Freud, Jung, and Lévi-Strauss, has shared initial versions of chapters of that work, and I have found it stimulating to compare her interpretations with my own. After writing the middle part of this section on Freud, I reread her perceptive essay, "Sigmund Freud and the Greek Mythological Tradition" (1975b), and realized how close is our perception of Freud's own use of myth. That essay also clarifies for me, however, that I see Freud as more reductionistic, less open to the polyvalence of symbolism, than does Downing; and I cannot but wonder whether her reading of Freud in the essay is not too charitably influenced by Jung's own understanding of "the interpenetration of the mythical and psychological in Freud" that Jung has taught us to see in retrospect—and that Downing herself notes in 1976.

I am also indebted to Paul Ricoeur's Terry Lectures (1970). This powerful reading of Freud (which is simultaneously a self-reading of Ricoeur) is not discussed here only because to do so would necessitate more space for exposition of

Ricoeur's thought—which has many ramifications for our comprehension of symbol and metaphor—than the scope of this volume will allow. I will cite just one image-laden statement: "A tradition exhausts itself by mythologizing symbol; a tradition is renewed by means of interpretation, which reascends the slope from exhausted time to hidden time, that is, by soliciting from mythology the symbol and its store of meaning" (1974a:29).

Bettelheim 1982 provides a useful corrective to the translation traditions that have erased for the English-speaking world Freud's profound concern with the "soul" (*Seele*) by translating it with "mind."

3. "Appearances" is used by Freud in 1924—originally lectures from 1915–17. See p. 190, where Freud compares the outward form of a dream in its relation to its latent thought with the facade of an Italian church in its relation to its general structure and layout.

4. Although there have been many studies of Freud's use of the Oidipous materials, I find one of the most convincing to be a study that argues from the basis of the inherent logics and societal contexts of Greek tragedy: Vernant, "Oedipus Without the Complex," in Vernant and Vidal-Naquet 1981:chap. 4. Twenty-four studies concerned with Oidipous are canvassed in Glenn:230–35.

5. The examples in the tenth and twelfth lectures of Freud's *A General Introduction to Psychoanalysis* seem especially arbitrary and reductionistic (1924; and note 1961a:37, where urinating into a fire is treated as a homosexual competition). Such correlations in fields other than dream analysis—especially within literary criticism—reached such an extreme stage that an anti-Freudian reaction has occurred in recent years; see for example Sontag:3–14.

6. Freud also depended upon the researches of J. J. Atkinson and W. Robertson Smith; Rainey:120 finds it odd that Freud never discussed the important works of William James or Rudolf Otto, which were of massive influence on other early-twentieth-century writers on the origins of religion. Gay provides a helpful workbook to accompany Freud's writings on religion.

7. So Downing can speak of Freud's use of the Oidipous story as his attempt to awaken the mythopoetic function in each of us: "To be Oedipus means to Freud to be fascinated with the search for one's own creation" (1975b:7); and "Freud's project was to awaken us to the mythological memories still alive in our unconscious, and also to that capacity for mythopoeic thought reflected in the form of the unconscious project" (12). But note that she stresses "ways in which Freud's thinking issues from a mythopoeic perspective, *despite* the *manifest* obeisance to a mechanistic and rationalistic outlook" (11, my emphasis), and hence wins her reading by means of a Freudian reinterpretation of Freud himself, a move not unlike what Jacques Lacan does in his Freudian interpretations of Freud.

8. It may be noted that Jung was so concerned to protect the confidentiality of his analysands that he rarely included such personal data when discussing archetypal themes encountered in his analytical practice. Several Jungian analysts have commented to me on the emphasis during their training upon the specific day-to-day contexts of analysands' personal materials—transpersonal elements being engaged primarily when an immediate contextual relationship

to unconscious material is not evident or when attempting to clarify a particular image that recurs frequently. On the importance of a series of dream images and "the context which the dreamer himself supplies," see Jung, *CW* 12:44–46.

9. On Kroeber's use of Freud, see Bourguignon:1078. It is striking in her review, and in Kennedy's "Cultural Psychiatry" (1973), both how meager was Freud's influence in these fields and how rapidly the two disciplines developed along sociometric and behavioristic rather than psychoanalytical lines.

10. Cf. Rank:84, "Myths are . . . created by adults, by means of retrograde childhood fantasies, the hero being credited with the mythmaker's personal infantile history." Rank includes Sargon, Moses, Karna, Oidipous, Paris, Perseus, and eight others. A later study by Lord Raglan (1937) studied an even larger group of mythological heroes in terms of birth narratives as well as the two other crucial rites of passage, initiations (accessions to the throne) and death. His 1934 essay, "The Hero of Tradition," is reprinted in Dundes 1965b; he argues for a ritual origin of myths and is highly critical of the Freudian interpretation. On Raglan (and other analyses of hero myths) see Dundes 1977. Campbell 1968b is appreciative of both Freud and Jung and is the most comprehensive of several modern studies of the meaning of hero cycles. Zinser summarizes the work of Rank and Theodore Reik before concentrating upon that of Géza Róheim.

11. This section reflects my study of about two-thirds of the *Collected Works* of Jung (published in the United States as Bollingen series 20, ed. Herbert Read et al.; individual volumes are cited here by *CW* rather than by separate titles—the publisher, Princeton University Press, has published several part-volumes in paperback). The abstracts section of Rothgeb and Clemens is helpful if one knows which writing one wants, but their index is keyed only to Jung's titles; the recently published *CW* 20, the *General Index,* on the other hand, is exhaustive and thematic. Extensive documentation of each point summarized seemed awkward, so I have given references only for quoted material. The volumes that would be most rewarding for someone who wishes to pursue study of Jung's approach to mythology would be the following: in *CW,* vol. 9, pt. 1, Jung's contributions to Jung and Kerényi; the papers on archetypes in *CW,* vol. 9, pt. 1; *CW* 18, and *CW* 8 (see index in each); and especially *CW* 5.

12. Evidently with Jung's approval, the book of essays by him and Karl Kerényi on the Child and the Maiden was entitled *Introduction to a Science of Mythology* in the British edition and *Essays on a Science of Mythology* in the American edition, although neither Jung nor Kerényi aspire to such a wide scope in that volume. On amplification of myths, see von Franz 1975:131–33; an elementary but clear and comprehensive introductory essay is W. M. Hudson.

13. See also Carloye:186. Needham:45 has sought to develop a non-Platonic use of archetypes in social anthropology, terming the archetype "the notion of a psychic constant in the form of an autonomous image to which the human mind is naturally predisposed."

14. To an important earlier study by Progoff we may now add Odajnyk. Some of John Layard's studies combined anthropology with a Jungian perspective, but the movement lacked the likes of a Géza Róheim.

15. See Hillman's many articles in the annual journal *Spring: An Annual of*

Archetypal Psychology and Jungian Thought, of which he is editor, and his monographs available for the most part from Spring Publications and Harper and Row. See also Hillman 1972b; 1975c; and the most accessible work to date, 1979.

16. MacCary's 1982 study of the figure of Achilleus treats very different aspects than did Nagy; if the latter brings Indo-European studies to fruition in Homeric studies, and Austin develops considerably the earlier work with oral poetics, MacCary turns now to psychoanalytical considerations, developing and correcting a number of Slater's analyses.

MacCary is curious about why we so easily find it possible to identify with the Homeric figures, and he finds an answer in our "recollection of the infantile struggle to define the self in terms of the mother's image, projected to the child, of [ourselves], a struggle which is erotic in Freudian terms and a response to sense impression in Hegelian terms" (xi–xii). It is primarily the struggle with narcissistic impulses that the figure of Achilleus represents, Achilleus, who "never even reaches the point of desiring the female: he is still trying to convince himself of his own existence and hence choosing as erotically and aggressively invested self-objects male doubles of himself, [namely] Patroklos and Hektor" (57). In the *Iliad,* "men define themselves in terms of other men, and women are only a means of strengthening and formalizing men's relations with each other" (135; cf. 157).

MacCary's discussion of "Narcissism in Homer and Homosexuality in Greek History" (sec. 2.9), as well as several other sections of his book, takes the discussion of archaic Greek psychosexuality to a new post-Freudian plane and should not be missed. The book is a major contribution not only to Homeric studies but to the contemporary development of Freudian thought.

I would also like to call attention to a relatively new journal that includes many studies relevant in the present context: the *Journal of Psychological Anthropology* (1/1–3/2), which changed its title to the *Journal of Psychoanalytic Anthropology* with issue 3/3.

17. Hence "*Religion* in its broadest sense . . . must be another term for that obscurity that surrounds man's efforts to defend himself by curative or preventative means against his own violence" (Girard:23), and "Ritual is nothing more than the regular exercise of 'good' violence" (37). A similarly reductive view is represented by La Barre 1970:11 and 24, when he implies a positive answer to his own question—"Is religion an autotherapy of the body politic when other cultural means fail?"—and then suggests that "Both neurosis and sacred culture are the frantic nonce-solutions of people under stress which are frozen into permanence by fear"; see the thoughtful review by Ricketts 1971.

Chapter 6

1. Frazer's "literary achievement," Vickery suggests, was "one to be ranked with that of Gibbon" (1973:109); "Without in the least denying the other contributory forces, we may legitimately suggest that *The Golden Bough* is also, in a very real measure, responsible for the form and shape of modern literature"

(120). Some additional literary features are charted by Vickery 1963 and by Hyman. The first part of J. Z. Smith 1973 traces the sequence of editions and changes in Frazer's own perspectives; Besterman's bibliography is almost exhaustive.

2. In 1972 Vickery published with another press his *Robert Graves and the White Goddess,* which is primarily a study of possible influences of Frazer on the corpus of Graves's poetry; Vickery considers Graves "the living writer most deeply affected not only by *The Golden Bough* but by the whole corpus of Frazer's writing" (1972:1). It would be helpful to have an analysis of Frazer's influence upon Graves's nonpoetic work, especially *The White Goddess* and his *The Greek Myths.* Cf. Weisinger 1966; and, on the quest/journey motif in several authors, the laconic book by Matthews. Something of the perspective contributed by Frazer can be seen in a book where it is entirely absent (Welsh), the heroic pattern being tracked according to entirely different principles. Certainly Frazer (1921, 1929) knew what the organization of myth cycles entailed: his multi-volume, heavily annotated editions and translations of Apollodoros, Ovid (*Fasti*), and Pausanias remain extremely useful.

3. Peter Munz's *When the Golden Bough Breaks: Structuralism or Typology?* (1973)—which in spite of its title makes little reference to Frazer—suggests that Frazer was just at "the point of bringing about a most fruitful and promising *rapprochement* between the study of mythology and traditional theology" (2). See also the editor's foreword and editorial notes in Gaster 1959. For extremely interesting insights into Wittgenstein's own reflections on thinking, stimulated by Frazer's, see Wittgenstein. Frazer's ritualistic bias is discussed by Ackerman, and *The Golden Bough* itself is considered "a work of literary criticism" by Northrop Frye (1967:30), the "myth of myth" by Weisinger 1961:397.

4. Frye himself notes: "I do not believe that there are different 'schools' of criticism today, attached to different and irreconcilable metaphysical assumptions: the notion seems to me to reflect nothing but the confusion in critical theory. In particular, the notion that I belong to a school or have invented a school of mythical or archetypal criticism reflects nothing but confusion about me. . . . I hold to no 'method' of criticism beyond assuming that the structure and imagery of literature are central considerations of criticism. Nor, I think, does my practical criticism illustrate the use of a patented critical method of my own, different in kind from the approaches of other critics" (1970:81–82).

5. Righter observes that *Anatomy* exhibits "a mythical structure devised for the explication of other mythical structures, bounded and defined by mythical limits"; the essay on Frye appeared earlier in *New Literary History* 3/2 (1972):319–44. Righter is very damning of Frye's typological genre classifications, especially of the way their global comprehensiveness provides little specific insight into particular literary works. He judges Frye's enterprise as "a remarkable if eccentric episode in literary history. . . . the last, and greatest, monument of a genre already well in decline" (79). A similar criticism is voiced by Ruthven:81, who suggests that "*Anatomy of Criticism* is itself a triumph of the mythopoeic imagination, a beautifully modulated address to an Academy of Fine Ideas, but not much use to the practising critic."

6. For the range, see in particular Bush 1963 (originally 1932); 1937 (reissued 1969); and 1968. Highet is now somewhat out of date but useful; Mayerson represents a more popular treatment. Feder 1964 sometimes gives modern references; Michael Grant 1962 usually does. Simpson's notes to Apollodoros's *Library* are especially thorough.

Chapter 7

1. The word *structurist* might be useful, but Bharati has appropriated it for "scholars who are concerned with structure *rather than with process or function* and who have some model in mind, *inclusive of, but wider than,* structuralist themes" (2, my emphasis)—distinctions that seem to me to be "poststructuralist" in derivation.

2. I have been reminded by Ninian Smart of another side to this issue: whereas historical accounts of the past used to be conveyed by mythical materials, the modern critical historian has come to be considered as working within the realm of science, and so most historical work now seems self-evident and convincing to us. But it is important to remember, notes Smart (81), that "modern history is like traditional myth: myths too commanded [i.e., in the past, before the modern period] that breathless authority, unquestioned reality." What gets raised here is the issue of competing historical constructions, inasmuch as the shibboleth of "myth" is now wielded freely by either side when one wishes to discredit the other.

3. For Lévi-Strauss, the principle reaches even further than the sort of self-consciousness implied by my term "human existence"—he was delighted at the cracking of the genetic code while he was composing Mythologiques, for the work on DNA substantiated for him the binary principle first analyzed by structural linguistics. In one of those tongue-in-cheek comments that perhaps only French intellectual writers can carry off, he remarks: "As can be seen, when Nature, several thousand million years ago, was looking for a model, she borrowed in advance, and without hesitation, from the human sciences: this is the [linguistic] model which, for us, is associated with the names of Trubetskoy and Jakobson" (1981:684).

4. Andriolo suggests that the process can be seen in the mediatory figure of Jesus Christ, who may be treated as a mediation between the deity and humankind—but, she would suggest, an unsuccessful one, necessitating yet another mediation, namely the figure of the saint.

5. Fiske and Hartley give a good résumé of the levels of significance of the codes, and they show the interconnections between this sort of semiology and what is usually developed under the rubric of "content analysis" in studies of popular-media materials. The range of specific narrative types, features, conventions, and other factors now being given focal attention in monographic studies is quite remarkable; but for a standard overview, indeed one upon which many of these studies are dependent, see Chatman.

6. In addition to the work by Via cited in the text, see Patte 1976b; Calloud; Barthes et al. 1974b; Polzin; and two thematic issues of journals, *Interpretation* 28/1 (1974) and *Soundings* 58/2 (1975). Further bibliography and studies are in *Semeia: An Experimental Journal for Biblical Criticism* 1 (1974), 2(1974), and 23(1982).

Chapter 8

1. After writing this section I discovered a similar statement in Weatherford's sketch of the American Congress (267): "The Americans reward with reelection that politician who can best blow-dry his tinted hair and bat his curly eyelashes, rather than the one who is at his desk working on the details of the disarmament treaty. They applaud the one who most frequently struts and frets across their television screen, but ignore the one who has hammered out a policy on nuclear non-proliferation. The politician who can most passionately deliver an enraged diatribe in the committee room and who knows how to exploit the pauses in the question and answer session receives more attention than the one who has dealt thoroughly but less dramatically with the real issue."

2. A recent work by Catherine H. Berndt and Ronald M. Berndt treats advertising and public language but does not move sufficiently within a grounded theory of communication. An older work by A. M. Hocart, recently reprinted, gives many insights into common cultural traits (snobbery, chastity) that betray deep mythological roots.

3. Bettelheim 1976:325–28 provides bibliography for general and interpretive studies (mostly German, some English and French); Jason and Segal represents one of the most contemporary collections of essays—see especially Claude Bremond's essay, "The Morphology of the French Fairy Tale: The Ethical Model," 49–76.

4. Useful on rethinking the issue of modernism (and "postmodernism"): Berman; Lears; C. Newman; and Spivey:chap. 1, which refers to "the tragedy of modernism." The most extensive bibliography I have found is in Davies. It will be evident that I do not restrict use of the term modernism to English-language literary writing between 1910 and 1930 (as one does within a literary-historical perspective such as Peter Faulkner's), to Hispanic literary criticism, or to the religious heresy condemned by Roman Catholicism in 1907. Calinescu traces the origins and subsequent uses of the terms modern, modernism, postmodern, and others.

5. See Kliever 1972 on the three different approaches to religious symbols in recent research: symbolic *reductionism,* symbolic *realism,* and finally symbolic *formism,* wherein "Reality is constituted by meaningful human experience rather than by objective ontological entities" (101); for this perspective, "there can be no uniform or absolute truths, but discriminating and relative judgments can be made about competing imaginative constructs."

6. Scharlemann demonstrates the parallels with Heidegger's "destruction" of

the history of ontology; but of course there is a certain terminological irony at play: the academic discipline within Christianity responsible for detailed elaboration of beliefs has been systematic—or "constructive"—theology. Schneidau 1976 argues that the Israelite prophetic/Yahwist traditions already provided a secularizing critique of culture and a relativizing of any scripted message. Schneidau 1982 explicitly develops the parallels between the biblical "radical way of appropriating history" and Derrida's perspectives.

7. I hope my recognition, in Chapter 1, of *levels* of myth reception in a society will be helpful toward distinguishing some of the dimensions of this issue: without distinguishing the different levels of "belief," arguments for disconfirmation can be established for almost any claim. See also Waardenburg's schema of seven sites of apperception (61–62) and the haunting, gnomelike observations of Charles Winquist that "belief in the content of myth as explanation is clearly a privilege of premodern experience" (1974:106) and of Wallace Stevens (*Opus posthumous*:163, cited in M. C. Taylor 1982:81): "the final belief is to believe in a fiction, which you know to be a fiction, there being nothing else. The exquisite truth is to know that it is a fiction and that you believe it willingly."

8. Gould:8. I assume "superior" here ought to be taken in the sense of indicating that myths come to have widespread public acceptance rather than the more limited acceptance of individual fictions, Winquist's "powerful sign" rather than a superiority of abstract definition.

9. Gould:71. This point is developed vis-à-vis the Lacanian concept of repression and desire—desire becomes "the metonymy in the metaphor of the self" (78); and "The mythicity of language lies in its control over the self as the site of the unconscious" (80). The very helpful companion to Lacan's *Écrits* by Muller and Richardson joins Wilden's (see Lacan 1968) in providing the explication and annotation necessary to introduce Lacan clearly and consistently in anglophone discussions.

10. See Ross-Bryant for an example of a recent textbook; many of the working groups within the American Academy of Religion have focused upon specific figures or issues. I note the attention given by well-known critics such as Robert Alter, Northrop Frye, and Frank Kermode to the Western biblical literature and the attention given by biblical critics themselves to contemporary critical theory as an aid to analysis of biblical materials: see for instance the use of reader-response criticism in Culpepper or the use of narrative criticism in Rhodes and Michie.

11. Gould:186. This is the basic contribution Gould thinks structuralist analysis, especially that of Lévi-Strauss, has to make; it is also the basis for Barthes's semiotic reading of "things," where "anything can be a myth which appropriates meaning through form," a position that Gould criticizes as lacking "expository tact" (187).

Selected Introductory Bibliography

Working one's way into the study of myths and rituals can remain a lifelong occupation, as perhaps it should. Just pursuing one particular scholar's works (I think of those of Joseph Campbell or Mircea Eliade or Robert Graves) can take months. And where does one begin and stop? . . . with anthropology, literary criticism, folklore, linguistics, religious studies, iconography . . . ?

References and footnotes to the chapters of this book have cited many works that will take the interested reader further, but some recommended readings are organized more programmatically here. Instead of trying to present an inclusive bibliography, I have noted books and articles (almost exclusively in English) that are fairly basic, or comprehensive, or of particular methodological importance. The format of the entries follows the practice of the rest of the book except that in every case I have included the year of publication.

General Introductions to Mythography

Chase 1969
Dorson 1973: mostly on folklore but with a wide scope; resists "whirr of the computer" approaches
Evans-Pritchard 1965b, and especially "The Comparative Method in Social Anthropology" in 1965a
Harris 1968
E. K. Maranda 1973
P. Maranda 1972a
Snyder 1979
van Baal 1971: weak in many areas, but a useful overview

Articles and books tracing the historical development of mythographic perspectives:

D. C. Allen 1970: extensively documented account of the rediscovery of classical mythological and mythographic materials during the Renaissance, their subsequent deployment, and the earlier Christian euhemerizing and allegorizing

Block 1980
Cohen 1969: brief but helpful summary
Cunningham 1973: critical analyses of Eliade, Douglas, Lévi-Strauss
Detienne 1981: valuable generally but also specifically on the origins of French
    classical mythography
Dörrie 1980: excellent on Greek and Roman uses of mythology
Feldman and Richardson 1972: a massive mythography for the years from
    1680–1860, with sources cited
Gruppe 1965 and de Vries 1961: the standard German mythographies
Hayward 1968
Vernant and Vidal-Naquet 1980:chap. 9: an excellent discussion of the my-
    thos:logos issue
Weissenberger 1980

On defining myth:

Banton 1965: seminal essays
Eliade 1963
Geertz 1973
Honko 1972
Leach 1982: restriction of "myth" to materials recorded in the field by
    contemporary ethnologists
Murray 1968b

General Introductions to Myths and Mythologies

Apollodoros—either Simpson 1976 or Frazer 1921
Boswell and Boswell 1980: genealogical charts for classical mythic figures
Campbell 1959, 1962, 1964
Cavendish 1980
Comstock 1972: highly recommended for a rapid overview, methodologically
    acute
Eliade—see pt. 1 of Beane and Doty 1975, both for selections from Eliade and
    for bibliography
Eliot 1976
Graves 1960
Guirand 1968: several subsequent reprintings; of uneven quality but often help-
    ful to begin setting the cultural and historical contours
Kerényi 1959
Kramer 1961
Morford and Lenardon 1971
Otto 1954
Pembroke 1981: brief overview of how Western classical mythology has been
    viewed

R. Smith 1981: the place to begin any search for collections of myths
Tripp 1970
Vickers 1973

Iconography of Myths and Rituals

L. A. Allen 1975: well-illustrated comparison of Australian aborigine arts and
  myth traditions
Boulter 1981: contemporary use of vase-painting iconography to reconstruct
  traditions
Campbell 1975: best in the cloth edition; splendidly illustrated
Carr 1979: reading a myth tradition from graphic evidence alone
Davidson 1977: excellent lectures from the Folklore Society
Henle 1973: elementary handbook with poor illustrations, but it gives a sense of
  the rich iconographic vocabulary of the Greeks
Hinks 1939
Jopling 1971: essays are very brief but comprehensive in scope
Lexicon Iconographicum Mythologiae Classicae 1984+: a multi-volume reference
  work, sure to become the new standard
Mallery 1893: still the most comprehensive illustrated account of Native North
  American iconography
Mitchell 1980: recent essays in aesthetics, ranging from antiquity to modern
  cinematic techniques
W. G. Moon 1983: a series of studies of classical images and art works; valuable
  bibliography
A. C. Moore 1977: poor illustrations but comprehensively focused upon the
  major religious traditions.
Munn 1973a: a work comparable in its philosophical perceptiveness to Wither-
  spoon 1977.
Panofsky and Panofsky 1962; Panofsky 1939, 1955
Jill Purce, general editor, Art and Imagination series (also entitled Art and
  Cosmos series, or the Illustrated Library of Sacred Imagination—from several
  publishers here and abroad): superb color plates, often mediocre black and
  white illustrations, texts of varying quality. Some of the most useful include: R.
  Cook 1974, de Rola 1973, Halifax 1982, Legeza 1973, Maclagan 1977, Wosien
  1974
Saxl 1970: rewarding collection of lectures
Schefold 1966
Seznec 1953: this book, along with Wind 1968, gives a comprehensive picture of
  Renaissance views of allegory and symbolism
Trendall and Webster 1971
V. Turner 1982a: essays accompanying a vast Smithsonian exhibit in the Ren-
  wick Gallery; for the well-illustrated catalog, see Office of Folklife Programs
  1982

van Baaren 1970–: a wide-ranging monograph series
Zimmer 1946: a glimpse into the sophistications of Eastern modes of expression, mostly slighted in this book

Anthologies and Collections of Essays; Journal Issues

Aycock and Klein 1980: recent essays of high quality
Campbell 1970b: from a stimulating series of lectures of the Society for the Arts, Religion, and Contemporary Culture
Cunningham 1973
Georges 1968; Murray 1968a; Sebeok 1958: the classic collections
P. Maranda 1972a: wide-ranging; useful for European perspectives
Natural History Press (a division of Doubleday): The American Museum Sourcebooks in Anthropology. The following, edited by John Middleton, are especially valuable for our purposes: 1967a, 1967b, 1967c
Watts, ed., Patterns of Myths series, of which only four were published, but they are excellent: Henderson and Oakes 1963; Long 1963; Perry 1966; and Watts 1963

Journal issues with thematic emphasis on myths/rituals:

Archē: Notes and Papers on Archaic Studies 6 (1981), "Transformations of Archaic Images"; *Chimera* 4/3 (1946); *Daedalus* 101/1 (1972), "Myth, Symbol, and Culture" (reprinted as Geertz 1971); *Parabola: Myth and the Quest for Meaning* (published quarterly since 1976; I have strong reservations about the snippet format from well-known authors); *Journal of American Folklore* 79/311 (1966), "The Anthropologist Looks at Myth"; *The Monist* 50/4 (1966), "Symbol and Myth"; *Zygon: Journal of Religion and Science* 18/3 (1983), "Ritual in Human Adaptation"

Studies of Ritual

Bascom 1957: the ritual-dominant theory surveyed
Bird 1980: résumé of phenomenology and function of rituals, and ritualism as a problem
Cafferata 1975: large-format paperback with a strange mixture of literature, illustrations, and bits of good critical commentary
Firth 1973: one of the most inclusive studies of ritual symbols from the perspective of anthropology
Fontenrose 1966
Grimes 1982a: sets out the major problematic issues for any contemporary study
J. E. Harrison 1924: remarkable scope in such a brief book; argues that ritual is the basis for myths, which in turn satisfy social needs

Jennings 1982: explores how one comes to ritual knowledge

Klapp 1956: elementary but inclusive discussion of the place of ritual in (American) society; a good starting point if supplemented by more recent methodological studies

LaFontaine 1972: Firth's microkinesic analysis and Leach's structuralist discussion of symbols are excellent essays in this book

Leach 1968: useful summary of modern approaches

Moore and Myerhoff 1977: one of the few full-scale collections on nontraditional, "secular" ritual

Munn 1973a: the symbolic systems of rituals

Scheff 1979: especially chap. 5

Shaughnessy 1973: provocative articles from modern discussions

Tambiah 1981: the subjective, semiotic, and social-referential aspects of ritual performances

V. Turner 1967, 1969b: the most explicitly ritual-focused of Turner's many works

Van Gennep 1960: classic in the field, refined and developed by Victor Turner and others

Wallace 1966b: anticipates in brief format his large book of the same year

Sociofunctionalism

Douglas 1980: helpful in viewing Evans-Pritchard as a theoretician and in his context

Firth 1975: retrospective reflections on sociofunctionalist approaches

Goode 1951

Hallowell 1941: a classic statement of sociofunctionalist views

Homans 1941

Jarvie 1964

Kirk 1962

Malinowski 1948: includes his famous essay, "Myth in Primitive Psychology"

Radcliffe-Brown 1952

Rappaport 1979: especially pp. 43–95, "Ecology, Adaptation, and the Ills of Functionalism"

Contemporary Anthropological-Ethnographic Studies

Banton 1965: essays that have been widely influential

Carmack 1972

S. Diamond 1974: always provocative and usually on target

Dolgin, Kemnitzer, and Schneider 1977: comprehensive reader in symbolic anthropology

Douglas 1966, 1970: good on comprehending the social matrix of myth; and 1975: some revisions of her earlier work

Harris 1976

Herdt 1981, 1982: extensive documentation of a ritualization of homosexual behavior as the normal socialization pattern

Jacobs and Greenway 1966: an early collection of essays on myth by anthropologists

Lessa and Vogt 1980: periodically revised, this reader is always a gold mine of current views

I. Lewis 1977

P. Maranda 1972b: bibliographic review, helpful for understanding background of current approaches

Spencer 1969: important articles on the interpretation of symbol, myth, and ritual

V. Turner: see bibliography cited in Chapter 3

Linguistic-Narratological-Semiotic Structuralism

Blumensath 1972: an inclusive reader from several languages, all translated into German, of some of the key studies; best international bibliography of applied structuralist literary studies to 1970

Durbin 1972: rather technical account of types of linguistic models currently employed

Ehrmann 1970: elementary but very helpful articles placing structuralism in its historical contexts

Hawkes 1977: the "later structuralism," showing clearly the recent emphasis upon semiotics

Jameson 1972: advanced but excellent on linguistic and Russian formalist backgrounds of structuralism as well as on recent French narratology

Lane 1970: includes many classic studies from early structuralism

Maranda and Maranda 1971a: important contributions by Greimas, Dundes, and others

Pettit 1977: critical of some of the uses of linguistics

Rossi 1974: diffuse and overlong but some excellent critiques included

Sebeok 1960: a good collection from a 1958 conference when the impact of linguistics first was being realized

Waugh 1966

Claude Lévi-Strauss

Perhaps the best way to begin is with a brief résumé of his whole program, such as Leach 1970; then move through the key articles in *Structural Anthropology*

(Lévi-Strauss 1963 and 1976), such as "The Structural Study of Myth," 1963:206–32, and "The Story of Asdiwal" and "Four Winnebago Myths," 1976:146–210. Then one is ready for the more advanced materials such as: "The Science of the Concrete" and "Systems of Transformation," 1966:1–34, 75–108. Of the four volumes of the Introduction to a Science of Mythology (Mythologiques), the first and last are especially important for seeing Lévi-Strauss's methodology; the first 200 pages of the first volume are condensed as pp. 250–98 in P. Maranda 1972a. Sperber 1979 and Hayes and Hayes 1970 are typical of the secondary, evaluative materials that this initial reading can introduce; Freilich 1977 is rewarding on mediations in myth sequences.

Psychological

Carloye 1980: critical of Jung, as of Lévi-Strauss

Edinger 1972 and Whitmont 1969: of many introductions to Jung's thought, these seem the most helpful

Fischer 1963: somewhat out of date but comprehensive; not, as the title suggests, restricted to folktales

Gould 1981: the most trenchant and constructive criticism and use of Jung's concept of the archetype

Henderson 1964: one of the best "plain language" applications of Jung's perspectives to mythology

Jones 1974: a wide range of essays in the two volumes, from an orthodox psychoanalytical (Freudian) stance

Jung and von Franz 1964: elementary presentations, approved by Jung just before his death; avoid the paperback edition, which destroys the conceptual design of the work

S. Moon 1970

Mullahy 1948: an entrée into the classical approaches within psychoanalysis; references to Freud's own works are given in Chapter 5

Neumann 1954, 1956: some of the most elaborate extensions of Jung's thought to world history and myth

Schneiderman 1981: broad, inclusive

Archetypal Criticism and Myth Analysis of Literature

Belli 1969; Bodkin 1934; Burrows, Lapides, and Shawcross 1973; Bush 1963, 1937, 1968; Feder 1971; Highet 1949; Mayerson 1971: these works all trace the various impacts of myths and mythical motifs in Western literature

A. Cook 1980

Ferrara 1975: multidisciplinary attempt to model the various structures in a literary work

Fiedler 1960

Fredericks 1982: the genre here is speculative fiction (sf, science fiction), and the author describes mythological influences as well as inherently mythologizing tendencies

Frye 1957, 1963, 1967: these will give a thorough overview of Frye's position

Gould 1981: the most penetrating of recent attempts to define the "mythicity" of modern literature

Herd 1969: inclusive but brief overview of myth criticism

McCune, Orbison, and Withim 1980: studies of specific works and writers; the bibliography, pp. 338–46, supplements that of Vickery 1966

Righter 1975: brief but full of insight

Slochower 1970: a widely influential post-Cassirer synthesis

Slote 1963: essays on specific authors and themes

Spivey 1980: after an excellent initial chapter, use of a Jungian patchwork as a critical tool

Stauffer 1948: resistance to myth-lit-crit

Strelka 1980: one of the best contemporary collections but, like most of them, lacking overall focus because of the range of essays included

Vickery 1966 and especially 1983

Wheelwright 1968: a plurisignificative view of symbol and myth that has been very influential

J. White 1972

Contemporary Religious and Theological Approaches

Altizer 1962

Barbour 1975

Crites 1971

Dudley 1967

Harvey 1966

Johnson 1974: with references to Bultmann's writings

Knox 1964

Miller 1970a, 1981

Niebuhr 1937: not exactly "contemporary" but displays the wisdom of Niebuhr's historical theology

Pieper 1965: a development and application of his earlier book (1952)

Rahner 1963: one of the few thorough studies of the early fusion of Greek and Christian horizons

Richardson 1967: generally positive evaluation of the role of myth in theology

Stevenson 1969: wrestling with new definitions of "history" vis-à-vis myth

W. I. Thompson 1981

Tillich 1971

Watts 1968: critical of Christianity's fusion of myth and history

Modern Appropriations of Myth; Contemporary Culture Analysis

Barthes 1972, 1979: translations from the massive collection of occasional essays for the popular press

Campbell 1968a, 1972

Cherry 1969: working toward mythological analysis of American political religiosity

Cuthbertson 1975: strong insights about political aspects of myth in an awkwardly written book

Dundes 1969: typical of Dundes's analytic applied to American behaviors

Ellul 1958

Finley 1956: the historian's wrestling with myth

Fiske and Hartley 1978: semiotic analysis of television programs

Greeley 1961/62

Halpern 1961

Harper 1966: philosophical exposition of the story of Sleeping Beauty

Jewett and Lawrence 1977a: the "new" American hero pattern

Lapham 1971: the military base as producing and supporting a mythological cosmos for its members

London and Weeks 1981: mythical or stereotypical aspects of American self-consciousness used as a platform for advocating a return to older values

Luckert 1979: shows then:now correlations in Navajo materials

Munz 1956

Patai 1972

Stevenson 1969: good on Bultmann and on Vico

Sullenberger 1974: American marketing and mythical figures

Transmission and Themes of Myths and Folklore

Bascom 1965: working toward standard definition of forms

Bauman 1975: good introduction to the new emphasis upon "performance"; excellent bibliography

Bauman and Sherzer 1974; 1975

Ben-Amos and Goldstein 1975

Downing 1981: Greek goddesses revisioned in a contemporary American woman's experience

Dundes 1962a, 1965b, 1975, 1980

Galinsky 1972

Jacobs and Greenway 1966: eight myths/tales/folktale genres still viable in their original social settings

Jason 1969

Lord 1960: the classic work on oral transmission by storytellers; see also Lord

1980; Austin's (1975) adaptation and supplementation for Homer; and Jason and Segal 1977

Lowry 1982: neither critical nor ideological but a sort of "soft archetypalism" in approaching mythic themes today

Maranda and Maranda 1971b: the title essay is a fine account of regularizing materials for subsequent analysis

Matthews 1968: the quest/journey motif, Oidipous onward

Merivale 1969

Paredes and Bauman 1972: emphasis upon performance rather than accumulation of context-free data

Propp 1968

Schneidau 1976: shows Western perspectives rooted in the (anti)mythological perspectives of ancient Israel—the home of a "sacred discontent" in the prophetic and Yahwist theologies that determined all subsequent Western cultures

Stanford 1963; Stanford and Luce 1974: on the figure of Odysseus/Ulysses

Vickery and Sellery 1971

Vinge 1967: a superior study, with original texts; comprehensive and exacting

Zipes 1979: neo-Marxian critique with many insights

Advanced and Specialized Studies

Babcock 1978: a truly thematic collection of essays around the central theme of inversion

Bachofen 1967: some of the last generation's most striking insights on myth and iconography

Blanchard 1983: develops an initial semiotics for aesthetics of ancient Greek art in relation to literature

Buchler and Maddock 1978: an Australian myth analyzed from several perspectives

Duncan 1968: how myth has been experienced as working inside a poet's personality; R. Newman 1965: shows how ritual-dominant school has influenced Newman's writing.

Godelier 1977: Marxian revisioning of Marx on "religion," "the primitive," in dialogue with Lévi-Strauss and other contemporary scholars

Leymore 1975: uses a structuralist/semiotic analysis together with industrial statistics, considers modern advertising to be analogous to tribal or Greek mythology

Lincoln 1981b, Littleton 1973, and Puhvel 1970: include summaries of Dumézil's tripartite Indo-European approach, which has not been developed here

MacAloon 1984: a wide range of topics but unified in use of ritual-performance perspective

Preston 1982: wide-ranging and inclusive collection of essays reflecting contemporary interest in the figure of the Mother/Goddess, in several cultures

Rudhardt 1972: mythic structures intend *themselves,* as symbols

Bibliographies

Andrew and Bruns 1973: highly recommended but not available to me
Boswell 1982: extensive (2,254 entries) catalog of uses of Greco-Roman themes/mythical figures/plots/and so forth in modern literature
Diehl 1956: comprehensive but out of date
Grimes 1984: preliminary version of a forthcoming bibliography for ritual studies containing more than 1,600 items
Hawkes 1977:161–87: annotated and subdivided usefully; includes major journals and series and a suggested sequence of readings on formalism, linguistics, structuralism, semiotics
Hecht 1982: studies of sacrifice
Isenberg and Owen 1977: comprehensive review of Mary Douglas's work
P. Maranda 1972a:299–309
Mercatante 1978: cursory annotations on popular collections or retellings of myths from many of the world's cultures
Peradotto 1973: the sort of desk tool every discipline ought to have at hand
Popenoe 1979
Ruthven 1976:84–100
R. Smith 1981
Stevens 1973: cited by others but unavailable to me
Vickery 1966

References Cited

Abrahams, Roger D. 1973. "Rituals in Culture." Ms. revision of "Ritual for Fun and Profit," paper read at Wenner-Gren Conference No. 59, 21–29 July 1973, Burg Wartenstein, Austria (cited by permission).

Abrahams, Roger D., and Richard Bauman. 1978. "Ranges of Festival Behavior." In Babcock:193–208.

Ackerman, Robert. 1975. "Frazer on Myth and Ritual." *Journal of the History of Ideas* 36:115–34.

Adolf, Helen. 1980. "Rilke—Transcended or Transcending?" In Strelka:95–108.

Aldiss, Brian, ed. 1975. *Evil Earths*. New York: Avon.

Aldrich, Charles Robert. 1931. *The Primitive Mind and Modern Civilization*. London: Kegan Paul; New York: Harcourt.

Alland, Alexander, Jr. 1976. "The Roots of Art." In Schechner and Schuman:5–17.

Allen, Don Cameron. 1970. *Mysteriously Meant: The Rediscovery of Pagan Symbolism and Allegorical Interpretation in the Renaissance*. Baltimore: Johns Hopkins University Press.

Allen, Louis A. 1975. *Time Before Morning: Art and Myth of the Australian Aborigines*. New York: Crowell.

Allen, Paula Gunn. 1975. "The Sacred Hoop: A Contemporary Indian Perspective on American Indian Literature." In Chapman:111–36.

Altizer, Thomas J. J. 1962. "The Religious Meaning of Myth and Symbol." In Altizer, Beardslee, and Young:89ff.

Altizer, Thomas J. J., W. A. Beardslee, and J. H. Young, eds. 1962. *Truth, Myth, and Symbol*. Englewood Cliffs, N.J.: Prentice-Hall.

Altizer, Thomas J. J., Max A. Myers, Carl A. Raschke, Robert P. Scharlemann, Mark C. Taylor, and Charles E. Winquist. 1982. *Deconstruction and Theology*. New York: Crossroad.

Ammons, A. R. 1977. *The Snow Poems*. New York: Norton.

Andrew, J. Dudley, and Gerald L. Bruns. 1973. "Structuralism, Narrative Analysis, and the Theory of Texts: A Checklist." *Bulletin of the Midwest Modern Language Association* 6:121–27.

Andriolo, Karin R. 1981. "Myth and History: A General Model and Its Application to the Bible." *American Anthropologist* 83/2:261–84.

Argüelles, José A. 1975. *The Transformative Vision: Reflections on the Nature and History of Human Expression.* Berkeley: Shambhala.

Armstrong, Robert Plant. 1975. *Wellspring: On the Myth and Source of Culture.* Berkeley and Los Angeles: University of California Press.

Arthur, Marylin B. 1976. "Review Essay: Classics." *Signs: Journal of Women in Culture and Society* 2/2:382–403.

Astrov, Margot. 1962. *American Indian Prose and Poetry: An Anthology.* New York: Capricorn. Originally published in 1946 as *The Winged Serpent.*

Augé, Marc. 1982. *The Anthropological Circle: Symbol, Function, History.* Translated by Martin Thom. New York: Cambridge University Press; Paris: Editions de la Maison des Sciences de l'Homme; Cambr. Stud. in Soc. Anth., 37.

Ausband, Stephen C. 1983. *Myth and Meaning, Myth and Order.* Macon, Ga.: Mercer University Press.

Austin, Norman. 1975. *Archery at the Dark of the Moon: Poetic Problems in Homer's "Odyssey."* Berkeley and Los Angeles: University of California Press.

Aycock, Wendell M., and Theodore M. Klein, eds. 1980. *Classical Mythology in Twentieth-Century Thought and Literature.* Lubbock: Texas Tech Press; Proc. Comp. Lit. Sympos. 1978, 11.

Babcock, Barbara A., ed. 1978. *The Reversible World: Symbolic Inversion in Art and Society.* Ithaca: Cornell University Press; Symbol, Myth, and Ritual ser.

Bachelard, Gaston. 1969. *The Poetics of Reverie: Childhood, Language, and the Cosmos.* Translated by Daniel Russell. Boston: Beacon.

———. 1971a. *On Poetic Imagination and Reverie: Selections from the Works of Gaston Bachelard.* Translated by Colette Gaudin. Indianapolis: Bobbs-Merrill.

———. 1971b. *The Right to Dream.* Translated by J. A. Underwood. New York: Grossman.

Bachofen, J. J. 1967. *Myth, Religion, and Mother Right, Selected Writings.* Translated by Ralph Manheim. Princeton: Princeton University Press.

Banton, Michael, ed. 1965. *Anthropological Approaches to the Study of Religion.* London: Tavistock; A.S.A. Monogr., 3.

Bär, Eugen. N.d. "Myth and Primary Process: A Psychoanalytic Approach." *Ars semeiotica* 1/5 (forthcoming).

Barbour, Ian. 1975. *Myths, Models, and Paradigms: A Comparative Study in Science and Religion.* New York: Harper and Row.

Barfield, Owen. 1977. *The Rediscovery of Meaning, and Other Essays.* Middletown, Conn.: Wesleyan University Press.

Barnard, Mary. 1966. *The Mythmakers.* Athens: Ohio University Press.

Barnett, J. 1954. *The American Christmas.* New York: Macmillan.

Barthes, Roland. 1972. *Mythologies.* Translated by Annette Lavers. New York: Hill and Wang.

———. 1974. *S/Z.* Translated by Richard Miller. New York: Hill and Wang.

———. 1977. *Image—Music—Text.* Translated by Stephen Heath. New York: Farrar, Straus and Giroux.

———. 1979. *The Eiffel Tower and Other Mythologies*. Translated by Richard Howard. New York: Farrar, Straus and Giroux.

Barthes, Roland, François Bovon, Franz-J. Leenhardt, Robert Martin-Achard, and Jean Starobinski. 1974. *Structural Analysis and Biblical Exegesis: Interpretational Essays*. Translated by Alfred M. Johnson, Jr. Pittsburgh: Pickwick.

Bartsch, Hans-Werner, ed. 1953. *Kerygma and Myth: A Theological Debate*. Translated by Reginald H. Fuller. London: S.P.C.K.; Vol. 1.

Bascom, William. 1957. "The Myth-Ritual Theory." *Journal of American Folklore* 70:103–14.

———. 1965. "The Forms of Folklore: Prose Narratives." *Journal of American Folklore* 78:3–20.

Bauman, Richard. 1975. "Verbal Art as Performance." *American Anthropologist* 77/1:290–311.

Bauman, Richard, and Joel Sherzer, eds. 1974. *Explorations in the Ethnography of Speaking*. New York: Columbia University Press.

———. 1975. "The Ethnography of Speaking." *Annual Review of Anthropology* 4:95–119.

Beane, Wendell C., and William G. Doty, eds. 1975. *Myths, Rites, Symbols: A Mircea Eliade Reader*. 2 vols. New York: Harper and Row.

Bedford, Gary S. 1981. "Notes on Mythological Psychology: Reimagining the Historical Psyche." *Journal of the American Academy of Religion* 49/2:231–47.

Beidelman, T. O., ed. 1971. *The Translation of Culture: Essays to E. E. Evans-Pritchard*. London: Tavistock.

Bell, Daniel. 1976. "Lévi-Strauss and the Return to Rationalism." *New York Times Book Review* (14 March): 23–24.

Bellah, Robert N. 1970. *Beyond Belief*. New York: Harper and Row.

———. 1975. *Religion in Time of Trial*. New York: Seabury.

Belli, Angela. 1969. *Ancient Greek Myths and Modern Drama: A Study in Continuity*. New York: New York University Press.

Belmont, Nicole. 1979. *Arnold Van Gennep: The Creator of French Ethnography*. Translated by Derek Coltman. Chicago: University of Chicago Press.

Belsey, Catherine. 1980. *Critical Practice*. London: Methuen; New Accents ser.

Ben-Amos, Dan, and Kenneth S. Goldstein, eds. 1975. *Folklore: Performance and Communication*. The Hague: Mouton; Approaches to Semiotics, 40.

Benamou, Michel, and Charles Caramello, eds. 1977. *Performance in Postmodern Culture*. Milwaukee: Center for Twentieth-Century Studies; Madison: Coda Press; Theories of Contemp. Cult., 1.

Berger, John, et al. 1972. *Ways of Seeing*. London: British Broadcasting Corporation and Penguin Books.

Berger, Peter L., and Thomas Luckmann. 1966. *The Social Construction of Reality: A Treatise in the Sociology of Knowledge*. Garden City, N.Y.: Anchor.

Berman, Marshall. 1982. *All That is Solid Melts into Air: The Experience of Modernity*. New York: Simon and Schuster.

Berndt, Catherine H., and Ronald M. Berndt. 1971. *The Barbarians: An Anthropological View*. London: Watts.

Besterman, Theodore. 1934. *A Bibliography of Sir James George Frazer, O.M.* London: Macmillan.

Bettelheim, Bruno. 1954. *Symbolic Wounds: Puberty Rites and the Envious Male.* Glencoe, Ill.: Free Press.

———. 1976. *The Uses of Enchantment: The Meaning and Importance of Fairy Tales.* New York: Random House.

———. 1982. *Freud and Man's Soul.* New York: Random House.

Bewkes, Eugene Garrett, Julius Seelye Bixler, Robert Lowry Calhoun, and others. 1937. *The Nature of Religious Experience.* New York: Harper and Row.

Bharati, Agenhananda, ed. 1976. *The Realm of the Extra-Human: Agents and Audiences.* The Hague and Paris: Mouton; World Anth. ser.

Bidney, David. 1958. "Myth, Symbolism, and Truth." In Sebeok 1958:3–24.

———. 1967. *Theoretical Anthropology.* 2d ed., augmented. New York: Schocken. See especially chap. 10: "The Concept of Myth."

Bierhorst, John. 1974. *Four Masterworks of American Indian Literature: Quetzalcoatl, The Ritual of Condolence, Cuceb, The Night Chant.* New York: Farrar, Straus and Giroux.

———. 1975. "American Indian Verbal Art and the Role of the Critic." *Journal of American Folklore* 88/350:401–08.

———. 1976. *The Red Swan: Myths and Tales of the American Indians.* New York: Farrar, Straus and Giroux.

Bird, Frederick. 1980. "The Contemporary Ritual Milieu." In Browne:19–35.

Blacking, John, ed. 1977. *The Anthropology of the Body.* New York: Academic; Assoc. of Soc. Anth. Monogr., 15.

Blanchard, Marc Eli. 1983. "In the World of the Seven Cubit Spear: The Semiotic Status of the Object in Ancient Greek Art and Literature." *Semiotica* 43/3–4:205–44.

Block, Haskell M. 1980. "The Myth of the Artist." In Strelka:3–24.

Blumensath, Heinz, ed. 1972. *Strukturalismus in der Literaturwissenschaft.* Cologne: Kiepenheuer and Witsch.

Bly, Robert. 1980. *News of the Universe: Poems of Twofold Consciousness.* San Francisco: Sierra Club.

Bodkin, Maud. 1934. *Archetypal Patterns in Poetry: Psychological Studies of Imagination.* London: Oxford University Press.

Bogan, Louise. 1946. "The Secular Hell." *Chimera* 4/3:12–20.

Bohannan, Laura. [Bowen, Elenore Smith.] 1954. *Return to Laughter.* New York: Doubleday/Natural History Library.

Boon, James A. 1972. *From Symbolism to Structuralism: Lévi-Strauss in a Literary Tradition.* New York: Harper and Row.

Boswell, Fred, and Jeanetta Boswell. 1980. *What Men or Gods are These? A Genealogical Approach to Classical Mythology.* Metuchen, N.J.: Scarecrow.

Boswell, Jeanetta. 1982. *Past ruined Ilion. . . : A Bibliography of English and American Literature Based on Graeco-Roman Mythology.* Metuchen, N.J.: Scarecrow.

Boulter, Cedric G. 1981. "The Study of Greek Vases." *American Journal of Archaeology* 85/2:105–06.

Bourguignon, Erika. 1973. "Psychological Anthropology." In Honigmann: 1073–1118.

Brandon, S. G. F. 1963. *Creation Legends of the Ancient Near East*. London: Hodder and Stoughton.

Brenneman, Walter L., Jr. 1979. *Spirals: A Study in Symbol, Myth and Ritual*. Washington, D.C.: University Press of America.

Brennert, Alan. 1980. "Stage Whisper." In Martin:123–55.

Brown, Norman O. 1947. *Hermes the Thief: The Evolution of a Myth*. New York: Vintage.

Brown, Peter. 1982. *Society and the Holy in Late Antiquity*. Berkeley and Los Angeles: University of California Press.

Browne, Ray B., ed. 1980. *Rituals and Ceremonies in Popular Culture*. Bowling Green: Bowling Green University Popular Press.

Buchler, Ira R., and Kenneth Maddock, eds. 1978. *The Rainbow Serpent: A Chromatic Piece*. The Hague and Paris: Mouton.

Buchler, Ira R., and Henry A. Shelby. 1968. *A Formal Study of Myth*. Austin, Tex.: Center for Intercultural Studies in Folklore and Oral History; Monogr. ser., 1.

Budapest, Z [Zsuzsanna E.]. 1976. *The Feminist Book of Lights and Shadows*. Edited by Helen Beardwomon. N.p.: Luna.

Bultmann, Rudolf. 1953. "New Testament and Mythology." In Bartsch:1–44.

———. 1958. *Jesus Christ and Mythology*. New York: Scribner's.

Burke, Kenneth. 1947. "Ideology and Myth." *Accent* 7/4:195–205.

Burkert, Walter. 1979. *Structure and History in Greek Mythology and Ritual*. Berkeley and Los Angeles: University of California Press.

———. 1983. *Homo necans: The Anthropology of Ancient Greek Sacrificial Ritual and Myth*. Translated by Peter Bing. Berkeley and Los Angeles: University of California Press.

Burrows, D. J., F. R. Lapides, and J. T. Shawcross, eds. 1973. *Myths and Motifs in Literature*. New York: Free Press.

Bush, Douglas. 1937. *Mythology and the Romantic Tradition in English Poetry*. Cambridge: Harvard University Press.

———. 1963. *Mythology and the Renaissance Tradition in English Poetry*. Rev. ed. New York: Norton.

———. 1968. *Pagan Myth and Christian Tradition in English Poetry*. Philadelphia: American Philosophical Society; Memoirs, 72.

Cafferata, John, comp. 1975. *Rites*. New York: McGraw-Hill.

Caldwell, Richard S. 1974. "Selected Bibliography on Psychoanalysis and Classical Studies." *Arethusa* 7/1:115–34.

Calinescu, Matei. 1977. *Faces of Modernity: Avant-Garde, Decadence, Kitsch*. Bloomington: Indiana University Press.

Callois, Roger. 1961. *Man, Play, and Games*. Chicago: Free Press.

Calloud, Jean. 1976. *Structural Analysis of Narrative*. Translated by Daniel Patte. Philadelphia: Fortress; Missoula, Mont.: Scholars; Semeia Suppl., 4.

Campbell, Joseph. 1959. *Primitive Mythology*. New York: Viking; Masks of God, 1.

_____. 1962. *Oriental Mythology*. New York: Viking; Masks of God, 2.

_____. 1964. *Occidental Mythology*. New York: Viking; Masks of God, 3.

_____. 1968a. *Creative Mythology*. New York: Viking; Masks of God, 4.

_____. 1968b. *The Hero with a Thousand Faces*. 2d ed. Princeton: Princeton University Press; Bollingen ser., 17.

_____. 1969. *The Flight of the Wild Gander: Explorations in the Mythological Dimension*. New York: Viking.

_____. 1970a. "Mythological Themes in Creative Literature and Art." In Campbell 1970b:138–75.

_____. ed. 1970b. *Myths, Dreams, and Religion*. New York: Dutton.

_____. 1972. *Myths to Live By*. New York: Viking.

_____. 1975. *The Mythic Image*. Princeton: Princeton University Press; Bollingen ser., 100.

_____. 1983. *The Way of the Animal Powers*. New York: Marck/Harper and Row; Hist. Atlas of World Mythol., 1.

Campbell, Joseph, and Henry Morton Robinson. 1944. *A Skeleton Key to Finnegans Wake*. New York: Harcourt, Brace.

Carloye, Jack. 1980. "Myths as Religious Explanations." *Journal of the American Academy of Religion* 48/2:175–89.

Carmack, Robert M. 1972. "Technohistory: A Review of the Development, Definitions, Method, and Aims." *Annual Review of Anthropology* 1:227–46.

Carr, Pat. 1979. *Mimbres Mythology*. El Paso: Texas Western Press; Southwestern Stud., Monogr. 56.

Carr, Pat, and Willard Gingerich. 1983. "The Vagina Dentata Motif in Nahuatl and Pueblo Mythic Narratives: A Comparative Study." In Swann:187–203.

Carroll, Michael P. 1982. "The Rolling Head: Towards a Revitalized Psychoanalytic Perspective on Myth." *Journal of Psychoanalytic Anthropology* 5/1:29–56.

Cassirer, Ernst. 1944. *An Essay on Man: An Introduction to a Philosophy of Human Culture*. New Haven: Yale University Press.

_____. 1946. *Language and Myth*. Translated by Susanne K. Langer. New York: Dover.

Cavendish, Richard, ed. 1980. *Mythology: An Illustrated Encyclopedia*. New York: Rizzoli.

Chapman, Abraham, ed. 1975. *Literature of the American Indians: Views and Interpretations. A Gathering of Indian Memories, Symbolic Contexts, and Literary Criticism*. New York: New American Library.

Chase, Richard. 1969. *Quest for Myth*. New York: Greenwood. Reprint from 1949.

Chatman, Seymour. 1978. *Story and Discourse: Narrative Structure in Fiction and Film*. Ithaca: Cornell University Press.

Cherniak, Christopher. 1981. "The Riddle of the Universe and Its Solution." In Hofstadter and Dennett:269–76.

Cherry, Conrad. 1969. "Two American Sacred Ceremonies: Their Implications for the Study of Religion in America." *American Quarterly* 21:741–45, 748–53.

Chicago, Judy. 1979. *The Dinner Party: A Symbol of Our Heritage*. Garden City, N.Y.: Anchor/Doubleday.

Clear, Val, Patricia Warrick, M. H. Greenberg, and J. D. Olander, eds. 1976. *Marriage and the Family Through Science Fiction*. New York: St. Martin's.

Cohen, Percy S. 1969. "Theories of Myth." *Man*, n.s. 4/3:337–53.

Colby, Benjamin N., and James L. Peacock. 1973. "Narative." In Honigmann:chap. 14.

Comstock, W. Richard. 1972. *The Study of Religion and Primitive Religions*. New York: Harper and Row.

Cook, Albert. 1980. *Myth and Language*. Bloomington: Indiana University Press.

Cook, Roger. 1974. *The Tree of Life: Image for the Cosmos*. New York: Avon.

Cooke, J. D. 1927. "Euhemerism: A Mediaeval Interpretation of Classical Paganism." *Speculum* 2:396–410.

Cords, Nicholas, and Patrick Gerster. 1978. *Myth and the American Experience*. 2d ed. Encino, Calif.: Glencoe.

Court, Earl W. 1960. "Myth as World View: A Biosocial Synthesis." In S. Diamond 1960:580–627.

Coward, Rosalind, and John Ellis. 1977. *Language and Materialism: Developments in Semiology and the Theory of the Subject*. Boston: Routledge and Kegan Paul. Reprint 1980.

Crites, Stephen. 1971. "The Narrative Quality of Experience." *Journal of the American Academy of Religion* 39/3:291–311.

Crocker, Christopher. 1973. "Ritual and the Development of Social Structure: Liminality and Inversion." In Shaughnessy:47–86.

Crocker, J. C. 1982. "Ceremonial Masks." In V. Turner 1982a:77–88.

Crumrine, N. Ross, and Marjorie Halpin, eds. 1983. *The Power of Symbols: Masks and Masquerades in the Americas*. Vancouver: University of British Columbia Press.

Culler, Jonathan. 1975. *Structuralist Poetics: Structuralism, Linguistics, and the Study of Literature*. Ithaca: Cornell University Press.

———. 1981. *The Pursuit of Signs: Semiotics, Literature, Deconstruction*. Ithaca: Cornell University Press.

———. 1982. *On Deconstruction: Theory and Criticism After Structuralism*. Ithaca: Cornell University Press.

Culpepper, R. Alan. 1983. *Anatomy of the Fourth Gospel: A Study in Literary Design*. Philadelphia: Fortress; Foundations and Facets ser.

Cunningham, Adrian, ed. 1973. *The Theory of Myth: Six Studies*. London: Sheed and Ward.

Cuthbertson, Gilbert Morris. 1975. *Political Myth and Epic*. East Lansing: Michigan State University Press.

Dames, Michael. 1976. *The Silbury Treasure: The Great Goddess Rediscovered*. London: Thames and Hudson.

d'Aquili, Eugene G. 1983. "The Myth-Ritual Complex: A Biogenetic Structural Analysis." *Zygon: Journal of Religion and Science* 18/3:247–69.

d'Aquili, Eugene G., and Charles D. Laughlin, Jr. 1975. "The Biopsychological

Determinants of Religious Ritual." *Zygon: Journal of Religion and Science* 10/1:32–58.

d'Aquili, Eugene G., Charles D. Laughlin, Jr., and John McManus, with Tom Burns, Barbara Lex, G. Ronald Murphy, S. J. Smith, and W. John Smith. 1979. *The Spectrum of Ritual: A Biogenetic Structural Analysis.* New York: Columbia University Press.

Davidson, H. R. Ellis, ed. 1977. *Symbols of Power.* Totowa, N.J.: Rowman and Littlefield; Folklore Soc. Mistletoe ser.

Davies, Alistair. 1982. *An Annotated Critical Bibliography of Modernism.* Totowa, N.J.: Barnes and Noble.

Davis, Kingsley. 1959. "The Myth of Functional Analysis as a Special Method of Sociology and Anthropology." *American Sociological Review* 24:757–72.

Dawkins, Richard. 1976. *The Selfish Gene.* New York: Oxford University Press.

Deely, John N., and Margot D. Lenhart, eds. 1983. *Semiotics 1981.* New York: Plenum Press; Proc. Sixth Ann. Meeting, Semiotic Soc. of Amer.

Delcourt, Marie. 1961. *Hermaphrodite: Myths and Rites of the Bisexual Figure in Classical Antiquity.* Translated by Jennifer Nicholson. London: Studio.

de Rola, Stanislas K. 1973. *Alchemy: The Secret Art.* New York: Avon.

de Rougement, Denis. 1956. *Love in the Western World.* Rev. ed. Translated by Montgomery Belgion. New York: Harper and Row.

de Santillana, Giorgio, and Hertha von Dechend. 1969. *Hamlet's Mill: An Essay on Myth and the Frame of Time.* Boston: Gambit.

Desmonde, William H. 1951. "Jack and the Beanstalk." *American Imago* 8:287–88. Reprinted in Dundes 1965b:108–09.

Detienne, Marcel. 1977. *The Gardens of Adonis: Spices in Greek Mythology.* Translated by Janet Lloyd. Atlantic Highlands, N.J.: Humanities; Eur. Philos. and the Human Sci., 2.

———. 1979. *Dionysos Slain.* Translated by Mireille Muellner and Leonard Muellner. Baltimore: Johns Hopkins University Press.

———. 1981. *L'invention de la mythologie.* Paris: Gallimard; Bibliothèque des Sciences Humaines.

Detienne, Marcel, and Jean-Pierre Vernant. 1978. *Cunning Intelligence in Greek Culture and Society.* Translated by Janet Lloyd. Atlantic Highlands, N.J.: Humanities; Eur. Philos. and the Human Sci., 4.

Detienne, Marcel, Jean-Pierre Vernant, Jean-Louis Durand, Stella Georgoudi, François Hartog, and Jesper Svenbro. 1979. *La cuisine de sacrifice en pays grec.* Paris: Gallimard; Bibliothèque des Histoires.

Detweiler, Robert, ed. 1982. "Derrida and Biblical Studies." Issue no. 23 of *Semeia: An Experimental Journal for Biblical Studies.*

Deutsch, Helene. 1969. *A Psychoanalytic Study of the Myths of Dionysos and Apollo: Two Variants of the Son-Mother Relationship.* New York: International Universities Press.

Devereux, George. 1967. *From Anxiety to Method in the Behavioral Sciences.* Paris and The Hague: Mouton.

———. 1978a. *Ethnopsychoanalysis: Psychoanalysis and Anthropology as Comple-*

mentary Frames of Reference. Berkeley and Los Angeles: University of California Press.

———. 1978b. "The Works of George Devereux." In Spindler:361–406.

de Vries, Jan. 1961. *Forschungsgeschichte der Mythologie*. Freiburg-Munich: Alber; Orbis Academicus ser.

Diamond, Stanley, ed. 1960. *Culture in History: Essays in Honor of Paul Radin*. New York: Columbia University Press.

———. 1971. "Primitive: The Critical Term." *Alcheringa: Ethnopoetics* 2:66–70.

———. 1974. *In Search of the Primitive: A Critique of Civilization*. New Brunswick, N.J.: Transaction.

Diamond, Stuart J. 1970. *The Social Behavior of Animals*. New York: Harper and Row.

Diehl, Katherine Smith. 1956. *Religions, Mythologies, Folklores: An Annotated Bibliography*. New Brunswick, N.J.: Scarecrow.

Diel, Paul. 1980. *Symbolism in Greek Mythology: Human Desire and Its Transformations*. Translated by Vincent Stuart, Micheline Stuart, and Rebecca Folkman. Boulder: Shambhala.

Dolgin, Janet L., David S. Kemnitzer, and David M. Schneider, eds. 1977. *Symbolic Anthropology: A Reader in the Study of Symbols and Meanings*. New York: Columbia University Press.

Donlan, Walter. 1970. "The Foundation Legends of Rome: An Example of Dynamic Process." *Classical World* 64/4:109–14.

Dorfman, Ariel. 1983. *The Empire's Old Clothes: What the Lone Ranger, Babar, and Other Innocent Heroes Do to Our Minds*. New York: Pantheon.

Doria, Charles, and Harris Lenowitz. 1976. *Origins: Creation Texts from the Ancient Mediterranean. A Chrestomathy*. Garden City, N.Y.: Anchor/Doubleday.

Dörrie, Heinrich. 1980. "The Meaning and Function of Myth in Greek and Roman Literature." In Strelka:109–31.

Dorson, Richard M. 1973. "Mythology and Folklore." *Annual Review of Anthropology* 2:107–26.

Doty, William G. 1972. *Contemporary New Testament Interpretation*. Englewood Cliffs, N.J.: Prentice-Hall.

———. 1975. "The Stories of Our Times." In Wiggins:93–121.

———. 1976. "Speaking in Images." *Parabola: Myth and the Quest for Meaning* 1/1:99–103.

———. 1980a. "Hermes' Heteronymous Appellations." In Hillman 1980:115–33.

———. 1980b. "Mythological Analysis of New Testament Materials." In Spenser:129–38.

———. 1980c. "The Subtle Gyves: Images of the Weavings of Fate in the 'Oresteia.'" *Archē: Notes and Papers on Archaic Studies* 4–5:83–120.

———. 1981a. "The Barbarian Without, the Darkness Within: Notes on the Image of the Primitive." *Archē: Notes and Papers on Archaic Studies* 6:150–72.

———. 1981b. "'Mythophiles' Dyscrasia: A Comprehensive Definition of Myth." *Journal of the American Academy of Religion* 48/4:531–62.

———. N.d. "A Lifetime of Trouble-Making: Hermes as Trickster." Unpublished ms., 43 pp.

Douglas, Mary. 1966. *Purity and Danger: An Analysis of Concepts of Pollution and Taboo*. New York: Praeger.

———. 1970. *Natural Symbols: Explorations in Cosmology*. New York: Pantheon.

———. 1975. *Implicit Meanings: Essays in Anthropology*. Boston: Routledge and Kegan Paul.

———. 1980. *Edward Evans-Pritchard*. New York: Viking; Modern Masters ser.

———, ed. 1982. *Essays in the Sociology of Perception*. Boston: Routledge and Kegan Paul.

Dover, K. J. 1978. *Greek Homosexuality*. Cambridge: Harvard University Press.

Downing, Christine R. 1975a. "Incestuous Fantasies: The Myths about Myth Spawned by Freud, Jung, and Lévi-Strauss." Paper for the Society for Values in Higher Education.

———. 1975b. "Sigmund Freud and the Greek Mythological Tradition." *Journal of the American Academy of Religion* 43/1:1–14.

———. 1976. "Toward an Erotics of the Psyche: In Tribute to Thomas Mann and Carl Jung." *Journal of the American Academy of Religion* 44/4:629–38.

———. 1981. *The Goddess: Mythological Images of the Feminine*. New York: Crossroad.

Dozios, Gardner R., ed. 1972. *A Day in the Life: A Science Fiction Anthology*. New York: Harper and Row.

Dresden, Sem. 1980. "Thomas Mann and Marcel Proust: On Myth and Anti-myth." In Strelka:25–50.

Dudley, Guilford, III. 1967. *The Recovery of Christian Myth*. Philadelphia: Westminster.

Duncan, Robert. 1968. *The Truth and Life of Myth: An Essay in Essential Autobiography*. Fremont, Mich.: Sumac.

Dundes, Alan. 1962a. "Earth-Diver: Creation of the Mythopoeic Male." *American Anthropologist* 64/5:1032–51.

———. 1962b. "From Etic to Emic Units in the Structural Study of Folktales." *Journal of American Folklore* 75/1:95–105.

———. 1965a. "On Computers and Folktales." *Western Folklore* 24:185–89.

———, ed. 1965b. *The Study of Folklore*. Englewood Cliffs, N.J.: Prentice-Hall.

———. 1969. "Thinking Ahead: A Folkloristic Reflection on the Future Orientation in American Worldview." *Anthropological Quarterly* 42:53–72. Reprinted in Dundes 1980:69–85.

———. 1975. *Analytic Essays in Folklore*. The Hague and Paris: Mouton; Stud. in Folklore, 2.

———. 1977. *The Hero Pattern and the Life of Jesus*. Berkeley: Center for Hermeneutical Studies in Hellenistic and Modern Cultures; Colloquy 25. Reprinted in Dundes 1980:223–61.

———. 1980. *Interpreting Folklore*. Bloomington: Indiana University Press.

Dupré, Wilhelm. 1975. *Religion in Primitive Cultures: A Study in Ethnophilosophy*. The Hague: Mouton; Relig. and Reason, 9.

Duràn, Gloria B. 1980. *The Archetypes of Carlos Fuentes: From Witch to Androgyne.* Hamden, Conn.: Archon/Shoe String Press.

Durbin, Mridula Adenwala. 1972. "Linguistic Models in Anthropology." *Annual Review of Anthropology* 1:383–410.

Durkheim, Émile. 1915. *The Elementary Forms of the Religious Life.* Translated by J. W. Swain. New York: Free Press.

Durkheim, Émile, and Marcel Mauss. 1963. *Primitive Classification.* Edited by Rodney Needham. Chicago: University of Chicago Press.

Edinger, Edward F. 1972. *Ego and Archetype: Individuation and the Religious Function of the Psyche.* Baltimore: Penguin.

Ehrmann, Jacques, ed. 1970. *Structuralism.* Garden City, N.Y.: Anchor. Originally published as *Yale French Studies,* 1966.

——, ed. 1971. *Game, Play, Literature.* Boston: Beacon. Originally published as *Yale French Studies,* 1968.

Eliade, Mircea. 1958. *Patterns in Comparative Religion.* Translated by Rosemary Sheed. New York: World.

——. 1960. *Myths, Dreams and Mysteries: The Encounter Between Contemporary Faiths and Archaic Reality.* Translated by Philip Mairet. London: Collins.

——. 1963. *Myth and Reality.* Translated by Willard R. Trask. New York: Harper and Row.

——. 1964. *Shamanism: Archaic Techniques of Ectasy.* Translated by Willard R. Trask. Princeton: Princeton University Press; Bollingen ser., 76.

——. 1967. *From Primitives to Zen: A Thematic Sourcebook of the History of Religions.* New York: Harper and Row.

——. 1969. *Yoga: Immortality and Freedom.* 2d ed. Translated by Willard R. Trask. Princeton: Princeton University Press; Bollingen ser., 56.

——. 1971. *The Forge and the Crucible (The Origins and Structures of Alchemy).* Translated by Stephen Corrin. New York: Harper and Row.

Eliot, Alexander, ed. 1976. *Myths.* New York: McGraw-Hill.

Ellen, Roy F. 1977. "Anatomical Classification and the Semiotics of the Body." In Blacking:343–73.

Ellenberger, Henri F. 1970. *The Discovery of the Unconscious: The History and Evolution of Dynamic Psychology.* New York: Basic.

Ellmann, Richard, and Charles Feidelson, Jr., eds. 1965. *The Modern Tradition: Backgrounds of Modern Literature.* New York: Oxford University Press.

Ellul, Jacques. 1958. "Modern Myths." *Diogenes* 23:23–40. Translated by Elaine Halperin.

Erikson, Erik H. 1966. "Ontogeny of Ritualization in Man." *Philosophical Transactions of the Royal Society of London,* ser. B, 772/251:337–50.

——. 1968. *Identity: Youth and Crisis.* New York: Norton.

Evans-Pritchard, E. E. 1965a. *The Position of Women in Primitive Society and Other Essays in Social Anthropology.* New York: Free Press.

——. 1965b. *Theories of Primitive Religion.* London: Oxford University Press.

Evers, Larry, ed., with Anya Dozier, Danny Lopez, Felipe Molina, Ellavina Tsosie Perkins, Emory Sekaquaptewa, and Ofelia Zepeda. 1980. *The South*

Corner of Time: Hopi, Navajo, Papago, Yaqui Literature. Tucson: University of Arizona Press. Reprint of an issue of *Sun Tracks: An American Indian Literary Series.*

Falk, Nancy A., and Rita M. Gross, eds. 1980. *Unspoken Worlds: Women's Religious Lives in Non-Western Cultures.* New York: Harper and Row.

Fast, Howard. 1975. "The Wound." In Aldiss:31–43.

Faulkner, Peter F. 1977. *Modernism.* London: Methuen; Crit. Idiom, 35.

Feder, Lillian. 1964. *Apollo Handbook of Classical Literature.* New York: Crowell.

———. 1971. *Ancient Myth in Modern Poetry.* Princeton: Princeton University Press.

———. 1980. "Myth, Poetry, and Critical Theory." In Strelka:51–71.

Feldman, Burton, and Robert D. Richardson. 1972. *The Rise of Modern Mythology: 1680–1860.* Bloomington: Indiana University Press.

Ferrara, Fernando. 1974. "Theory and Model for the Structural Analysis of Fiction." *New Literary History* 5/2:245–68.

Fiedler, Leslie A. 1960. *No! In Thunder: Essays on Myth and Literature.* Boston: Beacon.

Fingarette, Herbert. 1963. *The Self in Transformation: Psychoanalysis, Philosophy, and the Life of the Spirit.* New York: Harper and Row.

Finley, M. I. 1966. "Myth, Memory, and History." *History and Theory* 4:281–302.

———, ed. 1981. *The Legacy of Greece: A New Appraisal.* Oxford: Clarendon Press.

Firth, Raymond. 1967. *The Work of the Gods in Tikopia.* New York: Athlone.

———. 1972. "Verbal and Bodily Rituals of Greeting and Parting." In LaFontaine:1–38.

———. 1973. *Symbols: Public and Private.* Ithaca: Cornell University Press; Symbol, Myth, and Ritual ser.

———. 1975. "An Appraisal of Modern Social Anthropology." *Annual Review of Anthropology* 4:1–25.

Fischer, John L. 1963. "The Sociopsychological Analysis of Folktales." *Current Anthropology* 4/3:235–95.

Fiske, John, and John Hartley. 1978. *Reading Television.* London: Methuen; New Accents ser.

Foley, Helene P. 1975. "Sex and State in Ancient Greece." *Diacritics* 5/4:31–36.

———. 1982. *Reflections of Women in Antiquity.* London: Gordon and Breach.

Fontenrose, Joseph. 1959. *Python: A Study of Delphic Myth and Its Origins.* Berkeley and Los Angeles: University of California Press.

———. 1966. *The Ritual Theory of Myth.* Berkeley and Los Angeles: University of California Press.

———. 1978. *The Delphic Oracle: Its Responses and Operations, with a Catalogue of Responses.* Berkeley and Los Angeles: University of California Press.

———. 1981. *Orion: The Myth of the Hunter and the Huntress.* Berkeley and Los Angeles: University of California Press; Univ. Calif. Publ. in Class. Stud., 23.

Forster, Robert, and Orest Ranum, eds. 1982. *Ritual, Religion, and the Sacred.*

Translated by Elbourg Forster and P. M. Ranum. Baltimore: Johns Hopkins University Press. Reprinted from *Annales: Économies, Sociétés, Civilisations,* 7.

Foster, A. Durwood, Jr. 1966. "Myth and Philosophy: Theology's Bipolar Essence." *Journal of Bible and Religion* 34:316–28.

Foucault, Michel. 1970. *The Order of Things: An Archaeology of the Human Sciences.* New York: Vintage.

———. 1977. *Language, Counter-Memory, Practice: Selected Essays and Interviews.* Edited by Donald F. Bouchard. Translated by Donald F. Bouchard and Sherry Simon. Ithaca: Cornell University Press.

Frazer, James George, trans. 1921. *Apollodorus, "The Library."* 2 vols. Cambridge: Harvard University Press; Loeb Class. Lib.

———, ed. and trans. 1929. *Publii Ovidii Nasonis. Fastorum Libri Sex. The "Fasti" of Ovid.* 5 vols. London: Macmillan.

Fredericks, Casey. 1982. *The Future of Eternity: Mythologies of Science Fiction and Fantasy.* Bloomington: Indiana University Press.

Freilich, Morris. 1975. "Myth, Method, and Madness." *Current Anthropology* 16/2:207–26.

———. 1977. "Lévi-Strauss' Myth of Method." In Jason and Segal:223–49.

Freud, Sigmund. 1918. *Totem and Taboo: Resemblances Between the Psychic Lives of Savages and Neurotics.* Translated by A. A. Brill. New York: Random House.

———. 1924. *A General Introduction to Psychoanalysis.* Translated by Joan Riviere. New York: Washington Square.

———. 1939. *Moses and Monotheism.* Translated by Katherine Jones. New York: Random House.

———. 1958. "The Relation of the Poet to Day-Dreaming." Translated by I. F. G. Duff. In Nelson:44–54.

———. 1959. "Obsessive Actions and Religious Practices." In *Standard Edition* 11:126–27.

———. 1960. *Psychopathology of Everyday Life.* In *Standard Edition* 6.

———. 1961a. *Civilization and Its Discontents.* Translated by James Strachey. New York: Norton.

———. 1961b. *The Future of an Illusion.* In *Standard Edition* 21.

———. 1965. *The Interpretation of Dreams.* New York: Avon. Reprint of *Standard Edition* 4 and 5 in 1 vol.

Freund, Philip. 1965. *Myths of Creation.* New York: Washington Square.

Frey-Rohn, Lilliane. 1974. *From Freud to Jung: A Comparative Study of the Psychology of the Unconscious.* Translated by F. E. Engreen and E. K. Engreen. New York: Dell.

Fried, Martha Nemes, and Morton H. Fried. 1980. *Transitions: Four Rituals in Eight Cultures.* New York: Norton.

Friedländer, Paul. 1958. *Plato: An Introduction.* Translated by Hans Myerhoff. New York: Harper and Row; Bollingen ser., 59.

Friedman, Melvin J., and John B. Vickery, eds. 1970. *The Shaken Realist: Essays in Modern Literature in Honor of Frederick J. Hoffman.* Baton Rouge: Louisiana State University Press.

Friedrich, Paul. 1978. *The Meaning of Aphrodite*. Chicago: University of Chicago Press.

Frye, Northrop. 1957. *Anatomy of Criticism: Four Essays*. Princeton: Princeton University Press.

————. 1963. *Fables of Identity: Studies in Poetic Mythology*. New York: Harcourt, Brace and World.

————. 1967. "Literature and Myth." In Thorpe:27–41.

————. 1970. *The Stubborn Structure: Essays on Criticism and Society*. Ithaca: Cornell University Press.

————. 1976. *The Secular Scripture: A Study of the Structure of Romance*. Cambridge: Harvard University Press.

Gager, John G. 1975. *Kingdom and Community: The Social World of Early Christianity*. Englewood Cliffs, N.J.: Prentice-Hall.

Galinsky, G. Karl. 1972. *The Herakles Theme: The Adaptations of the Hero in Literature from Homer to the Twentieth Century*. Totowa, N.J.: Rowman and Littlefield.

Gallus, Alexander. 1972. "A Biofunctional Theory of Religion." *Current Anthropology* 13/5:543–68.

Gardner, Howard. 1972. *The Quest for Mind: Piaget, Lévi-Strauss, and the Structualist Movement*. New York: Random House.

Gaster, Theodor H. 1954. "Myth and Story." *Numen* 1/3:184–212.

————, ed. 1959. *The New Golden Bough: A New Abridgment of the Classic Work by Sir James George Frazer*. New York: Criterion.

————. 1961. *Thespis: Ritual, Myth, and Drama in the Ancient Near East*. Rev. ed. Garden City, N.Y.: Anchor/Doubleday.

————. 1969. *Myth, Legend, and Custom in the Old Testament: A comparative study with chapters from Sir James G. Frazer's "Folklore in the Old Testament."* New York: Harper and Row.

Gay, Volney P. 1983. *Reading Freud: Psychology, Neurosis, and Religion*. Chico, Calif.: Scholars; A.A.R. Stud. in Relig., 32.

Geertz, Clifford, ed. 1971. *Myth, Symbol and Culture*. New York: Norton. Reprint of *Daedalus* 101/1 (1972) (© 1971).

————. 1973. *The Interpretation of Cultures: Selected Essays*. New York: Basic.

————. 1982. *Local Knowledge: Further Essays in Interpretive Anthropology*. New York: Basic.

Georges, Robert A., ed. 1968. *Studies on Mythology*. Homewood, Ill.: Dorsey.

Gill, Sam D. 1982. *Native American Religions: An Introduction*. Belmont, Calif.: Wadsworth; Relig. Life of Man ser.

Girard, René. 1977. *Violence and the Sacred*. Translated by Patrick Gregory. Baltimore: Johns Hopkins University Press.

Glenn, Justin. 1976. "Psychoanalytic Writings on Classical Mythology and Religion: 1909–1960." *Classical World* 70/4:225–47.

Godelier, Maurice. 1977. *Perspectives in Marxist Anthropology*. Translated by Robert Brain. Cambridge: Cambridge University Press; Cambr. Stud. in Soc. Anth., 18.

Goethals, Gregor T. 1980. *The TV Affair: Worship at the Video Altar.* Boston: Beacon.

Goode, William J. 1951. *Religion Among the Primitives.* New York: Free Press.

Goody, Jack R. 1962. "Religion and Ritual, the Definitional Problem." *British Journal of Sociology* 12:142–64.

———. 1977. *The Domestication of the Savage Mind.* New York: Cambridge University Press; Themes in the Soc. Sci. ser.

Gordon, R. L., ed. 1981. *Myth, Religion, and Society: Structuralist Essays by M. Detienne, L. Gernet, J.-P. Vernant, and P. Vidal-Naquet.* Cambridge: Cambridge University Press; Paris: Editions de la Maison des Sciences de l'Homme.

Gould, Eric. 1981. *Mythical Intentions in Modern Literature.* Princeton: Princeton University Press.

Graff, Gerald. 1975. "Babbitt at the Abyss: The Social Context of Postmodern American Fiction." *TriQuarterly* 33:305–37.

Grainger, Roger. 1974. *The Language of the Rite.* London: Darton, Longman and Todd.

Grant, Mary, ed. and trans. 1960. *The Myths of Hyginus.* Lawrence: University of Kansas; Humanistic Stud., 34.

Grant, Michael. 1962. *Myths of the Greeks and Romans.* New York: New American Library.

———. 1971. *Roman Myths.* New York: Scribner's.

Grant, Richard. 1981. "Drode's Equations." In Randall and Silverberg:59–79.

Graves, Robert. 1960. *The Greek Myths.* Rev. ed. Harmondsworth: Penguin.

———. 1966. *The White Goddess: A Historical Grammar of Poetic Myth.* Rev. ed. New York: Farrar, Straus and Giroux.

Greeley, Andrew. 1961/62. "Myths, Symbols, and Rituals in the Modern World." *Critic* 20/3:18–25.

Greimas, A. Julien. 1971. "The Interpretation of Myth: Theory and Practice." In Maranda and Maranda 1971a:81–121.

Griaule, Marcel. 1965. *Conversations with Ogotommeli: An Introduction to Dogon Religious Ideas.* Translated by Ralph Butler, A. I. Richards, and Beatrice Hooke. London: Oxford University Press, for the International African Institute.

Griffin, Susan. 1978. *Woman and Nature: The Roaring Inside Her.* New York: Harper and Row.

Grimes, Ronald. 1975. "Masking: Toward a Phenomenology of Exteriorization." *Journal of the American Academy of Religion* 43/3:508–16. Reprinted as chap. 5 of Grimes 1982a.

———. 1976a. "Ritual Studies: A Comparative Review of Theodor A. Gaster and Victor Turner." *Religious Studies Review* 2/4:13–25. Reprinted as chap. 9 of Grimes 1982a.

———. 1976b. *Symbol and Conquest: Public Ritual and Drama in Santa Fe, New Mexico.* Ithaca: Cornell University Press; Symbol, Myth, and Ritual ser.

———. 1982a. *Beginnings in Ritual Studies.* Washington, D.C.: University Press of America.

————. 1982b. "Defining Nascent Ritual." *Journal of the American Academy of Religion* 50/4:539–55.

————. 1982c. "The Lifeblood of Public Ritual: Fiestas and Public Exploration Projects." In V. Turner 1982a:272–83.

————. 1984. "Sources for the Study of Ritual." *Religious Studies Review* 10/2:134–45.

Gruppe, Otto. 1965. *Geschichte der klassischen Mythologie und Religionsgeschichte.* Olms: Hildesheim. Reprint of 1921 ed. Suppl. to Roscher, ed., *Ausführl. Lexikon der Griech. und Röm. Mythologie.*

Guepín, J.-P. 1968. *The Tragic Paradox: Myth and Ritual in Greek Tragedy.* Amsterdam: Hakkert.

Guiart, Jean. 1972. "Multiple Levels of Meaning in Myth." Translated by John Freeman from *Archives de Sociologie des Religions* 26(1968). In P. Maranda 1972a:111–26.

Guirand, Felix, ed. 1968. *New Larousse Encyclopedia of Mythology.* New ed. Translated by Richard Aldington and Delano Ames. London: Hamlyn/Prometheus.

Gunn, Janet Varner. 1983. *Autobiography: Toward a Poetics of Experience.* Philadelphia: University of Pennsylvania Press.

Guthrie, W. K. C. 1957. *In the Beginning: Some Greek Views on the Origins of Life and the Early State of Man.* Ithaca: Cornell University Press.

Halifax, Joan. 1982. *Shaman: The Wounded Healer.* New York: Crossroad.

Hall, T. William, ed. 1977. *Introduction to the Study of Religion.* New York: Harper and Row.

Hallowell, A. I. 1941. "The Social Function of Anxiety in a Primitive Society." *American Sociological Review* 6:869–81; Bobbs-Merrill reprint ser., A-104.

————. 1966. "The Role of Dreams in Ojibwa Culture." In von Grunebaum and Callois:267–92.

Hallpike, C. R. 1969. "Social Hair." *Man,* n.s. 4:256–64. Reprinted in Lessa and Vogt 1980:99–105.

Halpern, Ben. 1961. " 'Myth' and 'Ideology' in Modern Usage." *History and Theory* 1/1:129–49.

Hampden-Turner, Charles. 1981. *Maps of the Mind.* New York: Collier.

Hannah, Barbara. 1981. *Encounters with the Soul: Active Imagination as Developed by C. G. Jung.* Santa Monica: Sigo.

Hardwick, Charles D. 1977. "Ironic Culture and Polysymbolic Religiosity." *Theologische Zeitschrift* 33:283–93.

————. 1982. "Elusive Religiosity, Illusions, and Truth Telling." *Journal of the American Academy of Religion* 49/4:657–69.

Harper, Ralph. 1966. *Nostalgia: An Existential Exploration of Longing and Fulfillment in the Modern Age.* Cleveland: Press of Western Reserve University.

Harris, Marvin. 1968. *The Rise of Anthropological Theory: A History of Theories of Culture.* New York: Crowell.

————. 1976. "History and Significance of the Emic/Etic Distinction." *Annual Review of Anthropology* 5:329–50.

———. 1979. *Cultural Materialism: The Struggle for a Science of Culture.* New York: Crowell.

Harrison, Helen A., Joseph P. Cusker, Gerald Wendt, Warren I. Susman, and Francis V. O'Connor. 1980. *Dawn of a New Day: The New York World's Fair, 1939/40.* New York: Queens Museum and New York University Press.

Harrison, Jane Ellen. 1957a. *Prolegomena to the Study of Greek Religion.* New York: World. Reprint of 1922, 3d ed.

———. 1957b. *Themis: A Study of the Social Origins of Greek Religion.* Cleveland: World. Reprint of 1927, 2d ed., with chapters by Gilbert Murray and F. M. Cornford.

———. 1963. *Mythology.* New York: Harcourt Brace and World. Reprint of 1924 ed. of Longmans, Green and Co.

Hart, Ray L. 1968. *Unfinished Man and the Imagination: Toward an Ontology and a Rhetoric of Revelation.* New York: Herder and Herder.

Hartlich, Christian, and Walter Sachs. 1952. *Der Ursprung des Mythosbegriffes in der modernen Bibelwissenschaft.* Tübingen: Mohr (Siebeck); Schriften der Studiengemeinschaft der evang. Akad., 2.

Harvey, Van A. 1966. *The Historian and the Believer: The Morality of Historical Knowledge and Christian Belief.* New York: Macmillan.

Hawkes, Terence. 1977. *Structuralism and Semiotics.* Berkeley and Los Angeles: University of California Press. (In its British ed., this is the first vol. in the New Accents ser.)

Hayes, E. Nelson, and Tanya Hayes, eds. 1970. *Claude Lévi-Strauss: The Anthropologist as Hero.* Cambridge: M.I.T. Press.

Hayward, John F. 1968. "The Uses of Myth in an Age of Science." *Zygon: Journal of Religion and Science* 3/2:205–18.

Hecht, Richard D. 1982. "Studies on Sacrifice, 1970–1980." *Religious Studies Review* 8/3:253–59.

Heilbroner, Robert. 1974. "The Human Prospect." *New York Review* 20 (14 January): 21–34.

Heinlein, Robert A. 1973. *Time Enough for Love: The Lives of Lazarus Long.* New York: Putnam's.

Helm, June, ed. 1967. *Essays on the Verbal and Visual Arts.* Seattle: University of Washington, for American Ethnological Society.

Henderson, Joseph L. 1964. "Ancient Myths and Modern Man." In Jung and von Franz:104–57.

Henderson, Joseph L., and Maud Oakes. 1963. *The Wisdom of the Serpent: The Myths of Death, Rebirth, and Resurrection.* New York: Braziller; Patterns of Myth ser.

Henle, Jane. 1973. *Greek Myths: A Vase Painter's Notebook.* Bloomington: Indiana University Press.

Henry, Patrick. 1979. *New Directions in New Testament Study.* Philadelphia: Westminster.

Herd, Eric W. 1969. "Myth Criticism: Limitations and Possibilities." *Mosaic* 2:69–77.

Herdt, Gilbert H. 1981. *Guardians of the Flutes: Idioms of Masculinity.* New York: McGraw-Hill.

———, ed. 1982. *Rituals of Manhood: Male Initiation in Papua New Guinea.* Berkeley and Los Angeles: University of California Press.

Hess, John. 1972. "The Mythical Lévi-Strauss." *New York Times Book Review* (20 February): 2, 28.

Highet, Gilbert. 1949. *The Classical Tradition: Greek and Roman Influences on Western Liberature.* New York: Oxford University Press.

Highwater, Jamake. 1981. *The Primal Mind: Vision and Reality in Indian America.* New York: Harper and Row.

Hill, Carol E., ed. 1975. *Symbols and Society: Essays on Belief Systems in Action.* Athens: Southern Anthropological Society Proceedings, no. 9.

Hillman, James. 1972a. "An Essay on Pan." In Roscher and Hillman:i–lxiii.

———. 1972b. *The Myth of Analysis: Three Essays in Archetypal Psychology.* Evanston: Northwestern University Press.

———. 1975a. "The Fiction of Case History: A Round." In Wiggins:123–73.

———. 1975b. *Loose Ends: Primary Papers in Archetypal Psychology.* Zurich: Spring Publications.

———. 1975c. *Re-Visioning Psychology.* New York: Harper and Row; 1972 Terry Lect.

———. 1979. *The Dream and the Underworld.* New York: Harper and Row.

———, ed. 1980. *Facing the Gods.* Irving, Tex.: Spring Publications.

Hinks, Robert. 1968. *Myth and Allegory in Ancient Art.* Nendeln, Liechtenstein: Kraus Reprint. Originally published as *Studies of the Warburg Institute* 6 (1939).

Hocart, A. M. 1970. *The Life-Giving Myth and Other Essays.* Edited by F. R. R. S. Raglan. London: Tavistock. Reprint from 1952.

Hofstadter, Douglas R., and Daniel C. Dennett. 1981. *The Mind's I: Fantasies and Reflections on Self and Soul.* New York: Basic.

Holder, Preston, ed. 1966. *Franz Boas, Introduction to "Handbook of American Indian Languages" and J. W. Powell, "Indian Linguistic Families of America North of Mexico."* Lincoln: University of Nebraska Press.

Homans, George C. 1941. "Anxiety and Ritual: The Theories of Malinowski and Radcliffe-Brown." *American Anthropologist* 43/2:164–72. Bobbs-Merrill reprint ser., S-121.

Honigmann, J. J., ed. 1973. *Handbook of Social and Cultural Anthropology.* Chicago: Rand McNally.

Honko, Lauri. 1972. *The Problem of Defining Myth.* Helsinki: Finnish Society for the Study of Comparative Religion; Stud. on Relig., 2 (pagination supplied, beginning with title page).

Hook, R. H., ed. 1979. *Fantasy and Symbol: Studies in Anthropological Interpretation.* London and New York: Academic.

Hooke, S. H., ed. 1933. *Myth and Ritual: Essays on the Myth and Ritual of the Hebrews in Relation to the Culture Pattern of the Ancient Near East.* London: Oxford University Press.

———, ed. 1935. *The Labyrinth: Further Studies in the Relation Between Myth and Ritual in the Ancient World.* London: S.P.C.K.

———, ed. 1958. *Myth, Ritual, and Kingship: Essays on the Theory and Practice of Kingship in the Ancient Near East and in Israel.* London: Oxford University Press.

Houston, Jean. 1980. *Lifeforce: The Psycho-Historical Recovery of the Self.* New York: Delacorte.

Hudson, Liam. 1972. *The Cult of the Fact: A Psychologist's Autobiographical Critique of His Discipline.* New York: Harper and Row.

Hudson, Wilson M. 1966. "Jung on Myth and the Mythic." In Hudson and Maxwell:181–97.

Hudson, Wilson M., and Allen Maxwell, eds. 1966. *The Sunny Slopes of Long Ago.* Dallas: Southern Methodist University Press; Publ. of the Texas Folklore Soc., 33.

Hughes, Richard E. 1975. *The Lively Image: Four Myths in Literature.* Cambridge, Mass.: Winthrop.

Hugh-Jones, Christine. 1979. *From the Milk River: Spatial and Temporal Processes in Northwest Amazonia.* Cambridge: Cambridge University Press; Cambr. Stud. in Soc. Anth., 26.

Hugh-Jones, Stephen. 1979. *The Palm and the Pleiades: Initiation and Cosmology in Northwest Amazonia.* Cambridge: Cambridge University Press; Cambr. Stud. in Soc. Anth., 24.

Huizinga, Johan. 1950. *Homo Ludens: A Study of the Play-Element in Culture.* Anonymous translation from the 1944 German ed.; Boston: Beacon.

Hultkrantz, Ake. 1966. "An Ecological Approach to Religion." *Ethnos* 31:131–50.

———. 1974. "Ecology of Religions: Its Scope and Methodology." *Review of Ethnology* 4:1–12.

———. 1981. *Belief and Worship in Native North America.* Edited by Christopher Vecsey. Syracuse: Syracuse University Press.

Humbert, Elie G. 1971. "Active Imagination: Theory and Practice." *Spring 1971: An Annual of Archetypal Psychology and Jungian Thought:*102–14.

Hunt, Robert, ed. 1967. *Personalities and Cultures: Readings in Psychological Anthropology.* Austin: University of Texas Press; Texas Sourcebooks in Anth., 3.

Hyman, Stanley Edgar. 1962. *The Tangled Bank: Darwin, Marx, Frazer, and Freud as Imaginative Writers.* New York: Atheneum.

Iglehart, Hallie. 1979. "Expanding Ritual: Personal and Collective Power." *Lady-Unique-Inclination-of-the-Night* 4:28–32.

Isenberg, Sheldon R., and Dennis E. Owen. 1977. "Bodies, Natural and Contrived: The Work of Mary Douglas." *Religious Studies Review* 3/1:1–17.

Jackson, Michael. 1979. "Prevented Successions: A Commentary upon a Kuranko Narrative." In Hook:95–131.

Jacobs, Melville, comp., and John Greenway, ed. 1966. *The Anthropologist Looks at Myth.* Austin: University of Texas Press; Publ. of the Amer. Folklore Soc., Bibl. and Spec. ser., 17.

Jacobsohn, Helmuth. 1968. *Timeless Documents of the Soul*. Translated by H. Nagel. Evanston: Northwestern University Press; Stud. from the C. G. Jung Inst., Zurich.

Jaeger, Werner. 1939–45. *Paideia: The Ideals of Greek Culture*. 3 vols. Translated by Gilbert Highet. New York: Oxford University Press.

Jaffé, Aniela, ed. 1963. *Memories, Dreams, Reflections by C. G. Jung*. Translated by Richard Winston and Clara Winston. New York: Pantheon.

James, E. O. 1969. *Creation and Cosmology*. Leiden: Brill; Suppl. to *Numen*, vol. 16.

Jameson, Frederic. 1972. *The Prison-House of Language: A Critical Account of Structuralism and Russian Formalism*. Princeton: Princeton University Press.

———. 1981. *The Political Unconscious: Narrative as a Socially Symbolic Act*. Ithaca: Cornell University Press.

Jarvie, I. C. 1964. *The Revolution in Anthropology*. London: Routledge and Kegan Paul.

Jason, Heda. 1969. "A Multidimensional Approach to Oral Literature." *Current Anthropology* 10/4:413–26.

Jason, Heda, and Dimitri Segal, eds. 1977. *Patterns in Oral Literature*. The Hague and Paris: Mouton; World Anth. ser.

Jennings, Theodore W. 1982. "On Ritual Knowledge." *Journal of Religion* 62/2:111–27.

Jewett, Robert. 1973. *The Captain America Complex: The Dilemma of Zealous Nationalism*. Philadelphia: Westminster.

———. 1979. *Jesus Against the Rapture: Seven Unexpected Prophecies*. Philadelphia: Westminster.

Jewett, Robert, and John Shelton Lawrence. 1968. "Comment" to issue on Psychohistory of the Cinema, *Journal of Psychohistory: A Quarterly Journal of Childhood and Psychohistory* 5/4:512–20.

———. 1976. "Norm Demolition Derbies: Rites of Reversal in Popular Culture." *Journal of Popular Culture* 9/4:976–82.

———. 1977a. *The American Monomyth*. Garden City, N.Y.: Anchor/Doubleday.

———. 1977b. "Mythic Conformity in the Cuckoo's Nest." *Psychocultural Review: Interpretations in the Psychology of Art, Literature, and Society* 1/1:68–76.

———. 1979. "The Problem of Mythic Imperialism." *Journal of American Culture* 2:309–20.

Johnson, Roger A. 1974. *The Origins of Demythologizing: Philosophy and Historiography in the Theology of Rudolf Bultmann*. Leiden: Brill; Suppl. to *Numen*, vol. 28.

Jones, Ernest. 1961. *The Life and Work of Sigmund Freud*. 1 vol. Abridged by Lionel Trilling and Steven Marcus. New York: Basic.

———. 1974. *Psycho-Myth, Psycho-History: Essays in Applied Psychoanalysis*. 2 vols. New York: Hillstone.

Jopling, Carol F., ed. 1971. *Art and Aesthetics in Primitive Societies*. New York: Dutton.

Jung, Carl G. 1953–79. *The Collected Works of C. G. Jung*. 20 vols. Edited by Herbert Read, Michael Fordham, Gerhard Adler, and William McGuire. Princeton: Princeton University Press; Bollingen ser., 20.

———. 1976. *The Visions Seminars*. 2 vols. Zurich: Spring Publications.

Jung, Carl G., and Karl Kerényi. 1963. *Essays on a Science of Mythology: The Myth of the Divine Child and the Mysteries of Eleusis*. Translated by R. F. C. Hull. Princeton: Princeton University Press; Bollingen ser., 22.

Jung, Carl G., and Marie-Louise von Franz, eds. 1964. *Man and His Symbols*. Garden City, N.Y.: Doubleday.

Kahn, Laurence. 1978. *Hermés passe ou les ambiguïtés de la communication*. Paris: Maspero.

Kallich, Martin, Andrew MacLeisch, and Gertrude Schoenbohm, eds. 1968. *Oedipus: Myth and Drama*. New York: Odyssey.

Kaplan, Bert, ed. 1961. *Studying Personality Cross-Culturally*. New York: Harper and Row.

Kavanagh, Aidan. 1973. "The Role of Ritual in Personal Development." In Shaughnessy:145–60.

Keiser, Albert. 1933. *The Indian in American Literature*. New York: Oxford University Press.

Kemp, Peter. 1982. "Death and Gift." *Journal of the American Academy of Religion* 50/3:459–71, with omission printed in 51/1 (1983): 125.

Kennedy, John G. 1973. "Cultural Psychiatry." In Honigmann:1119–98.

Kerényi, Karl. 1959. *The Heroes of the Greeks*. Translated by H. J. Rose. London: Thames and Hudson.

———. 1962. *The Religion of the Greeks and Romans*. Translated by Christopher Holme. London: Thames and Hudson.

———. 1967. *Eleusis: Archetypal Image of Mother and Daughter*. Translated by Ralph Manheim. New York: Schocken.

Kermode, Frank. 1962. *Puzzles and Epiphanies: Essays and Reviews 1958–1961*. New York: Chilmark.

Kirk, G. S. 1962. "Aetiology, Ritual, Charter: Three Equivocal Terms in the Study of Myths." *Yale Classical Studies* 22:83–102.

———. 1970. *Myth: Its Meaning and Functions in Ancient and Other Cultures*. Berkeley and Los Angeles: University of California Press; Sather Class. Lect., 40.

———. 1974. *The Nature of Greek Myths*. Baltimore: Penguin.

Klapp, Orrin E. 1956. *Ritual and Cult: A Sociological Interpretation*. Washington, D.C.: Public Affairs Press; Annals of Amer. Soc.

Klein, Theodore M. 1980. "Myth, Song and Theft in the Homeric *Hymn to Hermes*." In Aycock and Klein:125–44.

Kliever, Lonnie D. 1972. "Alternative Conceptions of Religion as a Symbol System." *Union Seminary Quarterly Review* 27/2:91–102.

———. 1978. "Authority in a Pluralistic World." In *The Search for Absolute Values in a Changing World*. New York: International Cultural Foundation, pp. 1257–73.

———. 1979. "Polysymbolism and Modern Religiosity." *Journal of Religion* 59:169–94.

———. 1981. "Fictive Religion: Rhetoric and Play." *Journal of the American Academy of Religion* 49/4:657–69.

Kluckhohn, Clyde. 1942. "Myths and Rituals: A General Theory." *Harvard Theological Review* 35:45–79. Often reprinted with omissions.

———. 1953. "Universal Categories of Culture." In A. L. Kroeber:507–23.

———. 1961. *Anthropology and the Classics*. Providence, R.I.: Brown University Press.

———. 1968. "Recurrent Themes in Myths and Mythmaking." In Murray 1968a:46–80.

———. 1973. "On Defining Myths." In Lee, Mourelatos, and Rorty:61–69.

Knox, John. 1964. *Myth and Truth: An Essay on the Language of Faith*. Charlottesville: University Press of Virginia.

Koester, Helmut, and James M. Robinson. 1971. *Trajectories Through Early Christianity*. Philadelphia: Fortress.

Koestler, Arthur. 1964. *The Act of Creation*. New York: Macmillan.

Kramer, Samuel Noah, ed. 1961. *Mythologies of the Ancient World*. Garden City, N.Y.: Doubleday.

Krieger, Murray, ed. 1966. *Northrop Frye in Modern Criticism*. New York: Columbia University Press; English Inst. Essays.

Kroeber, A. L., ed. 1953. *Anthropology Today: An Encyclopedic Inventory*. Chicago: University of Chicago Press.

Kroeber, Karl, ed. 1981. *Traditional Literatures of the American Indian: Texts and Interpretations*. Lincoln: University of Nebraska Press.

———. 1983. "The Wolf Comes: Indian Poetry and Linguistic Criticism." In Swann:98–111.

Krupat, Arnold. 1982. "An Approach to Native American Texts." *Critical Inquiry* 9/2:323–38.

Kuhn, Thomas S. 1970. *The Structure of Scientific Revolutions*. 2d ed. Chicago: University of Chicago Press.

Küng, Hans. 1979. *Freud and the Problem of God*. Translated by Edward Quinn. New Haven: Yale University Press; 1972 Terry Lect.

La Barre, Weston. 1958. "The Influence of Freud on Anthropology." *American Imago* 15:275–328.

———. 1961. "Art and Mythology: The Present State of the Problem." In Kaplan:387–403.

———. 1970. *The Ghost Dance: Origins of Religion*. Garden City, N.Y.: Doubleday.

Lacan, Jacques. 1968. *The Language of the Self: The Function of Language in Psychoanalysis*. Translated by Anthony Wilden. New York: Dell.

———. 1977. *Écrits: A Selection*. Translated by Alan Sheridan. New York: Norton.

LaFontaine, J. S., ed. 1972. *The Interpretation of Ritual: Essays in Honor of A. I. Richards*. London: Tavistock.

Lane, Michael, ed. 1970. *Introduction to Structuralism*. New York: Basic.

Langer, Susanne K. 1941. *Philosophy in a New Key.* Cambridge: Harvard University Press.

———. 1949. "On Cassirer's Theory of Language and Myth." In Schilpp:379–400.

———. 1953. *Feeling and Form.* New York: Scribner's.

Lapham, Lewis. 1971. "Military Theology." *Harper's Magazine* 243 (July): 78–85.

Larsen, Stephen. 1976. *The Shaman's Doorway: Opening the Mythic Imagination to Contemporary Consciousness.* New York: Harper and Row.

Larue, Gerald A. 1975. *Ancient Myth and Modern Man.* Englewood Cliffs, N.J.: Prentice-Hall.

Laughlin, Charles D., Jr., and Eugene G. d'Aquili. 1974. *Biogenetic Structuralism.* New York: Columbia University Press.

Lawson, E. Thomas. 1978. "The Explanation of Myth and Myth as Explanation." *Journal of the American Academy of Religion* 46/4:507–23.

Layard, John. 1972. *The Virgin Archetype: Two Essays.* Zurich: Spring Publications.

Leach, Edmund R. 1954. *Political Systems of Highland Burma: A Study of Kachin Social Structure.* Cambridge: Harvard University Press.

———. 1958. "Magical Hair." *Journal of the Royal Anthropological Institute* 88/2:147–64.

———. 1961. "Golden Bough or Gilded Twig." *Daedalus* 90/2:371–87.

———. 1968. "Ritual." *International Encyclopedia of the Social Sciences* 13:520–26.

———. 1970. *Claude Lévi-Strauss.* New York: Viking; Modern Masters ser.

———. 1976. *Culture and Communication: The Logic by Which Symbols are Connected.* New York: Columbia University Press; Themes in the Soc. Sci.

———. 1982. "Critical Introduction." In Steblin-Kamenskij:1–20.

Lears, Jackson. 1981. *No Place of Grace: Antimodernism and the Transformation of American Culture 1880–1920.* New York: Pantheon.

Lee, Alfred McClung. 1966. *Multivalent Man.* New York: Braziller.

Lee, E. N., A. P. D. Mourelatos, and R. M. Rorty, eds. 1973. *Exegesis and Argument: Studies in Greek Philosophy Presented to Gregory Vlasstos.* New York: Humanities.

Lee, Robert. 1964. *Religion and Leisure in America.* Nashville: Abingdon.

Leeming, David A. 1973. *Mythology: The Voyage of the Hero.* Philadelphia: Lippincott.

Legeza, Laszlo. 1973. *Tao: The Chinese Philosophy of Time and Change.* New York: Bounty.

LeGuin, Ursula. 1969. *The Left Hand of Darkness.* New York: Ace.

———. 1976. "Myth and Archetype in Science Fiction." *Parabola: Myth and the Quest for Meaning* 1/4:42–47.

Lentricchia, Frank. 1980. *After the New Criticism.* Chicago: University of Chicago Press.

Lesky, Albin. 1966. *A History of Greek Literature.* Translated by James Willis and Cornelius de Heer. London: Methuen.

Leslie, Charles, ed. 1960. *Anthropology of Folk Religion.* New York: Vintage.

Lessa, William A., and Evon Z. Vogt, eds. 1980. *Reader in Comparative Religion: An Anthropological Approach.* 4th ed. New York: Harper and Row.

Lévi-Strauss, Claude. 1963. *Structural Anthropology.* Vol. 1. Translated by Claire Jacobson and B. G. Schoepf. New York: Basic.

————. 1966. *The Savage Mind.* Chicago: University of Chicago Press; Nature of Human Soc. ser.

————. 1969. *The Raw and the Cooked.* Translated by John Weightman and Doreen Weightman. New York: Harper and Row; Intro. to a Sci. of Myth., 1.

————. 1971a. "The Deduction of the Crane." In Maranda and Maranda 1971a:3–21.

————. 1971b. *L'Homme Nu.* Paris: Plon; Mythologiques, 4.

————. 1973. *From Honey to Ashes.* Translated by John Weightman and Doreen Weightman. New York: Harper and Row; Intro. to a Sci of Myth., 2.

————. 1974. *Tristes Tropiques.* Translated by John Weightman and Doreen Weightman. New York: Atheneum. Earlier translated as *The World on the Wane.*

————. 1976. *Structural Anthropology.* Vol. 2. Translated by Monique Layton. New York: Basic.

————. 1978a. *Myth and Meaning: Five Talks for Radio.* Toronto: University of Toronto Press.

————. 1978b. *The Origin of Table Manners.* Translated by John Weightman and Doreen Weightman. New York: Harper and Row; Intro. to a Sci. of Myth., 3.

————. 1981. *The Naked Man.* Translated by John Weightman and Doreen Weightman. New York: Harper and Row; Intro. to a Sci of Myth., 4.

Levy, Marion J., Jr. 1968. "Functional Analysis. I. Structural-functional analysis." *International Encyclopedia of the Social Sciences* 6:21–29.

Lewis, Gilbert. 1980. *Day of Shining Red: An Essay in Understanding Ritual.* New York: Cambridge University Press.

Lewis, Ioan, ed. 1977. *Symbols and Sentiments: Cross-Cultural Studies in Symbolism.* London: Academic.

Lexicon Iconographicum Mythologiae Classicae. 1984–. Zurich: Artemis. Seven double volumes are projected.

Leymore, Varda Langholz. 1975. *Hidden Myth: Structure and Symbolism in Advertising.* New York: Basic.

Lifton, Robert Jay. 1971. "Protean Man." In Wolman:33–49; the most recently revised version of the essay.

Lincoln, Bruce. 1977. "Two Notes on Modern Rituals." *Journal of the American Academy of Religion* 45/2:147–60.

————. 1981a. *Emerging from the Chrysalis: Studies in Rituals of Women's Initiation.* Cambridge: Harvard University Press.

————. 1981b. *Priests, Warriors, and Cattle: A Study in Ecology of Religions.* Berkeley and Los Angeles: University of California Press; Hermeneutics: Stud. in the Hist. of Relig., 10.

Linenthal, Edward T. 1983. "Ritual Drama at the Little Big Horn: The Persistence and Transformation of a National Symbol." *Journal of the American Academy of Religion* 51/2:267–81.

Liszka, James Jakób. 1983. "A Critique of Lévi-Strauss' Theory of Myth and the Elements of a Semiotic Alternative." In Deely and Lenhart:459–72.

Littleton, C. Scott. 1973. *The New Comparative Mythology: An Anthropological Assessment of the Theories of Georges Dumézil*. Rev. ed. Berkeley and Los Angeles: University of California Press.

London, Herbert I., and Albert L. Weeks. 1981. *Myths that Rule America*. Washington, D.C.: University Press of America.

Long, Charles H. 1963. *Alpha: The Myths of Creation*. New York: Braziller; Patterns of Myth ser.

———. 1980. "Primitive/Civilized: The Locus of a Problem." *History of Religions* 20/1–2:43–61.

Lord, Albert B. 1960. *The Singer of Tales*. New York: Atheneum.

———. 1980. "The Mythic Component in Oral Traditional Epic: Its Origins and Significance." In Aycock and Klein:145–62.

Lowenthal, Leo. 1961. *Literature, Popular Culture, and Society*. Palo Alto: Pacific.

Lowry, Shirley Park. 1982. *Familiar Mysteries: The Truth in Myth*. New York: Oxford University Press.

Luckert, Karl W. 1979. "An Approach to Navajo Mythology." In Waugh and Prithipaul:117–31.

Lüthi, Max. 1970. *Once Upon a Time: On the Nature of Fairy Tales*. Translated by Lee Chadeayne and Paul Gottwald; introduction and reference notes by Frances Lee Utley. New York: Ungar.

MacAloon, John J., ed. 1984. *Rite, Drama, Festival, Spectacle: Rehearsals Toward a Theory of Cultural Performance*. Philadelphia: Institute for the Study of Human Issues.

MacCary, W. Thomas. 1982. *Childlike Achilles: Ontogeny and Phylogeny in the "Iliad."* New York: Columbia University Press.

McConnell, Frank. 1979. *Storytelling and Mythmaking: Images from Film and Literature*. New York: Oxford University Press.

McCune, Marjorie W., Tucker Orbison, and Philip W. Withim, eds. 1980. *The Binding of Proteus: Perspectives on Myth and the Literary Process*. Lewisburg, Pa.: Bucknell University Press; London: Associated University Presses.

McGuire, William, ed. 1984. *Dream Analysis: Notes of a Seminar given in 1928–30 by C. G. Jung*. Princeton: Princeton University Press; Bollingen ser., 99.

Macksey, Richard, and Eugenio Donato, eds. 1972. *The Structuralist Controversy: The Languages of Criticism and the Sciences of Man*. Baltimore: Johns Hopkins University Press.

Maclagan, David. 1977. *Creation Myths: Man's Introduction to the World*. London: Thames and Hudson.

Mahoney, Maria F. 1966. *The Meaning in Dreams and Dreaming: The Jungian Viewpoint*. New York: Citadel.

Major Trends of Research in the Social and Human Sciences. 1970. Part 1: social sciences. Paris and The Hague: Mouton/UNESCO.

Malinowski, Bronislaw. 1948. *Magic, Science and Religion and Other Essays.* Garden City, N.Y.: Anchor.

Mallery, Garrick. 1893. *Picture-writing of the American Indians.* Washington, D.C.: Government Printing Office; Accompanying Paper to 10th Annual Report (for 1888–89), Bur. of Amer. Ethnology.

Mannheim, Karl. 1936. *Ideology and Utopia: An Introduction to the Sociology of Knowledge.* Translated by Louis Wirth and Edward Shils. New York: Harcourt, Brace and World.

Manuel, Frank E., and Fritzie P. Manuel. 1972. "Sketch for a Natural History of Paradise." *Daedalus* 101/1:83–128.

Maranda, Elli Köngäs. 1973. "Five Interpretations of a Melanesian Myth." *Journal of American Folklore* 86/339:3–13.

Maranda, Pierre, ed. 1967. "Computers in the Bush: Tools for the Automatic Analysis of Myths." In Helm:77–83.

———, ed. 1972a. *Mythology: Selected Readings.* Baltimore: Penguin.

———. 1972b. "Structuralism in Cultural Anthropology." *Annual Review of Anthropology* 1:329–48.

———, ed. 1974. *Soviet Structural Folkloristics: Texts. . . .* Vol. 1. The Hague and Paris: Mouton; Approaches to Semiotics, 42.

Maranda, Pierre, and Elli Köngäs Maranda, eds. 1971a. *Structural Analysis of Oral Tradition.* Philadelphia: University of Pennsylvania Press.

———. 1971b. *Structural Models in Folklore and Transformational Essays.* The Hague: Mouton; Approaches to Semiotics, 10.

Martin, George R. R., ed. 1980. *New Voices III: The Campbell Award Nominees.* New York: Berkeley.

Mason, Carol, M. H. Greenberg, and Patricia Warrick, eds. 1974. *Anthropology Through Science Fiction.* New York: St. Martin's.

Mason, Herbert. 1980. "Myth as an 'Ambush of Reality.'" In Olson:15–19.

Massey, Irving. 1976. *The Gaping Pig: Literature and Metamorphosis.* Berkeley and Los Angeles: University of California Press.

Matthews, Honor. 1968. *The Hard Journey: The Myth of Man's Rebirth.* London: Chatto and Windus.

May, Robert. 1980. *Sex and Fantasy: Patterns of Male and Female Development.* New York: Norton.

Mayerson, Philip. 1971. *Classical Mythology in Literature, Art, and Music.* Waltham, Mass.: Xerox College Publishing.

Mead, Margaret. 1967. "The Life Cycle and Its Variations: The Division of Roles." *Daedalus* 96/3:871–75.

———. 1973. "Ritual and Social Crisis." In Shaughnessy:87–102.

Mercatante, Anthony S. 1978. *Good and Evil: Mythology and Folklore.* New York: Harper and Row.

Merivale, Patricia. 1969. *Pan the Goat-God: His Myth in Modern Times.* Cambridge: Harvard University Press; Harvard Stud. in Comp. Lit., 30.

Middleton, John, ed. 1967a. *Gods and Rituals: Readings in Religious Beliefs and Practices.* New York: Doubleday.

————, ed. 1967b. *Magic, Witchcraft, and Curing*. New York: Doubleday.

————, ed. 1967c. *Myth and Cosmos: Readings in Mythology and Symbolism*. New York: Doubleday.

Miller, David L. 1970a. *Gods and Games: Toward a Theology of Play*. New York: World.

————. 1970b. "Orestes: Myth and Dream as Catharsis." In Campbell 1970b:26–47.

————. 1976. "Fairy Tale or Myth?" *Spring 1976: An Annual of Archetypal Psychology and Jungian Thought:*157–64.

————. 1981. *The New Polytheism: Rebirth of the Gods and Goddesses*. 2d ed. Dallas: Spring Publications; with added materials by Henry Corbin and James Hillman.

Mitchell, W. J. T., ed. 1980. *The Language of Images*. Chicago: University of Chicago Press.

Moebius, William. 1981. "Founding the World in Myth and Nursery Rhyme." *Arche: Notes and Papers on Archaic Studies* 6:173–201.

Mol, Hans. 1976. *Identity and the Sacred: A Sketch for a New Social-Scientific Theory of Religion*. Oxford: Blackwell.

Montagu, M. F. A. 1949. "Cassirer on Mythological Thinking." In Schilpp:359–78.

Moon, Sheila. 1970. *A Magic Dwells: A Poetic and Psychological Study of the Navaho Emergence Myth*. Middletown, Conn.: Wesleyan University Press.

Moon, Warren G., ed. 1983. *Ancient Greek Art and Iconography*. Madison: University of Wisconsin Press.

Moore, Albert C. 1977. *Iconography of Religions: An Introduction*. Philadelphia: Fortress.

Moore, Richard E. 1972. *Myth America 2001*. Philadelphia: Westminster.

Moore, Sally F., and Barbara G. Myerhoff, eds. 1977. *Secular Ritual*. Assen and Amsterdam: Van Gorcum.

Moorman, Charles. 1980. "Comparative Mythography: A Fungo to the Outfield." In McCune, Orbison, and Withim:63–77.

Morford, Mark P. O., and Robert J. Lenardon. 1971. *Classical Mythology*. New York: McKay.

Muchembled, Robert. 1982. "Witchcraft, Popular Culture, and Christianity in the Sixteenth Century with Emphasis upon Flanders and Artois." In Forster and Ranum:213–36.

Mullahy, Patrick. 1948. *Oedipus: Myth and Complex. A Review of Psychoanalytic Theory*. New York: Grove.

Muller, John P., and William J. Richardson. 1982. *Lacan and Language: A Reader's Guide to "Écrits."* New York: International Universities Press.

Munn, Nancy D. 1973a. "Symbolism in a Ritual Context: Aspects of Social Action." In Honigmann:579–612.

————. 1973b. *Walbiri Iconography: Graphic Representation and Cultural Symbolism in a Central Australian Society*. Ithaca: Cornell University Press; Symbol, Myth, and Ritual ser.

Munz, Peter. 1956. "History and Myth." *Philosophical Quarterly* 6/22:1–16.
———. 1973. *When the Golden Bough Breaks: Structuralism or Typology?* Boston: Routledge and Kegan Paul.

Murray, Henry A., ed. 1968a. *Myth and Mythmaking.* Boston: Beacon. Reprint from 1959.
———. 1968b. "The Possible Nature of a 'Mythology' to Come." In Murray 1968a:300–353.

Myerhoff, Barbara G. 1974. *Peyote Hunt: The Sacred Journey of the Huichol Indians.* Ithaca: Cornell University Press; Symbol, Myth, and Ritual ser.
———. 1978. *Number Our Days.* New York: Simon and Schuster.
———. 1982. "Rites of Passage: Process and Paradox." In V. Turner 1982a:109–35.

Nagy, Gregory. 1979. *The Best of the Achaeans: Concepts of the Hero in Archaic Greek Poetry.* Baltimore: Johns Hopkins University Press.

Neale, Robert E. 1969. *In Praise of Play: Toward a Psychology of Religion.* New York: Harper and Row.

Needham, Rodney. 1978. *Primordial Characters.* Charlottesville: University Press of Virginia.

Nelson, Benjamin, ed. 1958. *Sigmund Freud on Creativity and the Unconscious: Papers on the Psychology of Art, Literature, Love, Religion.* New York: Harper and Row.

Neumann, Erich. 1954. *The Origins and History of Consciousness.* Translated by R. F. C. Hull. Princeton: Princeton University Press; Bollingen ser., 42.
———. 1956. *Amor and Psyche: The Psychic Development of the Feminine. A Commentary on the Tale by Apuleius.* Translated by Ralph Manheim. Princeton: Princeton University Press; Bollingen ser., 68.
———. 1963. *The Great Mother: An Analysis of the Archetype.* 2d ed. Translated by Ralph Manheim. Princeton: Princeton University Press; Bollingen ser., 47.

Neusner, Jacob. 1973. *The Idea of Purity in Ancient Judaism: The Haskell Lectures 1972–73.* Leiden: Brill; Stud. in Jud. in Late Antiq. . . . , 1.
———. 1975. "The Idea of Purity in Ancient Judaism." *Journal of the American Academy of Religion* 43/1:15–26.

Newman, Charles. 1984. "The Post-Modern Aura: The Act of Fiction in the Age of Inflation." *Salmagundi: A Quarterly of the Humanities and Social Sciences* 63–64:3–199.

Newman, Robert. 1965. "Myth and the Creative Process." *Centennial Review* 9:483–93.

Niebuhr, Reinhold. 1937. "The Truth in Myths." In Bixler, Calhoun, and Niebuhr:25–29.

Niethammer, Carolyn. 1977. *Daughters of the Earth: The Lives and Legends of American Indian Women.* New York: Collier.

Nock, Arthur D., ed. 1926. *Sallustius Concerning the Gods and the Universe.* Cambridge: Cambridge University Press.

Noel, Daniel C. 1981. "The Many Guises of the Goddess." *Archē: Notes and Papers on Archaic Studies* 6:93–111.

Nonnos. 1940. *Dionysiaca.* 3 vols. Translated by W. H. D. Rouse; introduction and notes by H. J. Rose; notes on text by L. R. Lind. Cambridge: Harvard University Press.

Norris, Christopher. 1982. *Deconstruction: Theory and Practice*. New York: Methuen; New Accents ser.

O'Brien, Joan, and Wilfred Major. 1981. *In the Beginning: Creation Myths from Ancient Mesopotamia, Israel and Greece*. Chico, Calif.: Scholars.

Odajnyk, Volodymyr Walter. 1976. *Jung and Politics: The Political and Social Ideas of C. G. Jung*. New York: Harper and Row.

Office of Folklife Programs and Renwick Gallery of the National Museum of Art. 1982. *Celebration: A World of Art and Ritual*. Washington, D.C.: Smithsonian Institution.

O'Flaherty, Wendy Doniger. 1980. "Inside and Outside the Mouth of God: The Boundary between Myth and Reality." *Daedalus* 109/2:93–125.

Ogilvy, James. 1977. *Many Dimensional Man: Decentralizing Self, Society, and the Sacred*. New York: Oxford University Press. Reprinted in 1979, with additions. New York: Harper and Row.

Olcott, William Tyler. 1911. *Star Lore of All Ages: A Collection of Myths, Legends, and Facts Concerning the Constellations of the Northern Hemisphere*. New York: Putnam's.

Oldfather, C. H., trans. 1952. *Diodorus of Sicily*. 10 vols. Cambridge: Harvard University Press.

Oliver, Harold H. 1980. "Relational Ontology and Hermeneutics." In Olson:69–83.

Olson, Alan M., ed. 1980. *Myth, Symbol, and Reality*. Notre Dame: University of Notre Dame Press; Boston U. Stud. in Philos. and Relig., 1.

Ong, Walter J. 1969. "World as View and World as Event." *American Anthropologist* 71/3:634–47.

Ortiz, Alfonso, ed. 1972. *New Perspectives on the Pueblos*. Albuquerque: University of New Mexico Press.

———. 1973. "Look to the Mountaintop." In E. G. Ward:88–104.

———, ed. 1979. *Southwest*. Washington, D.C.: Smithsonian Institution; Vol. 9 of *Handbook of North American Indians*, W. C. Sturtevant, gen. ed.

Ortiz, Simon. 1972. "From an Interview; Telling about Coyote." *Alcheringa: Ethnopoetics* 4:15–19.

Ortner, Sherry B. 1974. "Is Female to Male as Nature is to Culture?" In Rosaldo and Lamphere:67–87.

Otto, Walter F. 1954. *The Homeric Gods: The Spiritual Significance of Greek Religion*. Translated by Moses Hadas. London: Thames and Hudson.

———. 1965. *Dionysus: Myth and Cult*. Translated by Robert B. Palmer. Bloomington: Indiana University Press.

Panofsky, Dora, and Erwin Panofsky. 1962. *Pandora's Box: The Changing Aspects of a Mythical Symbol*. 2d ed. New York: Pantheon; Bollingen ser., 52.

Panofsky, Erwin. 1939. *Studies in Iconology: Humanistic Themes in the Art of the Renaissance*. New York: Oxford University Press.

———. 1955. *Meaning in the Visual Arts: Papers in and on Art History*. Garden City, N.Y.: Doubleday.

Paredes, Américo, and Richard Bauman, eds. 1972. *Toward New Perspectives in Folklore*. Austin: University of Texas Press; Publ. of the Amer. Folklore Soc., Bibl. and Spec. ser., 23.

Patai, Raphael. 1972. *Myth and Modern Man*. Englewood Cliffs, N.J.: Prentice-Hall.

Patte, Daniel, ed. 1976a. *Semiology and Parables: Exploration of the Possibilities Offered by Structuralism for Exegesis*. Pittsburgh: Pickwick.

———. 1976b. *What Is Structural Exegesis?* Philadelphia: Fortress; Guides to Bib. Scholarship ser.

Peacock, James L. 1969. "Society as Narrative." In Spencer:167–77.

Pearce, Roy Harvey. 1965. *Savagism and Civilization: A Study of the Indian and the American Mind*. Rev. ed. Baltimore: Johns Hopkins University Press. Originally published in 1953 as *The Savages of America: A Study of the Indian and the Idea of Civilization*.

Pelikan, Jaroslav, ed. 1971. *Twentieth-Century Theology in the Making*. Vol. 2. New York: Harper and Row. Selected from 2d ed. of *Religion in Geschichte und Gegenwart*.

Pembroke, S. G. 1981. "Myth." In Finley 1981:301–24.

Penner, Hans H. 1971. "The Poverty of Functionalism." *History of Religions* 11/1:91–97.

Penner, Hans H., and Edward A. Yonan. 1972. "Is a Science of Religion Possible?" *Journal of Religion* 52:107–33.

Peradotto, John. 1973. *Classical Mythology: An Annotated Bibliographical Survey*. Urbana: American Philological Association.

Perry, John Weir. 1966. *Lord of the Four Quarters: Myths of the Royal Father*. New York: Braziller; Patterns of Myth ser.

———. 1974. *The Far Side of Madness*. Englewood Cliffs, N.J.: Prentice-Hall.

Petersen, Norman R. 1974. "On the Notion of Genre in Via's 'Parable. . . .'" *Semeia: An Experimental Journal for Biblical Criticism* 1:134–73.

Pettazzoni, Raffaele. 1954. *Essays on the History of Religion*. Leiden: Brill.

Pettit, Philip. 1977. *The Concept of Structuralism: A Critical Analysis*. Berkeley and Los Angeles: University of California Press.

Piaget, Jean. 1970a. *Main Trends in Interdisciplinary Research*. New York: Harper and Row.

———. 1970b. *Structuralism*. Translated and edited by C. Maschler. New York: Harper and Row.

Pieper, Josef. 1952. *Leisure: The Basis of Culture*. Translated by Alexander Dru. New York: New American Library.

———. 1965. *In Tune With the World: A Theory of Festivity*. Translated by Richard Winston and Clara Winston. New York: Harcourt Brace Jovanovich.

Polanyi, Michael. 1962. *Personal Knowledge: Toward a Post-Critical Philosophy*. Chicago: University of Chicago Press.

Polanyi, Michael, and Harry Prosch. 1975. *Meaning*. Chicago: University of Chicago Press.

Polzin, Robert M. 1977. *Biblical Structuralism: Method and Subjectivity in the Study of Ancient Texts*. Philadelphia: Fortress; Missoula, Mont.: Scholars; *Semeia* Suppl. ser.

Pomeroy, Sarah B. 1973. "Selected Bibliography on Women in Antiquity." *Arethusa* 6/1:125–57.

_____. 1975. *Goddesses, Whores, Wives, and Slaves: Women in Classical Antiquity.* New York: Schocken.

Popenoe, Cris. 1979. *Inner Development.* Washington, D.C.: Yes! Inc.

Portmann, Adolf, Christopher Rowe, Dominique Zahn, Ernst Benz, René Huyghe, and Toshihiko Izutsu. 1977. *Color Symbolism: Six Excerpts from the Eranos Yearbook 1972.* Various translations. Zurich: Spring Publications.

Pouwer, Jan. 1974. "The Structural-Configurational Approach: A Methodological Outline." In Rossi:238–55.

Preston, James J., ed. 1982. *Mother Worship: Theme and Variations.* Chapel Hill: University of North Carolina Press; Stud. in Relig. ser.

Price, Theodora Hadzisteliou. 1978. *Kourotrophos: Cults and Representations of the Greek Nursing Deities.* Leiden: Brill; Stud. of the Dutch Archaeol. and Hist. Soc., 8.

Progoff, Ira. 1953. *Jung's Psychology and Its Social Meaning.* New York: Anchor.

Propp, Vladimir. 1966. "Struttura e storia nello studio della favola." In Italian translation of Propp, *Morphology, Morfologia della Fiaba.* Turin: Einaudi.

_____. 1968. *Morphology of the Folktale.* Translated by Laurence Scott; 2d ed. revised by Louis A. Wagner. Austin: University of Texas Press.

_____. 1972. "Transformations in Fairy Tales." Translated by Petra Morrison. Abridged in P. Maranda 1972a:139–50.

Puhvel, Jaan, ed. 1970. *Myth and Law Among the Indo-Europeans: Studies in Indo-European Comparative Mythology.* Berkeley and Los Angeles: University of California Press; U.C.L.A. Center for the Study of Comp. Folklore and Mythol., 1.

Radcliffe-Brown, A. R. 1952. *Structure and Function in Primitive Society: Essays and Addresses.* Glencoe, Ill.: Free Press.

_____. 1968. "The Interpretation of Andamanese Customs and Beliefs: Myths and Legends." In Georges:46–71.

Radin, Paul. 1915. *Literary Aspects of North American Mythology.* Ottawa: Government Printing Bureau (no. 1535); Canada Dept. of Mines, Geol. Survey, Mus. Bull. no. 16, Anth. ser. no. 6.

_____. 1956. *The Trickster: A Study in American Indian Mythology.* With commentaries by Karl Kerényi and Carl G. Jung. New York: Schocken.

Raglan, F. R. R. S. 1937. *The Hero: A Study in Tradition, Myth, and Drama.* New York: Oxford University Press.

_____. 1958. "Myth and Ritual." In Sebeok 1958:122–35.

_____. 1965. "The Hero of Tradition." In Dundes 1965b:142–57.

Rahner, Hugo. 1963. *Greek Myths and Christian Mystery.* Translated by Brian Battershaw. New York: Harper and Row.

Rainey, Reuben M. 1975. *Freud as Student of Religion: Perspectives on the Background and Development of His Thought.* Missoula, Mont.: American Academy of Religion, and Scholars; Diss. ser., 7.

Randall, Marta, and Robert Silverberg, eds. 1981. *New Dimensions 12.* New York: Pocket.

Rank, Otto. 1959. *The Myth of the Birth of the Hero and Other Writings by Otto*

Rank. Edited by Philip Freund. Translated by F. Robbins and S. E. Jelliffe. New York: Random House.

Rappaport, Roy A. 1968. *Pigs for the Ancestors: Ritual in the Ecology of a New Guinea People.* New Haven: Yale University Press.

———. 1979. *Ecology, Meaning, and Religion.* Richmond, Calif.: North Atlantic.

Reichard, Gladys A. 1944. "Individualism and Mythological Style." *Journal of American Folklore* 57/223:16–26.

Reverdin, Olivier, and Bernard Grange, eds. 1980. *Le sacrifice dans antiquité.* Geneva: Vanoeuvres; Entretiens sur l'antiquité classique, 27.

Rhodes, David, and Donald Michie. 1982. *Mark as Story: An Introduction to the Narrative of a Gospel.* Philadelphia: Fortress.

Richardson, Herbert W. 1967. *Toward an American Theology.* New York: Harper and Row.

Ricketts, Mac Linscott. 1966. "The North American Trickster." *History of Religions* 5/2:327–50.

———. 1971. "Anthropological Psychoanalysis of Religion." *History of Religions* 11/1:147–56.

Ricoeur, Paul. 1970. *Freud and Philosophy: An Essay on Interpretation.* Translated by Denis Savage. New Haven: Yale University Press.

———. 1973. "From Existentialism to the Philosophy of Language." *Philosophy Today* 17:88–96.

———. 1974a. *The Conflict of Interpretations: Essays in Hermeneutics.* Edited by Don Ihde. Evanston: Northwestern University Press.

———. 1974b. "Metaphor and the Main Problem of Hermeneutics." *New Literary History* 6/1:95–110.

———. 1975. *Paul Ricoeur on Biblical Hermeneutics.* Reprinted from *Semeia: An Experimental Journal for Biblical Criticism* 4.

Righter, William. 1975. *Myth and Literature.* London: Routledge and Kegan Paul.

Roazen, Paul. 1968. *Freud: Political and Social Thought.* New York: Knopf.

Rogerson, J. W. 1974. *Myth in Old Testament Interpretation.* Berlin: de Gruyter; B.Z.A.W., 134.

Róheim, Géza. 1945. *The Eternal Ones of the Dream: A Psychoanalytic Interpretation of Australian Myth and Ritual.* New York: International Universities Press.

———. 1950. *Psychoanalysis and Anthropology: Culture, Personality and the Unconscious.* New York: Internaional Universities Press.

———. 1971. *The Origin and Function of Culture.* Garden City, N.Y.: Doubleday/Anchor. Reprinted from 1943.

Rorty, Richard. 1979. *Philosophy and the Mirror of Nature.* Princeton: Princeton University Press.

Rosaldo, Michelle Zimbalist, and Louise Lamphere, eds. 1974. *Woman, Culture, and Society.* Stanford: Stanford University Press.

Roscher, Wilhelm H., and James Hillman. 1972. *Pan and the Nightmare.* Zurich: Spring Publications; Dunquin ser., 4.

Rose, H. J. 1930. *Modern Methods in Classical Mythology.* St. Andrews, Scotland: University Press.

———. 1934. *A Handbook of Greek Literature from Homer to the Age of Lucian.* London: Methuen.

Rosolato, Guy. 1972. "The Voice and the Literary Myth." In Macksey and Donato:201–17.

Ross-Bryant, Lynn. 1981. *Imagination and the Life of the Spirit.* Chico, Calif.: Scholars; Polebridge Books, 2.

Rossi, Ino, ed. 1974. *The Unconscious in Culture: The Structuralism of Claude Lévi-Strauss in Perspective.* New York: Dutton.

Rothenberg, Jerome. 1969. *Technicians of the Sacred: A Range of Poetries from Africa, America, Asia, and Oceania.* New York: Doubleday.

———. 1972. *Shaking the Pumpkin: Traditional Poetry of the Indian North Americans.* New York: Doubleday.

Rothgeb, Carrie Lee, and Siegfried M. Clemens, eds. 1978. *Abstracts of the Collected Works of C. G. Jung.* Rockville, Md.: National Institute of Mental Health; DHEW Publ., (ADM)78-743.

Rubenstein, Richard L. 1972. *My Brother Paul.* New York: Harper and Row.

Rudhardt, Jean. 1972. "Coherence and Incoherence of Mythic Structures." *Diogenes: An International Review of Philosophy and Humanistic Studies* 77:14–42.

Ruthven, K. K. 1976. *Myth.* London: Methuen; Crit. Idiom, 31.

Sagan, Eli. 1979. *The Lust to Annihilate: A Psychoanalytic Study of Violence in Ancient Greek Culture.* New York: Psychohistory Press.

Sahlins, Marshall. 1977. "Colors and Cultures." In Dolgin, Kemnitzer, and Schneider:165–82.

———. 1981. *Historical Metaphors and Mythical Realities: Structure in the Early History of the Sandwich Islands Kingdom.* Ann Arbor: University of Michigan Press; A.S.A.O. Spec. Publ., 1.

Samuels, Mike, and Nancy Samuels. 1975. *Seeing with the Mind's Eye: The History, Technique, and Uses of Visualization.* New York: Random House and Bookworks.

Sanders, Donald. 1979. *Navaho Symbols of Healing.* New York: Harcourt Brace Jovanovich.

Saxl, Fritz. 1970. *A Heritage of Images: A Selection of Lectures by Fritz Saxl.* Edited by Hugh Honour and John Fleming. Baltimore: Penguin.

Scharlemann, Robert P. 1982. "The Being of God When God is Not Being God: Deconstructing the History of Theism." In Altizer et al.:79–108.

Schechner, Richard. 1977. *Essays on Performance Theory: 1970–76.* New York: Drama Book Specialists.

Schechner, Richard, and Mady Schuman, eds. 1976. *Ritual, Play, and Performance: Readings in the Social Sciences/Theatre.* New York: Seabury.

Scheff, T. J. 1979. *Catharsis in Healing, Ritual, and Drama.* Berkeley and Los Angeles: University of California Press.

Schefold, Karl. 1966. *Myth and Legend in Greek Art.* New York: Abrams.

Schilling, Harold K. 1973. *The New Consciousness in Science and Religion.* Philadelphia: Pilgrim/United Church.

Schilpp, P. A., ed. 1949. *The Philosophy of Ernst Cassirer.* New York: Tudor.

Schneidau, Herbert N. 1976. *Sacred Discontent: The Bible and Western Tradition.* Berkeley and Los Angeles: University of California Press.

———. 1982. "The Word against the Word: Derrida on Textuality." In Detweiler:5–28.

Schneiderman, Leo. 1981. *The Psychology of Myth, Folklore, and Religion.* Chicago: Nelson-Hall.

Scholes, Robert. 1974. *Structuralism in Literature: An Introduction.* New Haven: Yale University Press.

Scholes, Robert, and Robert Kellogg. 1966. *The Nature of Narrative.* New York: Oxford University Press.

Scholte, Bob. 1973. "The Structural Anthropology of Claude Lévi-Strauss." In Honigmann:637–716.

Schorer, Mark. 1946. *William Blake.* New York: Holt.

Sebeok, Thomas A., ed. 1958. *Myth: A Symposium.* Bloomington: Indiana University Press.

———, ed. 1960. *Style in Language.* Cambridge: M.I.T. Press.

Segal, Robert A. 1983. "In Defense of Reductionism." *Journal of the American Academy of Religion* 51/1:97–124.

Seltman, Charles. 1960. *The Twelve Olympians.* New York: Crowell.

Sexson, Michael W. 1977. "Myth: The Way We Were or the Way We Are?" In Hall:35–47.

Sewell, Elizabeth. 1960. *The Orphic Voice: Poetry and Natural History.* New Haven: Yale University Press.

Seznec, Jean. 1953. *The Survival of the Pagan Gods: The Mythological Tradition and Its Place in Renaissance Humanism and Art.* Translated by Barbara F. Sessions. Princeton: Princeton University Press; Bollingen ser., 38.

Sharpe, Eric J. 1975. *Comparative Religions: A History.* London: Duckworth.

Shaughnessy, James D., ed. 1973. *The Roots of Ritual.* Grand Rapids, Mich.: Eerdmans.

Shepherd, William C. 1974. "On the Concept of 'Being Wrong' Religiously." *Journal of the American Academy of Religion* 42/1:66–81.

Sheridan, Alan. 1980. *Michel Foucault: The Will to Truth.* New York: Tavistock.

Simpson, Michael, trans. 1976. *Gods and Heroes of the Greeks: The "Library" of Apollodorus.* Amherst: University of Massachusetts Press.

Singer, June. 1976. *Androgyny: Toward a New Theory of Sexuality.* Garden City, N.Y.: Anchor.

Slater, Philip E. 1966. *Microcosm: Structural, Psychological, and Religious Evolution in Groups.* New York: Wiley.

———. 1968. *The Glory of Hera: Greek Mythology and the Greek Family.* Boston: Beacon.

———. 1974. "The Greek Family in History and Myth." *Arethusa* 7/1:9–44.

———. 1976. *The Pursuit of Loneliness: American Culture at the Breaking Point.* Rev. ed. Boston: Beacon.

———. 1977. *Footholds: Understanding the Shifting Sexual and Family Tensions in Our Culture.* Edited by Wendy Slater Palmer. New York: Dutton.

Slochower, Harry. 1970. *Mythopoesis: Mythic Forms in the Literary Classics.* Detroit: Wayne State University Press.

Slote, Bernice, ed. 1963. *Myth and Symbol: Critical Approaches and Applications.* Lincoln: University of Nebraska Press.

Slotkin, Richard. 1973. *Regeneration through Violence: The Mythology of the American Frontier, 1600–1860.* Middletown, Conn.: Wesleyan University Press.

Smart, Ninian. 1983. *Worldviews: Crosscultural Explorations of Human Beliefs.* New York: Scribner's.

Smith, Jonathan Z. 1970. "Birth Upside Down or Rightside Up?" *History of Religions* 9/4:281–303.

_____. 1972. "I am a Parrot (Red)." *History of Religions* 11/4:391–413.

_____. 1973. "When the Bough Breaks (A Critique of James George Frazer)." *History of Religions* 12/4:342–71.

_____. 1978. *Map Is Not Territory: Studies in the History of Religions.* Leiden: Brill; Stud. in Jud. in Late Antiq., 23.

_____. 1980. "The Bare Facts of Ritual." *History of Religions* 20/1–2:112–27.

Smith, Ron. 1981. *Mythologies of the World: A Guide to Sources.* Urbana: National Council of Teachers of English.

Snyder, Gary. 1979. *He Who Hunted Birds in His Father's Village: The Dimensions of a Haida Myth.* Bolinas, Calif.: Grey Fox.

Sontag, Susan. 1966. *Against Interpretation and Other Essays.* New York: Delta.

Spencer, Robert F., ed. 1969. *Forms of Symbolic Action: Proceedings of the 1969 Annual Spring Meeting of the American Ethnological Society.* Seattle: American Ethnological Society; distributed by University of Washington Press.

Spenser, Richard A., ed. 1980. *Orientation by Disorientation: Studies in Literary Criticism.* . . . Pittsburgh: Pickwick.

Sperber, Dan. 1979. "Claude Lévi-Strauss." In Sturrock:19–51.

Spindler, George D., ed. 1978. *The Making of Psychological Anthropology.* Berkeley and Los Angeles: University of California Press.

Spiro, Melford E. 1965. "Religion: Problems of Definition and Explanation." In Banton:85–126.

Spivey, Ted R. 1980. *The Journey Beyond Tragedy: A Study of Myth and Modern Fiction.* Orlando: University Presses of Florida.

Spretnak, Charlene. 1978. *Lost Goddesses of Early Greece: A Collection of Pre-Hellenic Mythology.* Berkeley: Moon.

_____, ed. 1982. *The Politics of Women's Spirituality.* Garden City, N.Y.: Anchor/Doubleday.

Sproul, Barbara C. 1979. *Primal Myths: Creating the World.* New York: Harper and Row.

Stacy, R. H. 1977. *Defamiliarization in Language and Literature.* Syracuse: Syracuse University Press.

Stanford, W. B. 1963. *The Ulysses Theme: A Study in the Adaptability of a Traditional Hero.* 2d ed. Ann Arbor: University of Michigan Press.

Stanford, W. B., and J. V. Luce. 1974. *The Quest for Ulysses.* New York: Praeger.

Starhawk. 1982. "Witchcraft as Goddess Religion." In Spretnak 1982:49–56.

Stauffer, Donald A. 1948. "The Modern Myth of the Modern Myth." *English Institute Essays 1947* 1:23–36.

Steblin-Kamenskij, M. I. 1982. *Myth.* Critical introduction by Edmund Leach;

epilogue and bio-bibliography by Anatoly Liberman; translated by Mary P. Coote with Frederic Armory. Ann Arbor: Karoma.

Stein, Murray. 1976. "Narcissus." *Spring 1976: An Annual of Archetypal Psychology and Jungian Thought:* 32–53.

Steiner, George. 1984. *Antigones.* New York: Oxford University Press.

Stevens, Gregory I. 1973. *Myth, Folklore, and Literature: A Bibliography.* Rev. ed. Ann Arbor: University of Michigan Center for the Coordination of Ancient and Modern Studies.

Stevenson, W. Taylor. 1969. *History as Myth: The Import for Contemporary Theology.* New York: Seabury.

Stewart, Kilton. 1969. "Dream Theory in Malaya." In Tart:161–70.

Stone, Merlin. 1976. *When God Was a Woman.* New York: Harcourt Brace Jovanovich; British title: *The Paradise Papers.*

Strelka, Joseph P., ed. 1980. *Literary Criticism and Myth.* University Park: Pennsylvania State University Press; Yearbook of Comp. Crit., 9.

Stuart, Grace. 1956. *Narcissus: A Psychological Study of Self-Love.* London: Allen and Unwin.

Sturrock, John, ed. 1979. *Structuralism and Since: From Lévi-Strauss to Derrida.* New York: Oxford University Press.

Sullenberger, Tom E. 1974. "Ajax Meets the Jolly Green Giant: Some Observations on the Use of Folklore and Myth in American Marketing." *Journal of American Folklore* 87/343:53–65.

Susman, Warren I. 1980. "The People's Fair: Cultural Contradictions of a Consumer Society." In H. A. Harrison et al.:17–27.

Sutherland, Anne. 1977. "The Body as a Social Symbol among the Rom." In Blacking:375–90.

Svenbro, Jesper. 1979. "Bibliographie du sacrifice grec." In Detienne et al. 1979:309–23.

Swann, Brian, ed. 1983. *Smoothing the Ground: Essays on Native American Oral Literature.* Berkeley and Los Angeles: University of California Press.

Tambiah, S. J. 1981. "A Performative Approach to Ritual." *Proceedings of the British Academy* 65 (1979): 113–69.

Tarn, Nathaniel. 1976. "The Heraldic Vision: A Cognitive Model for Comparative Aesthetics." *Alcheringa: Ethnopoetics,* n.s. 2/2:23–41.

Tart, C. T., ed. 1969. *Altered States of Consciousness: A Book of Readings.* Garden City, N.Y.: Doubleday.

Tate, Allen, ed. 1942. *The Language of Poetry.* Princeton: Princeton University Press; *Mesures* Ser. in Lit. Crit.

Taylor, Mark C. 1982. *Deconstructing Theology.* New York: Crossroad; Chico, Calif.: Scholars; Amer. Acad. of Relig. Stud. in Relig., 28.

———. 1983. "Deconstruction: What's the Difference?" *Soundings: An Interdisciplinary Journal* 66/4:387–403.

Taylor, Mark Kline. 1983. "Lévi-Strauss: Evolving a Myth about Myths." *Religious Studies Review* 9/2:97–105.

Tedlock, Dennis. 1980. "The Spoken Word and the Work of Interpretation in American Indian Religion." In Olson:129–44.

———. 1981. "The Spoken Word and the Work of Interpretation in American Indian Religion." In K. Kroeber 1981:45–64.

———. 1983. "On the Translation of Style in Oral Narrative." In Swann:57–77.

ten Raa, Eric. 1971. "The Genealogical Method in the Analysis of Myth, and a Structural Model." In Beidelman:313–47.

Thompson, Stith. 1946. *The Folktale*. New York: Holt, Rinehart and Winston.

Thompson, William Irwin. 1981. *The Time Falling Bodies Take to Light: Mythology, Sexuality, and the Origins of Culture*. New York: St. Martin's; Lindisfarne ser.

Thorpe, James, ed. 1967. *Relations of Literary Study: Essays on Interdisciplinary Contributions*. New York: Modern Language Association of America.

Tillich, Paul. 1971. "Myth and Mythology: The Concept and the Religious Psychology of Myth." In Pelikan:342–54.

Toelken, Barre. 1969. "The 'Pretty Language' of Yellowman: Genre, Mode, and Texture in Navajo Coyote Narratives." *Genre* 2/3:211–35.

Toelken, Barre, and Tacheeni Scott. 1981. "Poetic Retranslation and the 'Pretty Languages' of Yellowman." In K. Kroeber 1981:65–116.

Tompkins, Peter, and Christopher Bird. 1973. *The Secret Life of Plants*. New York: Harper and Row.

Tooker, Elizabeth, ed. 1979. *Native North American Spirituality of the Eastern Woodlands*. New York: Paulist; Classics of Western Spirituality ser.

Trendall, A. D., and T. B. L. Webster. 1971. *Illustrations of Greek Drama*. London: Phaidon.

Tripp, Edward. 1970. *The Meridian Handbook of Classical Mythology*. New York: New American Library.

Turner, Kay F. 1978. "Contemporary Feminist Rituals." In Spretnak 1978:219–33.

———. 1981. "The Virgin of Sorrows Procession: Mothers, Movement, and Transformation." *Archē: Notes and Papers on Archaic Studies* 6:71–92.

Turner, Terence. 1969. "Oedipus: Time and Structure in Narrative Form." In Spencer:26–68.

———. 1977. "Transformation, Hierarchy and Transcendence: A Reformulation of Van Gennep's Model of the Structure of Rites de Passage." In Moore and Myerhoff:53–70.

Turner, Victor. 1965. "Color Classification in Ndembu Ritual." In Banton:47–84.

———. 1967. *The Forest of Symbols: Aspects of Ndembu Ritual*. Ithaca: Cornell University Press.

———. 1968a. *The Drums of Affliction: A Study of Religious Processes Among the Ndembu of Zambia*. Oxford: Clarendon, for the International African Institute.

———. 1968b. "Myth and Symbol." In *International Encyclopedia of the Social Sciences* 10:576–82.

———. 1969a. "Forms of Symbolic Action: Introduction." In Spencer:3–25.

———. 1969b. *The Ritual Process: Structure and Anti-Structure*. Chicago: Aldine.

_____. 1974a. *Dramas, Fields, and Metaphors: Symbolic Action in Human Society*. Ithaca: Cornell University Press; Symbol, Myth, and Ritual ser.

_____. 1974b. "Liminal to Liminoid, in Play, Flow, and Ritual: An Essay in Comparative Symbology." *Rice University Studies* 60/3:52–92. Reprinted as chap. 1 in V. Turner 1982b.

_____. 1975a. *Revelation and Divination in Ndembu Ritual*. Ithaca: Cornell University Press; Symbol, Myth, and Ritual ser. Reprinted from 1961.

_____. 1975b. "Ritual as Communication and Potency: An Ndembu Case Study." In Hill:58–81.

_____. 1975c. "Symbolic Studies." *Annual Review of Anthropology* 4:145–61.

_____. 1977a. "Frame, Flow, and Reflection: Ritual and Drama as Public Liminality." In Benamou and Caramello:33–55.

_____. 1977b. "Process, System, and Symbol: A New Anthropological System." *Daedalus* 106/3:61–80.

_____. 1977c. "Variations on a Theme of Liminality." In Moore and Myerhoff:36–52.

_____. 1978a. "Comments and Conclusions." In Babcock:276–96.

_____. 1978b. "Encounter with Freud: The Making of a Comparative Symbologist." In Spindler:556–83.

_____, ed. 1982a. *Celebration: Studies in Festivity and Ritual*. Washington, D.C.: Smithsonian Institution.

_____. 1982b. *From Ritual to Theatre: The Human Seriousness of Play*. New York: Performing Arts.

_____. 1984. "Liminality and the Performative Genres." In MacAloon:19–41.

Turner, Victor, and Edith Turner. 1978. *Image and Pilgrimage in Christian Culture: Anthropological Perspectives*. New York: Columbia University Press; ACLS Lect. on the Hist. of Relig., n.s. 11.

Tyler, H. A. 1964. *Pueblo Gods and Myths*. Norman: University of Oklahoma Press.

van Baal, J. 1971. *Symbols for Communication: An Introduction to the Anthropological Study of Religion*. Assen: Van Gorcum.

_____. 1981. *Man's Quest for Partnership: The Anthropological Foundations of Ethics and Religion*. Assen: Van Gorcum.

van Baaren, T. P., ed. 1970–. *Iconography of Religions*. Several vols. Leiden: Brill.

Van Gennep, Arnold. 1960. *The Rites of Passage*. Translated by M. B. Vizedom and G. L. Caffee. Chicago: University of Chicago Press.

Vecsey, Christopher, and Robert W. Venables, eds. 1980. *American Indian Environments: Ecological Issues in Native American History*. Syracuse: Syracuse University Press.

Verene, Donald. 1966. "Cassirer's View of Myth and Symbol." *Monist* 50/4:553–64.

Vernant, Jean-Pierre. 1982. *The Origins of Greek Thought*. Anonymous translator. Ithaca: Cornell University Press.

_____. 1983. *Myth and Thought Among the Greeks*. Boston: Routledge and Kegan Paul.

Vernant, Jean-Pierre, and Pierre Vidal-Naquet. 1980. *Myth and Society in An-*

cient Greece. Translated by Janet Lloyd. Atlantic Highlands, N.J.: Humanities; Eur. Philos. and the Human Sci., 6.

———. 1981. *Tragedy and Myth in Ancient Greece.* Atlantic Highlands, N.J.: Humanities; Eur. Philos. and the Human Sci., 7.

Via, Dan O., Jr. 1975. *Kerygma and Comedy in the New Testament: A Structuralist Approach.* Philadelphia: Fortress.

Vickers, Brian. 1973. *Towards Greek Tragedy: Drama, Myth, Society.* London: Longman.

Vickery, John B. 1963. "*The Golden Bough:* Impact and Archetype." In Slote:174–96.

———, ed. 1966. *Myth and Literature: Contemporary Theory and Practice.* Lincoln: University of Nebraska Press.

———. 1970. "Mythopoesis and Modern Literature." In Friedman and Vickery:218–50.

———. 1972. *Robert Graves and the White Goddess.* Lincoln: University of Nebraska Press.

———. 1973. *The Literary Impact of "The Golden Bough."* Princeton: Princeton University Press.

———. 1980. "Literary Criticism and Myth: Anglo-American Critics." In Strelka:210–37.

———. 1983. *Myths and Texts: Strategies of Incorporation and Displacement.* Baton Rouge: Louisiana State University Press.

Vickery, John B., and J. M. Sellery, eds. 1971. *The Scapegoat: Ritual and Literature.* Boston: Houghton Mifflin.

Vinge, Louise. 1967. *The Narcissus Theme in Western European Literature Up to the Early Nineteenth Century.* Lund, Sweden: Gleerup.

Vivas, Eliseo. 1970. "Myth: Some Philosophical Problems." *Southern Review* 6:89–103.

Vlahos, Olivia. 1979. *Body: The Ultimate Symbol.* New York: Lippincott.

Vogt, Evon Z. 1976. *Tortillas for the Gods: A Symbolic Analysis of Zinacanteco Rituals.* Cambridge: Harvard University Press.

von Franz, Marie-Louise. 1968. "The Dream of Descartes." Translated by A. R. Pope. In Jacobsohn:55–147.

———. 1972a. *Patterns of Creativity Mirrored in Creation Myths.* Zurich: Spring Publications.

———. 1972b. *Problems of the Feminine in Fairy Tales.* New York: Spring Publications.

———. 1974. *Number and Time: Reflections Leading Toward a Unification of Depth Psychology and Physics.* Translated by Andrea Dykes. Evanston: Northwestern University Press.

———. 1975. *C. G. Jung: His Myth in Our Time.* Translated by William H. Kennedy. New York: Putnam's, for the C. G. Jung Foundation for Analytical Psychology.

von Grunebaum, G. E., and Roger Callois. 1966. *The Dream and Human Societies.* Berkeley and Los Angeles: University of California Press.

Waardenburg, Jacques. 1980. "Symbolic Aspects of Myth." In Olson:41–68.

Wallace, Anthony F. C. 1966a. *Religion: An Anthropological View.* New York: Random House.

———. 1966b. "Rituals: Sacred and Profane." *Zygon: Journal of Religion and Science* 1/1:60–81.

Ward, Anne G., ed. 1970. *The Quest for Theseus.* New York: Praeger.

Ward, E. Graham, ed. 1973. Vol 2. *Essays in Reflection.* Boston: Houghton Mifflin.

Warden, John, ed. 1982. *Orpheus: The Metamorphoses of a Myth.* Toronto: University of Toronto Press.

Warner, W. Lloyd. 1959. *The Living and the Dead: A Study of the Symbolic Life of Americans.* New Haven: Yale University Press; Yankee City ser., 5.

Watts, Alan W. 1963. *The Two Hands of God: The Myths of Polarity.* New York: Braziller; Patterns of Myth ser.

———, gen. ed. Patterns of Myths ser.; see Long 1963; Henderson and Oakes; Watts 1963; Perry 1966.

———. 1968. *Myth and Ritual in Christianity.* Boston: Beacon.

Waugh, Butler. 1966. "Structural Analysis in Literature and Folklore." *Western Folklore* 25:153–64.

Waugh, Earle H., and K. Dad Prithipaul, eds. 1979. *Native Religious Traditions.* Waterloo: Wilfrid Laurier University Press, for the Canadian Corporation for Studies in Religion; *SR* suppl., 8.

Weatherford, J. McIver. 1981. *Tribes on the Hill.* New York: Rawson, Wade.

Webster, T. B. L. 1954. "Personification as a Mode of Greek Thought." *Journal of the Warburg and Cortauld Institutes* 17:10–21.

Weigle, Marta. 1982. *Spiders and Spinsters: Women and Mythology.* Albuquerque: University of New Mexico Press.

Weinberg, Kurt. 1980. "Language as Mythopoesis: Mallarmé's Self-Referential Sonnet." In Strelka:141–76.

Weisinger, Herbert. 1961. "The Branch That Grew Full Straight." *Daedalus* 90/2:388–99.

———. 1964. *The Agony and the Triumph: Papers on the Use and Abuse of Myth.* East Lansing: Michigan State University Press.

———. 1966. "The Myth and Ritual Approach to Shakespearean Tragedy." In Vickery 1966:149–60.

———. 1968. "An Examination of the Myth and Ritual Approach to Shakespeare." In Murray 1968a:132–40.

Weissenberger, Klaus. 1980. "Mythopoesis in German Literary Criticism." In Strelka:238–73.

Wellek, René. 1963. *Concepts of Criticism.* Edited by Stephen G. Nichols, Jr. New Haven: Yale University Press.

Wellek, René, and Austin Warren. 1956. *Theory of Literature.* 3d ed. New York: Harcourt Brace and World.

Welsh, Alexander. 1981. *Reflections on the Hero as Quixote.* Princeton: Princeton University Press.

Wheelock, Wade T. 1982. "The Problem of Ritual Language: From Information to Situation." *Journal of the American Academy of Religion* 50/1:49–71.

Wheelwright, Philip. 1942. "Poetry, Myth, and Reality." In Tate:3–33.

_____. 1968. *The Burning Fountain: A Study in the Language of Symbolism*. Rev. ed. Bloomington: Indiana University Press.

White, John J. 1972. *Mythology in the Modern Novel: A Study of Prefigurative Techniques*. Princeton: Princeton University Press.

_____. 1980. "Mythological Fiction and the Reading Process." In Strelka:72–92.

White, Robert J., trans. 1975. *The Interpretation of Dreams. Oneirocritica by Artemidorus*. Park Ridge, N.J.: Noyes.

Whitmont, Edward C. 1969. *The Symbolic Quest: Basic Concepts of Analytical Psychology*. New York: Harper and Row.

Wicker, Brian. 1973. "Ritual and Culture: Some Dimensions of the Problem Today." In Shaughnessy:13–46.

Wiggins, James B., ed. 1975. *Religion as Story*. New York: Harper and Row.

Wiles, M. F. 1976. " 'Myth' in Theology." *Bulletin of the John Rylands University Library of Manchester* 59/1:226–46.

Wilson, Monica. 1954. "Nyakyusa Ritual and Symbolism." *American Anthropologist* 56/2:228–41.

Wimsatt, William K., Jr., and Cleanth Brooks. 1957. *Literary Criticism: A Short History*. New York: Knopf.

Wind, Edgar. 1968. *Pagan Mysteries in the Renaissance*. Rev. and enl. ed. New York: Norton.

Winquist, Charles E. 1974. "The Act of Storytelling and the Self's Homecoming." *Journal of the American Academy of Religion* 42/1:101–13.

_____. 1982. "Body, Text, and Imagination." In Altizer et al.:34–57.

_____. 1983. "Theology, Deconstruction, and Ritual Process." *Zygon: Journal of Religion and Science* 18/3:295–309.

Witherspoon, Gary. 1977. *Language and Art in the Navajo Universe*. Ann Arbor: University of Michigan Press.

Wittgenstein, Ludwig. 1979. *Bemerkungen Ueber Frazers/Remarks on Frazer's "Golden Bough."* Edited by Rush Rhees. Translated by A. C. Miles. Atlantic Highlands, N.J.: Humanities.

Wolman, Benjamin B., ed. 1971. *The Psychoanalytic Interpretation of History*. New York: Harper and Row.

Wosien, Maria-Gabriele. 1974. *Sacred Dance: Encounter with the Gods*. New York: Avon.

Wyman, Leland C. 1983. *Southwest Indian Drypainting*. Albuquerque: University of New Mexico Press; School of Amer. Res. Southwest Ind. Art ser.

Zahan, Dominique. 1977. "White, Red and Black: Colour Symbolism in Black Africa." Translated by Ruth Horine. In Portmann et al.:55–80.

Zimmer, Heinrich. 1946. *Myths and Symbols in Indian Art and Civilization*. Edited by Joseph Campbell. New York: Harper and Row.

Zinser, Hartmut. 1977. *Mythos und Arbeit: Studien über psychoanalytische Mytheninterpretation am Beispiel der Untersuchungen Géza Róheims*. Wiesbaden: Heymann; Stud. und Materialien der anth. Forsch., 3/2.

Zipes, Jack. 1979. *Breaking the Magic Spell: Radical Theories of Folk and Fairy Tales*. London: Heinemann.

Zolla, Elémira. 1973. *The Writer and the Shaman: A Morphology of the American*

Indian. Translated by Raymond Rosenthal. New York: Harcourt Brace Jovanovich.

Zuesse, Evan M. 1975. "Meditation on Ritual." *Journal of the American Academy of Religion* 43/3:517–30.

———. 1979. *Ritual Cosmos: The Sanctification of Life in African Religions.* Athens: Ohio University Press.

Zweig, Paul. 1968. *The Heresy of Self-Love: A Study of Subversive Individualism.* New York: Basic.

Index of Names Cited

About the Author

William G. Doty teaches religious studies at The University of Alabama and is chairman of the department. He received his bachelor of arts degree from The University of New Mexico, his master of divinity from The San Francisco Theological Seminary, and his doctorate from Drew University.